The Genesis of Rebellion

The Age of Sail has long fascinated readers, writers and the general public. Herman Melville, Joseph Conrad, Jack London et al. treated ships at sea as microcosms; petri dishes in which larger themes of authority, conflict and order emerge.

In this fascinating book, Pfaff and Hechter explore mutiny as a manifestation of collective action and contentious politics. The authors use narrative evidence and statistical analysis to trace the processes by which governance failed, social order decayed and seamen mobilized.

Their findings highlight the complexities of governance, showing that it was not mere deprivation, but how seamen interpreted that deprivation, which stoked the grievances that motivated rebellion.

Using the Age of Sail as a lens to examine topics still relevant today – what motivates people to rebel against deprivation and poor governance – *The Genesis of Rebellion: Governance, Grievance and Mutiny in the Age of Sail* helps us understand the emergence of populism and rejection of the establishment.

Steven Pfaff is Professor of Sociology at the University of Washington and serves on the board of the Association for the Study of Religion, Economics and Culture. He studies sociology, political science and economic history, and has received book prizes from the Social Science History Association and the European Academy of Sociology.

Michael Hechter is a fellow of the American Academy of Arts & Sciences and Foundation Professor of Political Science at Arizona State University. He is the author of various books, including *Alien Rule* (Cambridge University Press, 2013).

The Genesis of Rebellion

Governance, Grievance and Mutiny in the Age of Sail

Steven Pfaff
University of Washington
Michael Hechter
Arizona State University

CAMBRIDGE
UNIVERSITY PRESS

CAMBRIDGE
UNIVERSITY PRESS

University Printing House, Cambridge CB2 8BS, United Kingdom

One Liberty Plaza, 20th Floor, New York, NY 10006, USA

477 Williamstown Road, Port Melbourne, VIC 3207, Australia

314–321, 3rd Floor, Plot 3, Splendor Forum, Jasola District Centre, New Delhi – 110025, India

79 Anson Road, #06–04/06, Singapore 079906

Cambridge University Press is part of the University of Cambridge.

It furthers the University's mission by disseminating knowledge in the pursuit of education, learning, and research at the highest international levels of excellence.

www.cambridge.org
Information on this title: www.cambridge.org/9781107193734
DOI: 10.1017/9781108149853

© Steven Pfaff and Michael Hechter 2020

First published 2020

Printed in the United Kingdom by TJ International Ltd, Padstow Cornwall

A catalogue record for this publication is available from the British Library.

ISBN 978-1-107-19373-4 Hardback
ISBN 978-1-316-64515-4 Paperback

Cambridge University Press has no responsibility for the persistence or accuracy of URLs for external or third-party internet websites referred to in this publication and does not guarantee that any content on such websites is, or will remain, accurate or appropriate.

IN MEMORIAM

Edward Pfaff
and
Eliana Hechter

CONTENTS

The color plate section can be found between pp. 172 and 173.

PLATES

FIGURES

TABLES

Preface

The Age of Sail has long fascinated readers. Writers like Herman Melville, Joseph Conrad, Jack London and Herman Wouk treated ships at sea as microcosms, literary petri dishes in which they explored grand themes of authority, conflict and order. Popular novelists such as Patrick O'Brien and C. S. Forester have lovingly and perceptively rendered the naval world at the time of Nelson. Accounts of mutiny comprise a particular genre in maritime literature, stretching from *Mutiny on the Bounty* to *Billy Budd* and *The Caine Mutiny*. A host of successful feature films have followed in the wake of the books. The challenge before us lies in combining the excitement of maritime history with the methods that enable us to make broader claims about the mechanisms that explain rebellion.

In researching and writing this book, we have brought perspectives from the social sciences to bear on history. And we have sought to enrich the social scientific perspective by engaging in the kind of detailed and contextual analysis that the use of historical evidence allows. Drawing upon a host of primary and secondary sources, we trace the processes by which governance failed, social order decayed and seamen mobilized with systematic, multivariate analysis of ships that had mutinies and those that did not. These sources allow us to understand how seamen interpreted governance and why failures of governance instilled a sense of grievance in them. Our analyses reveal that the failure of governance is the single largest factor that explains the incidence of mutiny. Our findings show how seamen attained solidarity and why discipline and punishment played an ambiguous role in securing social order.

Unlike earlier inquiries into mutiny, the present one is motivated by a twin concern for the causes of rebellion and its antithesis, social order. Mutiny in the Age of Sail implicates both of these phenomena. Despite the harsh conditions that seamen faced aboard Royal Navy vessels, mutiny was a rare event. We argue that the infrequency of mutiny – like that of large-scale rebellions more generally – owes, in part, to people's tendency to tolerate accustomed levels of subordination and deprivation under normal conditions, and, in part, to the capacity of authorities to attain social order by governing fairly and effectively. If we want to understand the relationship between governance, social order and rebellion then and now, we need to rethink the genesis of rebellion.

ACKNOWLEDGMENTS

The idea for this book was born in 1996 in Oxford. As a fellow of New College living in college, I routinely dined at High Table. Like many things at Oxford, High Table has its own ritual. Shortly before the meal, participants gather in the Senior Common Room, and then walk into Hall to be seated in a random order. Once seated, the norm at the very long table is to converse with the people both on one's right and left. That evening there was a strange face to my right, and I struck up a conversation with him. It turned out that this individual was a postgraduate student in Naval History pursuing his DPhil. He was grousing about the long and tedious day he had just spent at the Public Records Office (PRO, now the National Archives). I was curious about the nature of the naval records to be found there. The student mentioned that the PRO had records of every sailor who had ever been on every ship since the founding of the Royal Navy in the seventeenth century.

Whereas there is a good deal of information about organizations in the historical record, ordinarily there is very little that identifies every individual in a given organization, especially over the *longue durée*. I immediately realized that this kind of evidence could be marshaled to create an innovative study of collective action – and of mutiny, in particular.

The idea lay dormant for quite a while. When I rejoined the Sociology Department at the University of Washington in 1999, I broached it to several of my colleagues there as a possible opportunity for collaboration. Steve Pfaff, who entered the department as an assistant professor that same year, became intrigued, and the two of us began thinking about applying for the funding that would be necessary to support the research. Years passed as we developed a proposal. In 2008 we succeeded in getting a seed grant from the University of Washington's Royalty Research Fund. A more substantial grant from the Harry Frank Guggenheim Foundation followed in 2009. Also in that year, I attended a conference organized by Sun-Ki Chai at the University of Hawaii-Manoa where I met Terence Lyons, then a program officer for the Air Force Office of Scientific Research (AFOSR). After mentioning the project, Lyons encouraged me to submit a larger grant to the AFOSR. This Steve and I did, and the agency came through with the bulk of the funds that enabled us to collect the data. Needless to say, we are deeply indebted to these institutions for the support that enabled us to tackle the substantial challenges that assembling our data from historical sources entailed.

Steve conducted exploratory research in the summer of 2008 as a visiting scholar at the Centre for Maritime Historical Studies at the University of Exeter. He benefited from conversations with outstanding historians at Exeter, in particular with Nicholas Rodger and Jeremy Black, world-renowned experts on the naval and military history of Georgian Britain. Professor Rodger graciously took on the ongoing role of informal advisor to our project. He also helped us to recruit Moira Bracknell, recently awarded a PhD in Maritime History, who we hired as a researcher on our project. We are thankful for her expert advice on sources and her mastery of the Admiralty records. She proved indefatigable, tracking down and photographing the archival records of hundreds of Royal Navy ships.

In the summer of 2009, we took another trip to the UK to work with primary documents. The data we collected enabled us to analyze the 1797 mass mutinies at Spithead and the Nore. This enriched our understanding of the dynamics of insurgency and informed the explanation of mutiny that we developed in this book. In order to carry out our work we had to take long westward rides on the Underground from central London to the National Archives at Kew, as well as long eastward rides on the Docklands Light Railway to the Caird Library at the National Maritime Museum in Greenwich. All the shuttling paid off handsomely. Working closely with the documents and using them to assemble systematic data gave us richer appreciation of the questions we were interested in tackling.

While in the UK that summer, we also visited the University of Oxford, where Eliana Hechter, a Rhodes scholar, was conducting research at St. John's College for her DPhil in Statistics. When we explained to Eliana the daunting sampling issues that we confronted in attempting a systematic study of a rare event (mutiny), she suggested an elegant solution. Rather than build a representative sample of Royal Navy ships in which we would inevitably have too few observations on the dependent variable and confront enormous expense in gathering so large and comprehensive a dataset, she suggested that we adopt the case-control method that is widely employed in epidemiology to study rare diseases. Subsequent consulting by the Health Sciences Library and the Center for Statistics in the Social Sciences at the University of Washington proved just how right Eliana was, and taught us how to use the method properly. Eliana's intervention opened up the pathway that led to a systematic analysis of mutinies, something that had never before been accomplished by researchers.

Our book has been substantially enriched by collaborations with Katie E. Corcoran and Patrick Underwood that resulted in earlier versions of some chapters that first appeared in the *American Sociological Review* (Chapter 4) and *Social Science History* (Chapters 5 and 6). We are grateful for their contributions and for the comments and suggestions that we received from the editors and reviewers of those journals. Portions of those papers appear by the kind permission of SAGE Publishing and Cambridge University Press.

Working to transform thousands of pages of handwritten documents into a machine-readable dataset required us to build a team of talented and hard-working coders. University of Washington students Lindsey Beach, Jayleen Bowman, Elizabeth Cady, Dale Coleman, Lauren Ho, Christopher Prather, Sarah Reinecke, Heather Reyes, Jocelyn Sayler, Kristin Smith, Samuel Stabler, Thomas Stanton, Timothy Thomas, Meral Tunador and Rachel Tweet proved to be patient and careful researchers without whom we could not have completed the book. Yuan Hsiao provided assistance with data visualizations.

Many colleagues provided commentary and criticism along the way. We are grateful to all of them, but we would single out a few who stand out for their contributions. These include Doug Allen, Yoram Barzel, Charles Causey, Bob Crutchfield, Aimee Dechter, Eliana Hechter, Phil Howard, Edgar Kiser, Ross Matsueda, Doug McAdam, Luis Fernando Medina, Karl-Dieter Opp, Nicholas Rodger, David Siroky, Karen Snedker and Andrew Walder.

Parts of this book benefited from presentations at a number of venues including the annual conference of the American Sociological Association; the Sociology Department at the University of Washington; the Quality of Governance Institute at Gothenburg University; the Center for Advanced Study in Madrid; the Juan March Foundation in Madrid; the Centre for Maritime Historical Studies at the University of Exeter; the Center for Advanced Study in the Behavioral Sciences at Stanford University; the Sociology Department at Umeå University; Nuffield College, Oxford; and the annual conference of the Association for the Study of Religion, Economics and Culture.

The story of this book opened at Oxford with me and it closed there with Steve. Nuffield College provided an academic visitorship that allowed him to spend the spring and summer of 2018 in a very congenial setting for the final effort to put our research together and complete a draft of the manuscript. Thanks are owed to the many friends and colleagues at the University of Oxford who have encouraged our work over the years and to the Department of Sociology and the Clarence and Elissa M. Schrag Faculty Fellowship for supporting Steve's sabbatical leave that enabled us to finish the book.

Michael Hechter

1 THE GENESIS OF REBELLION

1.1 Introduction

This book is a study of social order and rebellion in the Royal Navy in the period between 1740 and 1820. There have been previous scholarly books on naval mutiny, but for the most part they are disappointing. Although mutiny has long been regarded as a metaphor for social revolution, it usually has been treated on a case-by-case basis. Scholars have never systematically compared ships that experienced mutinies to those that did not.[1] This inattention to comparison makes dramatic sense, for each mutiny is unique and its story can be told by focusing on the nature of the Captain's leadership, the heroic – or dastardly – character of the ringleaders, and the loyalty of those seamen who resisted the mutineers. Yet this case study research strategy can shed little light on the nature of mutiny and, in particular, on the general circumstances that are likely to make it more probable.

A second family of studies compares the common features of naval rebellion across a range of mutinies. Since these studies are limited to instances in which mutiny occurred, however, they cannot determine what made these ships different from others that did not experience mutiny. Although comparative studies of mutinies can be insightful and well informed, they are unable to make causal claims.[2] As purely descriptive natural histories of mutiny, they cannot analyze their genesis.[3]

Because we regard mutiny as *rebellion* – that is, as an important instance of high-risk collective action – this book adopts an alternative form of analysis, one that combines systematic comparison of ships that experienced mutiny and those that did not with in-depth case studies of dozens of mutinies that allow us to make generalizations across different occurrences.

1.1.1   Revisiting the Mutiny on the *Bounty*

There is no mutiny more famous than the one that took place onboard HMS *Bounty* in April 1789. As an incident of British imperial or naval history, the mutiny on the *Bounty* is of trivial importance. What is important about the case is that, then and now, it has captured the popular imagination. Thanks to a host of books and several feature films, mutiny has become practically synonymous with the story of that ship.[4] More important for the questions that drive this book, however, the *Bounty* seems to encapsulate much about how we understand the genesis of rebellion.

In the wake of his misadventures in the South Seas, William Bligh, commanding Lieutenant of HMS *Bounty*, published an account of the mutiny. Bligh paused in his narrative to note that "It will very naturally be asked, what could be the reason for such a revolt?" He blamed it all on a conspiracy led by Fletcher Christian, a vain and unsteady junior officer, and comprised of seamen besotted by "female connexions" that they made on Tahiti. The mutineers had "flattered themselves with the hopes of a more happy life among the Otaheiteans, than they could possibly enjoy in England." Bligh argued that the revolt was facilitated by opportunities for rebellion that the mutineers had exploited: to wit, that the ship was isolated and his command included no Marines who could have come to his aid. Even so, given that mutiny was a capital offense, his readers no doubt assumed that his subordinates were driven by the strongest of grievances. But Bligh was at pains to assure them otherwise: "Had their mutiny been occasioned by any grievances, either real or imaginary, I must have discovered symptoms of their discontent."[5]

Bligh's critics, including some of the men subsequently captured and tried for the mutiny and backed by influential supporters, painted a different story. They claimed that the crew had been pushed to rebel by the injustice and deprivation that prevailed aboard the small ship. Bligh had shown little sympathy for the crew during a trying outward voyage that featured a fruitless, month-long effort to round Cape Horn in the teeth of severe winter storms. Having given up on that quicker but more perilous route, the ship then sailed eastward around Africa, reaching Tahiti only after a voyage that lasted more than ten months. Through it all, Bligh was said to be an erratic and overbearing commander. His frugal economizing deprived his men of adequate food and water even as he fiercely guarded his own petty privileges. Witnesses testified that Bligh relied on bullying and flogging to maintain shipboard order. Bligh's irascibility led him to demote his Sailing Master, John Fryer, replacing him with Fletcher Christian, who, in turn, later suffered Bligh's disfavor and became the chief ringleader of the mutiny.

These accounts portrayed the mutiny as being made by men who had reached the breaking point. Yet Bligh had patrons and supporters of his own: they contended that Bligh had been betrayed by weak and ungrateful subordinates. He and a handful of loyal seamen had returned to England thanks to an intrepid feat of survival and seamanship that included a harrowing passage of more than three thousand miles in an open launch. Having suffered betrayal and rebellion and lived to tell of it, some saw Bligh as a national hero. So was he a naval hero or a petty tyrant who drove his men to desperation? Two centuries later, neither depiction is especially convincing.[6]

The accusations lodged by Bligh's foes have resonated with audiences then and now because they match the conventional understanding of rebellion. The idea that rebellion occurs because suffering people are pushed to rebel when tyranny and oppression are severe and other ways out are blocked is widespread.[7] Injustice and deprivation are treated as causes of all manner of rebellion, ranging in scale from strikes and prison riots to revolutions and civil wars.[8]

One important elaboration of this idea is that rebellion is driven by relative deprivation. When people expect things to be getting better and they do not, or when the members of some important reference group are faring better than they are, frustration builds and can be channeled into aggression. Sometimes this occurs after sustained periods of improving conditions are followed by a downturn. It need not be the case that material conditions have actually worsened much or fallen to levels below those that previously had been endured peacefully. On the contrary, rebellion occurs because rising expectations have been thwarted. De Tocqueville noticed this in the coming of the French Revolution and it has been observed in other periods of rebellion as well.[9]

By contrast, Bligh's account of the mutiny on the *Bounty* has something that has more in common with the revisionist explanations of rebellion that took hold in the 1970s. Bligh blamed private incentives (the attractions of Tahiti), elite divisions (a rift between the officers) and favorable opportunities (the ship lacked Marines, it was alone in the South Seas, and so on) for the outbreak of rebellion on his ship. Prevailing theories of collective action similarly emphasize private incentives in motivating collective action.[10] The resource mobilization school of social movements discounts the causal role of grievances altogether, regarding political opportunities and resources instead as the key factors responsible for generating collective protest.[11]

In writing this book we sought to move beyond both the Bligh-like understanding of rebellion as a product of personal incentives, resources and opportunities, as well as the view that inequality and material deprivation are primary drivers of rebellion. What is at stake in the mutiny on the *Bounty* and the dozens of other mutinies that we will analyze, is less the personalities of a commander and his antagonists than the quality of governance. When seamen regard the governance of the ship as incompetent, reckless or heedless of their welfare, they are more likely to rebel. Every mutiny contains dramatic narrative details and takes place in the unique social ecology of a sailing ship. This alone makes the study of naval insurrection fascinating, but understanding mutiny sheds light on the general class of events known as rebellion.

1.2   What Is Mutiny?

The Royal Navy characterized mutiny broadly and imprecisely, variously defining it in the Articles of War as any form of individual or collective defiance of command, or any communication or planning to that effect.[12] What today we would consider to be relatively minor acts of defiance or refusal of duty could be construed as mutiny in the Articles of War. At one extreme, Captain Thomas Troubridge, known for the mutiny on HMS *Culloden*, declared, "Whenever I see a fellow look as if he was thinking, I say that is mutiny."[13] We are not interested in individual acts of insubordination, however broadly commanders defined it. Mutinies are classic examples of collective action. Collective action describes situations in which groups of people have to decide whether to undertake costly action that they believe would improve their shared situation. When collective action takes the form of rebellion against the state, the potential costs are especially high.

Our particular concern is with those mutinies that took the form of a *collective insurrection against the constituted order of a ship*.[14] We narrow our focus to mutinies that passed beyond the mere planning stage, in which the crewmen seized their ship or halted its operations by acting collectively. In some mutinies, the ringleaders sought to escape from naval service, whereas in others they wanted to compel their commanders or other naval authorities to redress their grievances. This book analyzes both types of mutiny.[15]

Full-fledged mutinies of this kind were rare (and dangerous) events, but they happened with enough frequency to have been a part of the shared experience of the sailing navy and its institutional ecology. Between 1756 and 1806, more than five hundred cases of mutiny (not including those of striking a superior officer) were tried by naval courts-martial, resulting in nearly four hundred convictions.[16] Most of these mutinies did not rise to the level of taking a ship or halting its operations – the forms that we shall study – but collective insubordination was a continual threat that concerned naval legal institutions and had a considerable influence on governance. The threat of mutiny influenced relations between seamen and officers, how commanders ran their ships and ultimately became an important impetus to legal and administrative reforms.

Studying mutiny in the Royal Navy enables us to understand the roles of governance, on the one hand, and grievances, on the other, in accounting for rebellion. The thorough record-keeping of the Navy makes it possible to track ships and their crews over time. This allows us to study scores of rebellions occurring in the same institutional setting in which practices and expectations about good governance were understood by seamen and officers alike.

At first glance, one would expect that seamen's grievances would be of little help in explaining mutiny. After all, it is widely understood that conditions in the Royal Navy were brutal. Sailors and

Marines in the Navy were subject to harsh conditions – as Samuel Johnson famously described their lot:

> No man will be a sailor who has contrivance enough to get himself into jail; for being in a ship is being in a jail, with the chance of being drowned ... A ship is worse than a jail. There is, in a jail, better air, better company, better conveniency of every kind; and a ship has the additional disadvantage of being in danger.[17]

If grievances were so ubiquitous, as Dr. Johnson colorfully suggests, why did most ships never face an insurrection and why did most seamen never take part in a mutiny?

Dr. Johnson, a man with no maritime experience, certainly exaggerated. Even so, conditions onboard naval ships were notoriously hard. A standard battleship of seventy-four guns was only about a hundred and sixty feet in length but bore up to five hundred men. This resulted in crowding, privation and a substantial risk of accident and disease. The officers were the lords of the ship and many infractions were punishable by flogging or, more casually, by a blow from a knotted rope or cane (this was known as "starting"). The quality and supply of food and drink often deteriorated during long voyages. Many seamen died of illnesses and shipwrecks. Seamen's pay was poor and its general rates had been set in the middle of the seventeenth century. Their liberties were routinely negated. For instance, commanders frequently denied seamen customary shore leave for fear that they would abscond. During wartime, the Navy relied on impressments to fill the ranks, and terms of service were indefinite.

Grievances can be causes of rebellion when they are severe and when they can be readily attributed to bad governance. Nevertheless, seamen did not regard *routine* hardship as grounds for mutiny. Eighteenth-century laboring people in England operated under different sets of expectations about their standards of living than do their modern counterparts. What were the relevant considerations? In some ways, conditions on merchant ships were harder than on naval ships. Most types of working people ashore were also poorly paid and faced coercive labor discipline. What seamen did seem to expect was that their commanders would maintain their safety, attend to their welfare, observe maritime occupational norms and rule in a predictable fashion. Incidents that threatened their safety and welfare, and indifferent or inappropriate responses to these threats, could stir unrest. In making Captains the supreme authorities on ships, the Navy also gave them responsibility for such failures. This made it easy for seamen to attribute blame to commanders for incidents that harmed or threatened them, regardless of the facts of the matter.

Mutiny tells us much about threats to social order and the exercise of command. Yet it not only reveals failures of social order, but also how shipboard cooperation is attained. The social order of a ship depended on cooperation between officers and men and between seamen of different skills and ranks. The scale of the Royal Navy in the eighteenth and early nineteenth centuries is impressive. In the Napoleonic era, the Navy employed more than a hundred thousand men. It was the western world's largest industrial unit, and among the most expensive and administratively demanding enterprises on the planet. Its warships were the technological marvels of the age. Attaining social order in so large and complex an enterprise was no small feat.

Inspired by now-classic explorations of social order at sea, our study explains how order was attained in the Navy and why it sometimes broke down.[18] In addition to correcting many misperceptions about mutiny that traditional approaches have fostered, our book stands solidly in the tradition of historical studies of social order and collective action.[19] It explores why people commit to participate in dangerous collective action, exploring the roles of grievances, coordination, leadership and dynamic mobilization processes. In this, it breaks with much of the literature on contentious politics, which focuses heavily on political opportunities.[20] We also differ from the micro-mobilization perspective adopted by many recent studies of rebellion that puts the emphasis on ideology and transformative experiences.[21] In analyzing the mass mutinies of 1797, our study takes on the arguments made by historians that the diffusion of revolutionary ideologies was the cause of rebellion by seamen, and the claims made by political scientists concerning the dynamic interactions between rebels and regimes that define armed insurgencies.[22]

We understand mutiny as the by-product of relations between the two principal collectivities onboard ship. On one side stands command (the Captain and his officers), and on the other stands the crew (the seamen). Relations between the two are shaped by the officers' ability to provide good governance, on the one side, and by the crew's grievances and its capacity to coordinate collective action, on the other. Mutiny, therefore, is the outcome of the conjunction of demand and supply. The demand for mutiny resulted from poor governance, especially the provision of insufficient collective goods like security, health and welfare. The failure of governance combined with inadequate monitoring and sanctioning by command led to the erosion of the shipboard social order. The demand for mutiny was shaped by the crew's perceptions that failures of governance were inappropriate and no mere accident.

The supply side of mutiny varies with a crew's capacity to undertake collective action in response to its grievances. Seamen varied in their capacity to act together, especially in so dangerous and uncertain a venture as mutiny. The everyday social practices of seamen, their informal organization and their occupational culture, provided them with resources that they could use in making a rebellion. They were accustomed to teamwork and had experienced shipmates with the skills and authority to act as leaders. In conflicts with command, they developed practices to activate group solidarity and bolster commitment to mutinies. Even so, mutinies were usually only risked when seamen saw shared threats to safety and welfare that were likely to worsen if they took no action. Situations like these naturally enhance coordination and mean that free riding does not pay.[23]

Planning a mutiny and mobilizing seamen to risk their lives represented a supreme test of the solidarity of seamen and their ability to coordinate their actions. Facing violent resistance from the authorities in the struggle to take and hold ships, and facing possible death by hanging in the wake of mutiny, rebellion in the Navy was not something that seamen undertook lightly. Most often, they mutinied when they felt that they had legitimate grievances and no other means of voicing them. Mutiny reflected badly on the governance of the ship by the Captain and his officers.

To evaluate these ideas, we conducted the first systematic study of naval mutiny in the British Navy during the Age of Sail. Unlike many studies of rebellion, ours includes both cases of ships in which documented episodes of mutiny did occur, and a larger set of nonmutinous cases randomly selected from the population of all ships. Our study compares a sample of mutinies that occurred on naval ships from 1740 to 1820 with a random sample drawn from the much larger population of ships that faced no such rebellion. Whereas scholars of mutiny have endorsed such a design, no previous study attempted it.[24] Fortunately, archival records were an excellent resource, providing comprehensive documentation that allowed us to analyze quantitative data and rich historical evidence about mutiny and its causes.

1.3 Understanding Rebellion

The goal of this book is to explain mutiny and, in so doing, better understand the causes of rebellion. Rebellion has played a central part in history. It has been a feature of human life ever since the emergence of authority in groups. Nevertheless, rebellion has been notoriously hard to predict.[25] De Tocqueville called rebellions the events that most "surprise and terrify" us.[26] This is partly because subordinates usually tolerate deprivation and inequality for a long time before rebelling. Another reason is that rulers seek to avoid rebellion by controlling their subjects. They try to make them dependent on the authorities for their well-being and fearful of punishment for defiance. This can make rebellion so dangerous a prospect that self-regarding people tend to avoid it in spite of their experience of deprivation. Finally, repression and social inequality often create a situation in which rulers know little about the extent or scale of popular grievances because subordinates have avoided voicing them either for fear of repression or because speaking up accomplishes little.[27]

What is clear – at least to us – is that grievances lie at the heart of rebellion. Nevertheless, a lot of previous scholarship suggests that grievances are *not* useful for explaining popular unrest. Inequality, it has been asserted, is the objective, material foundation of grievance. Yet inequality is ubiquitous and rebellion unusual. Trotsky remarked that if grievances were enough to cause insurrection, the masses would always be in a state of revolt.[28] If grievances are to be inferred merely from evidence of systematic inequality, then the relationship between them and social unrest is weak. A host of cross-sectional and cross-national empirical studies finds scant evidence that material grievances – understood as objective material deprivation – are linked to rebellion.[29]

Today, there is a renaissance in thinking about grievances. Some have argued that rebellion is one of the most important levelers of inequality.[30] Others argue that it is the only kind of voice that oppressed and exploited people have in seeking an improvement of their lot, and that authoritarian rulers only make concessions when they fear an imminent rebellion.[31] Around the world, unrest occurs in response to discontent with the provision of public goods, the removal or reduction of food subsidies and other threats to popular welfare.[32] In practice, the amelioration of collective grievances seems to be the main payoff that people who take part in rebellions expect.[33]

Part of the confusion about grievances lies in conflating an explanation of rebellion with the study of revolution. Rebellion may result in revolution, war or state collapse but it need not.[34] In fact, even if those macro-level events frequently begin with uprisings, rebellion is far more common than those outcomes. Since many factors besides the inception of rebellion explain why revolutions occur or states collapse, grievances might be thought of as mere background conditions. Explaining the *genesis* of rebellion means studying situations in which potential rebellions do and do not occur, as well as events that never rise to the level of a revolutionary assault on the social order. This is why studying mutinies in the Royal Navy is so valuable.

Another reason is that in studying mutinies we can observe the constitution of social order and its collapse in detail. Ships at sea are worlds in microcosm. Each ship has a political, social and cultural system in which authority must be enacted, compliance won and cooperation attained. Like the cultural historian Paul Gilroy, we are fascinated by "The image of the ship – a living, micro-cultural, micro-political system in motion," a sociological site with an underappreciated theoretical and historical importance.[35] Understanding the governance of ships and the establishment of social order, on the one side, and explaining why grievances flourish and social order breaks down, on the other, can teach us much about the genesis of rebellion across places and times.

1.4 Grievances and Governance

We argue that mutiny is the outcome of the conjunction of poor governance, the crew's perception that their situation requires concerted action to prevent decrements to their welfare, and their capacity to coordinate in response to their grievances. The conditions facing seamen in the Navy were not fundamentally different from those that face rebels today in circumstances as diverse as armed insurgencies, prison uprisings and militant strikes. Our study will show that two related factors, *grievances* and *governance*, explain the outbreak of mutiny in the Royal Navy and the genesis of rebellion in many other times and places.

A grievance is a wrong or hardship that the afflicted believe to be legitimate grounds for complaint. Rebellion is driven by grievances of different kinds. It is a response to perceptions of injustice, unfairness and failures of governance. We argue that grievances have an especially combustive potential when long-standing and suddenly imposed grievances have been combined in a particular time and place. In these moments, people urgently demand redress and may be inspired to rebel against the governing authorities whom they hold responsible for their situation but who are inattentive to their plight.

Governance is constituted by the structure of authority, social relations and the institutions used by those in positions of command to attain social order and produce collective goods. It refers to an authority's capacity to make and enforce rules and to deliver collective goods.[36] The conception of governance that we develop in this book, however, includes not only executive capacity and governmental outputs, but also the manner in which power is exercised. Governance is a set of techniques and institutions to achieve social order. One of the fundamental issues in human affairs is how to combine the actions of different people in a social setting to generate collectively beneficial outcomes.[37]

Governance shapes rebellious collective action because governing institutions help determine the shape that opposition to authority takes. Good governance provides routine mechanisms that allow for feedback from subjects. To the degree that authorities are isolated from their subjects and deny them meaningful and effective voice, the odds of rebellion increase. Of course, there are other factors besides poor governance and mounting grievances that determine whether discontent inspires rebellion. Would-be rebels usually have to perceive opportunities to act in effective ways. They have to share a common understanding of their situation that helps them to interpret their hardships and injuries as legitimate complaints deserving redress. They may be influenced by events elsewhere that change their perceptions about their situation and the vulnerability of their rulers. They have to be able, at least in a minimal way, to coordinate their actions behind a collective challenge to their rulers.

That poor governance and grievances are central factors in the genesis of rebellion is by no means a novel or counterintuitive argument. Nevertheless, systematically analyzing their contribution to the incidence of rebellion has often proven difficult. Governance is a notoriously difficult concept to measure. Even if we can measure the inputs invested in governing, that tells us little about the outputs of governance. Capturing the effects of governance means measuring performance and documenting shortfalls.[38] The excellent administrative data preserved in British naval archives provide us with an unusual opportunity to measure the performance of governance.

The obstacles to measuring legitimacy have led many to question the utility of the concept. The difficulties of capturing the dynamics of grievances have led some to treat them as constants, and therefore incapable of explaining rebellious collective action across different times and places. Others have erred by only studying outbreaks of rebellion and revolution.[39] Whereas they have been able to catalog a host of grievances in their anatomies of such cases, this approach cannot explicate how these situations differ from similar ones that did not lead to rebellion.[40]

Analyzing the role of grievances in the genesis of rebellion is complicated by several factors. The first is a tendency to start with known episodes of rebellion. Once a rebellion has begun, it is easy to find the grievances that putatively inspired it. Many of them will be long-standing. What made these grievances suddenly intolerable? Have similar grievances been tolerated in other times and places? If we want to make claims about grievances as causes of rebellion it is far better to have dynamic measures of grievances prior to the onset of rebellion, and to observe them in groups having different grievances.

A second problem, alluded to above, is the tendency to regard grievances as irrelevant for understanding rebellion. For a long time social scientists – rather counterintuitively – regarded grievances as ubiquitous; if so, they could not explain why rebellion breaks out in some times and places as against others. A constant cannot account for variable outcomes. Yet it seems obvious that grievances must lie at the heart of collective action. Unless there is some substantial payoff to the often dangerous and uncertain business of rebellion, why would people ever undertake it? The possibility of improving one's situation or remedying some kind of deprivation are the most common ends that participants seek in making a rebellion.

It strikes us that part of the problem has been reliance on an inadequate understanding of grievances. Too frequently, studies focus on those grievances that are assumed to flow from objective disparities between individuals and groups, rather than on participants' subjective interpretation of these disparities. Grievances are often inferred from observed intergroup differentials in income, health, incarceration or other measures of well-being.[41] The issue is that the members of many groups that suffer substantial forms of absolute deprivation tolerate it or see rebellion as a hopeless venture. Long-standing deprivations can create a sense of fatalism or despondence that often demobilizes aggrieved people. This means that in many instances rebellion and inequality are weakly related or wholly uncorrelated. Without dynamic measures of a range of grievances, including observations before and after incidents that sharpen existing grievances or create new ones, we lack the leverage to understand how and why they matter. Moreover, combinations of long-standing and immediate grievances – sometimes induced by accidents or unforeseen events – can increase one's sense of deprivation and help trigger rebellion.

We will show that combinations of grievances with different temporal frames inspire rebellions. Inadequate or unjust responses to suddenly imposed or incidental grievances reorient deprived people around a common focal point, providing ready targets in incompetent, corrupt or indifferent leaders.

1.5 Grievances and Collective Action

This book advances a grievance-based theory of collective action holding that groups of people who *share* grievances due to their subordinate positions in social and political structures are more likely to mobilize to enhance their welfare than those who bear *private* grievances, no matter how severe the sum of such grievances might be.[42] Grievances cannot generate collective action on their own, however. The immediate impetus to collective action is cognitive. Successful collective action proceeds from a significant transformation in the collective consciousness of the actors involved. Activists – sometimes motivated by private grievances – use collective grievances to construct legitimating accounts – or frames – to support their activism.[43]

Governance and grievances are linked because what transforms a hardship into a grievance is the perception or belief that the hardship is illegitimate. Governing institutions create the normative expectations that inform these beliefs. Because poor governance generates grievances, governance shapes rebellious collective action. Of course, grievances are far from unusual. Some are purely private, such as those feeding personal grudges. But others matter more because they are shared among people who belong to the same community or occupy the same social category. For a variety of reasons, people often feel that their group has been neglected or deprived, whether due to the circumstances they are compelled to inhabit or to the actions of others.

How can these shared grievances be measured? Sometimes they can be measured *directly* in sample surveys, but such studies are geographically and historically limited and liable to suffer from selection bias.[44] *Indirect* measures – based on the assumption that grievances can be inferred from individuals' subordinate positions in a social structure – can be used to study grievances arising from stratification and inequality across greater geographic and temporal space. For example, one can assume that political and economic inequalities affecting entire ethnic, class or racial groups tend to fuel resentment and justify attempts to fight perceived injustice.[45] Moreover, shared grievances are likely to have an emotional valence that makes collective identities more salient.[46]

In practice, however, structural variables often prove to be flawed predictors of collective action. For example, the poorest and most deprived people are usually not the most prone to rebellion, and crushingly bad oppression and poverty can be endured indefinitely without significant unrest. Does this mean that grievances can be ruled out as causes of rebellion? There is no warrant to believe that structural variables provide the *only* measures of grievances. Grievances can also emerge from a quite different source. Thinkers as diverse as Max Weber, Emile Durkheim and G. H. Mead all held that incumbency in a social role entails a set of behaviors that individuals are obligated to enact. For Weber, patrimonial rulers were obliged not to exceed the traditional limits to their power.[47] Serfs' existence was grim, but masters also had certain obligations toward serfs – providing access to the commons, and sharing food during famines – and any lord who failed to honor those obligations courted trouble. Likewise, Durkheim explained that individuals in nineteenth-century European societies had little expectation that their fortunes could exceed those of their parents. In consequence, they accepted (with resignation) norms about their place in the stratification system.[48] Last, Mead insisted that social roles made individuals act as if they were characters in a play or athletic contest. Given a set of rules of the game, everyone's action is normally oriented toward that of the other participants in predictable ways. The failure to honor these expectations is jarring: shortstops should not field a hit and throw it to the right fielder rather than the first baseman.[49]

This classical insight has been elaborated in recent social psychological research. For social psychologists, no compelling causal account of mobilization into rebellion can exclude grievances.[50] But there are at least two different kinds of grievances. *Structural* grievances derive from a group's disadvantaged position in a social structure, but *incidental* grievances arise from wholly unanticipated situations – incidents – that put groups at risk. Unlike structural grievances, incidental ones – like unexpected disasters, major court decisions and state repression – enhance a group's capacity to coordinate.[51]

This is because these two types of grievances have different psychological implications.[52] The incumbents who are confined to subordinate positions in a social structure tend to tolerate grievances like poor wages, difficult working conditions and political exclusion *so long as they remain at routine and predictable levels.* Norms and settled customs establish baseline expectations about the treatment that subordinates will encounter.[53] If they understand that bearing routine indignities is their lot in life, they are not likely to seek redress unless the magnitude of those grievances increases sharply. Under normal conditions structural grievances foster stable expectations that tend to discourage protest in spite of deprivation. The fear and shame associated with occupying lowly and degrading positions in a status hierarchy is ordinarily demobilizing. Moreover, since the members of oppressed groups typically are skeptical about whether their protest will accomplish much, they are all the more difficult to mobilize even when conditions are objectively poor.

When incidental grievances are severe, however, they are manifest to all affected and challenge expectations. Thus, it is easy for the victims of these unforeseen events to develop a collective identity.[54] So long as the group has some shared conception of fairness, injustice framing is relatively straightforward. The simultaneous experience of the same threat, injury or insult improves coordination by providing a common focal point among disparate actors, a substitute for formal organization that is especially powerful in socially dense settings.[55] For groups that lack many of the resources that enable collective action, incidental grievances help trigger rebellion even in the absence of formal organization or detailed planning.[56]

1.6 Coordination and Commitment in Collective Action

Grievances may be serious enough to trigger rebellion, but how are rebellions made? For large-scale rebellion to occur the members of aggrieved groups have to engage in collective action. Two principal obstacles stand in their way. The first is the tendency of people to stand on the sidelines of collective action, contributing nothing and expecting others to do all the work. This free-rider problem is most pronounced in situations in which everyone would enjoy access to a group good if it is achieved, regardless of his or her own contribution. If enough members of the group take this posture, the success of collective action is put in doubt, and the rebellion may never take off or simply sputter out for lack of participation. In situations in which the prospective collective action is dangerous and uncertain, the tendency for group members to free ride is even greater. Certainly, mutineers faced these conditions in the context of the sailing navy.

The second obstacle confronting would-be rebels lies in coordinating collective action. Even if grievances are widely shared and there is little interest in free riding among the members of a group, the failure to coordinate may make rebellion ineffective; it may never take off or quickly dissolve for lack of direction or concentrated effort. When group members can coordinate around shared grievances, employ similar tactics, adopt a common strategy and focus their efforts, their rebellion is much more likely to succeed. The problem is all the more acute in situations in which there is uncertainty about the outcome and in which participation is costly and potentially dangerous. In such situations, prospective rebels want to be assured that if they act, others will also act so that the costs and danger will be shared.[57] Again, these were precisely the circumstances facing mutinous seamen in the sailing navy.

Seamen were acutely aware of the obstacles and the dangers that they faced when they mobilized a rebellion against their commanders. Large-scale collective action is rarely easy even under favorable circumstances. The conditions that obtained in the Navy were especially unfavorable, however. Military discipline applied to seamen who were denied any form of organized response to grievances. Aboard ships, officers exercised surveillance and control over seamen. All forms of insubordination and the planning of insurrection violated naval statutes and could be harshly punished, including by hanging. Even if seamen managed to seize control of the ship or halt its operations, their success in redressing their grievances was anything but certain. All in all, from the perspective of seamen's collective action, the resources and opportunities enabling mobilization were few and far between.

In this book we argue that communal bonds and the cultural practices of seamen made it possible for them to attain solidarity. Informal organization, reinforced by face-to-face relations and social ties that knit seamen to one another helped to overcome free riding by creating community sanctions for those who exploited their shipmates. Informal organization facilitated coordination. The skill and authority that experienced seamen and petty officers acquired made them natural leaders, capable of coordinating a common response to grievances and mobilizing seamen's participation in mutiny.

Although on some ships seamen failed to engage in mutiny despite harsh conditions and poor governance, on others they overcame the barriers to collective action. We will show that this is because seamen possessed forms of social capital that enabled collective action, particularly the sense of community that developed among them on many ships. Impressively, seamen were sometimes able to attain the solidarity it took to mobilize a rebellion and stick with their shipmates in the face of danger and uncertain prospects for achieving their ends.

1.7   Outline of the Book to Come

Beginning with the example of the mutiny onboard the warship *Panther*, Chapter 2 describes how social order aboard naval vessels emerged as the joint product of governance and hierarchical control and more spontaneous cooperation among seamen. Despite the creation of a surprisingly flexible social order built on sound governance and the informal institutions that allowed seamen to organize themselves, social order in the Royal Navy also had its fragilities. When governance failed and grievances mounted, the everyday forms of social order that seamen created for themselves became resources that enabled rebellion.

Chapter 3 begins with the mutiny aboard the *Culloden*, an event in which the great body of seamen rebelled against a Captain whom they accused of poor governance, seized control of their ship and stuck together until betrayed in negotiations with naval authorities. We show why in cases like this seamen managed to cooperate in planning a mutiny and committing to the rebellion. Analyzing the different forms that mutinies took and the dominant strategies behind them, we document the central role played by Petty Officers and Able Seamen in mobilizing and leading their shipmates. Seamen used specific commitment mechanisms, including oaths and round-robin letters, to ensure that their shipmates would take part and stick with a mutiny.[58] We find that social ties among seamen helped bring them into rebellion and the extent to which private grievances heightened collective ones.

The point of entry into Chapter 4 is the infamous case of the *Hermione*, the bloodiest mutiny in the history of the Royal Navy. On that ship, poor governance by a tyrannical commander drove seamen to massacre their officers and sail the ship into enemy hands. The story of the *Hermione* is surely exceptional in its bloodiness, but the grievances that drove seamen to rebel in other cases may have been similar. To find out, we analyzed hundreds of pages of court-martial documents and official reports to uncover the motives that drove mutinies. Going beyond qualitative evidence, we test our propositions about the causes of mutiny by analyzing a random sample of hundreds of ships. We find strong evidence that backs our distinction between structural and incidental grievances and shows their additive effects in situations in which external conditions intensified the effects of poor governance.

The dynamics of large-scale insurgency and the problem of commitment are the focus of Chapter 5, which begins with the career and ultimate fate of Richard Parker, a seaman aboard the battleship *Sandwich* convicted of being the principal mutineer in the great naval insurrection at the Nore. We study the causes and outcomes of the mass mutinies at the fleet anchorages of Spithead and the Nore in the spring and summer of 1797. We show that a political and economic crisis, the failure of naval institutions to address seamen's mounting grievances and the capacity of seamen to coordinate explain why the mutinies occurred. But why did the mutiny at Spithead succeed while its counterpart at the Nore was a spectacular failure? Both insurrections were motivated by strongly held grievances and sealed by oaths, but the ships' companies under the control of the mutineers at the Nore varied dramatically in their commitment to the seaman's cause. Defection hastened the demise of the mass mutiny at the Nore. Many of the same processes that explain the decay of social order and mutiny in the Navy more generally explain why the leaders of the mutiny had trouble sustaining an armed insurrection against an intransigent government.

Chapter 6 is a study of discipline and punishment in the Royal Navy. It begins with the case of the frigate *Nereide* and the conflict between Captain Robert Corbet and his crew. Corbet sought to assert his authority and improve the efficiency of his command through frequent and severe flogging of his men. His men rebelled, leading to a trial of accused ringleaders and of Corbet himself for cruelty and excessive punishment. At trial, Corbet stated his confidence in the power of penal severity to attain compliance and improve his ship's performance. We show that Corbet's beliefs were anything but eccentric in the wake of the French Revolution aboard naval vessels, when the notion that severe discipline was necessary to maintain order became widespread among officers. Studying the disciplinary records of a sample of hundreds of ships, we find that flogging became more frequent and severe after 1789. The irony of the increasing reliance on flogging in the Navy was that, rather than making officers more secure from the threat of Jacobin radicalism, it increased the odds that seamen would rebel against excessive discipline.

If mutiny was a reflection of poor governance, did mutiny, or the threat of mutiny, motivate naval authorities to make reforms? In

Chapter 7, we begin with the incredible hardships endured by the crew of the *Wager* that motivated a rebellion to explore the consequences of mutiny. Although mutinies frequently did result in the redress of grievances, we show that despite the understanding among naval officials that mutiny was a symptom of poor governance, they often erred on the side of command. In the wake of rebellion, commanders who were primarily concerned with social order often insisted on zealous prosecution of accused mutineers. Surprisingly, the institutions of naval justice balanced the demand for revenge with adherence to the rule of law. Although seamen had no effective lobby, mutiny sometimes led to major reforms including improved pay and provisions, better attention to health and welfare and tighter controls on the discretion of commanders to impose summary punishment by flogging at will. In this sense, the indirect effects of mutiny improved the welfare of seamen and the operational performance of the Royal Navy.

We conclude by showing the implications of the book for the study of collective action, make a case for pursuing the link between governance and rebellion and consider what mutiny has to teach us about contemporary social unrest, insurgencies and revolutions.

Notes

1. See, e.g., Frykman 2010; Pack 1964; Pope 1963, 1987.
2. For surveys of naval mutiny see, among others, Gilbert 1983; Guttridge 1992; Hathaway 2001; Lammers 1969, 2003; Neale 1985; and Woodman 2005.
3. Jack Goldstone 2003, pp. 55–6, observes this of the natural history approach to the study of revolution, "Scholars working from this perspective aimed to study revolutions the way that the biologists studied natural history, namely, by gathering specimens, and detailing their major parts and processes. However, despite uncovering persistent patterns in the course of major revolutions, this approach failed to present a convincing reason why revolutions should occur at certain times and places but not others." The same approach has limited progress in the study of mutiny and many other domains of collective action.
4. For nonfictional accounts see, e.g., Alexander 2003 and Dening 1992.
5. See Bligh [1792] 1962, pp. 134–41.
6. We regard Bligh as a deficient leader who relied too heavily on the lash and unintentionally intensified grievances among his men. Personal conflicts were an important factor in the mutiny but we do not go so far as the eminent naval historian Nicholas Rodger (2004, p. 404), who contends that "Lieutenant Bligh was an outstanding seaman with an ungovernable temper and no idea how to get the best out of his officers; Fletcher Christian was a weak and unstable young man who could

not stand being shouted at." Poor governance intensified such clashes and created the grievances discontented officers could exploit.

7. See, e.g., Davies 1962, 1969; Gurr 1970; Simmons 2014; Useem 1998.
8. Carrabine 2005; Cederman, Gleditsch, and Buhaug 2013; Godard 1992; Goldstone and Useem 1999; Goodwin 2001; Useem and Kimball 1991.
9. Davies 1962, 1969; Gurr 1970; de Tocqueville [1856] 1955.
10. See, e.g., Lichbach 1998; Olson 1965; Popkin 1979.
11. On the insufficiency of grievances for the rise of social movements, see, e.g., Jenkins and Perrow 1977; McCarthy and Zald 1977; and Oberschall 1973. For overviews of resource mobilization theory and its extensions, see, e.g., Jenkins 1983; McAdam, McCarthy and Zald 1996; McAdam, Tarrow and Tilly 2001; and Tilly 1977.
12. Gilbert 1983; Rodger 1982.
13. Quoted in Woodman 2005, p. 100.
14. See, e.g., Dwyer 2017, pp. 16–17.
15. Eighteenth-century naval mutinies can be divided between those whose purpose was to seize a ship and escape from naval service (e.g., the *Bounty*) and others resembling a special kind of armed strike whose purpose was to gain leverage against naval authorities in pursuing the redress of grievances. In Chapter 3, we analyze the logic of these different kinds of mutiny.
16. Gilbert 1976, pp. 82–3.
17. Boswell [1791] 1934–50, p. 438.
18. See especially Lavery 2010; Rediker 1987; and Rodger 1986.
19. Important studies of social order and rebellion in the eighteenth and nineteenth centuries include Calhoun 1982; Gould 1995; Sewell 1980; and Tilly 1998.
20. On the political process model and its extensions, see McAdam et al. 1996; McAdam et al. 2001; Tarrow 1998; and Tilly 1977.
21. See, e.g., Loveman 1998; Viterna 2013; and Wood 2003.
22. Kalyvas 2006; Weinstein 2007.
23. Goldstone and Useem 1999; Kalyvas and Kocher 2007.
24. See, e.g., Lammers 2003 and Rodger 1986.
25. Finer 1997.
26. De Tocqueville [1856] 1955, p. 62.
27. Kuran 1997.
28. Trotsky[1932] 1959, p. 249.
29. Collier 2000; Fearon and Laitin 2003.
30. On violence as one of the "great levelers" in human history, see Scheidel 2017.
31. Acemoglu and Robinson 2006; Boix 2003; Gandhi and Przeworski 2006.
32. DeJuan and Bank 2015; DeJuan and Wegner 2017; Hendrix and Haggard 2015; Thomson 2017; Wallace 2013.
33. Medina 2007.
34. On the distinction, see the discussion in Tilly 1993.
35. Gilroy 1993, p. 4.
36. See the useful discussion of the concept of governance and a call to better specify it in empirical research in Fukuyama 2013 and 2016.
37. Hechter 2018 and Hechter and Horne 2009.
38. "We have little information about the inputs of governance that might allow us to judge the performance of governments ... we can infer little from the quality of government from how much governments are spending and where they are putting their money. Big government may not be better or worse than small government" (Gerring 2012, p. 182).

39. The technical term for this explanatory sin is sampling bias.
40. Goldstone 2003.
41. See, e.g., Goldstone et al. 2010. Scheidel 2017 offers a recent example.
42. Also see Cederman et al. 2013: ch. 2; such grievances may arise from members of dominant or privileged groups, often stemming from the perception of diminishing status-group advantages – see McVeigh 2009.
43. McAdam 1982, p. 34; see also Benford and Snow 2000; Gamson, Fireman and Rytina 1982; Walder 2009.
44. Indeed, the era of opinion surveys only began in 1948; see Bethlehem 2009.
45. Scheidel 2017.
46. Hechter 1978; Kemper 2001; Østby 2008; Stewart 2008.
47. Weber [1918–21] 1978, p. 227.
48. Durkheim [1897] 1966, pp. 249–50.
49. Mead 1934.
50. Klandermans 1997, p. 205.
51. Turner and Killian 1972: ch. 4; Useem 1998; Walsh 1981. Goldstone 2014 similarly makes the distinction between structural and "transient" or "accidental" grievances and finds that both are necessary to motivate rebellion.
52. Bergstrand 2014; Tausch et al. 2011; Van Stekelenburg and Klandermans 2013; Van Zomeren, Postmes and Spears 2008.
53. Kahneman 2011.
54. Klandermans 1997, p. 40; see also Gould 1995 on the activation of protest identities.
55. As Schelling 1960, p. 90, notes, "The role of 'incidents' can thus be seen as a substitute for overt leadership and communication."
56. As the historian E. P. Thompson (1971, pp. 78–9) observed of the disorganized English crowds of the eighteenth century, "An outrage to legitimate (moral) assumptions, quite as much as actual deprivation, was the usual occasion for direct action."
57. Lichbach 1998 calls this set of problems the "rebel's dilemma."
58. See Elster 1984 on commitment mechanisms.

2 GOVERNANCE AND SOCIAL ORDER IN THE AGE OF SAIL

In the spring of 1764, the men of the sixty-gun warship HMS *Panther* were desperate. Their ship had recently anchored at the steamy Dutch port of Batavia, a colonial town on the island of Java so infamous for tropical disease that it was nicknamed "the European cemetery." On June 1, the sun rose on another muggy day to find conditions aboard the ship growing ever more appalling. Nearly a third of the crew was sickened by debilitating illnesses. The healthy seamen were fearful of contagion and disgusted by the lack of attention that the sick had received. Food was scarce. For weeks, the crew had subsisted on spoiled and irregular provisions. Meals were frequently missed or served late.

The seamen understood the conduct of the ship's officers as the cause of their suffering. Launched in 1758, the *Panther* served in the East Indies during the Seven Years' War. She took part in the British invasion of Manila and seized a rich Spanish treasure galleon. Afterward, the ship passed to Captain Mathieson.[1] Assuming command after his chance for glory and plunder had passed, Mathieson decided to cruise the coasts of Malaya where he and his subordinate officers used the ship to engage in private trade in arms, opium, lumber and slaves. When Mathieson succumbed to disease, First Lieutenant Browne became the commanding officer. With the connivance of other senior officers, Browne continued the illicit business.

Through it all, the *Panther* had a tightly knit crew with a strong sense of their rights as seamen. By the time the *Panther* had reached Batavia, the ship's company had come to regard the officers as "rogues" who, as they later testified, "were going a-pirate with the ship." On reaching Batavia, the ship tied up at the wharf and the men expected their commander to begin reprovisioning. Instead, Browne told them that better stores were not to be found on the island. But Dutch seamen with whom they spoke told the crew something else; other ships calling at Batavia had been able to secure provisions, including the coveted salt-beef.

In angry conversations held below decks and out of the earshot of the officers, the men of the *Panther* became convinced that the corrupt officers were simply unwilling to improve their lot or share any part of their ill-gotten gains. For many months the seamen's pay had been left in arrears and victuals allowed to spoil. And the officers had forced the men to load and unload bulky private cargoes, including timber, without any payment for the work.

On that hot day in June, a group of disgruntled seamen acted. Browne had given orders to the Marine sentries not to allow any seaman to go ashore, even to purchase food in the marketplace. At noon, Browne and several other officers then left the ship to dine ashore. Meanwhile, the men's midday meal went unserved. At around two in the afternoon, guards rushed into the wardroom to warn the remaining officers that "the people were troublesome and could not be kept onboard either by the petty officers on the ship or the centinels [Marine guards] on the wharf." Third Lieutenant Garrow, left in command, was drunk but stirred himself, calling on the remaining officers to arm themselves and instructing the Master at Arms to bring some Marines with loaded muskets down to the wharf.

On gaining the deck, Garrow saw a crowd led by Petty Officer Daniel Hayslip down on the wharf. Hayslip was leading his shipmates to a nearby Dutch East Indies Company merchant ship. Some of the men were conversing with Dutch sailors. Garrow rushed down with a cane in hand and demanded that Hayslip return onboard. When he refused, Garrow warned him about the punishment he was facing for this apparent mutiny. But Hayslip persisted, declaring that he and the others "would go home in a Dutch Indiaman and he would never go on the

Panther again because she was but a merchantman and there was nothing but bad usage on board." Indignant, Garrow tried to take a Marine's cutlass in order to strike Hayslip but the soldier refused to hand it over. Enraged, he began to beat Hayslip with his cane, thrashing him senseless. Hayslip was dragged back to the ship.

On seeing Hayslip about to be put in irons, a shout of "one and all" went up among the ship's company. Some of the ship's most trusted sailors began rounding up seamen and shouting "that the captain and all the officers were scoundrels and they wanted to starve the people and go pirating with the ship." They declared that Hayslip was right and that they too would desert to foreign merchantmen.

Garrow responded with a drunken harangue, declaring that their poor treatment was not his fault, better provisions had been sent for and the men need only be patient. He also sent word to Browne and ordered that Hayslip be confined below decks. The mutineers prevented it. A riot was now underway and the officers remaining on the ship feared that the men would lynch Garrow. The ship's Sailing Master, Benjamin Lockyer, pushed forward to recover the unsteady Lieutenant from the mob. With a pistol in each hand, Lockyer turned to the mutineers and declared his "determination to shoot the first man through the head that should refuse to obey the orders of a commanding officer."

Lockyer's threat sufficed to rescue Garrow, but the disorder continued until Lieutenant Browne and a body of armed men returned onboard. Browne ordered Hayslip and three Able Seamen who had led the uprising against Garrow to be put into irons and confined below deck. Taking the quarterdeck, Browne asked the men why they had rebelled. They shouted back that they had not been given proper provisions and were forced to do work "which they had no business to do." Browne condemned them for staging an outrageous mutiny and told them he would not allow them to neglect their duty. But the angry seamen repeated that "if they were [to be] in a merchant ship then they would choose their own merchant ship" and hurled accusations that the officers had cheated them of their "proper allowance."

Backed by a group of armed Marines, Browne finally enabled the Master at Arms to shackle the supposed ringleaders. But as they were taken away, highly respected Petty Officer Matthew Sewell shouted, "What are they going into irons for?" and urged the ship's company to resist. He demanded that all unhappy men should be allowed to leave the ship on account of awful conditions, "improper usage," and years of unpaid wages. Just as it appeared that Browne too might lose control, the rebellion was quashed by the brutally decisive Master Lockyer, who came upon Sewell from behind and struck him on the head with a club. With Sewell falling in a heap, the Master at Arms clasped him in irons with the others. Its leaders silenced, the mutiny collapsed.

The *Panther* returned to British India where Browne sought an indictment against the accused leaders of the mutiny. But the commander of the East Indies Station realized that this was no ordinary case. Rather than try the case in India, the Admiral ordered the ship to return to England where a thorough investigation could take place. The five ringleaders endured a long journey in irons. On the *Panther*'s return, the official investigation into the affair and the circumstances that preceded it commenced, and it shocked naval officials.

***

More than a year after the events in Batavia, the mutiny's ringleaders went on trial. They faced the prospect of statutory death sentences. But during the trial many witnesses, including junior officers, attested to the severity of grievances aboard the ship. In an impressive display of solidarity with their accused shipmates, the Master at Arms, the Marines and several other seamen who were called to give testimony against the mutineers refused to incriminate them. Having gained a striking impression of incompetence and corrupt governance aboard the *Panther*, the court acquitted all the ringleaders, effectively nullifying the naval statutes concerning mutiny. The officers in the jury explained their highly unusual ruling by stating that the crew had obviously been abused and that the "general dissatisfaction among the ship's company" was justified.

The court was considerably less lenient in judging the conduct of the *Panther*'s officers, who faced not the prospect of hanging but rather dismissal and disgrace. The indictment had listed a string of infamies and abuses against them. Lieutenant Browne was found guilty for "behaving in a cruel, oppressive and fraudulent manner," which, besides the mistreatment of his crew, included compelling subordinates to assist in the illicit purchases of slaves and ordering the Master to falsify the ship's muster so as to enroll them for wages. As such actions violated the heart of the naval regulations that governed the conduct of officers, the court duly stripped Browne of his commission and banned him from future service as a naval officer. The Second Lieutenant was also found guilty of acting as a "common trader" rather than as a King's officer. He had dealt in opium and sold muskets and bayonets from the *Panther* for personal profit. He too was stripped of his commission.

Garrow and Lockyer fared better. Although variously accused of dereliction of duty, falsifying records, drunkenness and private trade in slaves and other goods, the court noted that they had been ordered to do so by their superiors or, at least, had the permission of senior officers who were judged to have been primarily responsible for the collapse of order aboard the *Panther*. Although both were admonished for their conduct, they retained their offices.[2]

The events surrounding the *Panther* present a clear case of the failure of governance, the multiplication of grievances and the decay of social order. In the dozens of cases of mutiny we studied we discovered that whereas mutiny frequently revealed failures of governance, courts-martial usually convicted the ringleaders. In this case, the failure of governance was so unusually blatant and so severe that it overcame the institutional controls meant to protect seamen from cruel, immoral and incompetent officers.

In addition to formal regulations, ships on the high seas were regulated by professional norms and customs of the sea that were supposed to constrain seamen and officers alike. On the *Panther*, corruption and poor oversight by the commanding officers had made the ship a black mark on the Navy's reputation. With norms of governance so badly breached by the officers, the court saw the seamen as having acted within their customary rights and acknowledged the moral leadership of the mutiny's ringleaders.

2.1 Order and Compliance in the Sailing Navy

Every ship in the Royal Navy had to be able to perform two functions. First, it had to maintain operational standards and be effective in battle. Second, it had to provide a stable social order onboard that promoted cooperation between officers and men, and between seamen of different skills and qualities. The episode aboard the *Panther* shows how that social order relied on parallel and, ordinarily, complementary forms of social organization. On the one side was the hierarchical control imposed on ships by commanders who were legally empowered agents of the Admiralty that administered the Navy. On the other was the largely informal, horizontal social organization based on teamwork and face-to-face ties that knit seamen into a community and made it possible for them to maintain everyday order.

In the ordinary operation of a warship, these two forms of organization worked together to attain the cooperation needed to operate the vessel and ply its armaments. Although tyrannical, corrupted and incompetent officers – particularly of the kind that outraged the men of the *Panther* – were exceptions, life aboard ship was poorly regulated and little was done officially to stop officers from misusing or brutalizing their crews.

As a result, sometimes seamen were treated brutally, overworked, neglected and even killed by their officers, but their formal means of seeking redress were limited. The Navy failed to institutionalize the routine use of voice by seamen. When command failed and grievances mounted, however, seamen potentially could use the resources their community provided to engage in collective action against command.

Historians have often painted naval labor relations in colors of naked exploitation and class conflict. This view coincides with the traditional depiction of naval commanders – in the mode of cinematic portrayals of William Bligh – as tyrants.[3] Yet if oppression was so severe, why was rebellion so rare? Repression surely played its part. Some depict the sailing navy as an authoritarian system based on the domination of seamen by their officers.[4] Naval law defined mutiny very loosely and gave commanders a great deal of latitude in using force to maintain order and suppress rebellion.[5] Naval officers were armed and the larger ships carried a complement of Marines providing extra security. According to the authoritarian view, naval law, shipboard organization and hierarchy combined to establish the dominance of commanders and the credibility of the threat of punishment for even minor expressions of insubordination. As a result, according to one historian, "A rough equilibrium between sullen defiance and conformity seems to have been the norm in naval ships."[6]

Yet social order in the Navy could not have rested so heavily on repression and coercion. Ships frequently sailed unescorted and far from port, providing seamen with abundant opportunities to seize them. The ranks of officers were thin and seamen always massively outnumbered them. Marines frequently sympathized with sailors and naval discipline was generally not as harsh as it has been commonly depicted.[7] More important, experienced sailors were skilled artisans who could not be flogged into providing the motivation and initiative that were required to survive and prosper at sea. Most seamen routinely went about their duties and endured hardship. We know this because despite the seamen's deprivation and subordination to command, mutinies were highly exceptional events.

The unmistakable success of the Royal Navy further undermines the authoritarian understanding of social order in the wooden world. Britain rose to world power on the shoulders of the sailing navy, prevailing in the perennial naval conflicts that occurred between 1740 and 1820.[8] It grew ever stronger over the course of the eighteenth century, imposing increasingly lopsided defeats on its enemies. As the French statesman André Dupin (1783–1865) ruefully acknowledged,

> Within the last 125 years, the British Navy has sustained six great maritime wars; and in each, successively, it has employed a force more formidable and better organized than in any of the preceding. It is since this period that England has realized its pretension to the sovereignty of the sea, by occupying all the important points which serve as the keys to that domain ... England conceived this by attacking nearly at the same time the navies of France, Spain, Holland, Denmark, Italy, and even America: it has in short, opposed itself to every maritime power of the world ... Let us, moreover, recall to mind that Great Britain has never, during the epoch, employed more than 145,000 sailors and marines in effecting these prodigies.[9]

Many factors played into that dazzling record of success, but the competence and reliability of the officers and seamen of the Navy made a substantial contribution.[10]

Although mutiny was a continual threat to the social order of sailing navies, it was a much greater hindrance to Britain's naval adversaries than to the Royal Navy.[11] This is telling in light of the fact that the Navy impressed many seamen and made them serve indefinite terms of service during wartime.[12] More than fear of punishment, it appears as if obedience was premised on the belief that seamen had in the competence and responsiveness of command, existing alongside the natural incentives for cooperation that arise when people working in teams must confront the terrors of nature and battle.[13]

Whereas factory workers who evade their responsibilities may not suffer the consequences, shirking sailors endanger the safety of all. Given the stakes, seamen preferred that competent commanders would provide adequate discipline and good order. Although the interests of officers and men often diverged, the conditions aboard ships limited the extent to which militancy and explicit class conflict could thrive. For their part, officers understood that morale was vital; they had to provide incentives for compliance, including the implicit commitment to safeguard seamen's interests and attend to their welfare. Patriarchal and personal relations between commanding officers and men further tended to soften the harshness of naval life.[14]

Cooperation on naval vessels was attained *vertically*, through reliable command and good governance, and *horizontally*, through seamen's own occupational culture and informal institutions. Part of why mutiny was uncommon is simple. The kind of poor governance that fatally undermined social order, as occurred on the *Panther*, was unusual in the Royal Navy. Under ordinary conditions, the Navy was remarkably successful in selecting and regulating commanders, providing ships with necessary provisions and in maintaining orderly and compliant crews.[15]

Finally, despite its strongly traditional practices and occupational culture, the ship of the line was the supreme machine of its age – technologically advanced, expensive and involving an enormous investment of skilled labor. The Navy required large cadres of motivated and skilled seamen to sail warships, ply their armaments, weather storms and win battles – not slaves or disaffected proletarians.[16] The Royal Navy prevailed, in large part, because it could rely on its officers and men to do their duty. It did so by providing incentives for commanders to govern well and for seamen to comply.

2.2 Governance aboard Royal Navy Ships: Vertical Organization

Good government is effective. It is a product of an organization's capacity to provide its agents with the resources they need to fulfill their missions and the ability to keep track of their performance, on the one hand, and, on the other, the degree of autonomy that it can afford to yield to those agents. Effective government is produced by agents who have the means to carry out mandates but sufficient discretion and appropriate incentives to do so energetically and creatively. As there is an obvious tension between these principles, authorities seek ways to exploit autonomy without enabling corruption or the shirking of responsibility. Because outstanding performance is rarely achieved through mere conformity, states seek to maintain control without stifling officials with excessive regulations and impractical controls.

In any situation of delegated authority, problems can emerge because agents do not always share the same interests as their principals and because agents often have better (local) information about their actions and performance than do their principals. Agency theory explains how principals attempt to control agents through selection and by monitoring and sanctioning their behavior.[17]

Navies in the Age of Sail faced substantial agency problems. Given the nature of naval operations, commanders usually were given general orders. They could not be readily monitored, particularly when sailing unaccompanied as cruisers, patrol vessels, convoy escorts or couriers. This created gaps in the information available to naval authorities when they tried to assess the performance of officers who, for their part, had good reasons to keep their day-to-day actions a matter of private information.[18] In response, the Navy sought to balance a variety of formal and informal means to ensure that commanders would fight and govern their ships well. Although there is no perfect solution to the conflicting imperatives of autonomy and control, the solutions that evolved in the Navy do much to explain why it was so militarily successful, why it was able to attain social order and why events like those that occurred on the *Panther* were uncommon.

Good governance in the Navy was built on practices that established control, as far as it was practical, by monitoring the performance of officers and establishing their dependence on naval authorities for their livelihoods and career advancement. In some respects, the Navy approximated a modern bureaucracy, but there were substantial and quite consequential deviations from that model.[19] Naval officers benefited from a clear chain of command, authority that was limited to a specific office and a delimited area of competence and responsibility. Commanders were installed by the Admiralty and held nonpurchasable royal commissions. Serving as a commissioned or warranted officer was a professional career and commissions and warrants could also not be purchased (as was typically the case in eighteenth-century armies, including Britain's) and could be resigned at will.

As in many bureaucratic organizations, commissioned naval officers enjoyed employment tenure. Commissioned officers (Lieutenants, Commanders, Post-Captains, Admirals) in good standing on the Navy List were guaranteed half-pay when not in active service. Career advancement was based on seniority. However, naval employment was different than the holding of other kinds of offices because it was shaped by a repeated cycle of boom and bust. During wartime, berths aboard ships were plentiful for officers, as were opportunities for promotion. Since maintaining large peacetime navies was ruinously expensive, the end of hostilities brought rapid demobilization, however. Only a fraction of those holding commissions could be employed aboard ships in peacetime. Unemployed officers might seek other employment or turn to careers as merchant seamen, making them unavailable at the onset of hostilities when rapid mobilization was essential.

The Navy's solution to this dilemma was to provide half-pay to demobilized officers and those awaiting assignments. This created a standing cadre of qualified officers who were available for mobilization as needed. The guaranteed income policy also increased officers' dependence on the Admiralty for their livelihoods. Disobedient or disgraced officers knew that they could be easily replaced from the deep pool of half-pay officers.[20] This provided what was probably the most effective disciplinary instrument available to the Admiralty in controlling the conduct of officers. Outright dismissal of deviant officers followed from their conviction by a court-martial made up of jurors who were fellow officers. Unless their behavior was especially heinous – as with the case of the Lieutenants on the *Panther* – courts-martial were unwilling to convict officers. It was far easier for the Admiralty to deal with troublesome officers administratively by passing them over for commands while letting them remain on the Navy list at half-pay indefinitely.

Naval authorities enforced a clear line of separation between private interests and the interests and property of the Crown. Officers were not permitted to practice a second occupation concurrently or engage in private trading, as did the disgraced officers of the *Panther*. Commanding officers were obliged to maintain accurate records of their operations that were submitted to the Admiralty at the close of their period of command or as evidence in the event of a court-martial. In principle, their conduct was always subject to review. For example, loss of their ship for any reason resulted in a compulsory court-martial to find fault. To prevent omission in reporting, the Captains of ships and their Masters, the highest-ranking warranted officers, were required to maintain separate logs. In addition to redundancy as a safeguard against inaccurate or falsified record-keeping, the career tracks of commissioned officers and warranted officers were kept separate so that Masters would not benefit from colluding with the Captains they monitored.[21]

In the modern bureaucratic model of governance, officials are promoted on the basis of a predictable timetable and paid solely on the basis of fixed salaries.[22] Since differences across officers in carrying out operations were hard to assess and measures of combat effectiveness were poor, naval authorities instead rewarded obvious evidence of energy and aggressiveness. Officers who distinguished themselves through valor in combat tended to be promoted even when they were not due for advancement.[23] Moreover, naval officers were encouraged to supplement their scheduled salaries by prescribed prize-taking – that is, the seizing of enemy ships and plundering of enemy countries. Of course, commanders might well prefer the soft prize to the hard fight. As the story of the *Panther* illustrates, the obsession with private gain could lead officers to shirk their duties, act like pirates or imperil their ships in the reckless pursuit of riches. Nevertheless, prize-taking created a powerful inducement for officers and seamen (who received a small share of prizes) to be aggressive in battle and zealous in the suppression of enemy trade. It also created a strong attachment to the naval profession among officers who, if lucky and able, stood a chance of making a personal fortune.

In an ideal bureaucracy, officers are selected solely on the basis of their technical qualifications. Here, naval institutions broke with bureaucratic rationalism in ways that had the potential to undercut good governance. In the Navy, patronage played a very important role. Successful naval operations required officers who were ambitious and resourceful. They also required officers who would get along with one another. The selection of officers with good reputations or from well-connected families, many of which had previously produced successful commanders, was an important mechanism for assembling a corps of Captains who could temper rivalry with cooperation.[24] Patronage gave naval authorities the confidence that commanders were loyal, able and socially appropriate – "gentlemen" worthy of the office and clubbable enough to get along in the wardroom.

Nevertheless, patronage had to be balanced against competence and reliability. Captains were entrusted with the lives of their subordinates and with extremely valuable ships. Because recklessness and incompetence could sink a ship or lose a battle, the need for loyal gentlemen-warriors was balanced against the need for competent seamen. Patronage and privilege were not enough to secure a commission: an officer's berth could not be purchased, every candidate was obliged to have spent several years at sea, including one as a midshipman or master's mate, and they had to pass a qualifying examination before they could be commissioned.[25] This gave some assurance that officers were not merely well-connected gentlemen in fine uniforms who had no idea how to sail or navigate a ship. Honor as the basis of claims to social standing gradually gave way to the ideals of duty and competence.[26]

Further assurance that the ship was in competent hands was gained by assigning a noncommissioned Sailing Master as the highest ranking Warrant Officer aboard each ship. Masters were technical experts in navigation and ship-handling. They were subordinate to the Captain but owed their promotion to a merit-based system administered directly by bureaucratic agencies without patronage or government favor. Masters (and First Lieutenants) kept separate logs from the Captains that were independent records of the voyage and its events. Having Masters on every ship put the navigation of expensive vessels in expert hands, and put an Admiralty watchdog in every ship's company.

Naval authorities also sought to control their officers through formalized regulations. Beginning in 1653, the Navy issued regulations to restrain abuses by commanders and encourage good governance aboard its ships. These were later confirmed and amended by various Acts of Parliament. The Articles of War sketched out a system of naval discipline, although they were not principally designed to regulate the conduct of seamen and did not provide a sound penal code to govern them. Rather, their real inspiration was to control naval officers in order to prevent the kinds of misconduct that overtook the *Panther*. Besides the Articles, officers also received *Fighting Instructions* and *Admiralty Instructions* to acquaint them with the rules and procedures of the Navy.[27]

As revised by Parliament in 1749, the Articles of War explicitly forbade trade with the enemy or the fraudulent seizure of prizes or property (Articles 6–9). Private trade in goods and the use of ships to transport cargoes for commercial purposes was also forbidden (§18). The wasteful expenditure of loss of Crown property was not allowed (§24) and officers were not to falsify records (§31). Commanders were responsible for the safety of their vessels, facing mandatory court-martial for the loss of ships, for dereliction of duty and incompetence. A sweeping article (§33) allowed for the dismissal of officers found guilty of "scandalous, infamous, oppressive or fraudulent" actions.

Although primarily concerned with issues of governance and military performance, the Articles also backed the authority of a ship's commanding officer. The commander of a ship had broad authority to maintain order, including the right to inflict summary punishment by flogging on seamen for a host of offenses. Seamen were forbidden to challenge their commander's authority or refuse to perform their duty. Desertion was made a capital offense (§16). Mutiny, also a capital offense, was defined rather capaciously as "mutinous assembly" (§19), mutinous conspiracy (§20), "stirring up disturbance" (§21) and striking superior officers (§22). The breadth of the definition made for poor penal policy but reinforced the discretion that commanders had in the day-to-day running of their ships, extending as far as the issuance of criminal indictments.[28]

The Navy needed its commanders to win battles and not to flinch from the very substantial dangers that they faced in engaging the enemy.[29] This was an important matter because the mortality rate of officers – who were exposed upon the quarterdeck during combat – was shockingly high in battle. Particularly when an encounter seemed dangerous and unlikely to result in the taking of prizes, officers might well shirk their duty or remain uncommitted to the fight. Hence, the Articles strongly attempted to suppress disobedience, opportunism and free riding among its officers, with consequences ranging from dishonor and dismissal through the penalty of death (§10–16).

It is a telling feature of the professional culture of the Navy that the worst offense an officer could be accused of was the failure to fight. The loss of a ship was forgivable, but to shrink from battle where victory was possible was ruinous. The Royal Navy was unique among sailing navies for having shot an admiral for alleged cowardice in 1757. Voltaire, shocked by the execution, remarked in *Candide* in 1759 that "in [England], it is found requisite, now and then, to put an admiral to death, in order to encourage the others to fight." The whole system was meant to make it better for a Captain to fight than to run. As the historian Nicholas Rodger has remarked about the naval ethos, "Many things might go wrong with an attack on the enemy, but the only fatal error was not to risk it."[30] Seamen also saw things this way, losing respect for commanders exhibiting cowardice. A telling instance occurred on the *Sunderland* in the spring of 1746. The crew objected to a commander who they thought "was afraid to fight" and was costing them the chance to take prizes, thus squandering "the making of our fortunes." One seaman went so far as to declare publicly that "Captain Crookshanks was a coward and would not look the enemy in the face." The general contempt for the commander aboard that ship undercut his authority, ultimately helping to provoke a full-fledged mutiny when junior officers tried to impose discipline on the increasingly disobedient crew.[31]

Severe sanctions for cowardice speak not only to combat readiness as an imperative but also to the problems that navy authorities faced in monitoring commanders; severe penalties that were only occasionally applied had to compensate for the problem of accurately judging performance in combat situations. At any rate, the balance of incentives was clearly in favor of aggressiveness. If British seamen were better skilled in fighting than seamen in other navies, as many contemporaries believed, at least part of the reason must lie with the strong incentives that commanders in the Navy had to make sure that seamen were battle-ready: their survival depended upon it.[32]

Formal rules like the Articles and the *Instructions* were important but not enough to secure good governance. The difficulty lay in the fact that the Navy could not fully adopt the strategies typical of a bureaucratic state that imposes strict discipline and control over officials through regulations and administrative oversight.[33] Although naval regulations were frequently ambiguous, no set of regulations could have perfectly resolved the tension between autonomy and control. Naval vessels were frequently assigned duties that put them out of sight of Admirals. This meant that commanding officers had to be given very general instructions and broad discretion in interpreting their orders, in conducting operations and in the day-to-day running of their ships. As a naval historian has noted, "The Admiralty's main problem was, of course, communications ... The lieutenant commanding a small sloop, or a senior captain commanding a two-decker, or an admiral commanding a squadron or a station frequently was in situations where uncertainties of war left him with a vital decision which he alone could make."[34] This was partly because messages could travel no faster than ships and it took about a month for a fast packet boat to sail from the south of England to the West Indies or New York.

The autonomy that naval commanders enjoyed was vital to the success of the Navy because it enabled officers to act with initiative and inventiveness. At the same time, autonomy also helps explain why officers could go badly astray, sometimes disastrously so, as with the *Panther*. Manifest corruption and misrule could lead to rebellion, but mutiny could also occur when seamen perceived failures in routine operations or bad labor practices as signs of poor governance. When the discretion of commanders was greatest, the likelihood that grievances were attributed to them was also greatest.

From the perspective of seamen, commanders enjoyed the broadest and most consequential area of discretion in discipline and punishment. In such matters commanders were practically the kings of their ships, delegated with the power to police behavior, encourage work by having men "started" with blows from ropes or canes and to inflict summary punishment by flogging at their own discretion. As we shall see in detail in Chapter 4, arbitrary and excessive punishment was an obvious expression of poor governance by commanders and a frequent incitement to mutiny.

Perhaps the most effective limitation on officers was informal. Officers could not afford a bad reputation; there were always surplus Post-Captains at the Admiralty's disposal who could replace them. Moreover, commanders themselves were required to recruit and retain the best seamen. These highly coveted sailors paid careful attention to officers' reputations and were unwilling to serve with officers they regarded as reckless, cruel or exploitative. Without a cadre of loyal and highly skilled seamen behind him, a commander was far less likely to succeed.[35]

The concern with reputation offset some of the weaknesses of formal control. The prosecution of officers was not very effective under the Articles. Admiralty officials worried that political meddling in naval trials, patronage, favoritism and other maneuvers led courts either to fail to convict or not to punish. Various amendments to the Articles failed to resolve this problem.[36] Since the naval profession was a distinctive and highly regarded status group, however, reputation was all-important to officers. Rather than being mere scions of the nobility, a greater share of naval officers was recruited from the middling than the upper classes of British society. Never a narrow bureaucratic caste, officers remained well embedded in British society throughout their careers.[37]

Whatever their origins, commissioned naval officers were gentlemen. Consequently, they jealously guarded their reputations not only as a source of livelihood, but as a mark of their social standing. Serious malfeasance was thoroughly dangerous to officers, as the loss of commission or dismissal from the service on the basis of a court-martial would be socially and professionally ruinous. Even the intimation of incompetence or poor character could impede career advancement or damage social standing. As a result, naval officers generally tried hard to be seen as honorable and professionally reliable. Triggering mutinies was taken as a black mark against an officer.[38]

In spite of the precautions, patronage sometimes resulted in the selection of officers who were either incompetent or temperamentally ill-suited to command. A number of mutinies can be explained in part by the protection that patronage afforded to officers who were tyrannical or psychologically unbalanced. Nevertheless, naval authorities allowed commanders broad discretion, and there was little direct oversight.[39] In order to make a complaint against officers seamen had to submit a petition to these very same officers. The Articles of War (§21) specified that "quiet" petitions were the only permitted form through which grievances could be voiced.[40] As petitions could be discouraged or disregarded by commanders, and those seen as organizing them often faced retribution, in suppressing the voice of the lower decks, this rule created an unintended incentive for mutiny.

2.2.1 Resources and Command

The striking military success of the Royal Navy was not the result of better ships or superior technology.[41] Rather, well-designed institutions that created formal and informal incentives for commanders to be aggressive and to practice good government over the seamen under their control played an unmistakable role in its success.

And yet, institutions do not tell the whole story of British naval success. One of Britain's great advantages lay in her superior fiscal-administrative resources. The government was able to support the Navy because it had an effective and highly extractive system of taxation and publically financed debt. These fiscal resources allowed the Royal Navy to maintain a larger fleet than her adversaries and a cadre of trained officers on half-pay *even during peacetime*. Commanders could count on the backing of a sound system of naval administration and provisioning. The suffering of the men on the *Panther* was not the norm. Even if their victuals were basic and their comforts few, seamen rarely went hungry.

Warships were the technical marvels of their age, and the ability to sustain a large fleet was the key to long-term advantage. This is because in the century between 1670 and the 1780, the world-wide carrying capacity of cargo ships nearly tripled.[42] British foreign trade doubled between 1700 and 1780 and then trebled by 1800.[43] As the volume of trade expanded, so did the pressure on trading states to expand their blue-water navies to protect merchant shipping and over-seas colonies. The result was an arms race in which ships became larger, more numerous and better armed. Ships-of-the-line became massive floating batteries capable of engaging in gunnery battles with rival fleets and imposing blockades on enemy coasts. Maritime powers also introduced a new class of ships, the frigates: fast, well-armed vessels that could serve as escorts in the defense of trade and colonies, or, conversely, as cruisers in a *guerre de course* against enemy shipping.

As it was immensely expensive to build, maintain and support vast fleets, the demands of naval warfare overtaxed the capacity of most European states. They all faced episodic naval crises owing to the inability to fund their fleets or maintain extensive naval operations. Seamen usually bore the brunt of these crises. Fleets were frequently undersupplied and wages left in arrears. Inevitably, hunger and the inability to pay wages were powerful instigators of rebellion, especially in the fleets of the continental European powers.[44]

For seamen, the incentives for compliance began with the material rewards for service. In the Royal Navy, seamen were paid according to a fixed schedule based on qualifications and rank. Their wages were broadly comparable to those of merchant seamen, with important exceptions. First, they did not rise with inflation, a cause of serious deprivation during wartime when prices tended to rise sharply (after the end of hostilities, prices would plummet), and which led to the gradual erosion of their pay over time. Second, during wartime European navies absorbed vast numbers of seamen as they mobilized their fleets, including many men either conscripted or impressed into naval service. The supply of civilian seamen necessarily contracted, leading to upward wage pressure on merchant shipping.

During wartime the wages of naval seamen thus tended to fall both absolutely and relatively. The resulting sense of grievance could be partially offset by the allure of prize-taking. When warships took prizes, even the lowliest member of the ship's company was entitled to a small share of the loot. But seamen's wages were understood more broadly. Proscribed levels of food and alcoholic drink were statutory entitlements for seamen and the quality and quantity of victuals were better in the Navy than in merchant ships. Seamen understood their victuals as part of their social wage, meaning that shortages of provisions or attempts to deny or restrict their rations or their grog were not only threats to their material well-being but de facto cuts in pay, as the men of the *Panther* understood.

The fact that British seamen were ordinarily guaranteed their accustomed food and drink was the result of an impressive administrative and procurement system that evolved to support the Navy.[45] This sustained bureaucratic and logistical effort was only possible because Britain had developed a reliable system of taxation and public finance, allowing it to extract resources from her people at a substantially higher rate than her competitors.[46] This resource base, coupled with the advantages of being an island nation that could afford to prioritize naval over land forces, gave the Royal Navy a considerable edge. The French, Spanish and Dutch navies faced perennial problems of adequately equipping and provisioning their fleets, manning their ships and paying their seamen. Not surprisingly, large-scale mutinies were more common in these navies than in the Royal Navy.[47] Of course, shortages of provisions that resulted in privation and illness among seamen did occur, as they had on the *Panther*, but these were exceptions and tended to occur when ships were engaged in long-distance operations in foreign waters.

Sound financing and naval administration created expectations among seamen concerning their "proper usage." Proper usage meant reasonable levels of work, regular payment of wages, timely distribution of prize money and normal levels of food and alcoholic drink. Violating these expectations reliably resulted in aggrieved sailors. The seventeenth-century administrator Samuel Pepys, one of the architects of the Navy, understood how vital victualling was for an effective navy, observing that "Englishmen, and more especially seamen, love their bellies above everything ... [they] do more bodily labour on their ships than the common seamen of Holland or France, as being better fed and really stronger."[48] As Pepys understood, better provisioning made it easier to constitute social order aboard ships and to gain the compliance of seamen. When food and drink were scarce, spoiled or served irregularly, seamen felt they had just cause to rebel, as with the *Panther* and many other ships that experienced mutinies (see Chapter 4).

Another source of unrest was matters related to pay. In many instances, wages were in arrears, either because of difficulties in obtaining or delivering the funds to pay seamen, or because commanders and admirals hoped to deter desertion by retaining unpaid wages.[49] The demand for back pay was a factor in many of the mutinies we found in naval records. Conflicts over unpaid wages could be particularly bitter as wartime hostilities began to come to a close. During the lengthy process of demobilizing the fleet, seamen wanted their unpaid wages and prize money, not least because many were eager to leave their ships and find berths among merchant vessels or risk unemployment. In the closing weeks of the War of American Independence, the seamen of the warship *Raisonnable* seized control of their vessel and held it for three days in an effort to compel their commander to pay outstanding wages and immediately release them from service. This was a serious breach of order and Lord Sandwich, the First Lord of the Admiralty, refused to negotiate or concede to any of their demands. He firmly instructed Captain Hervey that "the discipline and government of His Majesty's naval force as established by law should be preserved." Hervey was to retake the ship, identify ringleaders and "secure a number of those that refuse to obey that they might be made examples." The ship was duly retaken and, following trial, seven seamen were hanged for their part in the mutiny.[50]

When seamen perceived their commanders as being inattentive to their plight or holding their pay so as to control them, it created a powerful sense of grievance. More generally, commanders who failed to secure their timely release from service, the payment of wages or bonuses, or the securing of their prize-monies violated an implicit pact between a commander and his subordinates.[51] On the *Crown* in June 1764, the crew refused to take the ship to sea. Many seamen seized boats and fled ashore. In explaining the mutiny, the ship's company said that it had duly presented a number of grievances, including the Captain's failure to secure the bonus and a two-month advance of pay promised to volunteers, but nothing had been done. This left many of the men in rags and lacking the "necessaries" for going to sea. Moreover, the ship had outfitted at Woolwich near London, but Captain Treattus had confined the crew for weeks off Plymouth harbor without the shore leave that the seamen considered an entitlement before undertaking a long voyage. Although the seamen expected a Captain to protect their interests, Treattus stubbornly refused them the "customary indulgences" that "formerly had never been denied them" by any commander.[52]

Clearly, some grievances were out of the hands of commanders. Epidemic sickness could ravage a ship's company, and ships operating in tropical waters faced additional hazards of disease. Sharp increases in material deprivation resulting from inflation could be a powerful inducement to mutiny that owed nothing to problems of command. Nevertheless, seamen believed that commanders must be held accountable.

At sea, commanders were largely autonomous and their discretion had few effective limits; this was especially conspicuous in a commander's power to inflict flogging at will. In practice, bureaucratically assigned authority contended with the personalized, patrimonial authority of a ship's commander. Face-to-face relations managed tensions and, when things went as expected, the commander's authority and ability to gain willing compliance were naturally enhanced. But if his crewmen suffered, endured harsh treatment or had reason to doubt his competence, the same personalization of authority meant that they were prone to blame the commander. By dint of their great power, in the minds of seamen commanders were responsible for everything and liable for a variety of grievances.[53]

2.3   Social Order from Below: Horizontal Organization

Command is one side of the equation that produced social order, but the other side is the order that seamen themselves attained on the lower decks. Social relations onboard ships were regulated by naval statutes and conventions, including a fixed hierarchy of ranks. The commanders, their subalterns and Petty Officers gave direction to the crew, whose labor sailed the ship and fought its battles. In many settings, solutions to the problem of social order arise relatively spontaneously, crystallizing from below as small solidary groups nest within larger groups.[54] The everyday organization of Navy vessels permitted similar social processes.

Warships had a unique social ecology due to their crowding, which collapsed the social distance between people of different class positions and cultures. This was crucial because safety depended on cooperation between officers and skilled seamen. Innovations in formal organization also played an important role in boosting the informal community that emerged among seamen. In particular, a simple reform stabilized social order aboard naval vessels and, inadvertently, helped to provide seamen with the social capital that enabled them to mobilize. In 1755, Vice-Admiral Thomas Smith remade the everyday governance of the Royal Navy with a basic reform. Called the divisional system, it was a solution to the problem of scale that faced naval vessels as compared with merchant ships. Whereas merchant ships were generally much smaller than naval ships and had correspondingly smaller crews (due to economizing by merchants, and because heavy muzzle-loading artillery required large gun-crews), warships required greater organization and better supervision of seamen.[55] The customs and conventions that regulated life aboard merchant ships, which rarely bore crews exceeding two dozen men, functioned less well in ships that were growing ever larger, with the largest ships-of-the-line containing well over five hundred men.[56]

Smith solved the problem of scale by dividing a crew into administrative divisions presided over by a ship's Lieutenants.[57] Each would be responsible for the performance and well-being of the men of his division. Beneath each Lieutenant were subdivisions presided over by Midshipmen and Warrant Officers. The Master's Mate supervised the Petty Officers, who, in turn, supervised the men who organized themselves into messes. The men ate their meals on the gun deck, divided into groups of six shipmates who ate from small tables slung between the guns.[58]

The system was as brilliant as it was simple. It made subaltern officers directly responsible for the discipline, cleanliness and efficiency of the men in their charge. As a result, work performance improved, as did the health and welfare of seamen.[59] Just as important, it fostered informal social organization among seamen. The divisional system boosted the authority of Petty Officers and allowed them to develop reputations for trustworthiness. These seamen became intermediaries between officers and men, improving communication between decks. Moreover, seamen enjoyed the right to select their own messmates and could change their mess at the beginning of the month, a right they considered sacrosanct.[60] It bound them to a small group of shipmates upon whom they could count upon for support and through whom newcomers were socialized.

Hence, rather than a mass of seamen confronting a handful of officers aboard each ship, the divisional system fostered an extensive subnetwork of informal groups that provided a basis of everyday order. Petty Officers coordinated these informal groups so that they could be directed by the officers. The result was a system that exploited formal and informal, intentional and spontaneous sources of social order. From the perspective of naval authorities, the costs of monitoring and sanctioning the crews of warships decreased substantially because the divisional subunits did much of the work of controlling seamen.[61] The formal institutions of command mostly had to deal with conflicts across groups, with those who resisted informal control and with more serious forms of deviance that could not be contained informally.

In a hierarchical sense, the divisional system worked because it clarified the responsibilities of subordinate officers and encouraged them to work closely with Petty Officers to ensure good order.[62] But it also worked horizontally because it reinforced and exploited the community that naturally arose among seamen and encouraged self-policing. When seamen were disruptive, lazy or uncooperative, they could be straightened out by their messmates, and, failing that, identified as troublesome by their Petty Officers. Teamwork and mutual dependence created natural leaders among seamen, the Petty Officers and the highly skilled seamen who were relied upon to make things work, train others in seamanship and to socialize recruits and pressed men into the customs of the sea.

2.3.1 Authority in the Lower Decks

In everyday practice, naval social order relied heavily on an intermediate stratum between the officers and the mass of seamen. Whereas a Captain's authority stemmed from his office and his legal right to command, authority among seamen was based on professional competence, institutionalized through a division of labor that made Warrant Officers and Petty Officers their supervisors and foremen.

Skill and maritime experience created another basis of authority. Seamen developed a loose social ranking based on ability and professional qualifications that privileged the voices of skilled sailors and experienced seamen. The highly skilled sailors and craftsmen were indispensable to a commander's success. Handled properly, these seamen not only sailed the ship and maintained it in fighting trim, but were the allies of their officers. Such seamen tended not to object to authority or discipline in principle, so long as it was properly executed and focused on real troublemakers, shirkers and incompetent men.[63]

Especially on ships-of-the-line, a ship's company was a large and diverse population consisting of hundreds of officers and men. Not all were sailors. In addition to the companies of armed Marines that ships carried to fight in engagements, many relatively unskilled men were needed to handle the dozens of large guns borne by a typical warship. In the crews of the ships in our sample, fewer than half were Able Seamen and Petty Officers – those who actually were vital to the sailing of the ship. The rest were a diverse assortment of less-skilled seamen, soldiers, landsmen, servants and boys.[64]

The organization of work aboard a ship owed much to an informal arrangement predicated on the natural qualities of skill, fitness and experience. Seamen were divided into groupings reflecting the spatial division of the work aboard a ship. "Topmen" worked the masts and sails of the ship. These men were highly skilled, young and agile. Among all seamen, the topmen had the highest value in the sailing of the ship, recognized as "the most useful class of people on board."[65]

"Focslemen" worked the forward parts of the ship, often the "prime seamen getting on in years."[66] Most seamen aboard a man-of-war were young; the average seaman was about twenty-five years old. Only a handful aboard a large ship would have been above forty years of age.[67] From the perspective of terrestrial society, seamen were an exotic, even dangerous, tribe unto themselves. They spoke a sailor's argot, had distinctive dress and body adornment, wore their long hair in plaits and walked with a rolling gait. Older and experienced seamen were the repositories of the culture of seamen and dominated the forecastle and the gun deck, the portions of the ship reserved for their habitation. Here seamen ate, slept and socialized. The forecastle's relative seclusion from the officers gave seamen pockets of free space that allowed them to discuss their grievances and, if necessary, coordinate a response to them.[68]

In this seagoing world, the experience of senior seamen conveyed authority. They were repositories of knowledge and custom. It was largely up to them to socialize new recruits into a life at sea and manage conflicts among seamen. Richard Henry Dana, a middle-class New Englander who went to sea as a common sailor, recalled that it was in the forecastle that one really learned how to be a seaman:

> You hear sailors' talk, learn their ways, their peculiarities of feeling as well as speaking and acting; and, moreover, pick up a great deal of curious and useful information in seamanship, ship's customs,

foreign countries, and &c., from their long yarns and equally long disputes. No man can be a sailor, or know what sailors are, unless he has lived in the forecastle with them – turned in and out with them, and eaten from the common kid [dish].[69]

The "afterguard" of the ship's company was composed of the middling seamen who worked the rear section of the ship. The mass of lesser-trained sailors were the "waisters," assigned to the middle section of the ship. These members of the crew played little role in operating the ship but formed the bulk of the gun-crews. In addition to the seamen, the waist also included the "idlers," so called because they did not man a deck watch. These included the Cook, Carpenter and his mates, officers' servants and the like. Marines belonged to the waist and were not highly regarded by seamen.

Of course, seamen deferred to their officers, but in everyday matters they obeyed shipmates whom they acknowledged as superior members of crew. Jacob Nagle, a diarist who spent two decades in the Navy, provides insight into how the skilled and experienced sailors became the natural leaders of the ship. Status could be earned through age, experience and reliability. Nagle had entered the Navy as an impressed American Landsman but rose through the ranks to become an Able Seaman and, eventually, to the highest seaman's rank, Master's Mate. He earned a reputation as a seaman's advocate and his shipmates elected him to be their prize-agent. Men like Nagle were respected as leaders by fellow seamen and recognized as such by their officers. This gave them the ability to help regulate the everyday life of the ship and they took much of the responsibility for the training and management of seamen.[70]

As Dana's memoir suggests, leading seamen like Nagle did much of the work of producing useful seamen from the mass of boys and unskilled men who entered the Navy, particularly during wartime. The Navy system for coordinating work was preindustrial, relying largely on artisan labor and customary practices. Training was accomplished through the passing down of ways of work and skills from the experienced to the inexperienced seamen and from the Warrant Officers and Petty Officers to their crews.[71]

Each ship had a "Carpenter's crew," "Gunner's crew" and so on who were the seamen assigned to work under the Warrant Officers who were master craftsmen in their respective trades. When a seaman was entered onto a ship's books he was rated (usually by the First Lieutenant). In order to be rated "Able Seaman" a man was expected to "Steer, heave the lead, knot, splice, secure a gun, make points, robands and gaskets, set studding sails, make up sails, serve rigging, strip blocks, turn in a deadeye, and clap on a seizing."[72] The larger a ship in terms of the number of guns carried, the smaller the proportion of such seamen and other skilled ratings aboard the ship who could perform these specialist tasks, and the greater the proportion of unskilled landsmen and Marines who did the manual labor and the hauling of the guns.

Skilled seamen coordinated the routine work of the ships. Hierarchy played an undeniable role on ships through the top-down control over the seamen's work imposed by the commander via subordinate officers who acted as overseers. Direct intervention from above tended to occur in emergencies, however, when officers thought that the ship's efficiency was lacking, or when seamen refused their work or performed it poorly.[73] In a small-scale, directly managed setting like a ship, personal leadership is important. Petty Officers were the prototypical foremen; the "men in the middle" between seamen and commanders. As such, they were the key players in getting work done and maintaining shipboard discipline. Having assumed so many informal responsibilities, their intermediary role also put pressure on them to be the seamen's voice in articulating grievances and demanding their redress.[74]

Petty Officers became the indispensable shock-absorbers standing between command and the crew. Prudent naval officers understood this and sought to promote seamen who were not only skilled but loyal and reliable. The frigate Captain Basil Hall recounted that dedication and teamwork were the critical attributes:

> The higher ratings of quarter-master, gunner's mate, captain of the forecastle and of the tops, and so on, are given chiefly to men who may not, in fact, know more than every Able Seaman is supposed to be acquainted with, but who have recommended themselves by their superior activity and vigilance, and have not shown themselves fit to command others by their decision of character, but evinced a severe anxiety to see the work of the department well performed. It is of great consequence to assist in every way the authority of these leading hands over the other men stationed in the same part of the ship.[75]

As we show in Chapter 3, it was a grave threat when a commander lost the support of these crucial intermediaries. Not only were they the men upon whom he relied for the efficiency of his ship, but they were also the seamen most capable of instigating a rebellion against him.

2.3.2   Life at Sea and the Limits of Solidarity

Life at sea produced a community among seamen based on direct relationships, strong social ties and shared understandings.[76] When that community was strong on a given ship, it allowed seamen to produce social order from below that they used to regulate everyday life and foster cooperation. Nicholas Rodger observes of the "wooden world" that:

> It owed almost nothing to the authority of officers, and almost everything to the collective understanding of seamen. A ship at sea under sail depended utterly on disciplined teamwork, and any seaman knew without thinking that at sea orders had to be obeyed for the safety of all. This was not a matter of unquestioning obedience – those working aloft in particular had to exercise a great deal of initiative – but of intelligent co-operation in survival.[77]

Indeed, historians with very different ideological orientations agree that at sea "the ship's company became an effective, efficient collectivity, bound together in skill, purpose, courage, and community."[78] All concur that sailors had a sense of collective identity, distinctive traditions and belief in their rights and dignity. This occupational culture helped seamen to endure difficult conditions. It insisted on mutual assistance and provided seamen with a language with which to express grievances and the means to resist injustice. Seamen were able to stick together to get their jobs done under trying conditions, and, if necessary, to join together in protest.

There were limits to the solidarity that seamen were able to attain, however. Their capacity to commit themselves to the interests of the group depended on structural and relational characteristics of the ship's company that could bolster or undermine a ship's sense of community. One of the most substantial challenges to solidarity in a ship's crew was directly related to the size of the vessel. In many settings, social scientists have observed that social order and collective action are harder to attain in larger groups.[79] In the Navy, larger ships meant larger and more diverse crews, which strained the face-to-face relations that were at the root of seamen's sense of community and the informal institutions that regulated life at sea. With informal institutions overtaxed, the larger ships were subject to stricter discipline by command. Little wonder then that the best seamen preferred to avoid serving on the big ships-of-the-line where the sense of community was weaker and formal discipline stricter.[80]

Ships' crews were usually partially dispersed following a voyage. But commanders retained some sailors as followers, while other seamen stuck together while finding assignment to new ships, or were drafted in large number from one ship's company into another. Seamen having served together previously tended to have had greater mutual trust and this enhanced their ability to cooperate.[81] This source of community was depleted by rapid turnovers in a ship's company, as when seamen were dispersed into different ships, or when ships and fleets were flooded with newcomers. Under such circumstances, crews were often composed of people who had been strangers prior to their arrival on the ship. The spontaneous social order of the Navy was distressed, in particular, with the onset of sustained warfare, when the fleets were filled with thousands of new recruits and impressed men.[82]

Another source of strain in the Navy was the presence of many foreigners in the ranks. The Royal Navy had surprisingly ethnically diverse and polyglot crews – only about half of the seamen in our sample were Englishmen, as was typical of the Georgian Navy. In addition to the peoples of the British Isles, Swedes, Danes, Germans, West Indians and others found their way into ships' companies. Remarking on problems of command aboard the sloop *Albanaise* that mutinied in 1800, an officer blamed the trouble on the many Italian and Portuguese seamen aboard the ship. "Their behaviour was in general indolent, being foreigners they pretended not to understand anything said to them."[83]

The presence of large numbers of Irishmen was a particular source of tension, however. A new British national identity that included Englishmen, Scots and Welshmen was emerging over the course of the eighteenth century but it excluded the Irish because of religion and their colonial subordination.[84] Naval authorities were fearful that foreigners were particularly prone to rebellion and officers commonly regarded Irishmen as troublemakers.[85]

Nevertheless, owing to shortages of maritime labor and poor economic conditions in the Emerald Isle, Irishmen were heavily recruited and pressed, comprising up to a fifth of the Navy's total manpower. Despite constituting about a third of the population of the British Isles, there were few Irish officers and these few were only Protestants, as Catholics – the overwhelming majority of the Irish population – were forbidden to hold a commission.[86] Irish seamen faced discrimination and were often badly treated.[87]

Interethnic quarrels on ships were commonplace. The Scottish seaman John Nicol, who produced a memoir of his time aboard several Navy ships, recalled instances in which English seamen provoked fights with Irishmen. After having been paid prize-money on the frigate *Surprise*, a raucous party quickly turned into a brawl: "The crew were all fighting through amongst each other in their drink, English against Irish, the officers mostly on shore, and those on board looking on." It is not that ethnic differences trumped all sense of community; Nicol reported that if an Irish sailor were fighting a Marine or Landsman he might get the support of his English shipmates.[88]

International crews were not unique to the Navy. The seafaring trades were remarkably international in the Atlantic world, and naval service did not require that a seaman be a subject of the British crown. But ethnic diversity frequently strained the bonds of community and undercut solidarity. In many military organizations ethnic diversity has been found to undercut group cohesion and trust.[89] A host of comparative studies have found that units combining soldiers and sailors from ethnic or titular majorities with ethnic minorities from disadvantaged and colonized nationalities were more prone to insubordination and desertion than less diverse units.[90] In the Navy, too, ethnic differences among seamen had the potential to undercut a binding sense of community and this, in turn, made it harder for that crew to regulate itself.

2.4 Social Order and the Genesis of Rebellion

With respect to the management of seamen, one of the greatest shortcomings of the Royal Navy was that it had no reliable system for handling their grievances. The articulation of grievances relied almost entirely on informal channels, and the voice of the lower decks was not always effectively conveyed to commanders. It was even harder for seamen to bring their concerns to the Admirals who supervised fleets or to the central authorities in the Admiralty. Complaints could not be made without risking retaliation. Seamen might write petitions to fleet commanders or to the Lords of the Admiralty, but first they had to be passed on by their own commanders. True, naval authorities had informal means of monitoring allegations against officers, and a commander's reputation mattered a great deal. Still, protest could be easily muffled and patronage meant that influential or well-connected commanders usually had little to fear from seamen's complaints.[91]

All in all, the experience of life at sea informed stable expectations that generally kept grievances in check and regulated everyday conflicts. The failure of this equilibrium could tip a ship toward mutiny, however. A fascinating paradox of social order at sea is that the same informal and horizontal sources of social order that maintained control also help to explain why, under exceptional circumstances, seamen could undertake a mutiny. A ship's company was no mass of isolated seamen, but a hive of crosscutting, informal groups. Seamen counted on strong ties originating in these groups to survive a difficult life at sea. But those same ties had the power to persuade seamen to join a mutiny. When one's shipmates commit to rebellion, it becomes harder to stay on the sidelines or free ride on the risks that others are willing to take. Thus, everyday social relations that fostered social order through interpersonal ties could provide the mechanism that made mobilizing a large-scale mutiny possible as small groups of seamen, coordinated by experienced leaders, committed to their shipmates.

When grievances mounted and command was perceived as incompetent or ineffective, seamen turned to experienced shipmates accustomed to providing leadership. Chapter 3 will show that mutinies tended to be led by exemplary Petty Officers and the most skilled seamen. The loyalty of men like this to their commander could avert insurrection among an aggrieved crew; alternatively, their disaffection could instigate mutiny. Returning to the case of the *Panther* reinforces this point. At trial, witnesses identified five seamen as the ringleaders of the mutiny. Three of them were Able Seamen and two were Petty Officers. Matthew Sewell was the most prominent of them. Sewell was the Captain of the Forecastle, a position of great esteem. During the court-martial, officers testified that he was among the best seamen in the ship, with Lieutenant Garrow declaring that Sewell was "the last man I should expect mutiny from."

Nevertheless, like many of his counterparts on other ships that mutinied, Sewell played the role of the seamen's advocate and called for defying the officers. His standing among the men and his moral condemnation of command played an important role in the mutiny aboard the *Panther*. If the officers of a ship were incompetent, cruel or corrupted, men like Sewell knew that, even if mutiny was a dangerous recourse, it was one of the only ones available.

Social order in the Navy was produced vertically through formal institutions and professional practices that usually assured good governance. It was also produced horizontally through informal mechanisms that knitted seamen to one another, provided leadership and enabled cooperation. Under certain conditions, however, this social order could be fragile. Poor governance fomented grievances and incidents of misrule focused existing grievances on commanders. Ordinarily, the informal groups that bound seamen together helped defuse tension by mitigating everyday grievances and keeping deviance in check. As grievances mounted, the informal groups that gave coherence to seamen's lives could provide the basis of protest. The hard part for seamen was coordinating a response and attaining the solidarity necessary to achieve their collective goals.

Notes

1. On the later phase of the Seven Years' War in Asia, see Tracy 2012.
2. UK National Archive: Public Records Office, Admiralty (TNA: PRO ADM) file 1/5303. Please see Appendix A for more details.
3. Frykman 2009; Neale 1985; Rediker 1987.
4. Valle 1980, p. 3; also Neale 1985.
5. Rodger 1982.
6. Valle 1980, p. 16; also see studies by Byrn 1989; Claver 1954; Eder 2004; and Malcomson 2016 on the practices of naval discipline.
7. Underwood, Pfaff and Hechter 2018.
8. To put its success in numeric terms, in the wars against France and her allies between 1793 and 1815, the Royal Navy lost 166 ships of all kinds to the enemy (including just 5 ships of the line), but the combined enemy navies of France, Spain, the Netherlands, Denmark and the United States lost 1,201 ships to Britain (including 159 ships of the line). See Allen 2002, p. 207.
9. Quoted in Brenton 1837, pp. xiv–xv.
10. Allen 2002; Rodger 2004.
11. Dull 2009; Frykman 2007.
12. Brunsman 2013.

13. Stinchcombe 1995, p. 77.
14. See Rodger 1986.
15. Allen 2002; Rodger 1986, 2004.
16. A wage labor regime developed early on long-distance sailing ships because "the voyage required highly skilled, disciplined and cooperative labor that would perform the necessary procedures in emergencies, and would stick with the ship until the ship came home" (Stinchcombe 1995, p. 57). The Marxist historian Christopher Hill (1969, p. 227) noted that, "Technical skill was needed to sail a ship, and, for all the flogging, some minimum of cooperation and understanding with the crew."
17. For summaries of agency theory and its implications for governance, see Fukuyama 2013, 2016 and Kiser 1999.
18. "The captain had a large informational advantage over the Admiralty in terms of local conditions; in fact, it is hard to imagine a more severe case of asymmetric information" (Allen 2002, p. 205). Moreover, with all of the uncertainties and perils of sailing and navigation, "disasters, losses in battle, and other failures of duty could be blamed on the ill fortunes of nature" (p. 205).
19. On deviations from Weberian bureaucratic practice in the Navy, see detailed discussions in Allen 2002 and Rodger 1986, 2004.
20. On the supply and demand of officers, see Rodger 2001 and Wilson 2017.
21. For an insightful discussion of how the Navy instituted monitoring incentives, see Allen 2002.
22. The canonical source is Weber 1978.
23. Rodger 2001.
24. The Navy sought to balance "political loyalty, social suitability and professional competence" in its officers (Rodger 2004, p. 112).
25. Rodger 2001.
26. Rodger 2002; see also the discussion of naval professionalism in Elias 2007.
27. Rodger 1982.
28. On the legal and practical definitions of mutiny, see Gilbert 1983 and Rodger 1986. On the excessive penal discretion the Navy gave to commanders, see Chapter 6.
29. "Cowardice and indiscipline on the part of captains and flag officers was then [in the seventeenth century], and was to remain for at least a century, one of the gravest weaknesses of the Navy, and the Articles of War were largely aimed at curbing them" (Rodger 1982, p. 8).
30. Rodger 2004, p. 272.
31. TNA: PRO ADM 1/8289.
32. As Allen 2002, p. 206, argues, "The entire governance structure encouraged British captains to fight rather than run. The creation of an incentive to fight led to an incentive to train seamen in the skills of battle."
33. Kiser 1999, p. 159, argues that technologies of communication and transportation were the foundations of bureaucratic control. Where such capacities are limited, the greater the distance of agents from principals then the greater the monitoring problems and the higher the likelihood of deviance.
34. Pope 1981, pp. 30–1.
35. Earle 1998; Rodger 1986.
36. Rodger 1982, pp. 8–10.
37. Lewis 1960; Wilson 2017.
38. The military consensus is that mutiny is a command failure; see Lammers 2003, p. 480.
39. Lavery 1998, p. 622.

40. Consider for example:

    > If any Person in the Fleet shall find Cause of Complaint of the
    > Unwholesomeness of the Victual, or upon other just Ground, he shall
    > quietly make the same known to his Superior or Captain, or Commander
    > in Chief, as the Occasion may deserve, that such present Remedy may be
    > had as the Matter may require; and the said Superior, Captain or
    > Commander in Chief, shall, as far as he is able, cause the same to be
    > presently remedied.

41. Dull 2009; Rodger 2004.
42. Maddison 2001, p. 95.
43. Hill 1969, p. 226.
44. Dull 2009; Frykman 2009.
45. See Davey 2012; Knight and Wilcox 2010; also Rodger 2004, pp. 291–311.
46. Brewer 1989. The ability to tax and spend is a key feature of strong states; see Johnson and Koyama 2017.
47. Dull 2009; Frykman 2009.
48. Quoted in Lavery 2010, p. 89.
49. State capacity is clearly implicated in mutiny. As Geoffrey Parker 1973, p. 41, observes of the dozens of mutinies that plagued Habsburg forces in the Netherlands in the sixteenth and seventeenth centuries, "In all mutinies the payment of overdue wages was the principal point at issue." Today, mutiny afflicts the armed forces of developing countries in which weak state capacities continue to undermine good governance; see, e.g., Dwyer 2017 on contemporary Africa.
50. TNA: PRO ADM 1/5322.
51. Rodger 1986.
52. In this instance, naval authorities were unmoved; after order was restored twenty seamen were tried for mutiny and desertion. One ringleader was hanged. See TNA: PRO ADM 1/5302.
53. "The Admiralty, then, put virtually no restrictions on him [the commander] – in return for making him responsible for everything" (Pope 1981, pp. 61–2).
54. See Hechter 1987, 2018; Hechter and Kanazawa 1997; Ostrom 1990; and Richerson and Henrich 2009.
55. The average merchant ship in the 1770s was about 100 tons, with only the very largest East Indiamen even approaching the size of small warship (about 1,000 tons); Earle 1998, p. 8. On average, naval warships had about ten times as many men aboard as a comparably sized merchant ship; see Frykman 2009, p. 81.
56. See Rediker 1987, pp. 83–4, and Leeson 2010.
57. On the divisional system see Rodger 1986, pp. 216–17 and 60–1, and Lavery 2010, p. 177.
58. The naval system of dividing crews – a "ship's company" – into divisions bears resemblance to the organization of armies into companies. Costa and Kahn 2008 argue that the basic sense of community that prevailed in the Union Army was due to these smaller-scale units. The same has been found in the case of the German *Wehrmacht*, which is remarkable for the level of cohesion it maintained despite its impossible situation as the war progressed. See Shils and Janowitz 1948 and Van Creveld 1983, pp. 44–5.
59. Rodger 1986, pp. 60–1 and 216–17, and Lavery 2010, p. 177.
60. Lavery 2010, pp. 275–6.
61. The logic of this kind of arrangement is discussed in Chai and Hechter 1998.

62. In effect, the divisional system routinized the necessary role played by subordinate officers in mediating between command and seamen. See Baugh 1977, p. 143.
63. Rodger 2004, p. 321.
64. In our sample about a third of the men on the average ship were Able Seamen and about a tenth were Petty Officers.
65. Lavery 2010, p. 267.
66. See Rediker 1987, pp. 210–11, and Pope 1981, pp. 187–8.
67. The average seaman in our sample was twenty-six years old. Also see the detailed portrait of the seamen aboard the battleship *Bellerophon* in Cordingly 2003, pp. 208–10; the unusually detailed muster books of the armed cutters *Lord Duncan*, TNA: ADM 45/1 and *Camperdown*, TNA: ADM 41/2 18 01 08 24 provide insight into the characteristics of seamen.
68. On "free spaces" like this in the mobilization of rebellion, see Rao and Dutta 2012.
69. Dana 1911, p. 16.
70. Nagle [1802] 1988.
71. "Fleets fitting out for sea in the eighteenth century need a nucleus of experienced topmen, but they were also accustomed to receiving their share of human flotsam and jetsam, men with neither aptitude nor enthusiasm for life at sea. It was one of the grim achievements of the Georgian navy that this unpromising material was knocked into shape" (Glynn 1999, p. 19).
72. Lavery 2010, p. 267.
73. On the organization of work, see Earle 1998; Gill 1961; Lavery 2010; and Rodger 1986.
74. Working life in the Navy was not much different from work in merchant ships, or, for that matter, preindustrial workshops ashore. See Edwards 1979, especially pp. 19–25.
75. Quoted in Lavery 2010, p. 261.
76. On the sociological definition of community, see Calhoun 2012, p. 98.
77. Rodger 1986, p. 207.
78. Rediker 1987, pp. 134–5; see also Earle 1998; Lavery 2010; and Neale 1985.
79. Hechter 1987; Olson 1965.
80. See, e.g., the memoirs of Nagle [1802] 1988 and John Nicol [1822] 1997.
81. The American military refers to this as "unit cohesion."
82. Rodger 1986, pp. 216–17.
83. TNA: PRO ADM 1/5356.
84. Colley 2003; Hechter 1998. Hill 1969, p. 164, noted, "After negro slaves, Ireland was the principal victim of the navigation system which gave England her world hegemony." By contrast, naval service was a powerful force in assimilating Scotsmen into British society; see Caputo 2018.
85. Frykman 2009, p. 92; Neale 1985, p. 96.
86. Lewis 1960.
87. Officers were counseled in one advice manual that, "if two men make complaints about each other, if one is known to be turbulent or an Irishman, flog him without further question and show the ship's company the value of a good character" (Pope 1981, p. 250); on the treatment of Irish sailors also see Gill 1961, p. 14.
88. See Nicol 1997, pp. 48, 177.
89. Habyarimana et al. 2007, 2009.
90. Ethnic diversity has been a factor in insurrections and large-scale desertion in a host of cases, including sailors in the Austro-Hungarian Navy (Hathaway 2001; Sondhaus 2001), the German *Wehrmacht* during World War II (Shils and

Janowitz 1948), the British and Dutch Colonial navies (Lammers 1969, 2003), the French Army during World War I (Smith 1994) and the Union Army during the US Civil War (Costa and Kahn 2008), among others.

91. Rodger 1986, p. 229, takes a more sanguine view, noting that "The absence of any official mechanism for complaint meant in practice that any method was accepted as legitimate." He contends that naval authorities took note of discontent on ships and "A ship company's complaint was a powerful weapon against real oppression" (p. 233). If nothing else, the mass mutinies at Spithead and the Nore (see Chapter 5), provide some evidence to the contrary.

3 ONE AND ALL
The Anatomy of Mutiny

On January 13, 1795, Captain Thomas Troubridge of HMS *Culloden* noted in his logbook,

> At 8 received on board five of the prisoners that were condemned to death, three that were recommended to mercy being reprieved. At 10 fired a gun and hoisted a yellow flag forward. Read the Articles of War to the Ship's Company. Boats of the Fleet attending alongside, manned and armed. Marines under arms. Hung at foreyard Francis Watts, Cornelius Sullivan, Joseph Curtain, Jeremiah Collins, and James Johnson.

The execution on that blustery winter morning marked a bitter end to the mutiny on the seventy-four-gun warship *Culloden*. The events leading up to it began with the Battle of the Glorious First of June in 1794. *Culloden* played a part in that victory, suffering light casualties, including two men killed. Troubridge assumed command the following October. Thirty-six years old and the son of a baker, he made the difficult climb from the enlisted ranks to Post-Captain. Having been captured by the French, Troubridge was aboard an enemy vessel during the First of June and, now released, was eager to distinguish himself in the wars against revolutionary France.[1]

By all accounts an impressive officer, Troubridge was admired for his competence, bravery and professionalism. He had a reputation as being hot-tempered and devoted to strict discipline, however. He detested defiance or anything that reeked of insubordination on the lower decks;

recall that he once remarked, "Whenever I see a fellow look as if he was thinking, I say that is mutiny."[2] Any manifestation of indiscipline and every perceived threat made Troubridge "mad with rage."[3]

The men of the *Culloden* had been accustomed to a light hand, and within weeks after Troubridge assumed command they were complaining about tighter discipline.[4] A collision between commander and crew may have been brewing anyway when, on December 2, the ship ran aground during a squall off the Isle of Wight. The ship was badly damaged, took on water and was only saved by throwing off tons of shot, equipment and stores to get her floating again. As a result of the damage, *Culloden* limped into Portsmouth where shipwrights, joiners and caulkers began to make repairs.[5]

In the crowded, dimly lit lower decks of the ship seamen were complaining. Many became convinced that the ship was bad and unfit to go to sea. They feared that Troubridge was so eager to make a name for himself that he was rushing the repairs. Rather than merely being patched up, the crew wanted the ship to be overhauled and its hull thoroughly repaired. Failing that, they thought it right that they be assigned to other ships, safe from the *Culloden*'s defects and from the grasp of Captain Troubridge.

Witnesses later identified Jeremiah Collins, an old and experienced Able Seaman aged forty years, and his much younger friend, twenty-three-year-old Ordinary Seaman James Johnson as assuming leadership in planning a mutiny. Collins had three apparent followers, sailor Cornelius Sullivan, and Landsmen Joseph Curtain and David Hyman. These four seem to have known each other well, having all hailed from Cork. Besides the Irishmen, a second leadership group assembled around another old sailor, Samuel Triggs, an English Able Seaman forty-six years old. With the ship scheduled soon to return to sea, the conspirators resolved to act. After seizing control, they would bargain with naval officials, holding the ship until they were assigned to a new vessel, or, failing that, until the *Culloden* was overhauled. They also demanded the removal of the First Lieutenant whom they despised as too eager to enforce Troubridge's harsh regime.

In the shelter of the forecastle, they gathered discontented shipmates and felt out their willingness to join the mutiny. The ringleaders knew that sympathy with their goals was not enough; those who supported the mutiny would have to follow through. To deter "skulkers," they sought to bind seamen to their plan by imposing an oath on them. A seaman subsequently testified that he was given it on a Bible and that "The oath proposed to me was that I would not desert from them 'till it was all over and that I would not divulge any secret." Cornelius Sullivan – a rough fellow who had previously been flogged for fighting and striking a Petty Officer – was in charge of making sure that the oath was imposed, and of enforcing it once the ship was taken.

On the night of December 5, with Troubridge ashore, the mutiny's leaders began the insurrection with the prearranged sign of shot being rolled across the main deck. At around ten o'clock, the "greater part" of the ship's company arose, removing the ladders to the main deck and refusing to come to duty. Men led by Francis Watts disarmed the Marines guarding the gun room. The ringleaders ordered other sailors to "stand by the guns forward," seizing the heavy cannons that assured their control of the ship. Left in command, Second Lieutenant Griffith tried to force his way below decks despite the Boatswain's warning that he'd be "murdered" if he attempted it. Griffith went below anyway but could see little in the darkness and through the cover of barricades. Shouting at the men to return to duty, the Lieutenant was pelted with shot. Meanwhile, armed mutineers seized four Midshipmen, the Carpenter, the Clerk and the Master's Mate and brought them below decks, promising "not to hurt any of the Gentlemen."

The mutinous sailors quickly established order. They erected barricades for their defense and organized the crew into armed watches, with trusted sentries appointed to guard the ladders and hatchways with instructions to "let no one down nor no one up." They prepared cannons and pointed them toward the forward hatches, in case the Captain or naval officials attempted to retake the ship by force. Remarkably, the mutiny's organization mirrored the familiar routines of the ship; sailors were assigned to watches supervised by Petty Officers who oversaw the sentinels, distributed arms and provided the ammunition. The ringleaders sagely kept the spirit-room locked in order to maintain discipline in their own ranks.

Meanwhile, up on the quarterdeck, Griffith put the Marines under arms and sent a message about the mutiny to Troubridge, who rushed to inform Admiral Bridport, acting commander of the Channel

Fleet. Boarding the ship, Troubridge ordered the crew to return to duty but they refused, insisting on "a new ship or the old ship overhauled." Early in the morning of December 6, the mutineers released some of their hostages. An officer sent by the Admiral came aboard. Unsure of where the loyalties of the *Culloden*'s men might lie, Bridport ordered that a contingent of Marines from HMS *Barfleur* be brought aboard to bolster Troubridge. He sent word below insisting that the men return to duty but the cry rang up, "A new ship, a new ship." The mutineers insisted on negotiating with Bridport directly, which Troubridge flatly refused.

Taking stock of the situation, Troubridge ordered a muster of all the men who remained loyal. In addition to his officers, eighty-five seamen and all of the Marines save for six reported for duty. This left some three hundred men, or about 60 percent of the ship's company, taking part in the mutiny. Calling the muster established which men were on which side, but it failed to bring the mutineers to heel. On the upper decks, dozens of armed Marines stood at the ready. Below decks, the mutineers were armed with cutlasses and about fifty muskets. Determined to use what leverage they had, they let the officers know that they would blast anyone who tried to retake the ship by force. If the Navy could not be moved, they would blow up the ship or scuttle her.

Late in the afternoon, Admiral Bridport came aboard the *Culloden*. He agreed to speak with the mutineers, but insisted that they must surrender to Captain Troubridge. The mutineers rejected Bridport's demand, barring a guarantee that their grievances would be redressed and that they would be granted immunity from prosecution. They argued for a new vessel because the "ship was in a bad state" and might founder if she ran aground again or was beset by a winter squall. When Bridport reminded them that such decisions were solely matters for naval authorities to determine and that they could be compelled to resume their duties, they warned that, if so, then in the next battle, "they wouldn't fire a shot but would be taken by the French."

The standoff continued. Although Troubridge may have been keen to use force to retake his ship, Bridport recognized that this was a delicate matter and that, being in port, events on the ship had already come to the attention of the whole fleet. He was not eager to spill blood, lose a valuable warship or inflame the feelings of other seamen. On December 8, Bridport sent a delegation led by Sir Thomas Pakenham to negotiate a return to duty by the mutineers. Captain Pakenham, the son of an Anglo-Irish baron, was a highly respected officer who had distinguished himself at the Glorious First of June.[6] In spite of Pakenham's advice that they should immediately return to duty, the mutineers "refused to do so without the word and honour of the Captains that no person should be hurt" for his part in the mutiny.

The solidarity displayed by the mutineers posed a serious problem for the naval authorities. The seamen had remained firm in their commitment to one another and their demands for several days, were well armed, held hostages, controlled the ship's stores of provisions and had the capacity either to inflict heavy losses on their attackers or even sink the ship. In short, they had the ability to withstand a long siege, a situation that was intolerable to Troubridge and the Navy. Although meeting their demands might set a bad precedent, dislodging them by force was little better.

As a gesture of goodwill, on December 9 the mutineers complied with a request to send up food and drink from the ship's stores to feed the loyalists and Marines who remained above in a state of armed readiness. The next day, at three o'clock in the afternoon, Pakenham resumed negotiations with the mutineers. No record exists to document precisely what the agreement between him and the mutiny's leaders was because Pakenham was later excused from giving testimony before the court-martial. Apparently he persuaded the mutineers to return to duty on the condition that none would be punished. Sir Thomas's offer would have seemed credible. He was widely admired for his honor and "humane sympathies." Moreover, it was understood among seamen that mutinies could be resolved through negotiations. The customs of the sea allowed for the possibility that, if the authorities saw seamen's grievances as reasonable, if no serious injuries had been inflicted or damage done and if the seamen had maintained unity and purpose, mutinies might end without violent retaliation or a court-martial being called.[7]

With Bridport flatly refusing their demands, the seamen apparently saw little to be gained by maintaining the mutiny. Taking Pakenham at his word, they laid down their arms and climbed up to the main deck. Troubridge immediately ordered a muster to be held under Marine bayonets to document each man's participation. Consulting his officers, Troubridge indicted ten seamen as "principal mutineers" from that list. The waiting Marines put them in irons and removed them from the ship to await trial.

The court-martial began on HMS *Caesar* at Portsmouth on December 14 and lasted nearly a week. Troubridge blamed the mutiny on the influence of the "lower order of Irishmen" on the ship's company. However, the seamen identified as leading figures in the mutiny were generally acknowledged by their officers and shipmates as being "diligent," "sober," "orderly" and "deserving"; praised even as being "among the best men in the ship." Two of them were acquitted outright, but eight others were convicted of having been "principal ringleaders" of the mutiny and were sentenced to hang. The old seaman Triggs and two younger men were "recommended to mercy" as an acknowledgment of the "excellent character given to each of them by their officers." A royal pardon was forthcoming and they were spared the noose.

The seamen believed that Pakenham had given his "word of honour" that if they surrendered none would be punished or face a court-martial. Yet Pakenham's alleged betrayal could not be substantiated because Sir Thomas failed to testify on the grounds that he was suddenly taken ill. This was not the only irregularity. During the trial, some of the sailors called as witnesses were reluctant to give evidence because it would violate the oath of solidarity they had given to their shipmates. One sailor openly declared that he would stand by his oath as a matter of honor. In so doing, he might have made a mockery of Pakenham's duplicity, but he was sentenced to three months in the Marshalsea prison for his scruples. On the *Culloden*, the seaman's obligation to submit to formal authority clashed with obligations born of solidarity with shipmates. Mutiny was born from the resulting confrontation. But what shaped and determined such confrontations?

3.1   Mutiny in the Age of Sail

Two images tend to influence our thinking about mutinies. In one, they are romantic affairs in which seamen yearning for liberty or their sweethearts depose tyrannical commanders and sail away with the ship. The *Bounty* is the leitmotif for this image. The other is of a bloody uprising in which crazed and abused seamen slaughter their officers. The frightful case of the *Hermione* is the Royal Navy's exemplar.[8] Mutinies thus become idiosyncratic, driven by eccentric personalities and led by "a small knot of desperate men [who] took reprisals for the wrongs they had suffered." Whatever the romance and the terror they involved, mutinies were ultimately futile, since they were driven by fantasies of revenge and escape and could not change the system that exploited seamen.[9]

The case of the *Culloden*, which has much in common with the majority of the mutinies we have uncovered, tends to dispel such images. The lack of systematic research on mutiny as a form of rebellion made it easy to discount mutiny as collective action motivated by grievances, employing effective tactics and shaped by strategic considerations.

In contrast, our research reveals that the organization of mutinies can best be explained by the logic of collective action.[10] Mutinies resulted from the convergence of long-standing structural grievances among seamen combined with incidental grievances that intensified discontent and focused it on the person of the commander. The *Culloden* is typical in this regard. And the detailed narrative evidence on dozens of mutinies we assembled shows that seamen employed tactics that are consistent with different strategies to seek redress of their grievances.

As on the *Culloden*, the mutineers had to solve participation problems. That is, they had to overcome the social dilemmas that routinely obstruct the capacity of a group's members to act in their collective interest.[11] Foremost among these in high-risk collective action like rebellions is providing members of a group with the assurance that if they act, then others will join them.[12] When collective action is as perilous as mutiny can be, even highly disgruntled rebels are rightly worried about taking the initiative. The "who-goes-first" problem can prevent a mutiny from ever launching, or else cause its collapse before it has progressed very far. Seamen planning a rebellion have to be assured that, when the time comes, they will act together. Essentially, they face a coordination problem: even if shared grievances are intense and there is a willingness to act on behalf of the group, collective action fails if it is not directed and if participants have no confidence that others will also participate.[13]

The participation problem was especially acute in the case of mutiny. Seamen faced both grave dangers and profound uncertainty when considering rebellion. Part of the difficulty was that the Navy's

definition of mutiny was so broad that it treated all manner of disobedience – both individual and collective – and disorderly conduct as capital
crimes. In principle, planning a mutiny was just as subject to hanging as
was taking part in one or, for that matter, of having slain the officers. In
practice, however, not all mutineers were indicted, and not all of those who
were indicted hanged.[14] This ambiguity was compounded by uncertainty
concerning how the authorities would respond to mutiny – would they seek
a moderate settlement or crack down on the rebels?

In most instances, mutinies cannot succeed unless a substantial
portion of the ship's company backs them. If the salience of shared
grievances is great, it is easy for the ringleaders of a mutiny to win the
sympathy of their shipmates. Much more difficult is mobilizing them to
risk their necks and keeping them involved in the face of danger and the
threat of punishment. Many of those who sympathize with a mutiny in
principle will be content to remain bystanders, passively observing
events as they unfold. They will surely benefit if the crew's grievances
are redressed, but most of them will risk no personal danger. Even if they
choose to participate at early stages of the rebellion, they may drop out
later when their costs rise, or the prospects of success dim. This is part
and parcel of the notorious free-rider problem in collective action.
Seamen were well aware of it, and their motto insisting on "one and
all" was a plea for solidarity. Solidarity meant that seamen could
persuade or compel their shipmates to act in their common interest by
putting the needs of the group ahead of their narrow individual
interests.[15] Although the norm of solidarity was dearly held in the
maritime world, actually attaining it in a dangerous and uncertain
conflict was by no means assured.

In all the mutinies we studied, rebellious seamen intentionally
employed tactics that promoted *coordination* and secured the *commitment* of their shipmates. The occupational culture and social capital of
seamen provided them with resources – particularly the free spaces of
the forecastle and the lower decks, and the trust that emerged from face-
to-face relationships – that made coordination and commitment
possible.[16] Seamen developed ways of gauging and securing the commitment of shipmates to a prospective mutiny, the most important of
which were the drafting of protest letters and the swearing of illegal
oaths.[17]

Mutiny as a form of collective action can be thoroughly anatomized. We systematically examined dozens of cases of mutiny aboard specific ships during the Age of Sail. Although each episode of mutiny has distinctive features and, as it were, unique personalities, we find that mutinies assumed definite patterns. Despite the strong emotions that are generated in every rebellion, mutinies reveal deliberate strategies and tactics. We find that mutinies could be relatively spontaneous or well planned. They could be bloody or remarkably nonviolent. They could be well led or disorganized. They could be short-lived or involve a lengthy standoff.[18]

In general, however, mutinies varied across two dimensions. The first concerns the ability of seamen to coordinate a common response to grievances and to maintain control over their own ranks in the midst of rebellion. In this sense, we find that mutinies tended to be either *organized* or relatively *spontaneous*. Of course, compared with modern interest groups like labor unions, the organization of mutinies was always rather loose; seamen had neither the means nor the opportunities to attain formal organization, and in fact any such attempt would have been considered to be an illegal combination punishable by death. Nevertheless, many mutinies were launched by conspiracies in which "ringleaders" actively sought to mobilize and direct rebellions against command through informal organization. Other mutinies were more spontaneous, occurring in reaction to a situation with little advance planning or leadership. In these mutinies, too, leaders deliberately sought to activate solidarity and communicate a common purpose. Spontaneous mutinies were emotionally expressive but not necessarily irrational because of this. Rather, they occurred in response to situations that appeared to present opportunities to redress grievances and in which emergent rationality shaped collective action.[19]

In the second place, mutinies varied by their objectives. Although they were forbidden by law and punishable by the harshest of penalties, mutinies and the threat of mutiny were regular features of the social order of the sailing navy.[20] Whereas the specific demands and aspirations of seamen varied across mutinies, a clear pattern is nevertheless discernible. In broad terms, seamen either sought to *voice* their grievances and demand redress of them through mutiny or they sought to *exit*, to escape naval service through mass desertion or by seizing the vessel and sailing it to a foreign refuge or enemy power.[21] Table 3.1 categorizes our cases on these two dimensions of variation.

Table 3.1 *Mutinies in our sample by type*[*]

	Voice	Exit
Planning	Armed strike	Piratical seizure of ship
	Adamant (B), Alfred, Atlas, Barfleur	*Albanaise, Bounty,*
	(B), Blanche, Camilla, Canada,	*Chesterfield, Danae,*
	Crown, Culloden, Defence,	*Dominica, Ferret,*
	Dispatch, Egmont, Impeteux,	*Goza, Hermione,*
	Inflexible, Intrepid, Invincible,	*Hope, Jackal, Jason,*
	Janus, Namur, Raisonable,	*Lively, Marie*
	Romulus, Saturn, St. George,	*Antoinette, Prince*
	Suffolk, Swallow, Temeraire,	*Edward, Shark, Wager*
	Terrible, Tremendous, Winchelsea,	(n = 16)
	Windsor Castle (n = 29)	
Spontaneity	Riot	Collective desertion
	Adamant (A), Barfleur (A),	*Castor (A), Panther,*
	Beaulieu, Bedford, Berwick,	*Princess Royal,*
	Castor (B), Defiance (B),	*Royal Oak* (n = 4)
	Kingfisher, Minerva, Nereide,	
	Orion, Santa Monica,	
	Sunderland (n = 13)	

Note: [*] Successive ships with the same name are indicated serially.
Source: Hechter, Pfaff and Underwood 2016.

By voice, we simply mean that members who are dissatisfied with an organization can attempt to speak out against it. In most instances, voice does not take the form of collective action, and it can yield benefits without involving the members of a group. In some contexts, however, collective action alone can be expected to be an effective vehicle for voice. In the sailing navy and other authoritarian settings, voice means protest because there is no effective institutional practice for the airing of shared grievances. Individual complaint is ineffective and any attempt to voice grievances collectively is forbidden. In the Navy, exercising voice was mutiny. According to British law of the eighteenth and early nineteenth centuries, any collective defiance of legitimate authority was illegal and collective action was deemed to be a criminal conspiracy. "Combinations," secret societies and the taking of oaths were all specifically prohibited to sailors under civilian law as well as by the Articles of War.[22]

By exit, we mean the collective effort to escape service in the Navy. Desertion was the greatest threat to order and discipline in the armed forces of the eighteenth and nineteenth centuries. It severely hampered operations in armies as well as navies.[23] Seamen deserted for a variety of reasons. It was a way to escape discipline and the harsh conditions prevailing aboard naval vessels. It was appealing to seamen who had been impressed or who wanted to return to their families after long periods of service. For example, the married seaman John Nichol had served for seven years without shore leave when he finally got paid off in 1801 and managed to escape from a press gang ready to reenlist him in the Navy. Other seamen deserted simply to take a better berth aboard a civilian vessel offering superior conditions or wages.[24]

Ordinarily, desertion, unlike mutiny, requires no collective action. In fact, in our sample, about 6 percent of the average ship's company deserted in a given year. Desertions, either by isolated seamen or in small groups, tended to occur when a ship was in port or at an anchorage. Captains' and Masters' logs describe desertion in terms of opportunism, such as when seamen slipped over the side of a ship in port while on nighttime watch, stole a jolly boat or absconded when sent ashore on some errand.

That collective exit was a less common strategy than collective voice should be expected. Exit is ordinarily an individual response to the discontents that someone has with an organization and requires little or no coordination.[25] In the case of the sailing navy, seamen generally preferred to desert rather than to engage in collective action. Whereas large-scale mutinies were rarely attempted, desertion was commonplace – some forty thousand seamen deserted from the Navy in the period between 1793 and 1802 alone.[26]

In most instances, the desertion of disgruntled and disruptive seamen from a ship's company probably helped to stabilize social order, thereby reducing the chances that mutiny would occur. This is because in most contexts, exit is an alternative to voice, providing immediate relief from grievances and requiring no difficult coordination with others in order to succeed. However stabilizing that the desertion of highly disgruntled sailors probably was, the Navy could not afford to allow many seamen to abscond from its ships. Large-scale desertion worsened the endemic manpower shortage of the Navy, particularly during wartime when many seamen had to be pressed into service. In an effort to deter it, officers tightened discipline. The sanctions for desertion were harsh. Deserters who were caught in the act or captured afterwards faced either flogging at their commanders' discretion or trial by court-martial. Under the Articles, desertion was punishable by hanging (§16), although, in practice, most deserters were simply flogged.

Commanders usually made it hard to defect. The labor problem gave rise to the strategy of confining seamen on their ships for extended periods of up to several years. Seamen were rarely given shore leave during wartime. Moreover, when not at sea, naval vessels typically remained in anchorages off the coast rather than docking in ports. This was because very few seamen knew how to swim. In short, the costs of attempting desertion could be high, and opportunities to abscond were limited. Naturally, all these measures to deter seamen from running away tended to increase their disaffection.

One response to blocking exit and imposing indefinite confinement was the collective effort to escape the Navy. Depending on its level of organization, exit mutinies took two forms. The first was relatively spontaneous and poorly coordinated mass desertion. In this type of mutiny, rebellious seamen tried to flee a ship in great numbers. The case of the *Panther*, described in the previous chapter, is an example of this kind of mutiny. The other form of mutiny was the seizure of the ship in order to sail it into a foreign port or a remote territory safe from the grasp of the Navy.[27] The *Bounty* is a famous example of this kind of mutiny, which was especially abhorrent to naval authorities and treated as a species of piracy.

3.1.1 Organized Voice: Mutiny as Armed Strike

Although they had common features and common causes, not all mutinies were alike. Mutinies took different forms depending on the grievances that motivated them, the goals of the mutineers and the level of organization and planning. The case of the *Culloden* was an armed strike against naval authority, the most common form of naval rebellion, comprising about half of the mutinies in our sample.[28] The mutiny on the *Culloden* is fairly typical of mutiny as organized voice. In mutinies of this type, seamen refused to do their duty, and they would not work or take the ship out to sea until their demands were met. The idea of striking was familiar to early modern seamen. In addition to the knowledge they might glean about armed strikes in the Navy, naval seamen were mostly recruited from merchant vessels and were well acquainted with work stoppages.[29] Mutinies taking this form often followed from changes in policy, changes in command or the attempt to change the style of command or impose or enhance standards of discipline.

One such mutiny occurred in January 1797. Captain Henry Hotham was named to the frigate *Blanche* in the place of a well-liked commander. The ship's Petty Officers had heard rumors that Hotham was a cruel and arbitrary officer. They perceived his appointment as a punishment and a slight against the ship's company and organized the men to resist it. Hotham, in turn, decided to make a show of force by coming aboard with a party of armed officers. Seaman Jacob Nagle recounted the resulting showdown in his memoir:

> Captain Hotham bearing the name of such a tartar by his own ships crew, that our ship mutinisied and entirely refused him. He came on board, had all the officers armed on the quarter deck and all hands turned aft to hear his commission read at the capstain head. They [the ship's company] all cried out, "No, no, no." He asked what they had to say against. One of the petty officers replied that his ships company informed us that he was a dam'd tartar and we would not have him and went forward and turned the two forecastle guns aft with canister shot.[30]

The standoff was only resolved when Horatio Nelson himself, the Commodore of the squadron, came onboard and pledged to supervise Hotham and remove him if he mistreated the crew. As the story of the *Blanche* or the *Culloden* make clear, this kind of mutiny was a dangerous business and posed a daunting test of seamen's ability to coordinate an uprising and to maintain solidarity – what seamen called the commitment of "one and all" to the mutiny – in a confrontation with naval authorities.

If informal means of communicating seamen's grievances failed or commanders were indifferent to their complaints, a labor boycott was one of the only means of communicating their grievances and gaining leverage with naval authorities. In the economics literature, strikes emerge as a result of strategic interactions between the managers of firms and the leaders of organized labor. They occur because of imperfect or asymmetric information between the parties that leads them to misjudge the costs and incentives facing the opposite party. Whereas private information was an important element of the conflicts driving mutinies, the model of the two-player game can only go so far given the situation in the sailing navy. In the Age of Sail, mutiny leadership was informal and diffuse, and there were no institutions of collective bargaining. There was no right to strike or to organize; both were potentially capital offenses under the Articles of War. Furthermore, unlike in factories, commanders did not use lockouts or other measures to deny seamen wages as a means of winning concessions.[31]

Mutinies like this were something like unsanctioned, or wildcat, strikes in modern industrial relations. The objective was usually to voice grievances against specific commanders and their practices rather than against general conditions in the Navy (although the great mutinies of 1797 analyzed in Chapter 5 did just that). The protest often began with the drafting of a letter or petition that stated grievances and gave the reasons for defiance. The sailors at the core of a mutiny often pushed other seamen to add their names to the protest letter or take an oath of solidarity, as this was seen as the first step in getting their shipmates committed to a mutiny.

A strike halted the working of a ship, and during an armed standoff mutineers effectively had to control the ship, or at least some defensible section of it. Once in control, the point of such mutinies was not to abscond or take revenge on hated officers. Rather, mutineers sought to draw attention to their grievances and win improvements in their situation. They invariably promised to return to service once their demands were met, and sought assurances that no one would be punished for their participation.[32]

These mutinies were driven by deprivation compounded by the perception that commanders were strict, inflexible and insensitive to seamen's welfare. Mutiny became more likely when seamen believed that ordinary complaints communicated through Petty Officers and subaltern officers would be ineffective or, worse, invite reprisals. Given the obstacles to obtaining a transfer to another vessel and the danger and difficulty of desertion, highly discontented seamen were denied the exit option, compelling them to consider the possibility of an armed strike.

Armed strikes required leadership and resolve. Because of the high costs and uncertainty surrounding mutiny, nearly all mutinies that took the form of strikes required extensive coordination and extensive participation. To launch a mutiny like this and have any hope of prevailing in a standoff like the one on the *Culloden*, ringleaders had to make deliberate efforts to attain solidarity and frame mobilization in terms of "ill-usage," evoking norms of fairness and portraying their uprising as legitimate.[33]

As on the *Culloden*, mutineers armed themselves and erected barriers to acquire leverage in their negotiations and prevent the officers from easily restoring control by force. Armed strikes always occurred in ports or in anchorages – not in the face of the enemy or on the high seas, where a work stoppage would imperil the crew as much as the officers and would have undermined the legitimacy of the action. Ringleaders tried to maintain discipline in their own ranks and scrupulously avoided violence against officers or serious damage to the ship. Only by professing loyalty to the Crown, maintaining a disciplined approach and avoiding violence, could they ever hope to negotiate successfully with the authorities and avoid reprisals.

Petitions and oaths helped to attain solidarity in many of these mutinies. They were not always sufficient to secure the commitment of reluctant seamen, however. Sometimes ringleaders and their supporters resorted to more direct means of protest, including threatening recalcitrant seamen to join the mutiny, confining them below decks so that they could not defect to the officers, or assaulting those who opposed their plans. They recognized the clear incentives that bystanders had to free ride on the efforts of those who literally risked their necks. As one ringleader declared on the *Namur* in 1747, he would not tolerate shipmates who did nothing but "would be as willing to go ashore as any man" if the mutiny succeeded in winning their demand for shore leave. He and the other ringleaders backed up their determination by threatening free riders at sword point and wounding some with blows from cutlasses.[34]

Due to the constraints of naval discipline, mutiny was more dangerous and uncertain than were illegal strikes during the Industrial Revolution. With the odds against them, seamen were sensitive to political opportunities when considering an armed strike. In limiting mutinies to periods in which the ship was in port or anchorage, they made it possible to appeal to naval authorities above their commanders who they believed would be more likely to respond to their demands. In fact, they rarely addressed their petitions or protest letters to their immediate commanders, but rather to senior naval officials. Success in negotiations was by no means assured, however. Seamen tended to risk a strike only if they perceived that they had leverage. They thought that they had leverage if they considered their demands legitimate; that is, they were asserting no more than their "proper usage" and were acting according to accustomed maritime norms. If their commander seemed weak or compromised, or had acted in a clearly egregious or unacceptable fashion, seamen had greater confidence that he would yield or that naval authorities would not take his side in a dispute.

The perceived efficacy of the armed strike was greater when seamen thought that, through controlled disruption, they could impose significant costs on their commander or on naval authorities. This meant refusing to work and preventing the ship from being put into service. For this strategy to be effective, seamen had to be prepared to hold out, which could provoke a long standoff, as on the *Culloden*. Naval authorities were in a strong position to resist the holdout strategy if they had other naval vessels at hand, or a surplus of sailors who could be deployed in place of the armed strikers. Obviously, these conditions made it unlikely that an armed strike would succeed during peacetime and, in fact, all but a few of these strikes occurred during wartime.

Armed strikes were hard to resolve because the right to collective bargaining was unrecognized, and the leaders of mutiny had no legal standing to negotiate. Their only leverage came from withdrawing their labor that had to be backed, as one ringleader memorably put it, by "the power of gunpowder." Naval authorities, like Admiral Bridport in the *Culloden* mutiny, were reluctant to negotiate because concessions might encourage future mutinies. Moreover, they were also loath to recognize mutineers as having the standing to make demands. Seamen could only succeed if they convinced naval authorities that they could sustain their armed strike for a long period of time, and that dislodging it by force would be too costly, bloody or unpopular to risk. As on the *Culloden*, the result was often a standoff as mutineers and officers tried to wait each other out. Although both sides had clear incentives to avoid long standoffs, mutineers were generally less able to hold out than the authorities.[35]

Apart from the authorities' resource advantages, standoffs favored naval officials because their information was more complete.

For the leaders of an armed strike, the most important determinant of their leverage was the belief that solidarity in their own ranks was high.[36] Unless the majority of seamen took their side and were willing to stand by their shipmates, even in the face of threats of retaliation and a long standoff, mutineers could not hope to prevail.[37] Armed strikes only worked if seamen could redirect the fundamentals of naval power – numbers and organization – against the authorities. Long odds faced mutiny leaders because they had to maintain internal order, discipline fellow seamen and manage their meager resources in order to maintain and strengthen their negotiating clout. Imperfect information and uncertainty about the motives and true bargaining position of the authorities made settlements difficult to reach.

These mutinies were just as hard to bring to a satisfactory conclusion as they were to mobilize in the first place. Ironically, a strong sense of solidarity among the mutinous crew could complicate a settlement. On the one hand, without solidarity an armed strike was likely to fail. On the other, strong feelings of solidarity among crew members, combined with bitter grievances and the perception that officers were their adversaries and naval authorities untrustworthy, could promote a self-defeating militancy. Militancy made it more difficult to reach a compromise settlement, to concede defeat or to accept a return to duty under the same officers.

Sometimes voice mutinies succeeded outright, but about half the time they failed to win any of their objectives. Naval authorities might not give ground and the commanders opposed settlements that weakened their authority. If so, then a holdout by armed mutineers eventually would collapse either due to force or exhaustion. Afterward, concessions might be made, but ringleaders would be indicted and a court-martial would convene.

3.1.2 Organized Exit: Mutiny as Piracy

The armed strike was predicated on seizing temporary control of a ship to negotiate the redress of seamen's grievances. Organized exit was an entirely different response to grievances. It was premised on seizing a ship and using it as a vehicle to escape from the Navy altogether. This form of mutiny was the most violent and most feared kind in the Age of Sail. Seizing a naval vessel and sailing away with it was not only mutiny but piracy – an act of robbery at sea – because it involved the theft of Crown property. Since naval ships represented the most advanced technology of the era, they were extremely expensive to build or replace. Whereas this kind of rebellion has done the most to shape our conception of mutiny, it comprises only about a quarter of the mutinies in our sample.

Although they have been portrayed as having been driven by the strongest of passions, the evidence suggests that organized exit mutinies were largely crimes of opportunity. Attempting to seize a ship was a dangerous business. Several factors were necessary to convince seamen that a mutiny like this could succeed. Organized exit occurred when and where aggrieved seamen could not readily desert but thought that they had a reasonable chance of seizing the ship and escaping from retribution. Because seizing, holding and navigating a large ship presented nearly insurmountable difficulties, these mutinies took place on the smaller ships of the navy.[38] More than half occurred on unrated vessels – the smallest ships of the fleets, such as sloops, gun-brigs and cutters. These small ships were used as convoy escorts, for patrolling coasts, carrying messages and other services in support of the fleets. The remainder occurred on smaller frigates – fifth- and sixth-rate vessels – fast, lightly armed ships with a single gun deck. In short, this kind of mutiny did not occur on line-of-battle ships like the *Culloden*, but rather on ships that routinely sailed unaccompanied and away from home ports: "ships mostly used as 'cruisers and convoys,' for attack on, and particularly defence of, trade."[39]

Such ships were vulnerable to a *coup d'etat*. They usually operated outside of fleet formations, were commanded by less senior officers (Lieutenants and Masters), had fewer intermediate officers between the commander and the crew and, in the case of unrated vessels, lacked a contingent of Marines. A few organized exit mutinies, such as that aboard the *Jackal* in 1779, occurred in or near an anchorage of the Royal Navy. Much more commonly, organized exit mutinies occurred in locations that made it easier for the conspirators to seize power and escape. In fact, three-fourths of organized exit mutinies occurred at sea, generally remote from other naval vessels and close to foreign harbors. Consequently, they occurred along the far-flung reaches of Britain's seaborne empire, in the Mediterranean, Pacific, South America, West Africa and Asia. The greatest share took place in the West Indies. There sickness and difficult conditions intensified grievances while the many closely situated islands and coasts offered potential French, Spanish and American havens.

In organized voice mutinies, ringleaders faced the problems of large-scale coordination and overcoming free riding among the bulk of the seamen aboard a ship. Generally speaking, this was not the challenge confronting ringleaders in organized exit mutinies. These mutinies did not require the participation of a majority of the ship's crew. A tight cadre of mutineers could reasonably seize a small ship and abscond with it, particularly if the bulk of the sailors and Marines were expected to remain passive bystanders during the taking of the ship. In order to succeed, they required a well-coordinated band prepared to use force to take and hold the ship. They also needed a plan for sailing it to a foreign refuge. This was daunting because even skilled seamen did not know how to navigate a ship out of sight of the land. They usually had to persuade a specialist Petty Officer such as a Master's Mate who could perform the navigation, or else compel the ship's Master or another officer to do it.[40]

Given the secrecy and surprise required to launch these mutinies, ringleaders faced assurance problems. How could they be sure that the core of conspirators was reliable? Coconspirators had to be selected carefully, on the basis of their known grievances, discretion and abilities.[41] In the testimony given at courts-martial, it is evident that the core conspirators of these mutinies composed tight social networks of seamen who knew one another and had frequently served on previous vessels. Even if they relied on trusted shipmates to hatch the conspiracy, ringleaders also used round-robin letters to signal their commitment and bind them to the plot. They often sealed the plot with an (illegal) oath of solidarity. Evidence of oaths was revealed in many of the trials following these mutinies, conspicuously so on the *Albanaise, Danae, Ferret, Goza* and *Hermione*, and may well have been part of other conspiracies, as well.

Mutinies like this were especially terrifying because the instigators took advantage of surprise and used violence, or the threat of violence, to seize control of the ship. Although ringleaders generally tried to restrain their shipmates and convince officers that it was hopeless to resist, organized exit mutinies were the bloodiest type of mutiny. Deadly violence occurred in more than half of the cases in our sample. In some instances, mutineers murdered or severely injured officers who opposed them. With some exceptions, there was little gratuitous violence on the part of the mutineers. Nevertheless, organized exit mutinies could become bloody when officers tried to fight back or regain control of the ship by force.

On the *Hermione*, mutineers brutally slaughtered their abusive Captain and nine other officers. On the *Lively*, a Boatswain who resisted was hacked to death with an axe. The commanding Lieutenant of the *Goza* had his face slashed by a cutlass when he awoke to find a mutiny afoot and, on the *Danae*, Lord Proby was struck on the head when he tried to rally loyalists to his side. The mutineers on the *Marie Antoinette* were cruelly efficient; they swiftly overpowered their sleeping commander, carried him on deck and threw him to the sharks.

In the public mind, mutinies like this were as horrible as is terrorism today. The violence and the guile that characterized them were especially abhorrent to the naval profession, but they also offended because they revealed the fragility of the deference and subordination that presumably governed relations between the classes.[42] If they could be apprehended, principal ringleaders and mutineers were always tried and frequently hanged. Seamen involved in such mutinies were hunted across the globe and, thanks to a system of informants and posted rewards, often arrested years afterward. The Navy sent the frigate *Pandora* thousands of miles in search of the *Bounty* mutineers (after capturing fourteen of them, she foundered on the Great Barrier Reef).

In our cases, dozens of mutineers involved in the piratical seizures of their ships were subsequently arrested and tried. The sense of retribution that attended these pursuits and prosecutions is palpable. This was the only kind of mutiny after which convicted mutineers might not only be hanged but also gibbeted, a degradation in which their faces were blackened with pitch and their bodies hanged in chains to rot alongside the docks. Gibbeting may have been a forceful deterrent, but it also reeked of revenge.

Despite these manifold dangers, the potential advantages of "turning pirate" might have appealed to seamen. Pirates in the Age of

Sail were more than maritime bandits. They were organized criminals who elected their own officers and developed equitable institutions to govern their ships and divide the spoils.[43] By the 1740s, however, the "golden age" of piracy was a thing of the past. Due to the effective control of Atlantic sea-lanes by the European navies, seamen seizing their vessels during our time period did not expect that they would be able to become criminal entrepreneurs. Rather, they planned on holding the ship only as long as they could make a quick dash to an enemy port or foreign refuge. Once there, they hoped to escape the long arm of the Navy. Mutineers considered using a ship in the business of piracy in only a single case, the frigate *Chesterfield* that experienced a mutiny in 1748 off the coast of West Africa.[44]

The most obvious benefit to taking a ship was escape from naval service. As the *Bounty*'s William Bligh observed, exchanging an arduous life at sea for a life of ease on a South Sea island would have appealed to all but the most dutiful of seamen. Most of these mutinies, however, did not have an attractive refuge such as Tahiti as their objective. After seizing a naval vessel, the mutineers had to find a safe haven out of the reach of naval authorities. In practice, this meant that seamen had to seek refuge in a port that was either hostile to Britain, or that at least took a neutral position in her many wars. Mutineers would usually make for the closest refuge, whether a Channel port in France, a French- or Spanish-controlled territory in the Mediterranean, a Spanish dominion in the Caribbean or South America, or the United States. In this, it was not much different from the well-known seamen's strategy of absconding to foreign ships and ports – taking a "French leave" – as done by many individual deserters.[45]

A further inducement to piratical mutiny was that enemy powers sometimes granted seamen bounties for turning over their ship. In 70 percent of organized exit mutinies in our sample the seamen sought to turn their ship over to the enemy as a prize of war. This would have given mutineers a valuable incentive for the taking of the ship. This lucrative outcome was unusual, however. In some instances, the mutineers never reached their intended destination. In others, local maritime officials treated them coolly, regarding them as dangerous and untrustworthy, sometimes turning them over to British authorities. If not prize-money, a modest cash reward of some kind might be paid. Local authorities almost always urged the seamen to move on by signing on as sailors on privateers or neutral vessels. Some, especially the Landsmen, might settle in the new place, melting into the population. But skilled seamen, knowing no other trade, typically returned to the sea under an alias. This frequently led to the subsequent capture, trial and hanging of at least some of the mutineers after their ships were boarded by British naval vessels. In just three mutinies of this type did all the mutineers manage to elude naval justice.

Like terrorism today, the authorities usually blamed mutinies of this kind on the influence of foreign radicals.[46] Such claims were especially worrying during the wars that Britain fought against enemies espousing popular liberty, particularly the War of American Independence and those against revolutionary France. It is not easy to ascertain whether radical sympathies motivated seamen to commit mutiny because their private thoughts are not accessible to us. We rely instead on court documents and in just five cases witnesses testified that mutineers espoused radical ideologies, whether Irish nationalism, French Jacobinism or agreement with the American Revolution.

The case of the *Danae* in 1799 probably shows the clearest influence of radical ideas on the ringleaders of a mutiny. After seizing the ship in the English Channel, the mutineers took the ship to a French port. A few of the leading mutineers were clearly revolutionary sympathizers. During their detention, they put the revolutionary cockade in their hats, declared themselves Jacobins and proclaimed their intention to join the French Navy. Some of these men, despite having claimed American citizenship, had previously been impressed by the ship's Captain, Lord Proby. In hindsight, Proby conceded that these men were among the radical plotters:

> Every necessary measure was adopted to prevent any ill consequences arising from their bad dispositions; the midshipmen were put in a berth between the fore and main hatchways and all the officers had orders to watch these men narrowly but they behaved extremely well, till I was obliged to go to sea with a large proportion of the most attentive petty officers and near thirty of the best men absent in prizes; this opportunity they must have grasped to propagate principles which it is well known are but too easily adopted by men who seldom weigh the difference between unlicensed anarchy and the possession of real social liberty.[47]

In any event, one cannot easily explain the mutiny as due to French connivance or encouragement. These self-proclaimed Jacobins got a cool reception in France. The authorities refused to enlist them and "expressed their abhorrence of Treason." Although the mutineers hoped that they would receive prize money, they never got any. Rather, they were awarded just six Louis each to support themselves, given a passport and taken to the port of Brest in hopes that they would disappear into neutral ships or privateers. Some of those who did were later captured, tried and hanged.[48]

The *Danae* was exceptional. Time and again, ringleaders made clear that their foremost goal was not to take revenge or betray Britain, but merely to escape the Navy. Given the sense of confinement and coerced service that prevailed on naval vessels, particularly during wartime, this is hardly surprising. Mutineers sometimes did frame their mutiny in the language of liberty, which must have had a special resonance to seamen pressed onto ships for indefinite periods and denied shore leave. That language expressed grievances on the *Namur* in 1747 when mutinous seamen professed their loyalty and expectation of customary rewards in the wake of a battle that had left dozens of their shipmates dead or wounded, "It was liberty we fought for and liberty we will have. We have fought for King George and now we'll fight for liberty."[49] That language seems to have been in the minds of the mutineers on the *Jackal* in 1779 who declared to their stunned officers that, "Its liberty we want and liberty we'll have" before taking the vessel into a French port. Perhaps this language suggests American influence, but it also evoked customary entitlements such as shore leave and the traditional notion of the "rights of Englishmen."[50]

Perhaps radical ideas became widespread enough to have motivated mutinies, a theme explored in greater detail in Chapter 5. The evidence, however, suggests simpler motives. Fleeing naval service promised freedom. Despite its danger, seizing a ship and sailing it to a refuge where one might profit from its sale as a prize had an obvious appeal to impoverished seamen. That outcome could only be accomplished through force and deception, and this would have been enough to make the prospect of mutiny a potent source of terror for the authorities during the Age of Sail.

3.1.3 Spontaneous Voice: Mutiny as Riot

Mutinies taking the form of riots aboard ships were an extension of popular politics in the long eighteenth century. Riotousness and bursts of popular unrest were notorious features of British society.[51] This kind of disorder arose from the looseness of social control, common people's lack of political voice and the absence of any institutional means of asserting their demands. It tended to occur in reaction to incidents that threatened popular welfare. Riots were triggered by food shortages, dramatic increases in prices and efforts to deny people their customary privileges and entitlements, such as in the enclosing of rural commons. Generally, the British elite was surprisingly tolerant of riotousness, so long as it could be seen as venting steam in reaction to provocations and did not espouse radical aims.[52]

Social control in eighteenth-century Britain relied on a delicate balance of discipline, deference and negotiation. This was especially true in crowded naval vessels where the distance between rulers and ruled was vanishingly small and the exercise of authority was often intimate. In these conditions, commanders ruled as much through persuasion, habit and tacit consent as through coercion. Not surprisingly, when grievances mounted and antagonism between command and crew intensified, shipboard social order began to fray. Riots sometimes resulted from officers' clumsy efforts to restore control. From the seamen's point of view, a riot was one of their only means to attempt to enforce customary norms of proper treatment. Standing up for their accustomed rights and getting back at abusive officers could be expressions of emergent rationality.

Popular unrest had its counterpart in mutinies that were disruptive but poorly organized. A fifth of the mutinies in our sample took the form of spontaneous voice, most frequently a riot or a chaotic sit-down strike. They were tumultuous, loosely organized rebellions springing from incidental grievances related to the breakdown of social order.[53] They were reactions to provocations – particularly unpaid wages, flogging and discipline that violated the seamen's sense of justice, and violations of the customs of the sea. At the same time, however, these grievances also revealed strained social relations and frustrated expectations that grew among long-serving men on poorly governed ships. Whereas particular incidents provided the focal point for loosely organized rebellions, prior erosion of the officers' authority, a breakdown in accustomed routines and frustration growing from long periods without shore leave fostered these mutinies.

Research has shown that organization and planning are not necessary to generate collective action.[54] Although we tend to look for plots and instigators when we study the eruption of rebellion, mutinies could occur without much leadership or planning. Rioting tends to grow out of deprivation and disorganization.[55] Informal organization and shared identity are enough to provide a basis for loosely structured protest. Seamen who shared the same grievances and occupied the same social spaces could swiftly be drawn into an "us versus them" conflict. They required little preparation because they already shared common beliefs about their "proper usage," had a sense of collective identity and spoke the same language of grievances. When an egregious incident took place – such as the flogging of a popular sailor for a minor offense, depriving seamen of their accustomed ration of drink, withdrawing their petty privileges or witnessing a violent altercation between officers and men – it could become the focus for mass discontent.

Basic coordination appeared on the spot, evolving in response to the ongoing situation. Informal organization facilitated these mutinies, as seamen drew on personal networks to recruit their shipmates into the rebellion. Nevertheless, the outstanding feature of these mutinies is the social breakdown that propelled and enabled them. Social breakdown occurs when grievances are intense and people become detached from the communities that ordinarily mitigate them. Recall that social order in the sailing navy relied less on hierarchal authority than on the Petty Officers and old and experienced seamen who held the keys to maintaining compliance. If these senior seamen were invested in maintaining it, social order tended to be robust in all but the worst of conditions. Without the voluntary cooperation of these intermediate authorities, a commander will have difficulty maintaining control of his ship. When a substantial share of the leading seamen lose their investment in maintaining order and supporting command, discipline begins to erode. The most disruptive, incorrigible and rebellious seamen come to dominate the lower decks. This can unleash a cascade of conflict as mounting disorder provokes a harsh response by the officers, which, in turn, intensifies grievances among the bulk of seamen.

If, in response, Captains and their officers respond by cracking down after long periods of disorder, this risked mutiny. On ships including the *Barfleur, Beaulieu, Castor, Kingfisher* and *Sunderland* the outbreak of the rioting was a direct outgrowth of the prior decay of social order. On other ships, such as the *Minerva, Nereide* and *Santa Monica*, rioting broke out because seamen perceived their commanders to be martinets – too prone to flog seamen, and too willing to impose petty and unreasonable restrictions on them. Drunkenness was also a substantial factor in more than half of these mutinies: violence was sometimes triggered by officers limiting inebriation or preventing the theft of alcohol, as on the *Bedford, Defiance* and *Orion*. What might have been ordinarily regarded as routine discipline in a well-ordered ship violated the expectations that arose on poorly governed ships.

Disunity and conflict among the leading seamen help to explain why these mutinies lacked planning and careful coordination. Petty Officers were less likely to be identified as ringleaders in spontaneous mutinies. Whereas a divided body of Petty Officers might allow unrest to mushroom into rebellion, it also deprived mutinies of leadership and coherence. Some of the leading seamen became loud advocates for their shipmates and mobilized seamen into rebellion, but others opposed the mutiny or remained passive bystanders. The result was unplanned and poorly coordinated mutinies that failed to unify the leading seamen and provided little in the way of coherent strategy to gain redress of grievances.[56]

Although these mutinies were highly defiant in tone and featured much violence, naval authorities were surprisingly restrained in punishing the principal mutineers in their wake. No seamen were hanged afterward in nearly half (40 percent) of the spontaneous voice mutinies in our sample and only eight seamen in total were hanged in the remainder. Officials seem to have regarded mutinies of this kind as regrettable but inevitable reactions to poor governance and the distortion of expected patterns of naval life.

3.1.4 Spontaneous Exit: Mutiny as Mass Desertion

The least common form of mutiny was attempted mass desertion, comprising less than a tenth of mutinies in our sample. Like other mutinies that took the form of riots, they also reflected the breakdown of social order. In these mutinies, seamen shared grievances but did not seek any unified purpose except to flee the ship. In some ways, these were the simplest and most direct forms of rebellion. Seamen reacted in the same way at the same time to the opportunity to jump ship. Although prominent seamen led the way, these mutinies required little coordination and planning.

In 1763, the *Panther* had a mutiny of this kind; others also took place on the *Castor*, *Princess Royal* and *Royal Oak*. On all of these ships, disorganization and deteriorating conditions undermined social order. Mutinies occurred during the later phases of war when tensions had mounted after years of continuous service. Poor supervision and indiscipline allowed seamen to try to rush off their ships while in port or at an anchorage. Service for indefinite periods was especially galling to men who had been pressed, and many were looking for chances to escape. On the *Panther* and the *Royal Oak* groups of seamen overcame armed sentinels to storm off the ship and attempted to disappear into port cities or onto merchant vessels. On the *Castor* and the *Princess Royal* they assaulted officers and stole boats to make their way ashore. Although there were some seamen who played leading roles in these mutinies and who plotted to seize boats or get access to weapons, the dominant feature of these mutinies was confusion and the breakdown of authority.

The infrequency of this kind of mutiny reflects the fact that seamen routinely sought to desert, but rarely did so through large-scale collective action. The prospects of collective action only rose when commanders inflicted harsh penalties for desertion, confined men on ships while in ports for many months or even years at a time, and delayed wages so that would-be deserters would have to forgo back pay and prize-money. Although bounties were paid for captured deserters, and some were later recovered from boarded merchant ships, capture rates were low. Partly this is because sailors could disappear into the wide maritime world of dockside towns and outgoing ships, but also because the public was sympathetic to deserters from the Navy.[57]

3.2   Coordination: The Leadership of Mutinies

Given incentives to rebel, how did seamen actually make mutinies? Lacking coordination, discontent need never rise to the level of open rebellion. The documentary evidence shows that the coordination required some seamen to take on active leadership. A small minority of seamen played disproportionate roles in plotting mutinies, fanning unrest, drawing up protest letters and imposing oaths, and keeping order within their ranks. They mobilized seamen, appealed to bystanders and punished shirkers. They articulated grievances, made demands and tried to win concessions from naval authorities.

There was precious little anonymity aboard a ship. Seamen were reasonably well informed about one another and this facilitated monitoring. The confidence that one's shipmates shared the same grievances and were reliable allowed would-be mutineers to consider staging a rebellion. Yet this left coordinating a mutiny a substantial hurdle. Coordination grew out of the capacity of some seamen to provide leadership, and some mechanism by which shipmates made credible commitments to support a prospective mutiny.

Across time and places, rebellions tend to be led by alert, resourceful people especially interested in the redress of grievances.[58] Mutinies were no different. As with the case of the *Culloden*, they nearly always took shape around a small core of seamen who took the lead and devised the strategies.

In the records concerning the mutinies in our sample, we found nearly two hundred seamen identified as ringleaders, a status we confirmed through careful reading of the documentary evidence. In ships' muster books, we discovered that nearly half the ringleaders were rated as Able Seamen and another third were Petty Officers. This is not surprising insofar as these seamen occupied roles of authority in the everyday operations of the ship, and were the crucial intermediaries between the crew and command. As the theory of collective action would lead us to expect, this made them prone either to advocacy or to recruitment into leadership roles by their shipmates.

As anticipated, less-skilled seamen played a much smaller role. Just a tenth of the men identified as ringleaders were rated as Ordinary Seamen. Landsmen and Marines comprised another tenth. These categories of seamen generally had low status among their shipmates and were not accustomed to giving orders. Not surprisingly, the officers of the ship played leading roles only in exceptional circumstances, such as those aboard the *Bounty*. Only a handful of officers (less than 5 percent of all ringleaders), and most of them warrant rather than commissioned officers, helped to lead mutinies. Table 3.2 compares the characteristics of ringleaders with those of the crews from which they were drawn.

Table 3.2 *Comparing mutiny ringleaders to ships' companies*

Characteristic	% mutiny ringleaders	% ships' companies
Officers and Midshipmen	1.6	3.6
Warrant Officers	3.1	2.6
Petty Officers (all grades)	29.3	10.6
Able Seamen	50.7	35.8
Ordinary Seamen	9.4	13.9
Landsmen	4.2	12
Marines	1.6	13.7
Servants, Boys, and others	0	8.5
Foreigners (Irish or other foreign-born)	27.2	28.2
Recently pressed	11.5	6.5
Average age	26	22

Source: Court-martial documents and muster books in TNA: PRO ADM.

Several factors are associated with mutiny leadership. Rank and qualifications were not the only such factors, however. Seamen who became the ringleaders of mutiny bore a greater risk of punishment, and quite possibly hanging, than other seamen. What then could have motivated their excess contribution to the mutiny when the private benefits of a successful mutiny would be the same for less-prominent mutineers or mere bystanders? Being part of a group of long-serving seamen seems to have increased trust and provided potential leaders with the assurance that others would back them.

Certainly, social incentives that would have come from the respect and praise of one's shipmates appeared to have made a difference.[59] Descriptive evidence suggests an additional incentive. Private grievances appear to have made some seamen prone to adopt leadership roles. Being impressed into naval service and flogged within a year prior to the outbreak of the mutiny is associated with becoming a ringleader. By virtue of their experience and authority, ringleaders may have been especially offended by perceived injustice and ill-usage. Some ringleaders also nursed personal grudges against their commanders and may have been eager to settle the score. In the next chapter, we systematically evaluate the factors that increased the odds that seamen would take an active part in a mutiny and assume leadership roles.

3.3 Commitment: The Use of Petitions and Oaths

When grievances were widely shared by a crew and incidents of poor governance provoked indignation, the greatest hurdle in mobilizing a mutiny was not persuading seamen that they faced injustice, but rather obtaining assurances that they would rebel. Lacking this, a mutiny would fail. In these kinds of situations the assurance problem can only be overcome if people make credible commitments to one another. Commitments gain credibility if they are hard to fake. If there is some cost or danger to making a promise to participate in a high-risk collective action, people who do so generally mean it.[60]

In the Navy, seamen faced the commitment problem every time they considered initiating a mutiny. Despite this, they had resources that helped them to attain solidarity, particularly those emanating from the face-to-face relations making possible a difficult life at sea. When a seaman's trusted shipmates committed themselves to a mutiny, he was more likely to do so himself. A sense of community arises from informal groups rooted in shared identities and everyday routines. Seamen's solidarity grew from local social networks around which social order was built and that endowed social relations with meaning and purpose.[61] The social organization of seamen made it hard, if not impossible, to be anonymous aboard a sailing ship. This facilitated mobilization by making it easier for seamen to recruit others into a mutiny, to spot those who refused to commit and to know in advance who would be prone to defect or remain loyal to the officers.

Seamen also developed specific mechanisms that helped them to make commitments credible and to create expectations that an adequate number of their shipmates would rebel. Although seamen had clear incentives to conceal conspiratorial activities after the collapse of a mutiny or after their arrest, we found evidence of protest letters and oaths as part of the process of mobilization in more than a third of our cases of mutiny, and they probably played an undocumented role in many others.

3.3.1 Petitions

On *Adamant* in 1798, seamen secretly drafted a petition to the Admiral who was the Commander-in-Chief of their squadron expressing their "deplorable and unhappy state," listing their grievances and swearing to strike and hold the ship until they were given redress. The petition reads, in part,

> The grievances of the ship is as follows: Firstly, the officers take the prime of the meals [take part of their ration] ... [We are] deprived of every indulgence which every other ship gets after coming from sea, our wives and children turned out three days before the ship was payed [and] often ill-treated.

The document was signed or marked by 60 percent of the nearly three hundred seamen onboard (sixty-four seamen signed by making their mark). On the basis of the letter the ringleaders mobilized an armed strike a few days later.[62]

Why did seamen bother to draft such letters when mutinies were expressly forbidden under any circumstances? The customs of the sea played a part. Petitions like this were part and parcel of the repertoire of protest that had evolved in the maritime world. Seamen in the Navy circulated between merchant and naval vessels over the course of their careers. Contention was part of the seamen's lot, and they developed techniques for dealing with the commitment problems that inevitably arose when they challenged authority. In his autobiographical novel *Omoo*, Herman Melville provides a vivid example of how disgruntled seamen used a round-robin petition to organize a mutiny on a hapless whaling ship. He described the round-robin as a statement of grievances, signed by ship's crewmembers in such a way that individual ringleaders could not readily be identified: "Right beneath the note was described the circle about which the names were to be written; the great object of a Round Robin being to arrange the signatures in a ring, no man can be picked out as the leader of it."[63]

Round-robin letters developed in a maritime culture in which seamen were compelled to use rebellion and the threat of rebellion to protect their interests.[64] Round-robins were especially valuable because they helped to overcome the first-mover problem. Seamen would naturally expect that anyone regarded as a ringleader by the commander would be much more harshly punished, whether or not the mutiny ever advanced beyond the planning stages. The round-robin gave the organizers of a mutiny some protection; even if identified by witnesses as a ringleader, the charge would lack the substantiation of physical evidence.[65]

In effect, these letters were contracts drawn up among seamen pledging that all signatories stood behind the mutiny.[66] However ingenious, round-robins were developed on merchant ships and were meant for mobilizing rebellion in the small crews that were typical of these vessels. Their usefulness was much more limited on naval vessels, which usually contained hundreds of seamen. For larger ships operating under greater surveillance and much stricter naval discipline, it was hard to have every man sign a contract pledging rebellion in a small circle and more difficult yet to enforce.

Nevertheless, seamen on naval vessels were able to innovate on the basic idea. Even if protest letters were not signed by every member, the ringleaders of mutinies used petitions as frameworks for mobilization. Drawing up protest letters helped seamen assess support for a mutiny and reach a consensus about grievances. In 1799 the mutineers on the *Impeteux* at Bantry Bay in Ireland drafted a protest letter that they planned to deliver to the Admiral after seizing control of their ship. It read, in part,

> My Lord, we the Ship's Company of the *Impeteux* would wish to make known to your Lordship the usage we have received since Sir Edward Pellew commanded us is such we have never been used to this war by any other Captain we have sailed under it is unacceptable. Sir Edward has punished different people in the ship to the amount of forty-nine dozen and upwards for very frivolous crimes since we left Cawsand Bay [and] it is well known ... that we never deserved the barbarous usage we now experience at the hands of Sir Edward ... and his humanity to the sick is little better than to the well ... relying upon your Lordships goodness and wisdom we hope you redress our grievances with another Captain and second Lieutenant and a fourth Lieutenant.[67]

If it turned out that grievances were not severe enough, or that a consensus about them was lacking, the prospective leadership could abandon the mutiny in its planning stage. If seamen backed a petition, however, it suggested that they would be more likely to follow through once a mutiny was launched. Petitions had an added advantage in that they allowed ringleaders to exploit a bit of legal ambiguity. Written petitions for redress of grievances upon "just ground" were technically permissible under the Articles of War. This provided some small cover if it came to an officer's attention that a petition was being discussed.

Supporting a protest letter in the circle of one's shipmates compelled seamen to make a reputational investment in the mutiny. These commitments were especially binding for a seaman because he had to comply or explicitly break his commitment to his peers, thereby sullying his reputation. Reputation was everything in the maritime world. Seamen counted on mutual assistance with their shipmates to manage a difficult life at sea. Breaking one's word was a dire offense.[68] This bond was made even more explicit in the taking of illegal oaths of solidarity.

3.3.2 Oaths

Oath-taking was another common maritime practice that migrated between mercantile and naval vessels.[69] It was feared by the authorities because it smacked of self-organization, disloyalty and conspiracy. Expressly forbidden under punishment of death by the Articles of War, the giving and taking of oaths was dangerous in itself, but seamen believed that oaths would contain opportunism and achieve the norm of "one and all." A common refrain in the mutinies we have studied was the perception that oaths were necessary to attain solidarity and maintain order. As a Petty Officer who helped plan the mutiny on the *Ferret* explained, the belief was that without an oath, "we would not be able to stick to one another" once the mutiny was afoot.[70]

Although the texts of these oaths are mostly lost, evidence given at trials establishes the common practices that shaped them. The oaths pledged takers to the ship's company, made them promise that they would support the mutiny and obliged them not to inform on each other to the authorities. Seamen made of them solemn rituals, swearing men into the plotting of mutiny in small groups and compelling them to swear on Bibles or catechisms. On the *Danae*, for instance, witnesses later testified that the ringleaders had imposed an oath on the Bible that obliged the men "not to do any murder but only to take the ship."[71]

Why would seamen believe oaths to be binding, since they were not enforceable by law and, moreover, illegal? It is possible that ringleaders were able to leverage the superstitions of seamen to achieve compliance with the group's interests. Although they were not conventionally pious by all accounts, seamen were notoriously superstitious.[72] By swearing oaths on Bibles and other sacred objects, ringleaders probably sought to seal oaths with supernatural power. Seamen taking such oaths might have feared ill-fortune or punishment by a divine third party if they broke their solemn word to their shipmates.[73] Another possibility is the weight of social sanctions. Seamen giving their word to each other had good reason to fear the consequences of betraying their shipmates. In the maritime world, a seaman could not afford to be seen as untrustworthy or be shunned by his shipmates.

Perhaps the strongest incentives for complying with the oath was the fear of punishment. As on the *Culloden*, the ringleaders of some mutinies appointed armed guards as enforcers. Seamen who were seen as breaking the oath might have feared retaliation, whether during or after the mutiny. Finally, giving and taking oaths was strictly forbidden and subject to hanging. The severity of naval sanctions enhanced the credibility of commitments sealed by oaths. Mutineers may have hoped that by forcing sailors to take the oath – which, after all, was illegal and grounds for punishment by the authorities – they were in effect making these sailors guilty of mutiny at that very point. If seamen might be hanged for merely swearing an oath, defecting from a planned mutiny still posed substantial danger. In circumstances like these, indiscriminate retaliation by the authorities alters the logic of collective action, such that participation entails no collective action problem but nonparticipation does.[74] Oath-takers thus would have had an incentive to uphold the mutiny in the hope it would prevail, and they would either escape the Navy's clutches or be offered amnesty as a result of successful negotiations. In Chapter 5, we will test these explanations for solidarity in the case of a mass mutiny in which some seamen stuck by their oaths and others did not.

3.4 The Making of Mutinies

In the wake of the *Culloden* mutiny, word spread through the Navy about the betrayal of the ship's crew. If senior officers or naval representatives – "honourable Gentlemen" – could not trusted as brokers of a peaceful settlement, mutinies became that much more dangerous.[75]

No wonder that Troubridge noted that the hanging of the *Culloden*'s ringleaders was such a tense affair; neither side could be sure what the other might do.

Traditional accounts have it that mutiny was a hopeless undertaking and that, as with the case of the *Culloden*, mutiny led inevitably to failure and the noose. That is simply not true. In Chapter 7, we will show that, in spite of the obstacles that confronted seamen in achieving their goals, they sometimes succeeded in using mutiny to redress their grievances. Seamen addressed their petitions and protest letters to Admirals and other senior naval officials because they rightly perceived them as more likely to seek negotiated settlements than Captains. They might be persuaded to negotiate and provide an amnesty to mutineers if the rebels had leverage, made moderate demands and eschewed violence.

No matter their strategy in making a mutiny, or how great the restraint shown by the mutineers, the danger was greatest for those whom the authorities could identify as ringleaders. Nevertheless, every seaman who took part in a mutiny had no way of knowing whether he would walk away unscathed, suffer a flogging or hang from the yard-arm. All this made it hard to persuade seamen to join a mutiny but, paradoxically, having done so, could make them committed to holding out given the risks they had already assumed.

For commanders, control was paramount. They despised negotiations that might undermine their authority and preferred to regain the ship by force or threat. They detested settlements that allowed ringleaders to escape the noose. Admirals, on the other hand, wanted to minimize disruption, pacify labor relations across the fleet and avoid the costs and political complications of courts-martial. The different incentives facing Captains and Admirals are at least as important as the dispositions and worldviews of the individual commanders in explaining reactions to mutinies. The famous naval hero Horatio Nelson provides a telling example. As a Captain in 1794, he was incensed by Admiral Linzee's peaceful settlement and pardon of a mutiny aboard the *Windsor Castle*, a battleship in the squadron to which he belonged. He complained in a letter to his wife,

> I came in here two days ago, and found a most unpleasant circumstance a mutiny on board the *Windsor Castle*, Admiral Linzee's ship. The crew wish to change their captain and 1st lieutenant,

the officers have been tried at their own requests' and most honourably acquitted but the Admiral notwithstanding has removed them and forgiven the ship's company who richly deserved a halter. I am of the opinion 'tis mistaken lenity and it will be cause of present innocent people being hanged.[76]

Nevertheless, just two years later when Nelson was the Commodore of a Mediterranean squadron, he resolved a mutiny on the *Blanche* in just the same way.[77]

Our analysis of the historical evidence has revealed *how* seamen undertook mutinies. We want to dig deeper to understand *why* seamen made mutinies. What were the grievances most likely to inspire mutiny? Why did individual seamen risk their lives to take part in mutinies? To answer these questions, we now turn from how to why seamen rebelled.

Notes

1. Laughton 1899.
2. Goodman 2005, p. 100.
3. Crimmin 2004.
4. In fact, the number of floggings aboard the *Culloden* in the year preceding Troubridge was quite modest compared with contemporaneous vessels. See Captain's and Master's logs in TNA: PRO ADM 51/202, 1150 and PRO ADM 52/2876, 3014.
5. See TNA: PRO ADM 1/5331. For an extensive account see also Neale 1985, pp. 70–96.
6. For a favorable account of Pakenham and his involvement in ending the mutiny, see James 1837, pp. 60, 126–59, 185–6.
7. See Rodger 1986, pp. 237–43 on "orderly" mutinies.
8. See Chapter 4 for a detailed discussion of that case.
9. Lawrence 1987, pp. 13–15; McKee 1978. A few historians have tried to remedy this portrait with more comprehensive treatments that compare several mutinies and seek out their common features; see, e.g., Frykman 2010; Gilbert 1983; Neale 1985; Rodger 1986, ch. 6; and Rose 1982.
10. Olson 1965 is the *locus classicus* that has generated an enormous subsequent literature.
11. On social dilemmas, see Kollock 1998. For a comprehensive study of participation in rebellion, see Lichbach 1998.
12. On the problem of assurance and coordination games, see Hardin 1982 and Taylor 1997.
13. Lichbach 1998.
14. Between 1756 and 1806, about a third of all seamen indicted for mutiny (excluding charges of striking an officer) and tried by court-martial were hanged (Gilbert 1976, pp. 82–3). In our more restricted sample of sixty-two completed mutinies, hanging of at least one offender was inflicted in 60 percent of the cases.

15. For the theory of solidarity, see Hechter 1987. For an exemplary historical study of the determinants of solidarity in high-risk collective action, see Gould 1995.

16. By no means does face-to-face interaction always promote solidarity; in many cases it may promote conflict. Our claim merely is that such interaction is a necessary but insufficient determinant of solidarity.

17. On the role of commitment mechanisms in social conflict, see Schelling 1960. On costly signaling as a way to communicate commitment, see Gambetta 2011 and Hovi 1998.

18. For earlier efforts to classify and dissect the features of mutinies, see Lammers 1969, 2003 and Rose 1982.

19. Vernon Smith 2003 argues that the spontaneous enforcement of social norms is an expression of emergent, situational (or ecological) rationality.

20. In addition to the dozens of cases of full-fledged mutiny that we assembled in our sample and the fleet-wide mutinies of 1797, courts-martial tried more than five hundred seamen on charges of mutiny (excluding charges of striking a superior officer). Collective insubordination was a reoccurring part of naval life, especially when we consider that, in all likelihood, many attempted mutinies failed at the planning stages or at their inception and are less likely have resulted in documentary evidence. See Gilbert 1976, pp. 82–3, and Gilbert 1980 and Rodger 1986 on mutinies as regular features of naval life.

21. On the exit–voice framework in organizational analysis, see Hirschman 1970. On its implications for collective action see Dowding et al. 2000; Gehlbach 2006; Pfaff 2006; and Pfaff and Kim 2003.

22. See O'Donnell 1838, especially pp. 43–4, and, on naval statutes particularly, see Rodger 1982. "Combinations" were understood as any form of legally unsanctioned group activity.

23. On desertion in the Navy and in British merchant vessels see Earle 1998, pp. 168–72; Gilbert 1980; Gill 1961, p. 68; Rodger 1986; on desertion in the eighteenth-century British Army, see Way 2003; for studies of desertion in the US Civil War, see Berman 1991 and Costa and Kahn 2008; for an analysis of desertion in contemporary civil wars see McLauchlin 2015.

24. Nicol [1822] 1997.

25. For a discussion of the relative attractiveness of defection over collective action and the dynamic relationship between exit and voice, see Pfaff 2006 and Pfaff and Kim 2003.

26. Of course, some portion of them were reoffenders. See Frykman 2009, p. 83.

27. Since naval vessels were so valuable, mutineers delivering them to the enemy hoped for, but rarely received, ample rewards. As captured ships generally kept their original names, all of the European navies had prizes with foreign names.

28. See Appendix A for a description of the sample of mutinies in our study.

29. "Throughout the eighteenth century merchant seamen participated in many strikes ... Until the early nineteenth century strikes continued to erupt over rates of pay and volume of work, often only ended by the use of troops" (Coats 2011, pp. 43–5). See also Earle 1998 and Rediker 1987 on strikes in merchant vessels.

30. Nagle [1802] 1988, p. 209.

31. See, e.g., Cramton and Tracy 2003 and Hart 1989.

32. On this type of mutiny, also see Gilbert 1983, pp. 115–16; Neale 1985; Rodger 1986; and Way 2003.

33. On strikes as collective voice driven by norms of fairness, see Fantasia 1988 and Godard 1992.

34. TNA: PRO ADM 1/5290.

35. On the logic of strikes in the absence of collective bargaining, see Card and Olson 1995, pp. 43–4.
36. Godard 1992, pp. 163–5, calls this perception "strike power."
37. Card and Olson 1995 find that solidarity was a necessary condition for strike success. In their sample of nineteenth-century American strikes, the odds of success increased sharply when they involved at least 80 percent of a firm's workforce.
38. As Olson 1965 would have predicted.
39. Lyon 1993, p. xii.
40. On the similar conditions that obtained in mutinies aboard merchant vessels, see Rediker 1987, pp. 228–9.
41. For parallels in the business of organized crime, see Gambetta 2011.
42. On social order and the moral imagination of the naval profession, see Gilbert 1980, 1983.
43. On Atlantic piracy, see Leeson 2009 and Rediker 2004.
44. TNA: PRO ADM 1/5292.
45. See Earle 1998, p. 170; Frykman 2009, p. 83; and Gill 1961, p. 68.
46. Like the contemporary "war on terrorism," the international pursuit of mutineers raised legal and diplomatic problems as Britain pressured neutral countries to surrender suspects for trial and seized seamen holding foreign passports. In the case of the *Hermione* mutineers, many of whom took refuge in Spanish America or the United States, these issues arose with particular urgency. See Ekirch 2017.
47. Pope 1987, p. 248.
48. See TNA: PRO ADM 1/5353, 1/5353, 1/5356, 1/5358; and the detailed account in Pope 1987. Noting Proby's record as a martinet, a senior naval official discounted radicalism in explaining the mutiny in favor of a grievance interpretation; see Hughes 1957, p. 112.
49. TNA: PRO ADM 1/5290.
50. On the rhetoric of English liberty and traditional notions of rights, see Thompson 1980; also Calhoun 1982.
51. This kind of collective action has been dubbed "reactive" rather than radical or revolutionary because of its putative defensiveness and desire for restoration of customary conditions. See, e.g., Lanford 2004; Rudé 1964; Tilly 1995.
52. On social control and popular unrest as a safety valve venting social pressure in eighteenth-century England, see Brewer 1976; Brewer and Styles 1980; King 2000, 2006; Lanford 2004; McLynn 1991; Rodger 1986; Sharpe 1999.
53. On social breakdown see Useem 1998.
54. On informal groups and spontaneous collective action, see Goldstone and Useem 1999; Oberschall 1980, 1994; Opp and Gern 1993; and Pfaff 1996.
55. Kawalerowicz and Biggs 2015.
56. A similar process has been shown to trigger prison riots; see Goldstone and Useem 1999 and Useem and Goldstone 2002.
57. Earle 1998, p. 172; for a first-person account of a seaman who eluded capture for many years, see the memoirs of John Nicol ([1822] 1997).
58. On the critical mass in the inception of collective action see Centola 2013; Marwell and Oliver 1993; and Oliver and Marwell 2001.
59. See Calhoun 1991, 1997 and Chong 1991 for insights on how social pressure and reputational investments in a group create incentives to assume leadership in collective action.

60. Gambetta 2011; Hovi 1998.
61. On social identity theory and collective action, see Abrams and Hogg 1990, 2006; Hogg et al. 2004.
62. TNA: PRO ADM1/5345.
63. Melville [1847] 2007, p. 81.
64. Rediker 1987, pp. 234–5.
65. In the case of the Navy, see Gilbert 1983, p. 117.
66. Leeson 2010; on contractual solutions to social dilemmas more generally, see Lichbach 1998.
67. TNA: PRO ADM 1/5349.
68. See treatments in Earle 1998; Gill 1961; Lavery 2010; Rediker 1987.
69. "In situations of gravity and danger, seamen pledged oaths ... They pledged to be 'true to the crew.' Such pledges were often accompanied by ritual, drink, and cheer" (Rediker 1987, p. 166).
70. TNA: PRO ADM1/5375.
71. Pope 1987, pp. 76–7.
72. Rediker 1987, p. 185, argues that "The seaman's worldview was an amalgam of religion and irreligion, magic and materialism, superstition and self-help."
73. On how superstitious beliefs can be used to achieve cooperative outcomes, see Leeson 2017.
74. Kalyvas and Kocher 2007.
75. As Nicholas Rodger 2004, p. 445, observes, "After this no seaman would believe an officer's word of honour. An essential bond of trust had been severed."
76. Naish 1958, p. 187.
77. Nagle [1802] 1988, p. 209.

4 WHY SEAMEN REBELLED
The Causes of Mutiny

On the gloomy night of September 21, 1797, the frigate HMS *Hermione* was sailing off the western coast of Puerto Rico. Famous for their speed, armament and maneuverability, frigates were assigned to small squadrons but were frequently out of contact with other naval vessels. They were the most glamorous ships in the Navy, and the small number of officers who commanded them were heralded as stars. The commander of the *Hermione* was twenty-eight-year-old Hugh Pigot. A descendant of one of the first families in England, Pigot's father had been an Admiral. Pigot was both young and relatively inexperienced to command a frigate; no doubt his political connections had contributed to his good fortune. Sometime around 11 p.m., a half-dozen seamen approached his cabin. After knocking a sentry senseless, they kicked in the door and attacked their sleeping Captain. Pigot awoke in a flash and tried to defend himself with a dirk, but he was overcome with repeated blows from cutlasses and tomahawks.

On the deck above, Third Lieutenant Henry Foreshaw was the officer of the watch. He too found himself surrounded by armed men who wounded him and threw him overboard, cutting off his hand as he clutched the side of the ship. A few minutes later, the mutineers returned to Pigot's cabin to find him still alive and grasping his dirk. "You've showed no mercy yourself and therefore deserve none," declared Topman Joseph Montell, as seamen stabbed Pigot with bayonets and smashed his head with an axe. Finally, the mutineers threw Pigot into the dark, shark-infested waters of the Caribbean Sea.

The bloodletting did not end there. The mutineers broke into the gunroom, a mess for officers located between their small cabins. There they slaughtered the First and Second Lieutenants and a fourteen-year-old Midshipman. Witnesses reported that the mutineers paused, some thinking that enough blood had been spilled, but others, aided by strong drink and looking to settle old scores, insisted that all the officers must die. A self-proclaimed radical, Surgeon's Mate Lawrence Cronin, harangued the crew from a tabletop, calling on his shipmates to slay their oppressors. Others simply reminded their shipmates that murder had already been done and that they may as well finish the job.

One by one the remaining officers were dragged from their cabins or hiding places, hacked and stabbed by the mutineers and, to the cries of "Cut the buggers ... Launch the buggers! ... Heave the buggers overboard!" were hurled into the sea. Of the officers, Southcott, the ship's Master, and Midshipman Casey – who had earlier been victimized by one of Pigot's floggings – were allowed to live, along with the Cook, Carpenter and Gunner, and even then, only after they had had to listen to the men debating their fate for hours, eventually voting to spare them. Although many in the ship's company played no active role in the killings, they did little to stop the massacre.

Subsequent investigation and witness testimony revealed that the mutiny on the *Hermione* had been plotted by a group of eighteen men, supported by at least another forty active mutineers. According to one of the surviving officers, Edward Southcott, "All the best men were principals of the mutineers." A secret meeting had been called below decks to plot the mutiny. The precise timing of the mutiny was almost certainly decided by the departure of the *Diligence*, a brig-sloop in whose company the *Hermione* had been patrolling this section of the Caribbean.

The mutiny completed, the ringleaders appreciated that, although they had the ship under their control, they were hardly free men. Once their deeds were discovered they would be wanted by the Navy and face the hangman's noose. To avoid capture, they resolved to head for the port of La Guairá, five hundred miles south on the Spanish Main (in contemporary Venezuela), for Spain was then at war with Britain. Every man swore an oath never to speak of the mutiny, and most assumed aliases. Five days later they dropped anchor in La Guairá and a small party went ashore under a flag of truce. Using their aliases, they explained that the Captain had been overthrown because of his cruelty. Claiming that he and several officers had been set adrift in a boat (as on the *Bounty*, a story well known to the Spanish), they begged for asylum in exchange for surrendering the ship. The Spanish authorities believed them, and the men were taken ashore. Later, each mutineer was awarded $25 (about $500 in contemporary funds) for bringing in the ship. A few men who had taken no part in the mutiny, as well as the surviving officers, declared themselves prisoners of war and were eventually returned to the British. The rest were destined to remain wanted men for the remainder of their lives.

Not long after, word of the mutiny reached Sir Hyde Parker, the Commander-in-Chief of the Jamaica Station. He immediately ordered a manhunt to bring the mutineers to justice. As seafaring was the only trade that most of the men knew, many of those who went ashore at La Guairá soon found themselves on Spanish and French ships. Despite the mutineers' oath of silence, sailors drink – and when drunk, sometimes their tongues loosen. Within five months, five of the mutineers had been captured from a French privateer and brought to trial. Four were hanged and gibbeted at St. Nicholas Mole in present-day Haiti. Over the next nine years, thirty-two of the *Hermione*'s former crew were brought to trial and two dozen were hanged. More than one hundred and twenty seamen escaped justice by remaining in South America or by building new lives in the United States.

Casey, Southcott and the other surviving officers were tried for losing the ship, but honorably acquitted. As for the *Hermione* – or the *Santa Cecilia*, as she had been renamed by her new owners – the British authorities, furious at the Spanish refusal to hand over the mutineers, were determined to recover their ship. Two years after the mutiny, in a daring night attack, six small boats from HMS *Surprise*, a frigate under the command of Captain Edward Hamilton, stole into the heavily fortified Spanish harbor of Puerto Cabello (also in present-day Venezuela) where the *Santa Cecilia* lay at anchor. While some men used axes to cut the ship's anchor cable, others scrambled up her sides. After a desperate fight on the decks, British seamen took control of the ship and towed it away under heavy fire from the harbor's fortresses.[1]

***

The *Hermione* was a thirty-two-gun ship. She sailed to Jamaica in 1793 and took part in the French Revolutionary Wars in the West Indies. This was a bitter struggle, and the West Indies were of signal economic importance to the dueling empires. The war in the Caribbean proved a deadly one, with nearly half of the British forces dying of yellow fever and malaria. Islands were taken and then lost. Fighting triggered slave rebellions. Britain and her allies struggled to seize lucrative colonies from their enemies, restore royal authority and reimpose slavery.[2]

As a typical frigate intended for convoy and patrol duties, the *Hermione* harassed enemy shipping and captured many prizes. It also took part in operations supporting Britain's campaign to seize French possessions. Through it all, the men of the *Hermione* endured much hardship. Many were struck by tropical sickness, and mortality rates were high. The situation on the ship was about to grow much worse, however. Hugh Pigot was young, ambitious and hot-tempered. At the age of twenty-six he had been assigned one of his first commands in the West Indies, on the frigate *Success*. In the course of his command, an American ship in a convoy he was escorting ran into his vessel. Infuriated, Pigot demanded that the Master of the American ship come over to the *Success* where he had him soundly flogged for his ostensible carelessness. When news of the punishment reached the United States, it caused a furor, and this embarrassed the Admiralty, which called for an investigation. A subsequent court-martial reprimanded Pigot.

It was not Pigot's first collision nor the last time that he blamed someone else for a mishap. It happened again during his command of the *Hermione*. Thanks to incidents such as these, Pigot earned a reputation for impetuousness, brutality and arrogance. Being the son of an Admiral and the nephew of men who had prominent careers in the Navy and the Empire, his career went forward unimpeded. Despite his reputation and his tendency to fall into uncontrolled rages – which should have been considered character defects fatal to command – Pigot was awarded command of the *Hermione*.[3]

After accepting his new command, Pigot invited two dozen members of the *Success* crew whom he deemed sufficiently skillful and trustworthy to join him. Although these seamen could have remained on the *Success*, which was returning to England, most elected to serve under Pigot instead. This is surprising, since Pigot had been a harsh disciplinarian partial to frequent and severe floggings. In fact, two men on the *Success* had died after severe beatings. Despite his irascibility and harshness, however, Pigot had proven to be a successful raider. For the twenty-one seamen who accepted Pigot's invitation, the expectation of taking prizes evidently trumped the allure of escaping his command and returning home. Among those who followed Pigot onto the *Hermione* in February 1797 were some of the most important men on the ship, including a Midshipman, Master's Mate, Quarter Master, Bosun's Mate, Master at Arms and a number of Topmen who manned the tall masts.

The *Hermione* set sail from Cape Nicholas Mole on the eastern end of Santo Domingo (now Haiti) in April 1797. The ship had orders to patrol the Mona Passage, between the eastern point of Santo Domingo and Puerto Rico. Its quarry was French and Spanish ships. As the ship set out, the men may have been aware of turmoil in the fleet, or became aware of it during their cruise. In the spring of 1797, mass mutinies occurred in the Channel and North Sea Fleets.[4] In July, the crew of the small sloop HMS *Marie Antoinette* rose, murdered her commander and took her to a French port.

Under Pigot's command the *Hermione* was an unhappy ship, and his record is one of continual turbulence. Although tactically astute, Pigot was quick to blame subordinates for mishaps, and he alienated the junior officers. His rages led him to make very liberal use of striking the men with blows from ropes and canes ("starting"). Under his command floggings were common and often indiscriminate.[5] The tropics also took their toll: more than a dozen men were debilitated by sickness.

Two events seem to have tipped the ship's company from misery into mutiny. Following a dispute over the handling of the ship, Pigot ordered Midshipman David Casey to be flogged for his objection to Pigot's abusive language and increasingly unreasonable demands. Casey was a respected officer – he was to be spared in the massacre to come – and his humiliation fueled the men's loathing for their Captain, as well as the sense that no one was safe from his rages.

Then, on the evening of September 20, a few days after Casey's flogging, a tricky squall sent the tall masts gyrating wildly and the men worked frantically to reef the sails. On the quarterdeck below, Pigot, reportedly drunk, watched the men on the mizzentop mast with impatience and mounting fury. Convinced that the Topmen were slow and incompetent, he hurled up a chilling threat through his speaking trumpet: "I'll flog the last man down." In their panic and haste, three young sailors, one a lad of just sixteen years, lost their grip and fell screaming onto the deck fifty feet below. All three died. Pigot gave the crumpled bodies a contemptuous look before ordering the men to "throw the lubbers overboard" – derision that was a dreadful insult to professional sailors.

Pigot was far from done, however. He compounded the outrage by ordering those remaining on the masts to be whipped with ropes as they completed their tasks, swearing to flog them in the morning. The next day, as promised, the floggings took place. As Casey later observed, the shocking episode "greatly increased the previous dislike of the Captain and no doubt hastened, if not entirely decided, the mutiny."

4.1   Explaining Mutiny

Why did seamen rebel? Answering that question seems relatively straightforward in the case of the *Hermione*. But the mutiny on the *Hermione* is uniquely violent in British naval history. Fascinated and revolted by the rebellion, Edward Brenton's *Naval History of Great Britain*, published in 1837, considered it the direct consequence of the unusual cruelty and sadism of the ship's commander. In Captain Pigot, Brenton detected an irascible "martinet," whose brutality and unchecked "indulgence of passion" led to the abuse of power that drove his men to violent rebellion.

Brenton's assessment has been echoed by many subsequent historians.[6] In accounting for the mutiny, it is hard to ignore Pigot's tyranny and the shocking contempt for the seamen under his command as factors that propelled them to vengeance. Even if Pigot was an exceptionally grotesque figure, however, were the grievances of the seamen on the *Hermione* really so unique? Brutality, sadism and disregard for the dignity of seamen as practiced by Pigot were hardly commonplace in the Navy, but cruelty occurred frequently enough to be an object of concern among naval authorities. For instance, in an 1807 manual intended for naval officers, the reformist Admiral Phillip Patton hinted that not only personalities but institutional factors were at work. He observed that,

> The same possession of absolute power will account for the *fre-*
> *quent instances* which occur in the Navy, of men whose conduct has
> been unexceptional in subordinate situations, upon being advanced
> to the command of ships becomes capricious and tyrannical in
> a high degree, neglecting even the rules of justice and the rights of
> humanity, which are concealed from themselves under the mistaken
> idea of rigid discipline.[7]

Patton's reflections suggest that arbitrary and excessive punishment
may have been a systematic problem in the Navy.

More recently, some scholars have argued that the fate of the ship
was determined as much by the character of the sailors who manned the
ship as by the character of its commander. One account informed by
psychoanalytic reasoning sees the *Hermione* mutiny as the realization of
the universal desire of subordinated men to act on their fantasies of
bloody revenge.[8] Another, informed by Marxism, sees the mutiny as
a manifestation of the wider social conflict being waged between naval
authorities and seamen who had become part of a radicalized, international proletariat. This explanation contends that the mutiny was fueled
by the alienation between officers and seamen and by the growing sway of
Jacobin sentiments. When the radicalized worldviews of the seamen
converged with their brutalization at the hands of Pigot, the bloody
showdown on the *Hermione* was the inevitable result.[9]

Although we can learn from extreme cases of mutiny such as the
Hermione, we must tread very carefully when we seek to draw general
inferences from them. This caveat would apply just as well to our
argument that the volatile combination of severe grievances and poor
governance produced the explosion on that ship. Can we conclude the
same about other ships that experienced mutinies? And what of those
ships that did not experience mutinies: Did they too suffer from grievances and bad governance at similar levels?

In Chapter 3, we examined varieties of mutiny and their genesis.
Our analysis revealed common patterns across mutinies and the
mechanisms that seamen used to coordinate collective action and attain
solidarity. Yet our approach was limited; the detailed examination of
parts can explain *how* something works, but not *why* it came about.
This kind of dissection might explain a particular event, or perhaps
a few events, but not a whole class of events.

Having conducted a thorough anatomy of mutiny in the previous chapter, we now seek to determine its general causes. Etiology is the historian's counterpart to anatomy. It seeks to explain an outcome (such as an illness) by identifying its causes. Causation connects prior factors or agents with a subsequent effect. In the social sciences, as in medicine or genetics, causation is hardly ever simple; there is likely to be more than a single cause of the outcome of interest. Nearly every complex social behavior – such as mutiny – arises from the multiple and combined effects of several factors. This is especially true when a social outcome involves large-scale collective action.

4.2   What Caused Mutinies?

Social analysts commonly aim to sort out the vexing problem of causation by distinguishing between necessary and sufficient causes. A necessary cause is a factor that must be present in order to produce a given outcome. A factor is a sufficient cause if its presence alone determines the outcome. In reality, however, contributing causes often have to be present if a necessary cause is to have the expected effect. We find this to be true of mutiny. And there is a further complication. Causal processes can be of shorter and longer duration. Whereas some factors are very proximate to their effect, the causal effect of others takes a longer time to unfold. This is also true of mutiny. Take the example of the *Hermione*. Episodes involving immediate brutality converged with longer-term hardships like sickness and extended deployment to the West Indies to inspire the mutiny. Because proximate causes are not necessarily more important than distal ones, the challenge lies in designing studies that can include contributing factors having different temporalities.[10] Too often studies of rebellion and other forms of collective action cannot rely on the kinds of evidence that permit measurement of these kinds of factors.

Experiments in which treatments are randomly assigned to some cases with the untreated serving as the controls are the scientific gold standard used to infer causality. Regrettably, we cannot perform experiments on the past, and at any rate rebellions are impossible to study experimentally. To sort out causation in complex events like mutinies, a variety of methods must be deployed. Fortunately, the records of the Royal Navy are complete enough to support standard statistical methods. Moreover, detailed archival records permit causal process-tracing that allows us to piece together seamen's motives and the specific processes leading to mutinies.

Conventional historical approaches cannot reveal the relative importance of different factors contributing to the likelihood of mutiny. If we simply catalog lists of grievances and other potential causes of mutiny, we cannot know whether they were also prevalent on ships that never experienced mutiny.[11] In our study, we borrow a technique first developed to discover the factors increasing the odds that someone would acquire a rare disease. Called the case-control method, it involves comparing a group of cases in which a known outcome is unusual (in our study, a documented mutiny that satisfies our definition) to a larger group of randomly selected control cases similarly at risk, but that do not experience the outcome of interest. Like epidemiologists analyzing a rare disease, we searched for factors that increase the risk that any given ship belongs in the case (mutiny) rather than the control group (no mutiny).[12]

British naval records afford us the opportunity to trace ships over time through entries in daily logs. This allows us to capture a host of factors that may have influenced the likelihood of mutiny. By systematically comparing a sample of ships that underwent mutiny to a larger sample of similar ships that did not, we get closer to understanding the principal causal factors. Likewise, we can explain why individual seamen rebelled by systematically comparing seamen who took part in mutinies to those on the same ships that did not.[13]

4.3 Ill-Usage: The Understanding of Grievances

Seamen understood their grievances normatively. They interpreted them through the language of "ill-usage," a broad notion that included violations of fairness, insults to their dignity and occupational standing, and threats to their security and welfare. When long-standing deprivation combined with incidents that revealed the incompetence, disregard or injustice of their commanders, existing hardships were taken as ill-usage and seamen became more likely to rebel.

In Chapter 2 we saw how the crews of naval vessels were communities created by the prevailing conditions on ships – mutual dependence in the face of the dangers of the sea, and immersion in a shared occupational culture emphasizing skill, experience and loyalty. Like other members of the skilled working classes, British seamen had a sense of their own collective identity, distinctive traditions and beliefs in their rights and dignity. Their conception of "proper usage" came from this sense of community. They shared an occupational culture providing them with a potent framework for understanding deprivation and injustice that owed everything to their skill and experience and little to radical ideologies.[14]

Seamen had much to complain about. They resented their low wages that were not adjusted to inflation, inflicting serious hardship during times of war.[15] Impressment was another hardship, a "necessary evil" of involuntary servitude without fixed term that the British state inflicted on unlucky individuals who were caught up in recruitment drives during time of war.[16] Whether they were volunteers or pressed (or pressed men persuaded to "volunteer" to gain a boost in pay), during wartime seamen were retained at the Admiralty's pleasure. To deter attrition through desertion, this usually meant seamen faced confinement on their ships for long stretches of time.

Crowding aboard naval vessels was extreme. Even the largest warships were modestly sized by modern standards, an impression vividly conveyed to us by a visit to Lord Nelson's well-preserved flagship HMS *Victory* in Portsmouth harbor. Although that famous ship was large for its day, it is but two hundred and twenty-seven feet long and, at its broadest point at the beam, about fifty feet wide. Hundreds of seamen served on ships-of-the-line like this – indeed, the *Victory* often had a crew of more than eight hundred men – and even smaller vessels bore comparatively large crews. On the typical naval vessel seamen had between fourteen and eighteen inches of width in which to sling their hammocks. Cramped and unpleasant living conditions were an inescapable reality on a sailing warship.[17]

Discipline was harsh, as well. Seamen could be "started" at the whim of their officers. Captains had the right to inflict summary punishment by flogging for a wide range of offenses. Although on most ships moderate punishments were meted out, there was no effective brake on the abuse of seamen by their commanders. Pigot may have been unusually cruel, but "flogging captains" who inflicted frequent and severe floggings on their crews were all too common.[18]

Despite the deprivation that seamen faced, full-fledged mutinies were uncommon. Seamen rarely rebelled due to factors such as poor pay, crowding and its attendant discomforts, impressment and strict discipline because these hardships were all considered to be part of the seaman's lot. More generally, most seamen came from the British working classes who rarely enjoyed good wages and a comfortable standard of living and for whom corporal punishment was the norm.[19] It is not deprivation per se that inspires rebellion but rather the sense of grievance. A grievance offends not just because it does the bearers some harm, but because they regard it as wrong, unfair and illegitimate.

Seamen had a common language by which they understood and expressed their grievances. In the archival records, as well as in their letters and memoirs, seamen time and again strongly opposed what they called "ill-usage." Ill-usage was the obverse of proper usage. Proper usage implied order, routine and deference to the customary practices that protected seamen from cruel and capricious treatment, allowed them their small comforts of regular meals and grog and ensured reasonable standards of health and welfare. Treatment that indicated disregard and incompetent governance was intolerable in ways that the short, hard and poor lives expected as part and parcel of seamen's fate was not.

We find that some of the conditions that seamen faced generated greater grievances than others. In particular, grievances that resulted from what the seamen took to be failures of governance were especially galling. Such grievances not only offended them, but also refocused attention on existing hardships. Content analysis of the thousands of pages of official documents, court-martial transcripts and witness accounts assembled for this study reveals a range of grievances that were implicated in mutiny (see Table 4.1). Among them, governance failures loomed large, with seamen citing wage disputes, harsh discipline, shortages of food and water and spoiled rations (often linked in their minds to illness). Seamen were also offended by commanders who violated accustomed naval conventions and failed to address their concerns about sickness, safety or navigational competence following an accident.

Table 4.1 *Primary and secondary motives cited in sixty-two cases of mutiny*

Motive	First cited	Second cited	Total (%)
Cruelty/Excessive Discipline	15	10	25 (27%)
Wage Issues	13	2	15 (16%)
Victuals: Food/Water/Spirits	8	4	12 (13%)
Violation of Naval Customs	4	6	10 (11%)
Denial of Shore Leave	4	4	8 (9%)
Impressments	5	2	7 (7%)
Safety of Ship/Competence of Command	5	2	7 (7%)
Service in Foreign Waters	4	2	6 (6%)
Demand for Dismissal from Service	0	2	2 (2%)
Piracy	2	0	2 (2%)
			Total = 94

Source: Hechter et al. 2016.

A single grievance was rarely sufficient to trigger a mutiny. Usually grievances became intolerable in combination. In their statements, mutineers made clear that tyranny, overwork and disregard for seamen's well-being combined to constitute ill-usage. For instance, on the *Santa Monica* in 1781, mutineers cited an irascible Captain, the irregular service of meals, the denial of grog and the shortage of drinking water as proof of ill-usage.[20]

4.3.1 Wage Disputes

Wage disputes were cited in nearly a fifth of the mutinies. Apart from the great mutinies of 1797 analyzed in the following chapter, seamen rarely denounced their rate of pay or general exploitation. Rather, they objected to wages held in arrears by Captains as a means of deterring desertion, wages that the Admiralty had failed to pay for months or the denial of extra pay for unusual work. Captains were customarily expected to be advocates for their men, and seamen tried to remind them of their obligation. On the *Egmont* in 1779, the crew staged an armed strike against a Captain who administered the pay books improperly. The failure to deliver wages was regarded as an attack on the implicit contract between crew and command. Mutinies inspired by delinquent wages occurred on a number of vessels including the *Alfred* in 1801, the *Canada* in 1781, the *Crown* in 1764, the *Intrepid* in 1797, the *Invincible* in 1780 and the *Swallow* in 1762. These mutinies usually took the form of armed strikes. They could be swiftly and bloodlessly resolved if both sides were willing to bargain. On the *Invincible* in 1780, striking seamen shouted very plainly, "Give us money and we will go to sea! No sea without money!" They got it and off they went.[21]

As wars were winding down, seamen became anxious because wages were usually in arrears as hostilities ended. Seamen were eager to be released after long mandatory terms of service or, at least, to be paid their delinquent wages before setting off on another voyage. Mutineers on the *Inflexible* and *Janus* in 1783 and the *Dispatch* in 1815 wanted the wages due to them before being sent to the distant Indies. A delay in being released (mustering out) meant that skilled seamen might not find a berth in a merchant ship. As the War of American Independence came to a close, the mutineers on the *Raisonnable* in 1783 insisted on payment of wages and an expedited dismissal from service. The petition they delivered to Captain Hervey justifying their seizure of the ship read:

> My Lord, as the Ship's Company have taken it in their heads
> not to go to Chatham it is in vain to dissuade them from their
> resolution. As for your Lordship's character or your officers'
> being hurt, that shall not be, we intend to carry the ship into the
> harbour [at Portsmouth]. We had trouble to rig her to your
> Lordship's satisfaction and fit her out, so we shall leave her where
> we found her, we shall clean her and wash her and do everything
> that's wanted to the satisfaction of your Lordship and everybody
> else. Signed: Ship's Company.

The seamen failed to win the support of the Admiralty, however, and Hervey and his officers were able to secretly arm themselves and seize the ringleaders. The mutiny swiftly collapsed and seven men ultimately hanged for their part in the rebellion.[22]

Whatever their results, what episodes like that aboard *Raisonnable* show is that commanders who failed to muster seamen out swiftly, pay them their wages in timely fashion or make sure they received the prize-monies they had earned violated the implicit pact between a commander and his followers.

4.3.2 Customs of the Sea

Treatment that violated norms – what seamen understood as the customs of the sea, and their dignity as skilled craftsmen – often created a sense of grievance. In June 1798, the warship *Adamant* returned to England after a long period of service. The men were angered when they learned that the ship's company was to be drafted into several other ships rather than mustered out. They planned an armed strike to force naval authorities to address their "deplorable and unhappy state." The leading seamen drafted a protest petition against their Captain that was signed by half of the ship's crew. They were especially irritated by the disregard that the officers showed toward them. Recall that they wrote, in part,

> The grievances of the ship is as follows: Firstly, the officers take
> the prime of the meals ... [We are] Deprived of every indulgence
> which every other ship gets after coming from sea, our wives
> and children turned out three days before the ship was payed [and]
> often ill-treated when [the Captain] were absent.[23]

Seamen had a shared sense of the customs of the sea and what they permitted. Depriving them of customary "indulgences," such as family visits, and imposing indignities on them were attacks on their social status as skilled workers.

Seemingly trivial complaints had greater resonance when they were caused by commanders who failed to honor customary boundaries. On the *Defiance* in 1795, seamen objected to watered-down grog; they blamed the Captain who, in their view, arbitrarily denied them the comfort of the drink to which they were entitled. Seaman John Nicol, who was on a nearby ship, recalled:

> While we lay at Leith Roads [in Scotland], a mutiny broke out
> on the *Defiance*, seventy-four. The cause was, their captain gave
> them five-water grog; now the common thing is three-waters.
> The weather was cold. The spirit thus reduced was, as the

mutineers called it, as thin as muslin and quite unfit to keep out the cold. No seaman could endure this in cold climates.

In staging what proved to be a doomed rebellion, Nicol nevertheless thought the men of the ship proved themselves "stout, resolute dogs."[24]

Seemingly trivial grievances could turn into ill-usage if they grew from the violation of expectations about the proper relationship between crew and command. On the *Minerva* in 1794, seamen rebelled against the "unreasonable" rules of Captain Whitby who had banned loud noise and swearing from the decks and compelled them to dance for exercise. Enforcement of these policies included flogging, though usually fewer than a dozen lashes. Although the seamen did not regard the flogging as very harsh, it was frequent and "galling" because it violated customary usage. Seaman William Richardson explained that, "Though the punishment was light, it displeased the men very much, who had not had time to divest themselves of the new crime [cursing and swearing] they had been long accustomed to, and was nearly attended with serious consequences."[25]

Ill-usage was a powerful notion not because it referred to objective labor treatment standards, but because it captured transgressions of what was deemed to be culturally appropriate. The mutineers on the *Kingfisher* made this clear when they insisted that their ill-usage violated the moral standards that all Britons understood, grousing that "[m]en on this ship are treated like Turks and not as Christians."[26]

4.3.3   Sickness

Threats to life and limb also influenced how seamen understood the competence of commanders and their concern for the crew's welfare. Fatal accidents were taken as a sign of bad governance. For example, in a few months before the outbreak of mutiny aboard the *Berwick* in 1794, four seamen had perished in various accidents. Far worse than the all-too frequent deadly accidents was sickness, that great scourge of early modern warfare. Widespread outbreaks of sickness called governance into question. Seamen frequently employed the concept of ill-usage to describe disregard for their health.

At trial, the *Panther* mutineers saved themselves by being able to prove ill-usage that included the serving of spoiled food and the unconscionable neglect of sickened seamen. In the minds of seamen, illness flourished with ill-usage; thus sickness sharply increased grievances in a ship's company. For one thing, the greater the number of seamen who were debilitated by illness, the more work had to be done by the remainder of the crew. Besides the risk of contagion, unchecked sickness could also become a direct threat to the survival of a ship's company. Authority could collapse entirely when health was severely compromised, as on the *Wager* in 1741 when only a handful of seamen remained fit enough to sail the ship and the storm-tossed vessel ran aground before mutiny erupted.[27]

On the *Camilla* in 1783, yellow fever and smallpox overwhelmed the crew during its deployment in the West Indies. Leaving the sick and dying in port (as was the usual practice), the frigate had sailed with only two-thirds of its intended complement. The crew was convinced that sickness was still a threat and had created an undue burden on the remaining able crewmen. As the frigate prepared to depart Port Royal, Jamaica, a delegation of seamen came upon the quarterdeck and informed the officers they would not put the ship to sea. An officer later testified that "they wanted more men, and better usage or otherwise they could not, they would not, go to sea. That the ship was too weakly manned and, that if a squall came on – which were frequently in this country – they were not able to do their duty."[28] Refused their demands that their health and welfare be protected, the men mutinied.

Little wonder that seamen worried about sickness, particularly when serving in the tropics where fevers were endemic. Compared with disease, battle was infrequent and a comparatively trivial cause of death. During the Seven Years' War, the Navy lost more than a hundred thousand men to disease, whereas somewhat fewer than two hundred were killed in combat. Between 1793 and 1815, more than 80 percent of mortality in the Royal Navy resulted from disease – versus just 2 percent from battle. Annual mortality rates in the Navy could approach 15 percent as a consequence of disease.[29] Compared with the danger of inaction in the face of unchecked sickness, the dangers of mutiny might have seemed small.

In the seamen's minds, sickness was associated with disorder. The inability to manage sickness, above all communicable disease, was understood as a failure of command. If sickness were seen as inevitable and invariable across ships in similar circumstances, it would be surprising that it motivated mutiny. Keeping seamen healthy and avoiding the spread of infectious disease, however, were challenges that naval authorities indeed could meet. For instance, Horatio Nelson was a scrupulous administrator who ensured that the ships under his command were sanitary and well supplied with fresh foods. Health maintained shipboard order, and the remarkable operational effectiveness of the Royal Navy came about, in large part, because good commanders worked hard to avert health crises. By contrast, the health and welfare of seamen in the contemporary French, Spanish and Dutch navies were far worse, as was the problem of mutiny.[30]

Because very little was known about the precise causes of sicknesses, commanders were responsible for it and seamen blamed them when it went unchecked. William Bligh thought managing sickness was a commander's greatest responsibility on a long-distance voyage, remaking that "The scurvy is really a disgrace to a ship where it is at all common."[31] At the very least, commanders were expected to show solicitude toward sickened seamen and provide for the best care and comfort possible given the cramped and uncomfortable conditions that prevailed on their vessels. They were also expected to manage sickness so that it did not spread too widely or too quickly. Neither of these were easy tasks, and mishandling sickness aboard a sailing ship or disregard for the suffering were taken as signs of poor governance.[32]

4.3.4 Discipline and Punishment

Naturally, brutality and excessive discipline featured prominently in understandings of ill-usage. The *Hermione* is not the only case in which excessive and indiscriminate flogging directly inspired mutiny. More than a quarter of all the motives given for mutiny in our sample cited excessive discipline; severe and frequent punishment was ill-usage in its most extreme and obvious form. On the *Beaulieu* in 1797, mutiny was justified in terms of resistance to arbitrary and unnecessary punishments, with mutineers especially condemning their officers for punishing seamen for trivial offenses.[33] So strong was the resistance to excessive discipline that a commander's reputation for brutality could inspire mutinies against new commanders before they even assumed the commission, as occurred on the *Blanche* in 1797 and the *Barfleur* in 1809.[34]

Excessive discipline was objectionable not only because of the fear and injury that flogging caused, but also because it called the ability and mental fitness of a commander into question. On the *Ferret* in 1806, the inability of Captain Cadogan to manage a new command without threats, bullying of subordinate officers and frequent recourse to flogging was obvious from witness testimony. His crew especially objected to very severe lashings – one seaman was given ninety lashes by Cadogan.[35] A similar pattern is observable in the mutiny on the *Goza* in 1801. On that ship, the commanding Lieutenant had uncontrollable "passions" that led him to flog indiscriminately, including even influential Petty Officers.[36]

In many instances the irregular and humiliating character of punishment as much as its severity outraged seamen. Witnesses in the court-martial of the mutineers on the *Santa Monica* in 1781 reported "having been at different times beaten and knocked down with speaking trumpets, handspikes, blades of oars," and so on, by the officers of the ship. Shockingly, Captain Linzee personally struck sailors with his speaking trumpet or a knotted rope on many occasions. In their testimony, his officers conceded that Linzee had an uncontrollable temper and often lashed out in ways that were unbecoming in a gentleman. A commander was expected to assign punishment after due consideration, and to delegate the task of inflicting it to the appropriate subordinate. Linzee's lack of self-control violated unwritten rules about a commanding officer's relationship with his crew. Richard Wells, the Master, ruefully conceded in cross-examination that, based on two decades of service, "I cannot say I ever saw a Captain strike the men in any other ship I have been in."[37]

In justifying its mutiny, the crew of the *Tremendous* at anchor off the southern tip of Africa in 1797 drew up a detailed petition to Admiral Pringle that detailed a host of specific grievances such as the spoiled food and drink they were given and the denial of their proper rations and entitlements. The heart of their petition decried practices that violated their dignity and sense of their rights. These practices included Captain Stephen's enforcement of rules that were not stated in the Articles of War, irregular punishments and excessive starting and striking of seamen. Ill-usage of this kind undercut the consent without which teamwork cannot thrive. If the authorities refused to enforce this unwritten rule, then seamen would. In the Navy, they wrote, "We allow Laws to Punish, but no Tyrants to bear His Majesty's Commission."[38]

Unbridled anger and irregular discipline undercut social order and the legitimacy of command authority. Brutality and arbitrary punishments were not only demeaning but also suggested that a Captain lacked self-control. If he could not "govern his passions," he might not be able to govern a ship or bring it through danger.[39]

4.4   Testing the Relationship between Grievances and Mutiny

The motives expressed by rebellious seamen reveal how they connected poor governance to grievances through the master frame of ill-usage. Yet how do we know if such grievances really provoked mutinies when other factors also may have influenced mobilization? Do some kinds of grievances matter more than others in increasing the odds that a mutiny would occur on a given ship?

As the mutineers' grievances suggest, structural factors are far from the only ones that created a sense of injury. Building on classical insights in the social sciences, social psychologists have shown that there are at least two different kinds of grievances. *Structural grievances* derive from a group's disadvantaged position in a social structure, whereas *incidental grievances* arise from unanticipated situations – incidents – that put groups at risk. Unlike structural grievances, incidental ones – like unexpected disasters, accidents, major court decisions and state repression – tend to enhance a group's capacity to coordinate.[40]

The reason is that these two classes of grievances have different psychological implications. People who have long occupied subordinate positions in a society tend to tolerate grievances like poor wages, difficult working conditions and political exclusion so long as they remain at routine and predictable levels. If people understand that bearing such indignities is their lot in life, they are not likely to seek redress unless the magnitude of those grievances increases sharply. This seems clear in the case of seamen and the reasons they gave for mutiny.[41]

Under normal conditions, structural grievances foster stable expectations that tend to discourage protest. Members of subordinated groups are typically skeptical about what they can achieve through collective action. They know that open defiance of the authorities rarely wins advantages, and concentrate instead on their individual situations. Moreover, the fear and shame associated with low social standing tend to be demobilizing – a tendency especially evident among the least skilled seamen. When incidental grievances are severe, however, they are manifest to all who are affected. Incidental grievances impose injuries and pose threats that are shared by everyone belonging to the same category of people. It becomes easy for victims of these unforeseen events to develop an "us versus them" collective identity.[42] On ships, such incidents reinforced the boundaries between officers and men and between command and the crew.

So long as the group has some shared conception of fairness, as did seamen, framing a new injury as injustice is relatively straightforward. The simultaneous experience of the same threat, injury or insult improves coordination by providing a common focus among disparate people who might not otherwise make common cause. Where formal organization is lacking, experiencing an unfortunate incident can help people overcome the barriers that make coordination difficult. This mechanism is especially potent in socially dense settings such as those aboard ships.[43] For groups that lack many of the resources that foster collective action, incidental grievances therefore help trigger spontaneous mobilization.

Of course, structural and incidental grievances can concatenate, and when they do we expect them powerfully to increase the chances of rebellion. Structural grievances create a deep reservoir of resentment against those in power. They can remain at the threshold of tolerability until an incident occurs that focuses discontent on the authorities. In the wake of the new injury, failures of governance come sharply into focus and collective identities are made more salient, promoting mobilization.

Using a host of measures that we gathered from naval records – including from each ship's Captain's and Master's logs and muster books – we can test our argument about the combination of incidental and structural grievances as causes of mutiny.[44] Our unit of analysis is a given ship-year. With cases of mutiny, the relevant ship-year is the period one year before the date of the outbreak of the mutiny. For controls, the relevant ship-year is selected at random from the list of all possible ship-year combinations in the list of ships and their years of operation. We estimated multivariate logistic regression models predicting the incidence of mutiny. Then we compared the factors that, on average, significantly affected the odds of a mutiny on a given ship in a given year.

The analysis offers striking evidence in support of our thesis (for details of the model and estimation, see Appendix B). Incidental grievances – *sickness, reduced rations, accidents at sea* and the *last year of a war* – are all positively and significantly associated with mutiny even in the presence of other potentially confounding factors. Reduced rations indicates whether a ship's crew had been placed on reduced or restricted rations of food or drink by a ship's commander for a period greater than one day over the course of the relevant year. Seamen generally received less than their statutory rations due to shortages, the spoilage of provisions or disorganization aboard the ship. Sailing accident indicates whether a ship's logs reported an accident that endangered the operation of the ship or the crew (e.g., running around, a collision, a lost mast or a drowning) over the course of a relevant ship-year. By custom as well as naval law, a ship's commander was considered responsible for all failures of navigation and ship-handling. Both food shortages and accidents would have been indicative of bad governance.

In this era Britain was frequently at war. That fact could not be laid on a commander's doorstep, but how he managed wartime pressures and the competing interests of naval authorities and his crew was a different question. Last year of a war indicates if a relevant year was during the disruptive period of demobilization of fleets at the conclusion of Britain's wars. As we have seen, seamen blamed their commanders for delays in mustering out and receiving pay that was in arrears. These disruptive periods were real tests of governance and some commanders failed to meet them.

The association between mutiny and sickness was especially strong, occurring long before general debilitation. The average rate of sickness aboard the mutinous ships in our sample was about three times greater than in the controls. The risk of mutiny increased sharply after sickness crossed a threshold of about 10 percent of a ship's company. Our estimate of the effect of sickness is conservative, as it is measured as the proportion of the ship's company reported as sick by the ship's

Surgeon. This would exclude mere malingering or trivial complaints. Mortality would be of obvious interest to us, but it cannot be reliably captured, because the seriously ill were often transferred to naval hospitals or other sites prior to their death.

An outbreak of sickness that severely affected a tenth or more of a ship's company would have been highly destabilizing. Given the lamentable state of contemporary medicine, it created fear among seamen and imposed a challenge to a commander's abilities. Although one might think that sickness was important because it weakened the capacity of the officers to maintain control, this seems unlikely in most instances. Officers had a lower rate of sickness than seamen. On the contrary, it is more likely that widespread sickness and the perception of unchecked contagion operated by increasing grievances among seamen and demonstrating poor governance by commanders.

Structural grievances, however severe, were those arising from routine aspects of life at sea. Surprisingly, we find that many of the factors usually considered to be onerous to seamen – *impressment*, *crowding* and *foreign deployments* – are hardly associated with mutiny. Two structural grievances, however – *wages* and *punishment* – are significant in ways that our discussion of seamen's motivation to mutiny would lead us to anticipate. Periods when wages had greater buying power significantly decreased the odds of mutiny. Seamen were more likely to mutiny when they felt that the value of their wages had fallen and that authorities neglected to redress the situation. The problem of wage erosion gave rise to the mass, fleet-wide mutinies of 1797, which we analyze in detail in Chapter 5.

On the *Hermione* and many other ships, seamen cited excessive discipline as a grievance that motivated rebellion. Consistent with our discussion of egregious ill-usage, a high rate of flogging significantly increased the odds of mutiny.[45] Social historians have shown that seamen did not generally object to flogging, but rather to punishment that was arbitrary and indiscriminate. They expected commanders to sanction troublemakers who undercut effective teamwork. When flogging was frequent and applied for petty offenses irrespective of skill and qualities, however, it violated seamen's ideas about good governance.[46]

We expected that a structural grievance like punishment would be more likely to motivate rebellion at higher levels because it violated expectations about proper treatment. Flogging, in particular, should have a stronger effect on the odds of mutiny at higher levels as compared with low or moderate levels. To test this proposition, we examined the effect of flogging on the probability of mutiny.[47] We find that there is such a relationship. Figure 4.1 graphically illustrates the relationship between flogging and mutiny, displaying the estimated probability of mutiny across a range of the possible values of flogging, with all other factors in the model held at their average values. Figure 4.1 suggests that low and moderate levels of punishment did little to raise the odds of mutiny, but once punishment grew severe, crossing the threshold of about eleven floggings per capita in our model (this would mean that the average seamen on a given ship received eleven lashes in a year), it increases sharply. If the per capita number of floggings approached twenty, then, holding all other factors constant, mutiny became a near certainty.

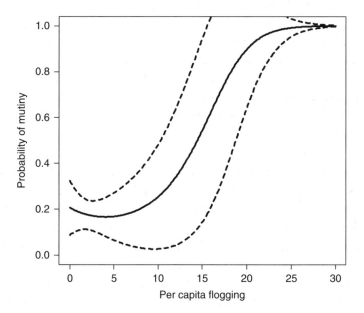

Figure 4.1 The relationship between flogging and mutiny: simulated probability of mutiny by per capita rate of flogging

Note: Dotted lines indicate 95 percent confidence interval.

Source: Hechter et al. 2016.

4.4.1   From Grievances to Mobilization

Our findings show that incidental and structural grievances combined to increase the odds of mutiny. Grievances alone cannot generate collective action, however. Seamen have to be able to cooperate and perceive some opportunity to succeed if they are going to mount a rebellion.

Considering the social structure of ships and related factors that might have influenced the capacity of a crew to mobilize, we wanted to see if the proportion of Irish seamen influenced the odds of mutiny. We chose to use the share of Irishmen on a ship in the Royal Navy because they were numerous among the ranks of seamen. Moreover, they were considered outsiders to the shared "Britishness" that by the end of the eighteenth century brought the English, Welsh and Scots into an emerging Protestant and imperial identity.[48]

Social ties among the members of a group and its sense of community can be important factors influencing its capacity to cooperate. To test whether varying levels of social capital across ships influenced the odds of mutiny, we measured prior service as the share of the ship's company reported as having served with other seamen on another ship prior to transfer to the current vessel.[49] Diversity among the members of a group may also influence cooperation. We measured rank heterogeneity, the stratification of the ship by rank and qualities as reported in muster books.[50] To our surprise, only the share of a ship's company that is Irish is positively and significantly associated with the risk of mutiny.

We found few interaction and nonlinear associations between the various factors in our model and no significant interaction effects between classes of grievances. We did, however, find interaction effects between the share of a crew that was Irish and the share that had previously served together. This finding suggests that very well-integrated crews were less prone to mutiny than more poorly integrated ones. Ships with high shares of Irishmen and seamen who were not closely tied to one another through previous experience were at greater risk of mutiny. Whereas research generally emphasizes how social capital enhances the capacity of protest groups to engage in collective action,[51] our finding points to a different relationship related to the problem of command. Probably crews with moderate levels of social integration were the most prone to mutiny – not cohesive enough to keep grievances in check through self-policing but with enough social capital to allow mobilization.

4.4.2 Opportunity and Contextual Factors

To consider whether differences in opportunities to take a ship influenced the propensity for mutiny, we included the share of Marines in a ship's company. Marines were supposed to engage the enemy in battle, but they also served as an onboard security force bolstering the authority of the commander. We also considered whether a ship was assigned to a fleet or squadron or engaged in detached service over the course of a relevant year. Although the presence of Marines did not deter mutiny, ships that were part of a fleet or squadron did have significantly greater odds of mutiny than did solitary ships. Given cases like the *Bounty* or the *Hermione* this may seem counterintuitive, but the finding is not surprising in the light of the qualitative evidence presented in Chapter 3. Mutineers rarely seized ships to sail away to a foreign haven. Most often seamen seized ships in order to negotiate with senior naval authorities, which meant that they wanted to be in port or at an anchorage close to the fleet.

Long periods of uninterrupted warfare could have increased tensions and fatigue and made the command of warships harder. We find, however, that the pressures of warfare and the duration of conflicts are not significantly associated with the risk of mutiny. In other studies, the association between mutiny and wartime can probably be explained by war serving as a proxy for a host of grievances that we measured directly.

Our analysis is limited in that we do not have measures about the personality of commanders, which doubtless played a role in motivating rebellions. We do have observations about how they governed, however, which is likely to matter more. An additional concern that could confound our causal interpretation is the assignment of commanders to ships. If commanders were selected for certain ships because of their reputation for toughness or strict discipline and the Admiralty considered this as a way to offset a crew with a reputation for rebelliousness, then this unobserved factor could also be influencing the odds of mutiny.

Fortunately, we can dismiss this possibility. The Royal Navy did not have a consistent, rationalized procedure for assigning commanders to specific ships. There was very little deliberate matching of officers to ships on the basis of the crews' characteristics, of which almost nothing was known by the Admiralty Lords who granted commissions. Assignments were the result of vacancies, patronage, social connections and reputation. Crews as collectivities were not considered important and were largely ephemeral because of turnover, mortality and the like. Not only did higher officials know next to nothing about ship's companies, the thinking (perhaps mistaken) was that any competent officer could govern any given crew.[52]

4.5   Why Individual Seamen Joined Mutinies

Our analysis of *crews* reveals the grievances and social factors that combined to cause mutinies aboard naval vessels. What explains why *individual* seamen took active part in a mutiny? Mutinies emerge as a result of interdependent behavior that cannot be reduced to the sum of the characteristics of individuals on a ship.[53] Just because a mutiny occurs on a ship does not mean that each individual seaman mutinies. Even if they shared the same grievances as their shipmates, each seaman would have had good reason to remain a passive bystander to rebellion. The logic of collective action is premised on the notion that individuals may have incentives *not* to behave in ways that contribute to the collective good. After all, seamen who took an active part in mutinies risked their necks, whereas bystanders got the same share of whatever collective benefit that was to be achieved through the mutiny. Given greater costs and more or less equivalent rewards, what motivated seamen to become mutineers?

In answering this question, the transcripts of the testimonies of defendants and witnesses in courts-martials provide limited insight. The handful of surviving memoirs by seamen who were present on ships experiencing mutinies are too few and their authors too unusual to be a reliable source of information about the average seaman. And at trial, the accused revealed little about their personal motives and had good reasons to minimize their roles.

Descriptive data like those presented in the previous chapter cannot tell us if seamen from certain categories were really more likely to have active mutineers or to have served as ringleaders. To answer that, we need to analyze the likelihood of being a ringleader based on systematic evaluation. In most instances, it is impossible to reconstruct a complete list of all of the seamen who took active part in a mutiny. Once a mutiny ended, no matter the outcome, seamen had little incentive to identify themselves and face punishment. In some mutinies, however, we have been able to assemble complete lists of all the seamen on a ship, including those taking part, and can measure whether they were identified as ringleaders in archival documents. The dataset allows us to consider several factors that might be associated with active participation and with leadership.[54]

The best option would be to systematically compare the seamen who did take active part in all of the mutinies with those who did not. Here an additional problem presents itself. Seamen tended to deny their involvement in rebellion no matter their role and, in some mutinies, no trial was held. We are fortunate, however, because we have been able to identify full lists of participants for some of the mutinies in our study. Although this subsample is limited to twelve of the mutinies in our sample, it includes diverse types of mutinies and kinds of ships; hence, it offers the best opportunity to explore the question of individual participation.[55] The dataset includes information on nearly two thousand seamen gleaned from musters and logbooks of whom five hundred (28 percent) were positively identified as mutiny participants. It affords us with sufficient statistical power to estimate models predicting the factors influencing the odds that individual seamen became mutineers.[56]

Turning first to those seamen identified as ringleaders, the results of the analysis show that Petty Officers and Able Seamen were more likely than other seamen to have played leading roles (see Appendix B). This is not surprising because in Chapter 3 we showed that the ringleaders of mutinies in our full sample were also more likely to have been Petty Officers and Able Seamen.[57] The findings reinforce witness testimony and other qualitative sources that reveal how coordination was achieved in the lower decks and the role that social standing played in selecting leaders.

More important, the results of the analysis help to divulge the motivations that led seamen to organize and lead mutinies. The decision to become a ringleader was shaped by individual incentives. Compared with their shipmates, ringleaders were more likely to have been flogged in the year preceding the mutiny and to have been pressed into service. These experiences may have made seamen more likely to nurse personal grievances against their commanders and thus more willing to assume the risks of leadership.

Analyzing active participation in mutinies rather than leadership reveals similar patterns. Personal grievances also help to explain why individual seamen risked their necks. As was the case with ringleaders, we find that having been pressed into the Navy significantly increased the odds of taking part in mutinies. Age deterred participation in mutiny. Older seamen may have steered clear of trouble or had the experience to know that mutinies were dangerous and unreliable ways to redress grievances.[58]

When controlling for other factors that could be associated with participation, we find that "foreigners" were more likely to have taken part in mutinies when compared with their British shipmates. Historical accounts are replete with evidence that foreign seamen, and especially Irish Catholics, were discriminated against at sea. Experiences at sea would have compounded the sense of grievance many would have already felt given the political and economic subordination that prevailed in Ireland. Even if motivated by prejudice, the opinion of naval authorities who considered foreigners and Irishmen as more prone to rebellion may have been partly right, if only because their biased treatment of them intensified ethnic grievances.[59] Other foreign seamen may have simply been less attached to the Navy and less likely to form attachments with their commanders. Finally, we find that Marines were less likely than sailors to be mutineers. Marines may have had greater attachment to command. Additionally, Marines may have been seen by other seamen as less reliable or more weakly attached to their occupational culture, making them less likely to be recruited by their shipmates.

Notably, the share of impressed seamen did not increase the odds of mutiny on a ship, but it did increase the odds of an individual seaman's taking part in mutinies and being identified as a ringleader. Perhaps the contrasting finding can be explained by the differences between individual and aggregate conditions. Impressment was an uncommon condition at the level of the group – in our sample, just 7 percent of seamen were pressed. However, the *personal* grievance of having been impressed could have been a very striking experience that primed individual seamen for rebellion.

In the light of our analysis, revisiting the *Hermione* reveals the unusual social dimensions of the conflict aboard that ship. It seems clear that on this ship a variety of grievances – incidental ones like accidents and sickness and structural ones like the system of discipline – combined to generate antagonism toward Captain Pigot. What drove the mutiny on the *Hermione*, however, appears to have been the unique situation created by combining the disillusioned men Pigot brought with him from the *Success* with those on his new command. Of course, it was not unusual for a Captain to bring a group of followers from his previous command with him when he went into a new ship. Carefully selected, highly skilled and loyal followers could be useful in assuring the success of his voyage. From the seaman's perspective, following a resourceful, ambitious and well-connected commander could mean gaining a share of his spoils and the all-important patronage that helped advance a naval career.

In the case of Pigot, however, the men who followed him onto his new command were highly skilled and influential. More importantly, they had long exposure to Pigot's brutality and uncontrolled rages. On the *Hermione* the contempt for Pigot that his followers had for him, and their fear that he was growing more dangerous and unpredictable probably played a key role in catalyzing the formation of the mutinous coalition that led the uprising.

Historical evidence and witness testimony from the trials following the mutiny tell us which seamen played leading roles in the mutiny, and which took active part in taking the ship and attacking the officers. We restricted our statistical analysis reported above to the ship's company of the *Hermione* (a total of 172 people), systematically comparing those who were ringleaders and active participants to other seamen. We found that personal grievances – having been pressed or flogged – were not associated with having been a ringleader on *Hermione* as they were on other ships. Instead, the men who came over to the ship with Pigot from the *Success* were the most likely to end up as ringleaders. Half the ringleaders of the subsequent mutiny were *Success* men. The *Success* men were a group selected for their talents and experience; Southcott called them the "best men" in the ship's company. They commanded respect on the *Hermione*, and were regarded as leaders by their shipmates. Controlling for rank and other factors, they were about seven times more likely than their shipmates to have been in the leadership of the mutiny and about four times more likely to have been active mutineers.

Although Pigot tried to win loyalty by showing favoritism toward the *Success* men and other seamen, apparently it won him little genuine affection because, controlling for other factors, having been promoted in the last year also increased the odds that a seaman would be identified as a ringleader in the mutiny against him. That so many of those who should have been Pigot's best defenders were at the core of the mutiny says much about his formidable capacity to alienate subordinates, and about the breadth of the grievances that drove the rebellion.

Pigot was capricious, his rages were unpredictable and his punishments were arbitrary and excessive. Despite his technical skills and record of performance, Pigot's arrogant misrule put everyone – such as Midshipman Casey or the unfortunate Topmen facing a sudden squall – at risk of humiliation and a thrashing, if not the loss of life. All of this generated strong collective grievances and violated the norms governing relations between officers and men. Rather than personal grievances, what seems to have mobilized men to join the mutiny was the conviction that Pigot was a tyrant who, due to patronage and privilege, could not be removed from command by any other means. Hatred and despair combined with a grim familiarity with Pigot among the *Success* men who knew him best shaped a coalition of seamen ready to slay a tyrant.

The *Hermione* is an extreme case, but it shows that even under conditions of severe collective grievances, other factors contribute to the making of a mutiny. In the context of long-standing structural grievances compounded by incidental grievances, a cadre of potential ringleaders has to be available and willing to risk initiating a rebellion. Seamen have to be persuaded to take an active part in spite of the dangers. Seamen on the *Hermione* were probably recruited to take an active part in a mutiny through social ties to others. Interpersonal ties can enable coordination and help members of a group to attain solidarity by encouraging conformity. Having served together for long periods and across different commands meant that seamen knew and trusted such shipmates. They probably had strong ties that fostered mobilization and discouraged free riding. Seamen with strong and abiding ties were probably key supporters whom ringleaders relied on as a mutiny was being planned or set in motion.[60]

It is important to reemphasize that some of the factors – impressment, flogging and ties to seamen through previous service – that were insignificant at the *group* level for predicting mutiny aboard ships are significant predictors of *individual* participation. How can we reconcile the ostensibly inconsistent findings? The pitfall of the analysis of groups is that we might be tempted to draw inferences about individuals from group-level characteristics. This fallacy of composition occurs whenever we implicitly assume that the attributes of an entity – a ship's crew – are merely the attributes of its constituent elements (individual seamen on that ship) and that we can draw inferences back to individuals from observations of the group.[61] Collective grievances propelled ships into mutinies. Those seamen who chose to play active roles in those mutinies were frequently motivated by private grievances in addition.

4.6 Ill-Usage and the Rhetoric of Moral Economy

Our ideas about grievances and the language of ill-usage are reminiscent of the literature on moral economy, which also links ideas about just governance to grievances. Historian E. P. Thompson famously argued that eighteenth-century English crowds were motivated to rebel by notions of traditional rights and customs. They believed that insurrection was justified by community norms. Common people were moralists, who applied traditional standards of the commonweal in judging the rightness of governance and economic exchange. Their moral economy emphasized balance and justice in social relations between rulers and subordinates.[62]

Thompson claimed that commercial and political elites in the early modern era were effectively constrained in their range of action by the traditionally-minded crowd. By engaging in bread riots and other local manifestations of rebellion, the English people kept their exploitation in check and applied pressure on their rulers to attend to their welfare. Protests inspired by conceptions of the moral economy lack leadership, organization and transformative goals, however. They are spontaneous and defensive. Above all, Thompson argued, it was the *threat* of rebellion, rather than the riots themselves, which was politically effective.

As applied to the Navy, the fact that the seaman's culture included the possibility of defiance – mutiny – in response to perceived exploitation can be seen as maintaining a balance in relations between commanders and their crews. Although it is true that Thompson specifically had in mind the claims that traditional communities make on the supply of commodities that are necessary for their livelihood, such as grain, the moral economy concept can be extended to seamen. In the Navy, labor relations are at stake rather than access to commodities, but seamen's ideas about their just compensation included their monetary wage as well as their victuals and other necessities of life.[63]

In spite of its insights, our theory differs from the moral economy thesis in several respects. Thompson was interested in condemning the rationalism and materialism of political economy in favor of cultural interpretation. This led to his rejection of the notion that people were acting strategically. The majority of the mutinies in our sample were clearly deliberate and strategic in their orientation, however. More broadly, we reject the primacy of either materially or culturally derived grievances as causes of rebellion. Whereas moral economy focuses on community action, we do not take norms or their enforcement as givens, but recognize that they require collective action to be effective. This means that individuals respond to incentives and actively shape grievance interpretations.

In its exclusive focus on outbreaks of rebellion, the moral economy framework has other notable limitations. One must consider the possibility that the language of ill-usage was a convenient justification for mutiny rather than a reflection of a set of commonly shared norms that determined the interpretation of grievances. Systematically comparing ships that did and did not have mutinies is thus of vital importance, because it allows us to measure the extent and intensity of grievances and statistically estimate their relationship to mutiny.

In practice, when applied to the authorities, ill-usage could be a capacious concept, covering sins of commission and omission. The causal importance of moral economy at the community level is suspect precisely because framing grievances in terms of ill-usage often required forging a consensus among seamen as to whom to blame for a hardship. Community norms are not a substitute for coordination, although they may enable it. We do not mean to suggest that framing grievances in moral terms does not matter. However, the framing of grievances had to be undertaken by influential seamen who used social influence to induce others to rebel and who were usually later identified as ringleaders in the wake of a mutiny. Even when loosely organized, mutinies required leadership, social influence and active coordination.

Instead, we point to the malleability and inconsistency of norms in practice and also to the fact that, whatever its normative basis, collective action is subject to the tension between self-interest and group interest.[64] Thompson claims that the "actual immediate benefits" of rebellion are rarely substantial, but that the credible threat of rebellion is an effective brake on exploitation and indifference. Lacking occasional rebellions, "the threat carries no terrors," hence, for the sake of the group, *someone* must act.[65] But who should act, particularly when action comes at great personal risk? Whenever there is a divergence between what is in the interest of an individual and what is "necessary" for the group, moral consensus may be a necessary factor but it is inadequate explanation for collective action.[66]

4.7 Revisiting Grievances as Causes of Mutiny

In 1970, political scientist Ted Robert Gurr published *Why Men Rebel*, a pathbreaking application of social psychology to the study of political violence. Gurr argued that rebellions occur because of a frustration–aggression complex. When large groups of people feel that their aspirations have been blocked, they become frustrated and angry. The situation is especially acute when individuals perceive they are disadvantaged relative to a given comparable (reference) group. Protest provides a release of these tensions. In the decades since, a host of studies tested the theory, but it received little empirical support. Because individual grievances are idiosyncratic, it is unsurprising that one's attitudes about such things as career satisfaction, economic well-being, living conditions and children's welfare do not turn out to be significant determinants of collective action.[67]

The analyses presented here and in the preceding chapter have revealed that mutinies occurred because of the combination of structural and incidental grievances that resulted, to differing extents, from poor governance. Grievances cause collective action by activating emotions connected with injustice and by creating a demand for their redress. Cases like the *Hermione* show that if grievances are severe enough, some people will risk everything to rebel against their source. They also show that there is an undeniable element of contingency in the making of mutinies. Incidental grievances are contingencies; unforeseen events and accidents that also worsen existing grievances. The personality of commanders also played a contingent role in triggering some mutinies, most obviously with Captains like Pigot.

Nevertheless, neither accidents nor personality suffice to explain mutinies. In his memoirs, Alexis de Tocqueville observed that the onset of rebellion often comes as a surprise to even the best informed. However great the deprivation people have been suffering, they typically endure bad conditions for a long time with little unrest. He argued that rebellions arise as a result of incidents that bring governmental brutality or incompetence into sharp relief. It is not that things were well with the regime before the unrest, but rather that incidental grievances served as "accidents that render the disease fatal."[68] De Tocqueville's insight that short-term events combine with longer-standing conditions to trigger rebellion still leaves us wondering which matters more, long-term deprivation or immediate injuries?

Across history, rebellion proceeds from a significant transformation in the shared consciousness of the people involved that makes deprivation a source of grievance. Protest leaders fashion legitimating accounts – or frames – to support their actions. We have seen how seamen used the language of ill-usage to express their grievances and how ringleaders catalogued varieties of ill-usage to justify mutiny. Our study design allowed us to include a variety of these grievances directly in our models. In the historical and comparative social sciences many scholars may rely too heavily on indirect measures of grievances, based on the assumption that grievances can be inferred from people's subordinate positions in a social structure.[69]

Structural deprivation often poorly predicts the outbreak of rebellion. The worst-off people and the worst-off societies are not necessarily the most likely to rebel, a fact that has complicated the understanding of the relationship between grievances, rebellion and revolution for decades. This has led some to take the view that grievances are so ubiquitous that they cannot explain the outbreak of rebellion.[70] We have better specified the relationship between grievances and collective action, however, and shown that both immediate and long-term grievances predict the risk of rebellion. Grievances are necessary causes of mutiny. Moreover, as our exploration of the relationship between punishment and the risk of mutiny suggests, at higher magnitudes grievances may even be sufficient causes of rebellion.

Nevertheless, our findings show why it is hard to predict rebellions and revolutions. The problem of predicting rebellions is a perennial issue in the social sciences, with each large-scale revolutionary situation provoking another round of debate surrounding whether social scientists could have, or should have, predicted it.[71] Our models help identify the factors that put ships at risk of mutiny, but we cannot predict when a crew would mutiny. This is because of the difficulties of coordinating collective action and the contingent nature of the incidental grievances that appear to be necessary to trigger a mutiny even in a structurally deprived crew. Our findings speak to a general problem that confronts not only the study of rebellions but also the study of other phenomena. For instance, geologists know very well where fault lines lie and the magnitude of the pressure along them. They can predict where earthquakes will occur but have greater difficulty in predicting the moment in which a tectonic slip will trigger an earthquake. Events like rebellions occur because of a combination of sudden causes with longer-term causes. This does not leave us entirely in the dark, however. Governance connects these different causes and shows that deliberate action can help to institute and maintain social order.

4.8   Large-Scale Rebellion and Macro-Level Social Order

Alongside the *Bounty*, the mutiny on the *Hermione* is the most famous case of insurrection in the history of the Royal Navy. Having left its commander and his officers butchered and the ship treasonously surrendered to the enemy, the mutiny was bound to shock British public opinion. Many saw in the mutiny the spirit of Jacobin radicalism and the Terror that proceeded from the French Revolution. The *Hermione* affair was all the more shocking because it came on the heels of the great mass mutinies at Spithead and the Nore, which had threatened the Empire and nearly paralyzed the Navy during the spring of 1797. Now there was widespread fear that radicalism had invaded British shores and threatened the integrity of the country's "wooden walls."

We have established the causes of mutinies occurring aboard single ships. But large-scale mutinies in which rebellion spreads from one ship to another and collective action takes places both within and across ships is a much different phenomenon. In the next chapter, we uncover the grievances that drove the remarkable mass mutinies of 1797, the mobilization and organization of seamen into a mass mutiny involving dozens of ships, the factors that enabled seamen to attain group solidarity and why the uprising at the Nore failed.

Notes

1. For detailed accounts of the *Hermione* mutiny, see Ekirch 2017; Frykman 2010; and Pope 1963. Also see TNA: PRO ADM 1/5344, 1/5344, 1/5346, 1/5347, 1/5348, 1/5350, 1/5350, 1/5357, 1/5360, 1/53/75 and 1/5409.
2. Duffy 1987.
3. No doubt this was due partly to Pigot's important patron in the Caribbean – Sir Hyde Parker, who at this time was Commander-in-Chief at the Jamaica Station, and later was promoted to Admiral.
4. See Chapter 5.
5. There is a good description of flogging in Pope 1963, pp. 61 ff. Also see Appendices B and C in Pope 1963 that present the data on floggings on the *Success* and the *Hermione* under Pigot's command.
6. Brenton 1837, pp. viii, 408. Also see Frykman 2010; Pope 1963.
7. Quoted in Lavery 1998, p. 624, emphasis added.
8. McKee 1978.
9. Frykman 2010.
10. On causation in the social sciences see Dowding 2016; Mahoney 2007, 2008; and Sobel 1996. On conceptualizing "slow" and "fast" causal processes in the social sciences, see Pierson 2004 and Sewell 2005.
11. Conventional descriptive approaches cannot assess the relative importance of any factor, no matter how frequently it occurs in an outcome of interest. Hence, in discussing the relationship between sickness and disorder on sailing ships, Lamb 2002, p. 128, asserts that "It is impossible to say how frequently, or to what degree, scurvy conspired with other causes to provoke a mutiny." Such assertions notwithstanding, it is possible to sort out the correlation between sickness and mutiny given the right data and the right research design.
12. See Appendix A for a detailed discussion of the case-control method and how we drew the sample of cases and controls.
13. On the logic of combining case-study research designs with quantitative research designs, see Brady and Collier 2010; Gerring 2007; and Seawright 2016.
14. On the subjective understanding of injustice as lying at the heart of rebellion, see the classic study by Moore 1978, as well as more recent studies by Goldstone 2000, 2014 and Selbin 2010.
15. Inflation eroded the value of a seaman's wages, which were not regularly adjusted and remained basically fixed at seventeenth-century levels until a general wage increase was granted by Parliament in 1797 and again in 1807. Rates of pay for most seamen remained unchanged from 1658 until 1797 (Rodger 2004, pp. 618–27).
16. Brunsman 2013.
17. On the size of naval warships and their social ecology, see Gerstenberger 2007; Pearson 2017; Pope 1981; and Rodger 1986.
18. See Underwood et al. 2018.
19. Rodger 2004, p. 212; on the condition of working classes in the eighteenth century more generally, see Ashton 1955 and Porter 1991.
20. TNA: PRO ADM 1/5318.
21. TNA: PRO ADM 52/2354.
22. TNA: PRO ADM 1/5322.
23. TNA: PRO ADM 1/5345.
24. Quoted in Nicol [1822] 1997, p. 164; see also the account in Neale 1985.

25. For accounts of the mutiny, see Richardson 1908, p. 105 and Rodger 2004.
26. TNA: PRO ADM 1/5340.
27. TNA: PRO ADM 1/5288 and also the detailed account in Pack 1964.
28. TNA: PRO ADM 1/5323.
29. On disease, mortality and living conditions at sea see studies by Dull 2009; Earle 1998; Gill 1961; Pope 1981; and Rodger 2004.
30. On the management of sickness, see Bowden-Dan 2004 and MacDonald 2006; on the problem of sickness across European navies, see Dull 2009 and Frykman 2009.
31. Quoted in Lamb 2016, p. 52.
32. See Allison 1943; Convertito 2011; and Keevil 1958.
33. TNA: PRO ADM 1/5340.
34. Nagle [1802] 1988, pp. 208–9.
35. TNA: PRO ADM 1/5375.
36. TNA: PRO ADM 1/5359.
37. TNA: PRO ADM 1/5318.
38. Theal 1898, pp. 161–85.
39. On this point, see Dening's 1992 perceptive analysis of the cultural dynamics of mutiny.
40. Klandermans 1997; Turner and Killian 1972; Useem 1998; Walsh 1981. Goldstone 2014 distinguishes between "structural" and "transient" causes of revolution and finds that both are necessary causes of revolution.
41. See Bergstrand 2014; Tausch et al. 2011; Van Stekelenburg and Klandermans 2013; Van Zomeren et al. 2008.
42. Gould 1995; Pfaff 1996.
43. As Schelling 1960, p. 90, argues, incidents can function as a substitute for coordination and overt leadership. For an application of this concept to the onset of revolution, see Pfaff 2006.
44. Appendix A provides a detailed description of the sampling and estimation strategy that informed our analysis.
45. One could treat punishment as an incidental grievance because episodes of excessive punishment may have done much to trigger rebellion, as in case of the *Hermione*. The logic of our argument constrains us from doing so, however. Flogging was an expected part of life at sea and was the institutionalized form of naval punishment. We explored whether incidents of excessive punishment (floggings greater than two dozen) were associated with risk of mutiny and found no significant association, suggesting that our operationalization of punishment as a structural grievance is probably correct.
46. This is the consensus view among several naval historians including Earle 1998; Lavery 2010; Pope 1981; and Rodger 1986, 2004.
47. A monotonic relationship is a causal association between two factors whereby if one increases then the other will respond either increasing or decreasing at the same rate. A nonmonotonic relationship between two factors violates the assumption of a linear relationship between them.
48. Colley 2003 shows how a British national identity had been forged by wars with Catholic powers and by an imperial project that united the English, Scots and Welsh. Excluded were the Irish, subjects of the British Crown, albeit in a separate kingdom, a population that included both the Catholic majority and Protestant minorities, with the latter considered much less alien by Britons. Although ships' musters provide no way of differentiating between these groups, the great majority of those marked as Irish were Catholics, as was at least 80 percent of the Irish population in 1800. On discrimination against foreigners and Irishmen in the Navy, see Frykman 2009 and Gill 1961. Other categories of foreign seamen –

from continental Europe, the Americas, Africa and Asia – could be found in the Navy but we discovered that they were rarely numerous on any ship in our sample.

49. Admittedly, our measure is a crude proxy for social network structures, but it does suggest the extent of social capital at the aggregate levels and such ties may have facilitated participation in mutiny.

50. We calculated a Shannon entropy score for each ship's company using the following groups by rank/quality: Officers, Warrant Officers, Petty Officers, Able Seamen, Ordinary Seamen, Landsmen, Marines and other (e.g., servants). Lower scores indicate less rank diversity.

51. See Diani and McAdam 2003 and the critical discussion in Kitts 2000.

52. On the assignment of commands and the careers of sea officers, see Rodger 1986, 2001, 2004 and Wilson 2017.

53. See Hechter 2018.

54. We do not have complete lists of mutineers for all of the ships in our sample. The lists that we do have exist either because a Captain took a muster that identified participants (as with Troubridge on the *Culloden*), or because lists were produced based on witness testimony during trial. There do not appear to be any substantial differences between the mutinies that left behind lists and those that did not. Of course, not all the leaders of a mutiny were necessarily indicted as such, and the role of others may have been exaggerated. Courts-martial were thorough, however, and naval authorities took care to identify leaders of unrest. It seems unlikely that they pinned mutinies on convenient scapegoats given the frequency with which officers conceded at trial that mutiny leaders were reliable, dutiful and orderly; "among the best men of the ship."

55. See the discussion of these data sources in Chapter 3 and Appendix B. Note that the sample that allows comparison of participants and nonparticipants contains a diverse set of ships and mutinies belonging to the whole range of types we described in Chapter 3.

56. Caution has to be exercised in comparing the results of the analysis of the factors increasing the odds of mutiny on ships to the results of the analyses of the factors increasing the odds of individual participation or leadership. Given the different units of analysis (ships' crews, individual seamen), direct comparison of regression results is invalid.

57. The omitted category, or reference group, in the analysis is officers (commissioned and warranted).

58. A similar negative relationship between age and participation in criminal activities has also been identified, see, e.g., Hirschi and Gottfredson 1983; Kanazawa and Still 2000.

59. Particularly after the French Revolution and the rebellions in Ireland in the late eighteenth century, naval officials commonly blamed mutiny on the activities on foreigners and Irishmen; see Frykman 2009, p. 92, and Neale 1985. British seamen may have been less likely to forge solidarity with "foreigners" and ethnic diversity may have undercut social order. See, e.g., Jaffer 2015.

60. Siegel 2009.

61. Hardin 1982, 2007.

62. This theme is explored in Thompson 1980 and is further elaborated in Thompson's 1971 paper on the moral economy of the English crowd.

63. Thompson's ideas have been widely influential despite his aversion to general concepts in the social sciences and his claim that the logic of moral economy was limited to the early modern era. See, e.g., Scott 1976, 1985, 1990, on peasant societies and

everyday forms of resistance that, in turn, informed an expanding range of research in the social sciences (Götz 2015). For a persuasive application of moral economy to modern labor relations, see Kopstein 1996.

64. Hechter and Opp 2001.

65. Thompson 1971, p. 120.

66. For a compelling critique of the moral economy perspective see Popkin 1979.

67. Gurr 1970; see discussion of the empirical tests of the theory in Brush 1996.

68. De Tocqueville [1856] 1955, ch. 1.

69. For example, we might assume that political and economic inequalities affecting entire groups are likely to fuel resentment and justify attempts to fight perceived injustice. See, e.g., Cederman et al. 2013.

70. McCarthy and Zald 1977; Skocpol 1979; Tilly 1977; but see the attempted correctives by Goldstone 1991, 2014.

71. On the revolutions of 1989 and the fall of communism, see Collins 1995; Goldstone 2000; Hechter 1995; Kiser 1995; Kuran 1995; and Tilly 1995; for the more recent debate on the Arab Spring rebellions, see Asongu and Nwachukwu 2016; Bellin 2012; Gause 2011; and Howard and Hussein 2011. On the general problem of prediction with combined causation and diverse causal temporalities, see Pierson 2004.

5 INSURGENCY AND SOLIDARITY
The Mass Mutinies at Spithead and the Nore

The yellow flag signaling an impending execution was raised aboard HMS *Sandwich* on June 30, 1797. Marine guards in dress uniforms stood polished and ready. The deck of the ship was crowded with seamen, naval officers and political notables who had gathered to witness the hanging of the mutineer Richard Parker. Parker's notoriety was so great that a grandstand had been erected on a nearby shore to accommodate the many spectators who could not fit on the deck. The sea around the *Sandwich* was jammed with boats filled with gawkers seeking a closer view of the execution. In one of them, distraught and dressed in mourning clothes, sat Anne Parker, the mutineer's wife.

Parker had been convicted of having been the "president" of the naval insurrection at the North Sea anchorage at the Nore, located just east of the mouth of the Thames estuary. A mass mutiny unprecedented in the history of the Royal Navy, it had drawn in nearly three dozen vessels and thousands of seamen, paralyzing the fleet and imposing a crippling blockade on Thames shipping. Writing decades later, Edward Brenton, who had been a Lieutenant on one of the ships taking part in the mutiny, could still marvel at the "flame of discord which had suddenly burst forth in the British fleet," calling the Nore mutiny the event that had "most endangered the safety of the British empire."[1]

Facing the noose as the first ringleader among dozens who would be hanged, Parker cut an undeniably impressive figure. He was thirty years old, of middling stature, but with dark, handsome looks. Dressed in black, Parker slowly approached the scaffold led by a priest who knelt with him in a final prayer. After rising, Parker was given a glass of wine. He then approached his former commander and prosecutor, Captain James Mosse, and asked to shake his hand. Agreeing, Mosse permitted Parker to speak briefly.

Parker addressed the crowd respectfully, professing his loyalty to the kingdom but acknowledging his guilt and the justice of the punishment. Hoping that his death would atone for the errors committed by the men of the fleet, he bade his shipmates and companions a calm farewell. He revealed no bitterness toward the seamen who had abandoned the mutiny and helped to decide his fate. Mosse was impressed, describing Parker's conduct as "decent and steady." Ascending the scaffold, Parker put his neck in the noose and a hood was placed on his head. He stepped briskly over the edge of the ship. A group of sweating seamen hauled him up to the yardarm. Parker's body stopped convulsing halfway up and a great gun was fired to mark his death. He remained hanging for more than an hour.

In her rowboat, Anne Parker fainted as the gun boomed across the water. She had fought hard to save her husband's life, organizing a petition to Queen Charlotte begging that royal mercy be shown toward the ringleaders of the mutiny. Now, having failed to save Parker's life, she was determined to decide the fate of his corpse. George III and senior naval officials had wanted Parker gibbeted but, fearing popular unrest, the authorities on hand took Parker to the nearby Sheerness Fort where his body was laid in an unmarked grave.

The indomitable Mrs. Parker wanted her husband to have a proper Christian burial. Learning of the location of the grave, she enlisted the aid of three women with whom she scaled the walls and disinterred the corpse. She then spirited it away in a hired cart and brought it to London. The Nore mutiny had not only divided seamen for and against the rebellion, but the British public as well. For a week, the body lay in a tavern, visited by sympathizers as well as the merely curious. Alarmed by the attention that Parker was still attracting, a magistrate took him away to be buried at St. Mary's Church in Whitechapel. The strange afterlife of Richard Parker finally ended when his wife persuaded the parish priest to perform funeral rites over his remains.[2]

***

Parker's path to the scaffold began in early 1797 when, driven by sheer desperation, he accepted a bounty of £30 (less than $5,000 in contemporary terms) to reenlist in the Navy. For a few years after leaving the service he had been living with his wife and their children in Edinburgh, but various attempts to earn a living failed, leaving him destitute. Imprisoned for an outstanding debt of £23, the bounty redeemed his debts and provided a little income.

Parker was paid to help fulfill the quota of recruits that the port of Leith and other coastal towns were obliged to provide the government under the 1795 Quota Act. The legislation was intended to solve the manpower crisis by bringing thousands of seamen into the Navy to fight revolutionary France. Parker received a good bounty because he was an experienced seaman. Born in Exeter in the coastal county of Devon, he had received an education, learned navigation and went to sea in 1782. Rated an Able Seaman, Parker served on several ships during the last months of the War of American Independence. He became sick on a voyage to the Gambia on the coast of West Africa, was hospitalized and released from naval service when the war ended in 1783. Following his discharge, Parker sailed on merchant ships bound for the Mediterranean and the East Indies. He married Anne McHardy in 1791, and they began a family.

In 1793, Parker was lured back into the Navy by the prospect of gaining a commission. He was rated a Master's Mate, soon promoted to Midshipman and began his training to become a Lieutenant. But his path was blocked by a petty dispute with a superior officer. Although intelligent and well spoken, Parker was also vain and boastful. Charged with insubordination, he was convicted and stripped of his rank by a court-martial. After suffering the humiliation of returning to the service as a regular seaman, Parker was hospitalized for rheumatism. He was discharged upon recovery in 1794, his naval career apparently finished.

Little wonder that Parker was despondent when he arrived on the squalid *Sandwich* at the end of April 1797. The vessel was a large ninety-gun warship that had been launched in 1759. No longer fit to be a ship-of-the-line, the *Sandwich* was permanently assigned to the anchorage at the Nore sandbar and consigned to duty as a floating battery and receiving ship for the North Sea Fleet. It also served as the flagship of

Admiral Charles Buckner, the Commander-in-Chief of the Nore fleet. In addition to her regular crew, the ship was crowded with hundreds of recent enlistees, some of them volunteers, others pressed men and Quota-men. Conditions on the ship were very poor and discontent ran high.

Parker was certainly nursing a grudge when he came aboard the *Sandwich*, but he was also reentering the Navy at a time in which general discontent was at its highest level in a century. Seamen of all ranks were angered by wages that had been eaten away by wartime inflation, the poor quality of provisions and reductions in their victuals and the harsh discipline that prevailed in the Navy. Parker was not long aboard the *Sandwich* when mutiny overtook the vessel. Inspired by the ongoing mutiny of the ships-of-the-line of the Channel Fleet that had erupted at the Spithead anchorage south of Portsmouth in the previous month, the men of the *Sandwich* rose on May 12 and seized control of the vessel. The mutiny soon spread across the Nore and, eventually, to ships of the North Sea Fleet at other ports.

As a newcomer who had been on the ship for fewer than two weeks, Parker played no role in planning or conducting the initial mutiny aboard the *Sandwich*. As the mutiny spread to other ships, however, the ringleaders organized a Council of Delegates to govern a confederation of vessels that was derided as the "Floating Republic" by its detractors. Composed of representatives from each ship, the Council would take part in decision-making and negotiations with the government. In spite of his limited role in the mutiny up to that point, the Committeemen appointed Parker to the *Sandwich*'s ruling council and elected him to be the President of the Delegates of the Fleet. Why they did so is uncertain. Most likely, they regarded Parker as a good spokesman given his naval experience, attractiveness and verbal eloquence. For his part, Parker appears to have been attracted to the role by his bitterness toward the Navy, his genuine dedication to the seamen's cause and, not least, his vanity.[3]

Despite his subsequent notoriety and vilification by the press and the government as the personification of treason, it is not clear that Parker's actual role in the mutiny went much beyond that of a figurehead.[4] There is no evidence that he had any radical attachments prior to the mutiny. He did not exercise power directly, but acted through the Committeemen that ran each ship. He did, however, preside over meetings of the Council of Delegates, played an active part in negotiations with the government, helped to enforce the Council's decisions and visited the various ships of the mutinous fleet to prop up mutineers' commitment and morale.

In the end, the mutiny unraveled without winning any additional demands beyond those that had previously been granted at Spithead. Parker's authority, such as it was, effectively collapsed on June 9. He was promptly arrested, brought to the jail at Sheerness and then transferred to the *Saturn* where he was tried for mutiny, treason and piracy. In a four-day trial in which many witnesses testified, Parker attempted to defend himself by claiming that he had been motivated by patriotism, had only acted as president to avert greater violence and was a moderate influence on the mutiny's more radical ringleaders. Following his conviction, Parker was brought to the *Sandwich* where he met his doom.[5]

Previous mutinies had demonstrated that the best way for all seamen to avoid punishment and achieve their goals was to maintain a united front (see Chapter 3). When the Nore mutiny collapsed, no concessions had been won and hundreds of seamen were referred to courts-martial. As the trials progressed, scores were punished with severe flogging and imprisonment, and more than two dozen ringleaders were hanged.

How can we explain a mass insurgency like the Nore mutiny? Why did Parker and his comrades fail – and hang – when their counterparts at Spithead succeeded and walked away without suffering any repercussions? Why, despite the extensive mobilization that brought thousands of seamen into a defiant rebellion, was insurgent solidarity so fragile that the mutiny repeatedly suffered from defections that hastened its collapse – without the government even having to fire a shot?

5.1   Reconsidering the Mass Mutinies at Spithead and the Nore

The mass mutinies of 1797, first at Spithead and subsequently at the Nore, triggered a political crisis. Not only did they immobilize the ships that were Britain's "wooden walls" against the threat of invasion by

revolutionary France and her allies, but they also indicated that radicalism might have gained a firm foothold at home. That possibility led the
distinguished conservative political theorist and statesman Edmund
Burke to bewail the fate of "our Navy, that has already perished with
its discipline forever."[6]

The mutinies stunned the public because they were unlike any
previous rebellion. They occurred not on isolated ships but among
dozens of ships in the principal fleets stationed in home waters. The
mutineers seemed republican both in their demands and in their self-
organization. Public views held that "Jack Tar" – the common English
term referring to seamen of the Royal Navy – was brave and loyal but
impetuous, prone to drunkenness and in need of stern command. Yet
what occurred at Spithead demonstrated the canny assertiveness of the
seamen, their capacity for discipline and impressive solidarity.[7] The
mutineers elected Delegates who maintained order, pledged to protect
the country and patiently demanded the redress of their grievances.
After a period of extensive negotiation with the Admiralty, they were
rewarded with an act of Parliament that raised their wages, as well as
a royal pardon to ensure that no one would be punished for their
participation in the rebellion.

The Nore mutiny, which followed hard on Spithead's heels,
seemed to embody radical excess, however. The mutineers made
broad demands for the reform of naval governance, imposed an
embargo on Thames shipping and were unable to prevent the eruption
of violence and disorder. Unlike the fleet at Spithead, the bargaining
position of the "Jacobins" at the Nore was undermined by the defection
of many of their ships. When the Nore mutiny finally collapsed, no
concessions had been won and hundreds of seamen were referred to
courts-martial to face capital charges.

Taken together, the mutinies of 1797 have fascinated scholars
of eighteenth-century radicalism, but these were very different events.[8]
Whereas at Spithead the mutineers maintained a united front long
enough to successfully negotiate on behalf of their demands, at the
Nore solidarity was compromised by the defection of entire ships'
companies from the rebellion. Despite widely shared grievances and
an impressive feat of mobilization that pulled thousands of seamen
into the rebellion, commitment varied dramatically across crews at the
Nore.

At the Nore, as Brenton observed, the defection of ships' companies from the mutiny "had very important consequences; it spread distrust among them [the seamen], and led them to doubt the firmness of each other; and everyone sought, by indirect means, to make his peace and secure his own safety."[9] The defection by ships across the fleet was an acute problem because the mass mutinies were more than simply a collection of individual mutinies. Combined into a single movement, the rebellious ships comprised an armed insurgency directly challenging naval and political institutions in the midst of a wartime crisis.

The stories of individuals like Parker who became active players in the drama of rebellion tell us something about its causes and consequences. Social forces, however, were also at play. Research on high-risk collective action seeks to identify the general processes that underlie involvement in dangerous and uncertain political causes, such as armed insurgencies. For obvious reasons, much of the literature stresses the initial hurdles facing such movements: recruitment and mobilization.[10] Yet far less attention has been paid to the reasons why insurgents might continue to support a rebellion when dangers grow and the prospects for its success dim. This is a vital issue not only for understanding the fate of the Nore mutiny, but for all sustained rebellions. The most important determinant of an insurgency's effectiveness does not reside in its initial mobilization, but rather its capacity to sustain group solidarity and contain defection in the face of growing adversity.[11] Lacking staying power, a large-scale armed strike like that at the Nore cannot hope to win concessions from the government.

We focus on analyzing the forces that drove defection at the Nore because defection is the mirror image of solidarity. Solidarity exists to the extent that a group possesses the capacity to act in the collective interest by motivating its members to meet their corporate obligations.[12] Anyone can profess solidarity to a cause that enjoys widespread support and bright prospects for success, but what really matters is whether one sticks with it when the outlook darkens. In previous chapters, we have seen that mobilization on the basis of broad us-versus-them appeals may be effective in persuading large groups of seamen to join a mutiny. This kind of collective action can also be vulnerable to rapid collapse, however, as cascades of defectors abandon a cause that has become too costly, dangerous or uncertain.

This was precisely the situation that developed at the Nore. In response, the Nore mutiny's leaders struggled to maintain control over the ships of the fleet by monitoring the activities of the loyalists (and suspected loyalists) and punishing their opponents. The seamen relied on the mutiny's leadership to negotiate a victorious settlement, including an amnesty, in what the leadership portrayed to them as an all-or-nothing dispute. This bargain depended on information about alternative resolutions of the conflict. Because the Admiralty could dangle the prospect of amnesty to the seamen on defecting ships, thereby inducing them to abandon the rebellion, the key tool in the hands of mutiny leaders was control over this information.

5.2   The Problem of Solidarity in Rebellious Collective Action

Solidarity at Spithead and the Nore was predicated on an oath: "I, A. B. do voluntary make oath and swear that I will be true in the cause we are embarked in …"[13] Why did seamen honor their oaths to the mutiny in the absence of third-party enforcement, and continue to do so on many ships up until the very last moment, long after prospects for success had receded?

Most explanations of solidarity in the mass mutinies of 1797 have emphasized the roles of ideology and community among seamen. To the degree that individuals share a common ideology, they internalize a set of norms that may be sufficient to sustain solidarity in the absence of material incentives or social rewards.[14] This view is well grounded in a historiography that traditionally has attributed insurgent commitment at the Nore to the ideology spread by the French Revolution, the English radical societies and the writings of Thomas Paine.[15] Some historians have painted a picture of a radicalized Atlantic proletariat, with naval authorities regarding the "Irish and Foreigners" as the most ideologically contaminated.[16] If ideology is largely responsible for the maintenance of insurgent solidarity, then radicalism should have been widespread at the Nore and should have deterred defection.

By contrast, a second explanation holds that solidarity is fostered not by ideology, but by close-knit communities. Oath-takers at the Nore may have been constrained by social ties and reputational incentives to honor their commitments.[17] It is well known that labor militancy tends to be greatest in communities of geographically or socially isolated groups of workers who are highly interdependent – just like seamen.[18] We have seen that seamen had a strong sense of occupational identity and belief in their "due rights and privileges." Aboard ships, seamen created communities that were united by skill and teamwork.[19] Their commitment to one another was reinforced by each individual's investment in his reputation for professional reliability. Without it, life at sea would be hard, if not impossible.[20] If social ties were primarily responsible for the duration of mutiny, then those ships bound by tight communities would have been least likely to defect from the mutiny.

Both explanations for insurgent solidarity are plausible, but the evidence from the Nore suggests that neither can account for it. Rather than crews united by radical worldviews or knit together into tight communities, each ship appears to have had distinct factions of seamen – active mutineers, loyalists and bystanders – who sought both to improve their lot and secure their own safety. The bystanders – probably constituting the majority of seamen – could be swayed by either side, and thus were crucial to the fate of the mutiny on most ships.

Commitment to the mutiny relied primarily on techniques used by the leadership to increase dependence and control over rank-and-file seamen. People accept obligations to a group to the extent that they are dependent on it to attain goods that they cannot provide for themselves. In the case of the mass mutinies of 1797, seamen wanted to increase their wages and improve their living conditions. Experience taught them that armed strikes could redress grievances. Seamen also knew that the best way to avoid being sanctioned for mutiny was to win a general pardon as a condition of settling. Hence, seamen were dependent on the mutiny's leaders to win the strike and to protect them from attack or retaliation by the authorities.

Dependence is influenced by a number of factors, including the availability of close substitutes, the cost of obtaining those goods someplace else and information about alternatives. All of these elements are sensitive to situational considerations and changing circumstances that are beyond the group's control. This was certainly true at the Nore, where much was out of the hands of the mutiny's leadership.

Although dependence may convince individuals to accept obligations imposed on them by the group, the probability that they will comply with these obligations rests in the control capacity of the group. Solidarity is binding to the extent that the group has the ability to monitor compliance and sanction deviance from the obligations that it imposes. Throughout the rebellion, the mutiny's leaders sought to maintain control over the ships of the fleet. In so doing, they monitored the activities of the loyalists (and suspected loyalists), and threatened to punish those who wanted to return their ship to the Admiralty. As is typical of the back-and-forth struggles at the heart of insurgent conflicts, the loyalists and mutineers on each ship sought to attain the support of the bystanders, whose tilt to one side or the other would determine whether the ship would maintain solidarity with the fleet-wide mutiny or defect from it.

Seamen relied on the mutiny leadership to negotiate a victorious settlement, including an amnesty, in what was framed as an all-or-nothing struggle. For its part, the government responded by threatening the mutineers with force: it mobilized troops on land to isolate the insurgency and persuade the seamen to abandon their leaders. Early in the standoff, these threats appear to have increased seamen's dependence on the mutiny leadership by convincing them that only by prevailing over the government could they secure their safety.[21]

Yet the belief that the leadership was most able to protect the lives and well-being of seamen depended on the latter's knowledge about alternative settlements to the conflict.

In this regard, a key instrument in the hands of mutiny leaders was control over information. To enhance the seamen's perception that their best option was to stand by the mutiny, the leadership tried to deny them access to information that capitulation was by far the safer course. If dependence and control explain the duration of the mutiny rather than ideology or community ties, then those ships with large cadres of activist mutineers and those whose crews were unaware of the government's offer of amnesty for defectors would have remained with the mutiny the longest.

5.3 The Context of Rebellion: The Crisis of the 1790s

In 1797, Britain and her allies had been at war with France for four years, suffering numerous defeats at the hands of revolutionary armies. At sea, however, the kingdom fared much better. In 1794, the Channel Fleet had defeated a French fleet, and in 1796 an invasion of Ireland –

which had no love of English rule – was thwarted by logistical difficulties and stormy weather. In February 1797, the Spanish fleet, allied with France, attempted to reach Brest to unify with the French Navy in order to launch an assault on Britain. The Royal Navy defeated the Spanish off Cape St. Vincent, however.

Nevertheless, in April 1797, Austria – Britain's last continental ally – began to sue for peace, and some politicians at home also began to call for a peace treaty. The threat of an invasion continued to loom: a French raiding party landed in Wales, setting off a financial crisis in London. Plans continued to be drawn up that would combine France's Atlantic fleet with the Spanish and Dutch fleets to coordinate an invasion of the British Isles. Intelligence revealed that the Dutch republican government that was allied with France was assembling its fleet. Responding to these threats, the Navy stationed large fleets in home waters and continued to impose a costly blockade on French ports.[22]

At home there were mounting political threats. Although the kingdom was governed by the pro-war conservative William Pitt (the Younger), many in the opposition Whig party were sympathetic to France, eager for reform and a peace treaty. In 1791 Thomas Paine had published *The Rights of Man*, which quickly became the bible of English radicals, and inspired the formation of a network of underground republican activists – most importantly the London Corresponding Society, or LCS. In 1795 the LCS, whose principal demands were for universal male suffrage and annual Parliaments, helped organize a demonstration demanding reform, peace and bread at George III's opening of Parliament. Instead, the result was the passage of new sedition acts, as elite fears of revolution intensified.[23]

Through it all, Britain's economy was groaning under the pressures of war and military expansion. Government expenditure rose to nearly a third of total economic activity. Spending on arms and operations led to severe civilian shortages; consumer prices rose by more than a third over 1790 levels.[24] In the winter of 1797, the Bank of England was obliged to abandon the gold standard and financial insecurity endangered England's capacity to carry on the war.

The severe economic pressure on working people begot an upsurge of strikes and industrial disturbances on land – about a third of all eighteenth-century English strikes occurred during the 1790s.[25] Inflation threatened no group more than naval seamen, whose wages were frequently delayed or in arrears, and whose general rates of pay had not been raised since 1652.[26] Many seamen's wives and families became deeply impoverished. In 1792, increased pay and provisions had been granted to the soldiery, largely to counter desertion, and in 1797 a second increase in pay was given in order to ensure the loyalty of the Army as a safeguard against domestic insurrection.[27] Meanwhile, discontent was rampant in the Navy; seamen were excluded from a pay raise because it was more costly than the government thought it could afford.

In the 1790s it became clear that naval manpower requirements – more than a hundred thousand seamen – approached the entire domestic supply of maritime labor. The Navy had been forced to expand rapidly, more than tripling the number of ships in service and more than doubling its required manpower. Impressments had long been relied upon to fill the ranks, but the Pitt government passed Quota Acts in 1795 and 1796 that placed naval levies on British counties and ports. The Acts flooded the Navy with some thirty thousand recruits; unlike Richard Parker, most of them were unskilled. This dismayed experienced seamen who were obliged to train and accommodate the newcomers.[28] In addition, many "foreigners," whose origins were not in England, Scotland or Wales, were brought into the Navy.[29] The foreigners included deserters from continental armies and navies, but Irishmen were recruited and pressed in much larger numbers and some Irish prisoners were brought into the fleet as a result of the Insurrection Act.[30]

In a context of such severe material grievances and the influx of foreigners and newcomers, naval authorities feared that seamen were becoming ripe for mutiny. As we have seen, mutinies had occurred occasionally in the Navy and collective defiance was hardly unusual in the seagoing trades from which naval seamen were drawn.[31] Dozens of mutinies occurred on individual ships whose aggrieved seamen seized their vessels and refused to perform their duty until their demands were met. In some instances, particularly when the seamen refrained from violence, negotiated with officers and remained united, naval authorities gave in to moderate demands and agreed not to prosecute any seaman for his involvement in the mutiny. Common knowledge of these episodes evidently informed the strategy of the Spithead and Nore mutineers.[32]

To the government and its supporters, it seemed that radicalism had gotten firm footing in the Navy of the 1790s. Radicals reportedly visited dockyards and Portsmouth was in the hands of Whigs who sympathized with seamen's grievances and favored peace with France.[33] Animosity between seamen and their commanding officers appeared to be growing. In June 1794 seamen on the warship *Culloden* had armed themselves, erected barricades and refused to go to sea on the grounds of poor treatment and an unsafe ship. The matter appeared to be settled when an officer negotiated an end to the standoff. As seen in Chapter 3, the seamen were betrayed and five ringleaders were hanged. The trust between officers and men was severely undermined.[34]

5.3.1 The Spithead Mutiny

As early as 1796, Captain Thomas Pakenham – the same officer who had been involved in ending the *Culloden* mutiny – had warned of the dangers of a general mutiny in the Channel Fleet. Victors over the French in 1794 and cognizant of the false assurances given on the *Culloden*, the seamen of the fleet had a strong sense of collective identity, firm leadership and a definite strategy. In the months prior to the outbreak of mutiny in April 1797, seamen discussed grievances and distributed "round-robin" letters stating their demands for better pay and living conditions.[35] Out of these clandestine activities came a number of petitions to the various commanders and ultimately to the Admiralty, but all were ignored. By March 30, Lord Bridport (de facto commander of the fleet) had received petitions from eleven of the ships in the fleet. After informing the Admiralty that mutiny was afoot, Bridport was told to put the ships to sea on April 15. The following day sixteen line-of-battle ships disobeyed the order.

Over the course of a tumultuous month, the mutiny held together in spite of the authorities' many attempts to weaken the fleet's solidarity.[36] Ringleaders on each ship – later elected as Delegates who governed the mutiny from the flagship *Queen Charlotte* – planned the mutiny and played a critical role in coordinating the different ships.

The ringleaders of the Spithead mutiny took deliberate steps to enhance their chances of success. First, they controlled access to the mutiny. Scores of ships besides the battleships of the fleet sympathized with the mutiny. When the crews of frigates and sloops – the ships used as scouts and convoy escorts – sought to join the mutiny, however, they were declined on the grounds that the men of Spithead would do nothing that might imperil the safety of England or damage her trade. This not only communicated the fundamental patriotism of the mutineers, but it also ensured that the mutiny would be a confederation among like vessels, ships-of-the-line with large but well-established crews. Onboard the ships in the fleet, the mutiny's Delegates won the support of the Marines by taking up their demands for improved pay and conditions.

Second, they took steps to bind the entirety of ships' companies to the mutiny, chiefly by imposing an oath on all the seamen aboard the ships of the fleet. The organization of the mutiny reflected the same principles that drove previous, isolated armed strikes in the Royal Navy. Each seaman was expected openly to support the mutiny and its demands. Individuals were obligated to sign their name to petitions to demonstrate their loyalty to the Delegates. One of the few pieces of surviving correspondence from Spithead was discovered on the *Royal Sovereign*. It indicates that seamen were expected to take an oath that pledged that "[the ship's company be] firmly united in so just a cause and resolve[d] to have every means and Redress. They Likewise ... determined not Be Separated either men or officers."[37]

Leadership likewise reflects similar patterns to those of the mutinies that occurred on single ships. Of thirty-two Delegates, fifteen were Petty Officers, a dozen were Able Seamen and five were Midshipmen. Their average age was thirty years old, somewhat older than the typical seaman by a few years. Just five of them were "foreigners" – four Irishmen and an American. Despite the myth that the leadership included radical intellectual Landsmen caught up in the press or the Quota Act, none of the Delegates were Quota-men or had been recently pressed. Rather, they appear to have been the "best men" of their respective ships drawn from the most experienced and respected seamen.[38]

Valentine Joyce was the Council's leader and spokesman. Twenty-eight years old, Joyce was born on the island of Jersey and entered the Navy rated as an Able Seaman in 1788. Highly respected by officers and seamen alike, Joyce proved an effective leader and a savvy negotiator. He artfully defended himself in the press against accusations of radicalism and of having been an Irish Quota-man – a "Jacobin" and "Belfast tobacconist" – according to his detractors in Parliament and the press. Joyce deserves much of the credit for keeping order in the fleet and for seeing that the chief demands of the mutineers were met. Admiral Lord Howe, who was involved in the negotiations that settled the mutiny, was impressed by the character and conduct of the Delegates, praising Joyce especially. It is telling that Joyce never faced the noose. What is more, he must have enjoyed goodwill in spite of his leading role in the mutiny. In the years following the events at Spithead, Joyce was repeatedly promoted. He was a Midshipman when he lost his life in the shipwreck of the sloop HMS *Brazen* in 1800.[39]

Precisely how the fleet managed to maintain solidarity through thick and thin can never be known in full because of the absence of documentation. All seamen were pardoned and there were no trials of mutineers. Most of the correspondence to and from the fleet and other documents were subsequently destroyed by naval officials.[40] We do know, however, that when individual ships began to waver in their support for the mutiny, they were moved closer to the guns of the *Queen Charlotte*, which was the seat of the Delegates and effectively enforced the collective action. When the Admiralty issued revised orders to the Admirals on May 1 calling for enhanced discipline and tighter order on ships, it outraged men of the Channel Fleet. Along with encouragement from radical politicians who warned the seamen not to trust the government's promises, this stiffened the seamen's resolve. There were provocations by the officers on some ships of the fleet, including the *London* where three seamen were killed. Nevertheless, the Delegates managed to contain the incident. Despite the challenges and political pressure, discipline and unity of purpose prevailed at Spithead.

The Delegates' achievement was remarkable. They maintained order in the fleet and negotiated a peaceful end to the mutiny. They engaged in adroit public relations, including correspondence with politicians and with newspapers. Insisting that their demands required not just a policy change but legislation, the mutineers won an Act of Parliament to improve wages and victuals. The wage increase was modest, about 10 percent for the average seaman, but more importantly they won a royal pardon to ensure that none would hang. All told, by May 15, the Admiralty and the Parliament had granted the Spithead mutineers their demands and they received a pardon from the King. The mutiny was over. Public opinion, initially shocked by the rebellion, was elated by its peaceful conduct and moderate resolution.[41] Things would go very differently at the Nore.

5.4 The Nore Mutiny

Before the final resolution at Spithead, news of the rebellion spread throughout home waters, from Plymouth in the west to Yarmouth in the east. Grievances were intense in the North Sea Fleet. As in other mutinies, poor governance added to the shared experience of deprivation. The surviving evidence suggests that seamen objected most strenuously to their low wages, but also to tyrannical officers and ill-usage that included harsh discipline and disregard for their health and welfare.[42] We know that the Nore mutiny was directly inspired by Spithead because emissaries had been sent there to gather the lessons learned. On May 6, a committee secretly formed on the unhappy *Sandwich*. It called on other ships to organize themselves and elect Delegates for a fleet-wide mutiny.[43]

On May 12, they acted, and Captain Mosse's log indicates how well the Committeemen were prepared to seize control: "At half past 9 (AM) the people cheered and came aft and demanded the keys of the magazine and the store rooms. Pointed the fore castle guns aft and gave charge to the Master."[44] After seizing the ship, the mutineers raised a red flag – the traditional symbol of defiance – and gave three cheers. Immediately, mutinies followed on several nearby ships and in the following weeks spread across the eastern coast.

The mutineers had to establish order aboard each ship and across the fleet. The ships joining the mutiny anchored close by one another, all within sight of the flagship *Sandwich*. Each ship was governed by a committee that, in turn, elected two fleet Delegates who assembled in council aboard the *Sandwich*. On each ship, ringleaders administered an oath of solidarity to all. A witness explained the nature of the oath and how it was given:

> "I, A. B. do voluntary make oath and swear that I will be true in
> the cause we are embarked in, and I will to the laying down of
> my life be true to the Delegates at present assembled, whilst they
> continue to support the present cause . . ." the man going on to

swear that he would discover and report any activity subversive of "our present plan," or likely to fray the texture of "our present system." When a sufficient number had been sworn, so that their weight would be preponderant, and secrecy hopeless, the rest were dealt with in batches.[45]

The Delegates derived a set of articles to govern the rebellion, specifying "unanimity" among the ships of the fleet, "strict discipline to be maintained" and "all unsuitable Officers to go ashore."[46]

Although they emulated what their counterparts had done at Spithead, organizing the mutiny as a democratic confederation posed a greater challenge at the Nore. The ships were drawn from a large area, and those that joined the mutiny were diverse and had originated in several different North Sea ports. The North Sea Fleet itself had been hastily assembled to counter the threat posed by the Dutch Navy. It included many old warships and repurposed merchant ships. Not all of the ships' companies that joined the mutiny did so spontaneously. The mutiny enveloped several ships whose crews had been induced to join after being boarded by Delegates. These included the small vessels *Hound*, *Firm* and *Comet*, but also two frigates, *Iris* and *San Fiorenzo*. The ships' companies of the *Hound* and the *San Fiorenzo* were only persuaded to join the mutiny after having been fired on by other mutinous ships. On more than one occasion, the *Sandwich* nudged reluctant mutineers forward by the threat of her guns.[47]

The *Sandwich* was unquestionably the headquarters of the Council. Following the inception of the mutiny on the *Sandwich*, Delegates from each ship joining the rebellion met in council and acted both as representatives and agents of the fleet-wide mutiny. Parker and his colleagues exercised their authority at meetings of the Council in frequent visits to other ships to inquire into shipboard conditions and political dispositions, and even by rowing to the port of Sheerness to lead supportive rallies.

5.4.1   The Dynamics of the Nore Mutiny

The mutiny progressed through four distinct phases. The first was the outbreak on May 12 on the *Sandwich* followed by its spread to other ships. The government reacted slowly because it saw the mutiny as a mere continuation of the Spithead affair, and expected it to falter once the seamen realized that they would gain the same concessions as the Channel Fleet. In the following weeks, however, as the Delegates stated demands beyond those granted at Spithead and the mutiny spread to the Yarmouth squadron, the government realized that a new rebellion was afoot.[48]

On May 20, the mutineers addressed their enlarged demands to Admiral Buckner, hoping to negotiate a favorable settlement. The Delegates expected "every indulgence granted to the Fleet at Portsmouth" and, in addition, wanted to improve the rights and status of seamen. Their list of demands went to the heart of the issue of governance in the Navy and reflects almost precisely the grievances that drove seamen to rebel in the mutinies that we documented in the previous chapter (see, e.g., Table 4.1).

They wanted opportunities for shore leave, limits on the holding of pay in arrears, the right to petition for the replacement of abusive or incompetent officers, pay advances for pressed men, clemency for deserters, trial by jury in courts-martial, more equitable distribution of prize money and the immediate payment of bounties to volunteers.[49] These demands went substantially beyond those that had been won at Spithead, and the government was determined to resist giving in to new pressure. Brenton claimed that "[t]he mutiny from this moment assumed the character of rebellion, and as such the government and the nation, justly incensed, determined to treat it."[50]

Indeed, beginning on May 21, the government began to tighten the noose. Unauthorized communication with the mutinous fleet was forbidden by a parliamentary act and press censorship was imposed. The purpose of the embargo was to prevent coordination with supporters abroad and to seek evidence of sedition and radical connections.[51] Although scant evidence was found of radical entanglements, the mutineers were largely cut off from contact with the public.

Even if the government was resolved not to make any concessions to the Nore insurgents' new demands, it could not simply crush the mutiny. It had no trustworthy naval force in home waters that could rout the insurrection, and the Army, for its part, could do little beyond reinforcing the coast. Moreover, the ships held by the mutineers had enormous value as the most technologically advanced military machines of their day, and they also contained many officers who effectively were hostages. Finally, armed action threatened public disapproval, and might well have drawn naval attacks by France and her allies. Instead, the government gradually cut the mutineers off from supplies and tried to block all letters going in and out.

For their part, the mutiny leaders responded by limiting shore access to active and trusted mutineers, selectively distributing messages of support, and suppressing correspondence that might inform seamen about the royal pardon and the prior wage concessions at Spithead. Nevertheless, the slow drip of defections of some ships brought the mutiny into a state of crisis from which it never entirely recovered.[52]

Over the course of the mutiny, a seesaw struggle transpired as both pro- and anti-mutiny factions battled for the support of the less committed seamen, many of whom played little active role. Surviving letters from ships at the Nore make it clear that sentiments were divided between firm supporters of the Delegates, those who were cautiously hopeful that demands would be met and determined opponents of the insurrection.[53] In some instances, loyalist plotting to retake the ship and exit the rebellion commenced almost immediately after the ship joined the mutiny. But on most ships, the frustrated negotiations between the fleet's Delegates and the government and the defection of ships from the mutiny – beginning with the *Clyde* on May 29 – encouraged loyalists to act.

In retrospect, the mutineers' policy of keeping most of the officers onboard was a mistake. It left in place a core around which loyalist factions could take shape, and this invariably worked to undermine the mutiny. Although the mutineers forced some despised officers and loyalists ashore, in practice this was not widely done, partially because the Delegates wanted to signal that the ships remained in readiness, and partially because officers were hostages who could be used as potential bargaining chips. The *Espion*'s Surgeon noted in his journal that remaining officers were generally treated with respect, in spite of

> The great uncertainty that every day prevailed, respecting what
> mad attempts these deluded men [the Delegates] might make ...
> However, owing to the excellent discipline maintained in the Navy,

> [the seamen] went readily to accustomed habits of order and reg-
> ularity. All the duties of the ship were conducted as if no distur-
> bance had ever happened.[54]

Although the good order and deference did speak to their capacity for self-organization, Brenton shrewdly observed that it was precisely the prevailing uncertainty – particularly after the first defections – that led seamen, save "the most guilty adherents," to curry favor with the remaining officers.[55]

Facing government intransigence, loyalist plotting and defections, the mutineers became increasingly militant, maintaining their unity by threat and firing on ships seeking to exit the mutiny by sailing upstream toward London. A blockade on Thames shipping, imposed at the end of May, detained more than a hundred merchant vessels. In retrospect, the blockade too was a serious miscalculation. Brenton recalled, "The extent and value of the trade detained at the Nore was immense, and the consternation in London and throughout the empire proportionately great."[56] The government's position hardened and the seamen found it increasingly difficult to harmonize their claims with the patriotic loyalty that the public expected.[57] As the Admiralty tightened its noose around the fleet, movement became restricted and provisions began to run short. The Delegates countered by seizing and distributing provisions from merchant ships. The take from these seizures was small, however, and disputes surrounding the distribution of supplies heightened tensions.[58]

The third phase commenced with the mutiny of the greater part of Admiral Duncan's squadron at Yarmouth and its arrival at the Nore. Morale was poor; Duncan had warned the Admiralty and called for improvements of the seaman's lot.[59] Toward the end of May, committees formed on some of his ships. Duncan responded by having his officers assemble their crews and read the details of the Spithead settlement. Nevertheless, on May 30 as the squadron departed on patrol, many crews rebelled. Duncan quashed an incipient uprising on his flagship, but a dozen vessels made their way to the Nore. Although their appearance was an enormous boost to morale, on arrival the Yarmouth men proved to be just as highly factionalized as the other ships of the fleet.[60]

The final phase of the mutiny began after June 6 when the Delegates, led by Parker, restated their demands to the Admiralty, warning that if they were not met, "such steps will be taken by the Fleet as will astonish their countrymen."[61] Meanwhile, the maintenance of the blockade had entrenched the government's position and was turning public opinion against the mutineers. The government sent troops to occupy seaports and passed an act that made it a capital crime to assist the rebels.

On June 7, the Admiralty positioned batteries on nearby shores and ordered the removal of buoys and channel markers, making escape by sea more difficult. In the fleet, the situation became increasingly dire, as factional struggles divided crewmen, supplies began to run short and more ships defected. The blockade was abandoned and the Council's authority effectively collapsed. With no apparent way out, the last of the mutineers finally surrendered on June 15. In the following days, authority was restored. Officers identified the activists on each ship, leading to the arrest of hundreds of men and their referral to courts-martial. Trials progressed for months but on October 11, the North Sea Fleet under Duncan's command annihilated the Dutch fleet off Camperdown. Grateful for a momentous victory that ended the immediate threat of an invasion, the Crown pardoned the remaining indicted mutineers.

5.4.2 Oaths and Collective Action at the Nore

Because the officers always comprise a very small minority of the ship's company, if a large proportion of seamen refuse to accept their authority they can readily gain control of the ship. Given the severe, widely shared grievances that incensed the men of the Royal Navy in the 1790s, their capacity for self-organization and the stunning prior example of Spithead, the problem facing the mutiny's leadership was hardly initial mobilization but rather how to sustain the commitment of seamen to the cause. Historians of the Nore mutiny observed that the ringleaders considered the oath to be the "firmest shackle" binding seamen to the mutiny.[62] But why did the leaders believe that oaths would be so binding?

Oaths facilitate distinct stages of collective action. During the *first* stage – mobilization – coordination is the fundamental obstacle. However, in the *second*, more extensive stage of collective action, the great problem facing insurgencies is how to overcome defection and free riding.[63] In the case of the Nore, we know that the activist core of mutineers had taken secret oaths in the first phase, prior to seizing their ships. As seaman Matthew Barker explained, "There warn't so many led into the secret of the mutiny as was first imagined; but then they were chiefly petty officers and able seamen, who possess a strong influence on all hands, fore and aft."[64] Outside the core group of conspiratorial ringleaders and their supporters, mere oath-taking could not be taken as a reliable signal of allegiance.[65] Bowing to social pressure, seamen could always affirm their support for the mutiny insincerely. Why then did the leadership demand that all seamen take the oath?

It is likely that, in the second stage of the mutiny, the oath was intended as a "doomsday" pact – victory or death – that puts signatories at risk regardless of their subsequent behavior.[66] Evidence indicates that the leaders appreciated the difference between the conspiratorial oaths they had sworn to in the planning stage, and those they administered to an entire crew after taking a ship. For example, the conspirators aboard the *Leopard* used the oath to establish that they could take the ship, assessing loyalties one by one. Once they gained control of the ship, the leadership swore the rest of the seamen. One mutineer explained "that when they had got about 150 or 160 then they thought they were the strongest party and they were not afraid and they called them in three or four together afterwards . . . getting all the ship's company sworn."[67] By taking an oath in the presence of witnesses the activists clearly sought to bind all seamen into the "sin" of rebellion.

Loyalists may have taken the oath under duress with no subjective compunction against defecting or subsequently informing on mutineers. Even so they would have been constrained, at least to some extent, since they had no assurance that the authorities would ultimately believe claims that they had taken oath disingenuously. Moreover, by "roving the ropes" (making a gallows on a yardarm) the ringleaders made it clear to potential defectors that betrayal risked deadly reprisal from the mutineers, as well. Seaman Robert Dodson, a mutineer on the warship *Nassau*, wrote his wife, "We have a yard rope riv'd for hanging any man that refuses the Proposals that they've sworn to."[68] The loyalist John Wells wrote his wife that he believed the punishment for defying the committee aboard his ship was death. Wells (erroneously) thought that loyalists had been hanged on other ships and that "the first man who denies will certainly share the fate [of hanging]" on the *Leopard* as well.[69]

Even if some seamen discounted the odds that the government would punish all the oath-takers, uncertainty put everyone at risk. As such, they had reason to stick with the mutiny in the hope that it would prevail and win a general amnesty. What made the doomsday scenario credible was that hanging was the statutory punishment for mutiny under the Articles of War, and that the government had taken an unmistakably hostile posture. The threat of general retaliation bolstered the insurgency by changing the logic of collective action such that *nonparticipation* seemed to pose greater costs to the individual seaman than participation.[70]

In such situations, defection does not pay off. So long as uncertainty prevailed concerning the outcome of the rebellion, attempted defection could be catastrophic, with seamen risking being hanged either by the ringleaders or by the government for having taken the treasonous oath in the first place. Under these conditions, individuals will remain with an insurgency until changes in available information strongly suggest that one of the two outcomes is less likely.

5.5 Why Did Mutineers Stand by Their Oaths? The Sources of Solidarity

To evaluate our theory of solidarity we can exploit different types of evidence. Detailed analysis of the social dynamics of the Nore mutiny is possible because there is a rich trove of relevant evidence – including the daily logbooks and sixteen verbatim trial transcripts of the more than one hundred defendants tried by courts-martial before remaining indictments were dismissed after the Camperdown victory. Because the logs and muster books are complete for the thirty-three ships involved at the Nore, we were also able to consider a host of important factors about ships, their crews and their experiences in the mutiny. We used these systematic data to determine what led a ship to defect from the mutiny.

From the inception of the mutiny on the *Sandwich* on May 12, the Council of Delegates insisted on "unanimity" and "strict discipline." As we have seen, it threatened to severely punish any oath-taker who betrayed the cause, signaling this by roving the ropes after it took control of a ship. Court-martial testimony makes clear that the fleet Delegates and Committeemen on each ship were the eyes and ears of the Council. They donned red cockades to symbolize their power, carried cutlasses and pistols and posted armed sentries. Confrontations with loyalists aboard some ships left several seamen dead. Parker explicitly used the threat of the noose and, when he visited other ships to exhort his supporters or quell dissent, he had a rope roved.[71]

On each ship, governing committees enforced both shipboard order and punished political offenses. In practice, the control of a ship was most secure where a sizable cadre of committed mutineers could be relied on, if necessary, to back up the Council's decisions by force. For instance, on May 26, two seamen were flogged for defiance on the *Sandwich*; one of them was not only given two dozen lashes but was also dunked overboard.[72] On other ships with sizable activist cadres – including the *Ardent*, the *Standard* and the *Monmouth* – mutiny leaders publically flogged and humiliated loyalists whom they saw as posing threats to the mutiny. On the *Monmouth*, six loyalists were severely flogged and, so that no one missed the point, the offenders had their heads shaved and were forced to wear a halter around their necks to show that they had passed "within a few inches of the rope." Their degradation concluded with their being sent ashore in a launch that paraded through the fleet.[73]

Inflicting political punishments like these required the active participation of committed mutineers. By contrast, on ships in which the committees were weakly supported, there was tentative enforcement of the Delegates' instructions and loyalists acted with less fear of reprisal. Parker and the Delegates visited a number of ships that they perceived as wavering. Several ships with suspected loyalist majorities, including the *Iris*, *Tisiphone* and *San Fiorenzo*, were ordered to moor within range of the *Sandwich*'s guns. When loyalists gained control of ships and attempted to escape from the Nore, insurgent ships opened fire on them. Although the casualties were light, probably because the mutineers aimed at sails and riggings in an effort to stop or slow the ships, those attacks deterred other defections.[74]

These examples should not be taken to imply that the leaders of the mutiny had installed a reign of terror, or that they managed to coerce thousands of seamen into supporting the mutiny against their will. The testimony of William Gregory, later hanged as a ringleader, summarizes the matter nicely:

> Could it be reasonably supposed that twelve men armed, whom
> they armed themselves, should command that band of people? ...
> There were six times the number of Officers in the King's ship than
> there were of the Committee and if those Officers were not able to
> exert their authority how could the Committee do it?[75]

At least initially, the mutiny spread as widely and quickly as it did because seamen were strongly aggrieved and the rebellion enjoyed substantial support. Throughout the struggle, however, the leadership buttressed its control by the threat of force, particularly against suspected loyalists.[76] Although they hanged no defectors – in spite of the very visible threat that was conveyed by roving the ropes – prominent loyalists were flogged, beaten, dunked overboard or ceremonially drummed off ships, particularly on vessels whose ringleaders were emboldened by the support of a large mutinous cadre. On some vessels divided by contending mutinous and loyalist factions, violent struggles erupted, killing or wounding several seamen.[77]

Besides imposing discipline, mutiny leaders deliberately increased seamen's dependence on the Delegates by controlling available information. To enhance the seamen's perception that their best option was to stand by the mutiny, the leadership selectively denied them access to information suggesting that capitulation was the safer course. As the committee on the *Sandwich* had dispatched a fact-finding mission to Spithead, it knew all about the settlement, which included a general increase in wages and a pardon for defecting mutineers. For the leadership, this knowledge was private information that they withheld to maintain support behind a united bargaining position.

The facts surrounding the Spithead settlement and pardon were not shared with the crews of the ships at the Nore and, on those ships where these facts had become known, the leadership insinuated that the settlement was fraudulent. Delegates who permitted the disclosure of this information were expelled from the Council. Loyalists responded by trying to reduce seamen's dependence by spreading this information, usually by arranging to have officers publically read the pardon, or by spreading rumors of news from shore.

Taken together, the credible threat of retaliation from the mutineers for breaking their word, combined with uncertainty regarding possible naval sanctions, apparently bolstered the commitments sealed by the oath. The evidence provides strong support for our proposition that dependence and information control were essential features of insurgent solidarity at the Nore. However, evidence is scantier for explanations based on seamen's attachment to radical political movements and revolutionary ideology, or for others emphasizing the primacy of community attachments.

True, the Council's stated goals went beyond wage issues – including a demand for enhanced seamen's rights and status – that the government perceived as radical. Certainly, some radicals could be found among the leading mutineers. Court-martial testimony and surviving letters indicate that republican sentiments were held by some of the Delegates.[78] For instance, William Gregory openly declared, "Is there not many among you here as fit to be our Sovereign as George Rex? He has power and we have the force of gunpowder."[79] According to Lieutenant Forbes of the *Sandwich*, red cockades – radical symbols even then – distinguished the prominent members of the mutineers' party: "Only those that appeared to me to be the most active and the leading men in the mutiny ... I apprehend between forty and fifty of the ship's company [of several hundred men] might have worn them at different times."[80] Other witnesses claimed that as the mutiny dragged on, radicals said that if the government would not budge then ships should variously be scuttled, defect to France or the Netherlands, find refuge in Ireland and so on, though none of these ideas gained widespread support.

Courts-martial were eager to find members of radical underground organizations among the mutineers, but they identified none at all. This was also the finding of a simultaneous investigation undertaken by the Home Office, which sent agents across the country to interrogate radicals and question relatives and acquaintances of the mutineers (Anne Parker among them).[81] Despite their radical reputation, the Delegates did not endorse revolution. They saluted the King's birthday, played patriotic songs and forbade "communication with Jacobins or Traitors."[82] Seamen's political complaints seem to have owed more to ideas of traditional English liberties and just reward for service than they did to foreign Jacobinism. A surviving song from the Nore mutiny, the "Sailor's Lament," put the matter this way:

If Liberty be ours O say why are not all protected?
Why is the hand of Ruffian sway 'Gainst Seamen thus Directed?
Is this Your proof of British rites? Is this rewarding Bravery?
Oh shame to boast Your Tars Exploits then Doom those Tars to
Slavery.[83]

Nor is there much evidence to back the claim that foreign seamen represented a radical cadre spoiling the otherwise loyal Jack Tar. Although Irishmen and other "foreigners" were among the hundreds of active mutineers, they do not appear to have asserted any particular ideological rationale for the mutiny (see Table 5.1). Although a few of the surviving seamen's letters from the Nore indicate support for Irish nationalism, there is no evidence that this ideology played any part in the mutiny.[84]

Most striking in the composition of the most active mutineers is the disproportionate role played by the highly experienced Petty Officers. As we have seen in the leadership of mutinies generally (Chapter 3), skilled seamen, men used to bearing some authority, were key coordinators of the ruling committees aboard the ships of the fleet.

Critics of the Nore mutiny also blamed it on the influence of pressed and Quota-men. Indeed, the leading mutineers were more likely to have been compelled to serve. Their overrepresentation, however, may have been largely due to private grievances rather than radicalism. This is shown by the fact that the mutineers' demands did not include abolishing impressment. Seamen with personal grievances like Richard

Table 5.1 *Comparison of indicted ringleaders at the Nore mutiny against population of seamen on ships at the Nore*

Characteristic	% Nore ringleaders	% population of Nore ships
Petty Officer	32.4	12
Foreign (Irish or other foreign born)	25.9	18.9
Pressed or Quota-man	16.4	10
Age (years)	27.7 (mean)	25 (mean)

Source: Pfaff et al. 2016.

Parker or Irishmen with ethnic grievances may have helped to constitute a critical mass around which the mutiny mobilized.[85] Nevertheless, there is little in the backgrounds or actions of the most active mutineers, much less the bulk of the seamen who supported the rebellion, suggesting that the Nore seamen were the vanguard of a radicalized proletariat.[86] Rather, as was typically observed of ringleaders, Captain Parr of the battleship *Standard* attested, "I am very sorry to say that the active mutineers that are here were amongst the best of the ship's company."[87] Beyond the activist core, there is no evidence that radical ideology promoted commitment or solidarity; court-martial testimony and surviving seamen's letters actually show that radical ideologies were divisive.

If ideological attachments are unconvincing causes of solidarity at the Nore, what of social ties across the seamen of the fleet? In the context of increasing danger, one might expect that a feeling of community bolsters solidarity.[88] In eighteenth-century Britain, secret societies bound by oaths were often recruited from villages, artisanal occupations and sects. E. P. Thompson's Luddites who stuck by their oaths even after being arrested were rooted in particular villages and rural districts.[89]

Moreover, in a more religious age fear of otherworldly sanctions may have restrained oath-takers. In traditional societies it is commonplace for leaders to leverage the supernatural beliefs of their followers to secure compliance to rules that benefit the community.[90] Even if seamen were superstitious, they were notoriously impious.[91] The history of rebellions suggests that the fear of hellfire may be powerful, but social ostracism is probably more so. For example, the social costs that traitors to the Luddite cause faced in their homogenous villages were little short of ruinous. The Parisian Communards felt intense social pressure to fight and feared the disapproval of their homogeneous, densely knit "urban villages." As one explained when encouraged to defect, "I can't leave; what would my comrades from the *quartier* say?"[92]

In contrast to rural communities and stable working-class neighborhoods, eighteenth-century maritime life was much more socially fluid. The Atlantic world had more than a hundred and fifty thousand English-speaking seamen. As we have noted previously, there was substantial turnover in many ships' companies, and crews were discharged at the end of each voyage. The ships that took part in the

Nore mutiny had suffered unsustainably high levels of desertion in the year before the mutiny; on average, about 7 percent of ships' companies absconded. In the 1790s the Navy had been flooded with tens of thousands of newcomers, many of them inexperienced Landsmen and foreigners. The influx of replacements like these tends to detract from unit solidarity.[93] Once the war ended, sailors could expect to find employment outside the Royal Navy in the merchant ships of several oceangoing countries. Finally, seamen who betrayed the ringleaders of the mutiny may have expected to be assigned to other ships. In exchange for his testimony against the Committeemen, for example, a witness on the *Monmouth* expected a transfer to the Marines, out of reach of his old shipmates.[94]

Seamen belonged to an occupation but not necessarily to a broader community. Whereas local ties may have been strong and dense on particular ships, the bonds of community would have been hard to extend across the fleet. In some instances, strong community bonds aboard *particular* ships might have introduced social cross-pressures that worked against fleetwide solidarity. A powerful illustration of these crosscutting commitments is provided by the early defectors from the mutiny, the crews of the frigates *Clyde* and *San Fiorenzo*. On May 29, under fire, the *Clyde* became the first ship to defect. This occurred after "Captain Cunningham harangued the ship's company and read to them the King's most gracious pardon on the condition that they would return to their duty – they gladly accepted and expressed their grateful thanks by three cheers."[95] The *San Fiorenzo* quickly followed suit.

Why were these seamen disloyal to the rest of the Nore fleet? The sense of *local* community appears to have been stronger on these ships than the sense of community existing across the remaining ships in the mutiny. The crews of these two early defecting ships had served together for a long time. They had emotional attachments to their commanding officers that persisted even after being enveloped in the mutiny. In neither instance were the mutinous factions numerous; the mutineers aboard the *San Fiorenzo* were so weak that they had required the armed assistance of other vessels before they could seize the ship.[96] Unusually, the Captains of these ships were not confined to quarters, and it is worth noting that both crews would have had reason to be relatively satisfied with shipboard conditions. Both had long-serving commanders, moderate punishment and tiny rates of desertion compared with what was typical of ships at the Nore.[97]

As these cases of early defection make clear, the Nore's leaders, unlike those of most other insurgent groups, could not select their followers. As such they were unable to exclude seamen who lacked strong grievances or ideological conviction. Nor could they provide special incentives to reward compliance, take loved ones as hostages or make a credible threat to avenge disloyalty on a traitor's family, all tactics that have been successfully employed by other kinds of insurgent groups to bolster their solidarity.[98]

The role of radical ideology or the bonds that knit the wider seafaring community in the mutiny are impossible to dismiss entirely, however. Even though the great bulk of seamen were not radicals, they shared norms that claimed that, under particular circumstances, mutiny was justified. And seamen, like members of other occupational groups characterized by strong interdependence, had norms that vaunted solidarity. The existence of these norms has no necessary implications for the attainment of compliance among group members, however. What made sustaining solidarity difficult at the Nore was not simply the problem of enforcement; radicalism was not widely diffused among seamen, and community bonds were attenuated, creating cross-pressures that undercut commitment.

5.5.1 Testing Dependence and Control as Bases of Solidarity

Narrative evidence tracing the processes responsible for attaining solidarity reveals the importance of dependence, chiefly through withholding information about the Spithead settlement, and control, through the discipline and monitoring of seamen by armed Committeemen. But the events on the ships whose active mutineers were tried by court-martials are much better documented than the others. How confident can we be that the factors we have identified hold across all the ships at the Nore?

Since muster books and the daily logbooks of the thirty-three ships participating in the Nore were complete, we were able to code both cross-sectional and time-varying variables for every ship. Logbooks contain daily observations of events aboard each ship, and muster books allow us to see how the demographic and social structure of the crews influenced solidarity. Together, these data made it possible to model the influence of structural and situational factors on the duration of mutiny aboard each ship. The duration we are modeling is the number of days from when a ship entered the mutiny until its defection. Ships varied as to when they entered and exited the mutiny. The average ship at the Nore remained in the mutiny for twenty-two days.

To assess the role of control, we considered the relative strength of the mutinous faction on Nore ships. This is not simply a measure of popular support for the mutiny aboard a given ship. Several facts speak against this interpretation. First, there is no evidence that militant seamen were more likely to be assigned to some ships than to others. Second, on no ship were these cadres large enough to constitute a majority (on average, only 6 percent of the crew were activists, and on no ship were they more than a fifth of the crew). Third, the logbooks show that ships with large activist cadres had *more* episodes of punishment and violence against loyalists – this hardly suggests consensus.

Perhaps the proportion of indicted mutiny activists doesn't capture control because of biases in prosecution. The number of activists might have been underreported, as the authorities could have had an incentive to minimize the prosecution of the valuable, highly trained sailors. Blaming a few troublemakers would also imply that grievances did not run very deep. The manner in which seamen were indicted and their characteristics, however, suggest otherwise. Commanding officers provided the list from each ship. Given a strong desire to rid themselves of militants, this list would tend to provide a reliable estimate of core mutineers. This tendency was balanced by the value of many of the seamen who were actively involved in the mutiny. More than two-thirds of the indicted men were highly skilled and qualified Petty Officers and Able Seamen, who would not have been cast away lightly.

To capture the selective disclosure of information, we include the date on which the pardon was read. We used logbooks to identify whether the settlement at Spithead and the terms of the royal pardon were read to a ship's crew and, if so, on what date. On some ships, such as those of Duncan's squadron, the details were read at the first show of unrest, and on others, if read at all, they were disclosed at later points during the confrontation with the authorities.[99]

We included several other factors to capture the possible effects of community and foreign radicalism, as well as grievances such as having been pressed or induced to serve through the Quota. Our models do not presume that decisions by ships' companies were taken independently. We also included the spread of defection in the mutiny as a diffusion variable that captures the influence on a given ship by previous defections by other ships.

Our analysis allows us to predict defection from the mutiny, focusing on the relationship between the duration of mutiny and key variables such as the share of *active mutineers, share Irish, pardon read* and the *diffusion variables* as the predictors.[100] Our findings strongly support the role of control and dependence in bolstering solidarity. Having the *pardon read* has a positive and significant association with defection in all of our models. The risk of defecting is nearly three times greater for ships in which the pardon was read compared to ships in which it was not read. Figure 5.1 represents that relationship graphically, providing an estimate of the effect of the pardon on time of defection.

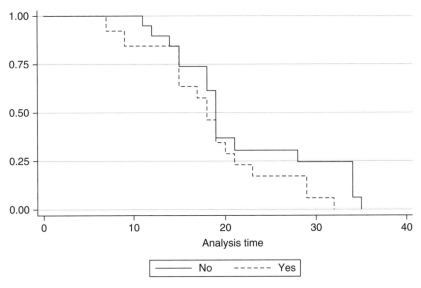

Figure 5.1 Kaplan-Meier estimate of time to defection at the Nore (in days) by pardon having been read

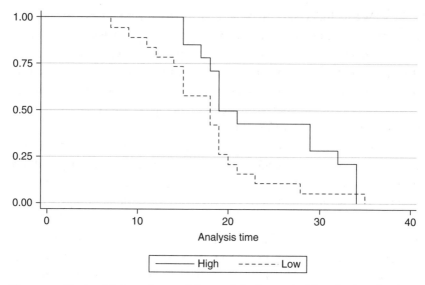

Figure 5.2 Kaplan-Meier estimate of time to defection at the Nore (in days) by share of active mutineers in the ship's company above or below mean

As expected, we also found that the *share of active mutineers* on a ship has a significant and negative effect on the hazard rate in each model. A larger proportion of active mutineers decreased the odds of a ship defecting from the fleet at the Nore, a relationship that is consistent with the narrative evidence that we have traced. Figure 5.2 shows the relationship between the high and low shares (above and below the mean value) of active mutineers on the duration of the mutiny.

Further results show that the larger the proportion of Irish on a ship, the higher a ship's probability of defection, thus hastening its exit from the mutiny. This finding reinforces our argument that, although there is some evidence of Irish nationalism among seamen in the 1790s, it appears to have played no substantial role in mobilizing or sustaining the insurgency at the Nore. Far from bolstering the mutiny as many have presumed, the share of Irish seamen in a ship's company appears to have diminished solidarity, possibly due to anti-Irish feelings among the English sailors that would have undercut community.[101]

Finally, the hazard of defecting from the mutiny increases as the number of ships that defected increases, whether measured as all defections prior to a given time, or as defections one day or three days prior. This squares with the historical evidence that the departure of ships threw the mutiny into uncertainty and disorder. Ships that defected attracted attention, sailing away under fire from other ships. Defections were an obvious signal of the mutiny's diminishing chances of success and, unlike the news of the Spithead settlement, were common knowledge wholly out of the leadership's control.

The fact that learning about the pardon retains its statistical significance despite the role of previous defections provides striking support for our argument. In ships in which information about the pardon was unavailable, seamen were more likely to have stuck with the leadership until the general capitulation partly because they believed that they might be severely punished – and perhaps hanged – even if they tried to defect. And on ships with large mutinous cadres, the threat of retaliation by one's own shipmates was highly credible and deterred defection.

5.6   Why the Mass Mutiny Succeeded at Spithead and Failed at the Nore

Whereas the mutiny at Spithead was a celebrated success, that at the Nore was an abject failure. Valentine Joyce triumphed whereas Richard Parker hanged. Why did the oath of solidarity prevail at Spithead and unravel at the Nore? It is impossible to trace the process whereby solidarity was established and maintained at Spithead due to the lack of documentation and the fact that none defected, depriving us of the variation we would need to gain analytical leverage. Nevertheless, several factors stand out as possible reasons for the difference in outcomes.

One basic difference is timing. Coming on the heels of the Spithead mutiny in which the government had already made substantial concessions that applied to seamen across the Navy, Parker and the Nore Delegates were at a fatal disadvantage in making additional demands. To many in the government as well as in public opinion, the Nore mutiny was redundant and risked radicalizing the situation in Britain if the government did not take a firm stand against insurrection.

In addition, the demands made by the mutineers at the Nore were probably too broad. Acceding to them would have dictated substantial changes in naval governance. In the midst of a serious military crisis that demanded unprecedented fiscal and manpower commitments, naturally the government was ill-disposed toward such sweeping reforms. The kingdom wanted a Navy ready for action, not one in which long-standing institutions were put into question and seamen's subordination was subject to contention. Although the mutineers of the North Sea Fleet had leverage by threatening the government's war policy and the country's economic stability, they lacked sufficient clout to force radical changes in the organization and manning of the Navy.

Finally, compared with the leaders of the Spithead mutiny, the Delegates at the Nore appear to have blundered by admitting so many ships into their mutiny. Whereas a strong sense of community backed the authority of the Spithead Delegates, nothing comparable bolstered the mutiny at the Nore. Joyce and his comrades built their insurgency around the crews of ships-of-the-line with a strong sense of their identity as a victorious fleet, reinforcing a firm line of division in an "us versus them" conflict. The diverse collection of ships at the Nore mutiny had no such overarching identity or long-term connections. There was too much diversity and too little stability in the ships of the North Sea Fleet to nourish a strong sense of community.[102] Loosely connected, the seamen at the Nore were willing to abandon the cause when it began to look as if the mutiny might not be able to protect them from retaliation or provide redress of their grievances. Rather than solidarity born of deep attachments, the leadership at the Nore was compelled to rely heavily on dependence and control secured through selective disclosure of information and coercive power.

5.7 The Nore Mutiny and the Study of Rebellion

The problem of solidarity in a sustained rebellion obtains not only in mobilizing people with grievances but in a group's capacity to compel them to follow through with their commitments in spite of costs and uncertainties. The organizers of the mutinies at Spithead and the Nore rightly believed that they had to maintain a united front to prevail in the struggle with the government and to avoid punishment. Although seamen desired better pay and working conditions, the leaders of the mutinies sought to bind them to these collective goals by imposing an oath of solidarity. Under the oath, seamen promised to obey their leaders and persevere until their goals were attained.

Yet, as Thomas Hobbes famously observed, "covenants without the sword are but words, and of no strength to secure a man at all."[103] Although benefiting from large-scale, apparently enthusiastic mobilization, the mutineers at the Nore soon found themselves facing a lengthy standoff with the government. Neither ideological commitments nor community ties were adequate to maintain solidarity. As pressure mounted, the leadership was compelled to control seamen in order to deter defection. They exploited informational asymmetries to persuade seamen to stand by the insurgency, even as its prospects for success faded.

Our analysis shows that the greater the control they could exert through force and the more that insurgent leaders were able to limit access to information concerning alternative settlements, the greater a ship's commitment was to the mutiny. Whereas conventional accounts of the binding power of oaths stress tradition or supernatural beliefs, such accounts do little to explain oaths' variable success in binding members of insurgent groups to their cause. Many who take oaths later violate them in spite of the norms adhering to ideologies and communities.[104]

We have shown that illicit oaths like the one that seamen took at the Nore can have a fundamentally strategic character. First, they sharpen the divisions between groups in a conflict, imposing a clear boundary between camps.[105] Second, since a government may threaten punishment for taking illegal oaths, this means that the costs of maintaining control are lower for insurgent leaders. Oath-takers must reckon not only with the threat of retaliation from their comrades but also with possible punishment by the government if they fall into its hands. This situation increases the dependence of group members on the leaders of a rebellion to provide safety and reduces the incentive to defect. This may be why oaths are signature features of anti-government insurgencies across times and places.[106]

Sometimes ideology or the bonds of community can attain the requisite commitment to sustain a rebellion in the face of concerted opposition, but not at the Nore. In their struggle to cement an often shaky confederation of ships, mutiny leaders used information control, surveillance and credible threats to compel seamen to stand by their cause. Insisting on an "all or nothing" resolution, mutiny leaders sought to raise the probability that seamen who were party to the oath would hold fast. Where mutiny leaders were able to exploit informational asymmetries, they persuaded seamen to stand by the insurgency, even as its prospects for success faded. The ability of leaders to exploit information asymmetries like this may be a crucial, if largely unacknowledged, feature of social activism generally.[107]

One of the implications of the mass mutinies of 1797 is that rebellion can be an effective way to win concessions and compel the authorities to reform governance. Poor governance of the Navy in the 1790s magnified grievances among seamen. They coordinated an armed rebellion in response that gave effective voice to their discontent. If insurgent groups can attain solidarity and have the leverage to compel the government to negotiate, they can win at least partial redress of grievances. The lesson of Spithead is that, despite the disaster at the Nore, the situation of seamen in the Royal Navy improved as a result of the mass mutinies of 1797. The government was forced to act and wages and provisions improved for all seamen.

Another implication is that poorly informed militants fearing reprisals may be the most committed to strikes, uprisings and armed insurgencies. The lesson of the Nore is that, in such situations, the most effective counterinsurgency strategy may be to isolate the rebels while offering an amnesty that makes individual defection less costly. The more credible the amnesty, and the better the odds that defectors will be protected from retaliation, the more likely that it will erode solidarity by decreasing dependence on the rebellious group. If that is achieved, one of the conditions necessary for sequential defections will have been set in place. This dynamic may help explain the frequently observed paradox that large-scale, radical and seemingly determined strikes and rebellions may arise suddenly but collapse just as quickly in a reverse cascade of collective action.

Finally, the mass mutinies occurred in the context of a political crisis. Revolutionary France posed an existential threat to the British monarchy. The crisis encouraged a reactionary posture and a spirit of intransigence that undercut better governance. It led the government to misunderstand the goals of the Spithead mutineers, at least initially.

Illustration 1 John Webber, portrait of William Bligh, c. 1776
Source: National Portrait Gallery, Australia.

Illustration 2 Robert Dodd, "The mutineers turning Lt Bligh and some of the officers and crew adrift from His Majesty's Ship HMS *Bounty*," c. 1790
Source: National Maritime Museum, UK.

Illustration 3 "A SHIP of War of the third Rate" and "Section of a SHIP of War, of First Rate," c. 1728

Illustration 4 Thomas Rowlandson, "Picture of a Naval Captain," c. 1799

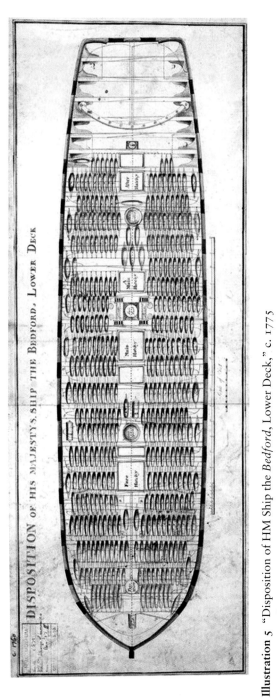

Illustration 5 "Disposition of HM Ship the *Bedford*, Lower Deck," c. 1775
Source: National Maritime Museum, UK.

Illustration 6 George Cruikshank, "Saturday Night at Sea," c. 1840
Source: National Maritime Museum, UK.

Illustration 7 Thomas Rowlandson, picture of a sailor, c. 1799
Source: National Maritime Museum, UK.

Illustration 8 Picture of a Petty Officer of the Napoleonic Wars

Illustration 9 Thomas Rowlandson, "Portsmouth Point," 1811
Source: National Maritime Museum, UK.

Illustration 10 William Beechy, portrait of "Sir Thomas Troubridge"
Source: National Maritime Museum, UK.

Illustration 11 Caricature of a press gang, c. 1780
Source: National Maritime Museum, UK.

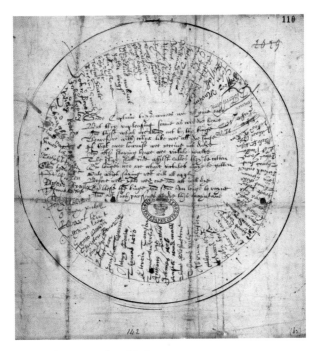

Illustration 12 "Sailors Round Robin"
Source: National Archives of the UK.

Illustration 13 John Augustus Atkinson, "British Sailors Boarding a Man of War" (capture of the *Hermione*), 1815

Source: National Maritime Museum, UK.

RICHARD PARKER.

PRESIDENT of the DELEGATES in the late MUTINY in his MAJESTY'S FLEET at the NORE.

For which he suffered DEATH on board the SANDWICH the 30 of June 1797.

Illustration 14 William Chamberlain, "Richard Parker, President of the Delegates," 1797
Source: National Maritime Museum, UK.

Illustration 15 Isaac Cruikshank, "The Delegates in Council, or, Beggars on Horseback," 1797
Source: National Maritime Museum, UK.

THE MUTINY AT PORTSMOUTH.

Illustration 16 "The Mutiny at Portsmouth"
Source: iStock by Getty Images.

Illustration 17 "Mutiny at the Nore. Richard Parker . . . tenders the Sailors'
Grievances"
Source: Almay Image.

Illustration 18 William Joy, "Escape of HMS *Clyde* from the Nore mutiny," 1830
Source: National Maritime Museum, UK.

Illustration 19 George Cruikshank, "The Point of Honour," 1825
Source: National Maritime Museum, UK.

THE WRECK OF THE 'WAGER'

The Captain shoots Mr. Cozens

Illustration 20 "The Wreck of the Wager. The Captain Shoots Mr. Cozens"
Source: iStock by Getty Images.

Illustration 21 Thomas Hudson, portrait of George Anson, before 1748
Source: National Maritime Museum, UK.

Illustration 22 J. M. W. Turner, "The Fighting *Temeraire* tugged to her last berth to be broken up," 1838
Source: National Gallery, UK.

Illustration 23 Lemuel Abbott, portrait of Rear-Admiral Sir Horatio Nelson, 1799
Source: National Maritime Museum, UK.

Fear of radicalism stiffened resistance to the Nore mutiny, permitted no further reforms and ensured that the government would see the ringleaders hanged.

The mutinies of 1797 reinforced the belief among naval officers that stricter discipline and harsher punishment were needed to counter the revolutionary threat. The campaign to stifle radicalism, however, came at a great price. In the following chapter we shall see why the perception of threat led to a harsher disciplinary regime that inflicted much misery on seamen and undermined good governance. Cruel and indiscriminate punishment had an unintended consequence, however: it actually increased the odds of mutiny aboard Navy ships.

Notes

1. Brenton 1837, p. 276.
2. On Parker, see Coats 2008. On Anne Parker's struggles to bury her husband, see Easton 2017.
3. Dugan 1965, p. 199, wryly comments, "Parker was intelligent, discontented, vain and enthusiastic. The seamen picked him to lead because he was comparatively well-educated, literate, attractive . . .. Above all, Parker was willing to be president, which most of the other Delegates were not."
4. As Watt and Hawkins 2016, p. 401, note, Parker may have been "less of a leader to them and more of a focus of public attention."
5. See TNA: PRO ADM 1/5486 and ADM1/5340. On Parker's role, also see Coats and MacDougall 2011; Dugan 1965; Gill 1913; and Manwaring and Dobrée 1987.
6. Rodger 2004, p. 441.
7. Land 2009; London 2001.
8. See, e.g., Coats 2011; Linebaugh and Rediker 2001; Thompson 1980; and Wells 1983.
9. Brenton 1837, p. 289.
10. See, e.g., Diani and McAdam 2003; Gates 2002; and Gould 1995.
11. See Berman 2009; Kalyvas 2006; Kalyvas and Kocher 2007; and Weinstein 2007.
12. For an elaboration of the theory of solidarity that informs our analysis, see Hechter 1987.
13. Manwaring and Dobrée 1987, p. 131.
14. See, e.g., Fantasia 1988 and Wood 2003.
15. Gill 1913, p. 4; also see Rodger 2003; Thompson 1980, p. 168; and Wells 1983.
16. Frykman 2009, p. 92; Glasco 2004; and Rediker 1987, p. 155.
17. Chong 1991; Cook, Hardin and Levi 2005.
18. See studies of labor-based collective action in Gould 1995; Kerr and Siegal 1954; and Wolcott 2008.
19. Rediker 1987, pp. 134–5, 154; also see detailed studies by Earle 1998; Lavery 2010; Neale 1985; and Rodger 1986.
20. Leeson 2010, p. 302.

21. Dynamics like these are not peculiar to the Nore; Wood 2003, p. 116, describes how guerrillas secured peasant support by making them dependent on the movement for protection from government repression. Kalyvas 2006, pp. 124, 157, argues that general threats of retaliation "allow insurgents to solve collective action problems by turning the protection of civilian populations into a selective incentive" and notes that "the force inherent in control solves collective action problems."

22. On the wars of the French Revolution, see Doyle 1990. On the Navy during the crisis of the late 1790s, see Dull 2009, pp. 123–50 and Rodger 2004, p. 429.

23. McLynn 1991, pp. 336–8; on English radicalism, see Goodwin 1979 and Thrale 1983.

24. Oliver 1941 and Twigger 1999.

25. McLynn 1991, p. 332.

26. Lavery 2010, p. 213; also Rodger 2004, p. 446.

27. Fortescu 1902; Wells 1983.

28. Lavery 2010, p. 211; Rodger 2004, p. 444.

29. On the treatment of the Irish, see Colley 2003 and Hechter 1998.

30. Frykman 2009; Gill 1961, p. 70; Rodger 2004, p. 444.

31. The Spithead and Nore mutinies were strikes, albeit in a context without institutionalized labor relations and rights to collective bargaining.

32. Gilbert 1983; Neale 1985; Rodger 1986. See also the discussion of mutiny success in Chapter 7.

33. See Coats and MacDougall 2011; Dugan 1965, p. 68; Rodger 2004, p. 442; and Wells 1983.

34. Neale 1985; Rodger 2004, p. 445.

35. Round-robin letters and petitions as coordination devices are discussed at length in Chapter 3.

36. For narrative accounts, see Dugan 1965; Gill 1961 and Manwaring and Dobrée 1987.

37. Hattendorf et al. 1993, pp. 543–5.

38. Manwaring and Dobrée 1987; on the essentially moderate leadership at Spithead also see Rodger 2004, pp. 448–9.

39. Coats 2004; London 2001.

40. Systematic research on Spithead is almost impossible to carry out because of the paucity of archival records: due to a general amnesty, no courts-martial were held and the loss of letters and documents related to the mutiny did away with crucial evidence. See Brown 2006 and Watt and Hawkins 2016, pp. 373–4.

41. Land 2009.

42. See the sixty-six letters related to the Nore collected by Watt and Hawkins 2016.

43. Dugan 1965, pp. 179–80.

44. TNA: PRO ADM 51/1173.

45. Manwaring and Dobrée 1987, pp. 131–2.

46. Gill 1913, p. 110.

47. For example, on May 13 the Master's Log of the *Swan* reported that a cutter came alongside the ship "with three men in the stern-sheets and asked for the captain of our forecastle. The commanding officer refused to let them on board. They insisted on coming on board and said they would drop the *Sandwich* astern and blow us out of the water." TNA: PRO ADM 52/3472. For another such episode, see letter B13 in Watt and Hawkins 2016, p. 420.

48. Wells 1983.

49. See the letter from the Delegates to the First Lord of the Admiralty, dated June 6, 1797, found in the Caird Library, National Maritime Museum Greenwich, Ms X94/062.

50. Brenton 1837, p. 287.
51. MacDougall 2011 and Watt and Hawkins 2016.
52. Wells 1983, pp. 88–90.
53. See the sixty-six letters connected with the Nore mutiny collected by Watt and Hawkins 2016.
54. Thursfield 1951, pp. 87–8. The *Isis*'s Surgeon reported that the remaining officers were treated with "every mark of respect and attention"; see Watt and Hawkins 2016, p. 424.
55. Brenton 1837, p. 289.
56. Brenton 1837, p. 268.
57. Land 2009.
58. Gill 1913, pp. 220–1.
59. Dugan 1965, pp. 123–9.
60. Brenton 1837, pp. 287 –90; Rodger 2004, pp. 448–9; see also Watt and Hawkins 2016.
61. Caird Library, Ms X94/062.
62. Manwaring and Dobrée 1987, pp. 131–2.
63. Heckathorn 1996.
64. Glasco 2004, p. 47.
65. Gambetta 2011.
66. We owe this interpretation to Doug Allen. On the logic of such pacts and their role in fostering cooperation, see Rasmussen 2007, p. 123.
67. TNA: PRO ADM 1/5486.
68. See letter B4 in Watt and Hawkins 2016, p. 410; see also letter B35, p. 444.
69. See letter B12 in Watt and Hawkins 2016, p. 419.
70. Kalyvas and Kocher 2007.
71. TNA: PRO ADM 1/5486.
72. TNA: PRO ADM 51/1173 and 52/3397.
73. TNA: PRO ADM 1/5486; see also the Captain's log of *Ardent* for June 9, 1797, TNA: PRO ADM 51/4411 and the trial of the *Standard* mutineers TNA: PRO ADM 1/5486. A letter from the seaman John Waters to his father described his degradation at the hands of the "villains" aboard the *Monmouth*; letter B51 in Watt and Hawkins 2016, p. 462.
74. Wells 1983, pp. 88–9.
75. TNA: PRO ADM 1/5340.
76. See the evidence presented in the trial of *Leopard* mutineers, TNA: PRO ADM1/ 5486.
77. See, e.g., the *Isis*'s Captain's log of June 10, 1797, TNA: PRO ADM 51/1185; and the Captain's log of the Leopard for June 18, 1797, TNA: PRO ADM51/1168.
78. See, e.g., letters B29, 34, 35, 37, 38, 41 and 58 collected in Watt and Hawkins 2016.
79. TNA: PRO ADM 1/5340.
80. TNA: PRO ADM 1/5486.
81. Goodwin 1979, p. 408.
82. TNA: PRO ADM 1/5486; also see trial transcript of the remaining *Sandwich* mutineers in TNA: PRO ADM 1/5340.
83. TNA: PRO ADM 1/727/C370a.
84. On the Irish, see Brown 2006; Kennedy 1990; and Rodger 2004; see also letters B37, 38 and 41 in Watt and Hawkins 2016.
85. See Centola 2013 and Oliver and Marwell 2001 on the critical mass in collective action.

86. For different interpretations that stress nascent class consciousness among the sea-going proletariat, see, e.g., Frykman 2009; Glasco 2004; and Rediker 1987.

87. Trial transcript of *Standard* mutineers, TNA: PRO ADM 1/5486.

88. Hovi 1998.

89. Calhoun 1982; Thompson 1980.

90. Leeson 2017.

91. Rediker 1987.

92. Gould 1995, p. 181.

93. See studies of military cohesion by Costa and Kahn 2008; Shils and Janowitz 1948; and Van Crefeld 1983.

94. See, e.g., letter B51 in Watt and Hawkins 2016, p. 462.

95. See Master's logs of *Clyde*, TNA: PRO ADM 52/2864/17960701.

96. Master's log of *San Fiorenzo*, TNA: PRO ADM 52/3388/17970114.

97. The rate of desertion was *Clyde* 1.4 percent; *San Fiorenzo* 0.9 percent; average of Nore ships 7.1 percent, and the flogging rates in the year prior to the mutiny were also low, being a per capita rate of 1.0 for *Clyde*; 0.33 for *San Fiorenzo*; and an average of ships at the Nore of 1.9.

98. See studies by Berman 2009; Kalyvas and Kocher 2007; and Weinstein 2007.

99. See Appendix C for a description of the hazards models we used to estimate the time to defection. Ships have a value of 0 up until the day in which the pardon was read (if it was read). From that day onward, a ship receives a value of 1 for the rest of the duration of its mutiny. Ships that never had the pardon read receive a value of 0 for their entire mutiny duration. There is no pattern in the evidence that suggests that this variable is endogenous to our dependent variable.

100. Alternative models were also estimated for *size of the ship's company*, *share unskilled landsmen*, *share previous service* and *share pressed men*. Despite their potential theoretical importance, none of these variables is significantly correlated with the duration that a ship's company remained with the mutiny, however. They were excluded from the final models.

101. Colley 2003, p. 8; also see Hechter 1998 and Lavery 2010, pp. 233–4.

102. Calhoun 1982, p. 156.

103. Hobbes [1651] 1996, p. 111.

104. See, e.g., Leeson 2017; Luongo 2011; MacKenzie 1967.

105. Kalyvas 2006.

106. Historical studies of the role of oaths can be found in Alam 2007; Ownby and Heidhues 1993; Thompson 1980; and Wells 1983.

107. Lichbach's (1998, pp. 89–91) survey of the literature on rebellion notes that "dissident entrepreneurs try to set up a 'smoke screen' for their rank-and-file followers" and "try to take advantage of incomplete information." Typically, "Leaders try to convince followers that the probability of winning is higher than it really is ... by overestimating the government's willingness to be pressured into concessions" (p. 91) and by withholding information about favorable terms of surrender. In strikes, leaders often withhold information about the employer's position and the terms being offered so as to maintain unity and reach a collective settlement. See Ahlquist and Levi 2013; Cramton and Tracy 2003; and Martin 1980.

6 DISCIPLINE, PUNISHMENT AND THE FEAR OF INSURRECTION

In early February of 1808, five distinguished naval officers assembled in the frigate *Nereide*'s great cabin with its large windows spanning the width of the stern. The scene was pleasant enough, with the ship at anchor in summer weather in Table Bay at the Cape of Good Hope. But the task at hand of the officers attired in dress blue and gold braid was grave. They had been given the unpleasant duty of trying a brother officer on serious charges of misconduct, including brutality and the oppression of his crew.

The accused, Captain Robert Corbet, was a bold and talented commander whose career nevertheless had been dogged by accusations of cruelty. Most recently, Corbet had clashed with Sir Edward Pellew, the Commander-in-Chief of the East Indies Station. While at Bombay, the crew of the *Nereide* had managed to smuggle a letter of complaint detailing Corbet's ill-usage to Pellew. Their grievances seemed well founded. Although Corbet had earned a strong professional reputation, he had also imposed harsh discipline on his crews. Starting and flogging occurred with savage frequency. In the year prior to his trial, Corbet inflicted thousands of lashes on the crew of his ship, amounting to the staggering rate of about twenty-five lashes per seaman – or about five times the average rate during this era. Moreover, this was hardly an aberration; in one seven-month period between August 1806 and March 1807, Corbet had inflicted 134 floggings on his crew with an average severity of seventeen lashes.

When Pellew reproached him for his cruelty, Corbet insisted on a court-martial to clear his good name. Pellew assented, but the trial would have to be held at the Cape because there were not enough officers of rank (the juries of courts-martial had to be composed of officers of at least the Post-Captain rank) in the vicinity to hear the case. In early January, when the ship made ready to depart Bombay with no apparent action taken on their complaint, the seamen of the *Nereide* believed that their grievances had been ignored. Corbet made no effort to inform them otherwise, and a mutiny followed as the "major part" of the ship's company staged a strike, refusing to take the ship to sea. Corbet suppressed the mutiny with the aid of armed Marines and put ten ringleaders in irons. He steered for the Cape at once, where he would soon see the mutineers tried by the same court that would hear the charges against him.

At the end of January 1809, the mutineers faced the officers who would also sit in judgment of Corbet just a few days later. Courts-martial were highly ritualized affairs, designed to display the majesty of justice and the restoration of hierarchy and order. A gun was fired to summon the members of the court and the Union Jack was raised to the top of the mainmast. The officers of the jury assembled in full dress uniforms. One by one, the defendants were led in by an armed guard who remained at their side throughout the trial. As their commanding officer, Corbet served as the prosecutor. The defendants called witnesses but did not themselves benefit from counsel. Once the evidence had been presented, the jury of officers deliberated privately and covered their heads as the dreadful sentence was announced.[1]

All ten of the accused ringleaders were convicted of mutiny and sentenced to the statutory penalty of death by hanging. The testimony laying out Corbet's exceptional harshness was not ignored, however. The jury recommended nine of the convicted seamen to royal mercy and, in the end, only one of them hanged.[2]

Whatever sympathies the members of the jury may have felt toward the seamen of the *Nereide* would have been balanced by admiration for a dashing Captain whose rise had been promoted by none other than Horatio Nelson. Corbet, the son of a naval officer, was commissioned a Lieutenant in 1796. He came to the attention of the then Vice-Admiral Nelson in 1803, who was impressed by Corbet's "officer-like and regular" conduct. Nelson's patronage brought him assignments as an acting

Captain on frigates in Nelson's squadron until Corbet received his official commission in 1806. As the commander of the *Nereide*, Corbet proved to be a talented officer, taking several prizes. In 1807, the ship departed from Portsmouth as part of a squadron setting off to invade the Rio de la Plata region of Spanish America. After the failure of that expedition, the *Nereide* was sent to the Cape and then to Bombay for a refit.

As it happened, Corbet was fortunate to have drawn a favorable jury. The officers composing it were hard-driving and aggressive, cut from the same cloth as Corbet. Captain Josias Rowley, the most senior officer, served as the president of the court. Rowley was a tough and battle-hardened commander impressed by officers who liked to fight and seize prizes. At the trial, Corbet made a spirited defense of his actions that was crafted to appeal to officers of his ilk. He reminded them that naval regulations granted commanders discretion to maintain discipline as they saw fit. He insisted that "Severity must depend upon circumstances, and whenever I have been severe, circumstances have rendered it necessary." Although Corbet had been severe, he claimed that harshness was justified by the lazy and insubordinate tendencies of seamen.

Concluding his own defense, Corbet shared his personal view concerning the importance of giving commanders unlimited license to inflict corporal punishment. Flogging, he asserted, was a moral necessity and an indispensable tool of British naval supremacy in an age of revolution and insurrection:

> Convinced as I am that whenever discipline is relaxed, whenever a captain feels his power incompetent to support subordination, activity and exertion, that the service I delight in has passed its zenith; that our discipline constitutes its superiority over all others, that we meet enemies as brave as ourselves, that our country has experienced its greatest damage from relaxing on its support and safety from infliction of discipline. Under these ideas I count the public character of a strict and rigid discipline.

Corbet's candid acknowledgment of his severity did not condemn him in the eyes of his brother officers on the jury. They acquitted him of most of the charges, going so far as to call many of them "unfounded," "litigious" and "vexatious." They did find, however, that the charge of "cruelty and oppression" was partially proven because of "Punishment having been inflicted on board the ship with sticks of improper size and such as are not usual in His Majesty's Service." Accordingly, they declared, "The Court do therefore adjudge said Robert Corbet to be reprimanded, and is hereby reprimanded." For all the misery inflicted on his seamen, in the end naval justice did no more than admonish Corbet not to use large sticks when beating them. Back in Britain, however, Admiralty officials considered the affair to be a stain, and the outrageous conduct of Corbet and other "flogging Captains" prompted growing public concern that a reform of the system of discipline by summary flogging and casual beatings ("starting") at the discretion of commanding officers was desperately needed.[3]

***

Following his acquittal, Corbet remained attached to the Cape Station where the *Nereide* became engaged in a campaign against French commerce raiders in the Indian Ocean. British and French frigate squadrons fought for control of the French possessions of Isle-de-France (Mauritius) and Ile Bourbon (Réunion). Corbet distinguished himself in an attack on Ile Bourbon in 1809. In recognition of his achievements, he was given the command of the heavy frigate *Africaine*. By this time, Corbet had such a reputation for brutality that desertion rates on ships under his command were high; it was joked among fellow officers that his crewmen would desert even into cannibal territory. The seamen aboard *Africaine* nearly mutinied as Corbet assumed command, but they were induced to submit because the Commander-in-Chief at the Cape had the forethought to surround the ship with armed vessels.

The *Africaine* was an unhappy ship under Corbet but, as it happened, his command did not last long. On September 13, 1810, Corbet engaged two French frigates in a battle off Ile Bourbon. In close ship-to-ship combat, the French raked cannon fire across the quarterdeck, leaving dead and wounded men in their wake. Corbet was among the casualties, his legs crushed by a cannon ball. The *Africaine* ultimately surrendered, but not before two more hours of bitter fighting that left nearly fifty men aboard the ship dead or mortally wounded and a third of the crew injured. Despite the Surgeon's amputation of his shattered foot, Corbet died after six hours of agony.

In the aftermath of the surrender it was rumored that the seamen of the *Africaine* had thrown the battle to the French out of hatred for their Captain and, moreover, that they refused to attend to his wounds. Although Corbet was despised by his crew for his notoriously brutal system of discipline, such charges are almost certainly unfounded. The battle was hard fought against long odds and many seamen gave their life in defense of the *Africaine*. Even so, the posthumous reputation of Captain Corbet never fully recovered.[4]

6.1 Discipline and Punishment in the Royal Navy

The period from 1740 to 1820 was especially turbulent in British history. The country witnessed the difficult birth of an industrial proletariat and soon found itself facing both the stirrings of overt class conflict and rebellious Irish nationalism – developments that shook the boots of its ruling elites. Their collective confidence was further eroded by momentous geopolitical events. These years saw the War of American Independence (1775–83), the French Revolution (1789) and the Napoleonic conquest of most of the European continent. Britain was a prime target in all of these events, and its sense of vulnerability increased markedly. If the country had been defeated by a ragtag group of fledgling American colonists with French help, how on earth would it be able to withstand political threats, both domestic and international, flowing from the French Revolution and its aftermath?

This chapter assesses the effect of these grave challenges on the practice of discipline in the Royal Navy. It demonstrates that the Navy experienced a turn to much greater penal severity after 1789. Yet this reaction did nothing to increase the safety of her ships or the security of the country. The policy of punishment by summary flogging at the discretion of a ship's commander was part of a system of discipline meant to achieve and sustain social order (see Chapter 2). In the wake of the French Revolution, many in the British establishment came to agree with Corbet. The preponderance of the British elite believed that making more aggressive use of the lash would make the Navy's ships more secure. However, the greater penal severity enacted in the wake of revolution did not improve onboard security. On the contrary, it increased the risk of mutiny (see Chapter 4).

The irony is all the greater because the naval policies governing punishment had been intended to create a moderate disciplinary regime based on principles of general deterrence. For the most part, prior to the revolutionary crisis a loose system of social control prevailed allowing for much give and take between officers and seamen and the moderate use of flogging. But this social compact frayed with the coming of the French Revolution, as officers became more fearful of disorder, intolerant of petty deviance and, consequently, more punitive. What went wrong?

6.1.1   Why Did Commanders Excessively Flog Seamen?

Corporal punishment is one means by which authorities enforce discipline. Resort to punishment is costly, however, and the incentives to punish are not immediately self-evident. In inflicting flogging on the seamen under their command naval officers faced a dilemma. On the one hand, most officers were confident that flogging was necessary to maintain discipline, particularly if they felt their authority was threatened or that the ship's performance was compromised. On the other, the officers were aware that most deviance could not be detected, and that flogging could inspire seamen's antipathy. We know that excessive flogging was one of the chief grievances that motivated mutinies (see Chapter 4). Moreover, commanders had almost no way of ascertaining the effectiveness of their punishment. If indeed it did suppress disorder, what was the optimal level of severity or frequency needed to maintain shipboard order? Given these informational limits, it is not obvious that commanders would flog frequently or intensely.

People are most prone to sanction those who violate norms in the context of high social interdependence, as aboard naval ships.[5] Beyond mere professional norms, commanders had natural incentives to use punishment to enhance their security, the safety of a ship at sea and the ultimate success of their command. In the sample of ships that we assembled, flogging was both commonplace and normative. Captains who failed to flog seamen were exceptional (less than 10 percent of the commanders in our sample avoided flogging seamen in a given year).

We expect that flogging would be more frequent and severe aboard ships whose commanders perceived threats to their authority and control. Yet the severity and frequency of punishment did not simply vary across particular ships, as might be expected, but also over time. It turns out that punishment increased markedly during the

1790s – the rate of flogging appears to have trebled in the Navy – as "flogging Captains" like Pigot and Corbet became more common. What accounts for this dramatic increase? We think that the revolutionary age prompted naval officers to be increasingly insecure and distrustful of the lower classes, and that this led them to make greater use of the lash. Commanders became increasingly fearful of "mob rule," sedition and the radicalization of their crews, fears that were probably exaggerated but no less consequential.

Social-psychological research suggests that there are good reasons to expect that such sentiments resulted in a greater willingness to flog seamen. When confronted with threats to social order, people are more severe in assigning punishment, chiefly as a result of emotional states that justify retribution.[6] The desire for retribution increases punitiveness. Even quite general threats to social order, such as the notion that "crime is on the rise," increases the willingness to punish.[7]

Corbet, Pigot and other severe commanders did not regard themselves as brutal or tyrannical. People in authority usually perceive themselves as acting on a sound moral basis when they punish, even though their moral judgments may be emotionally malleable and their actions inconsistent. No matter how cruel or arbitrary their behavior may be, like Corbet they can readily justify the punishments that they mete out.[8]

The revolutionary age influenced the disposition of naval commanders to punish in excess because they were responding to threats to British social order that reached crisis levels in the years following the French Revolution. From that point forward, commanders were more likely to flog to demonstrate their authority, suppress disorderly behavior and deter potential troublemakers. Not all Captains exposed to this shifting climate became tyrants, of course. But the situation encouraged commanders like Pigot and Corbet to inflict a brutal penal regime on seamen they deemed disorderly or insubordinate. All in all, commanders inflicted greater punishments on crews on ships sailing after 1789.

The sense of threat was no mere paranoid fantasy; France and her allies indeed were Britain's mortal enemies, and the Jacobins actually did hope to foment insurrections in Great Britain and Ireland. Other threats were more proximate. At sea, collective insubordination – generally considered under the rubric of mutiny even when it was not prosecuted as such – was one of the most direct threats that officers confronted.[9] Those who had experienced collective insubordination may have been more prone to interpret all kinds of deviance as threatening. We expect that commanders who had faced collective insubordination flogged more severely.

We explore these propositions by reconsidering the history of naval discipline in the Georgian era. Rather than assessing the putative *effects* of punishment on the commission of crimes, as has been done in most research on social control, our data enable us to take quite another tack. We analyze the *punishments* that commanders inflicted in their efforts to secure social order, thereby shifting the focus from offenders to enforcers. We can analyze the prevalence of flogging based on a random sample of naval vessels drawn from a complete set of ship-years between 1740 and 1820.[10] Daily records allow us to assess the incidence and severity of flogging on these ships over the course of a given year and to identify the factors associated with flogging.

6.2   Deterrence and Naval Discipline

The traditional depiction of life at sea in general, and in the Royal Navy in particular, focuses on adversarial relations between officers and seamen and the routine violence that putatively backed the exercise of command.[11] Although traditional accounts dwell on the horrors of the lash, many contemporary historians argue that the Navy's reputation for brutal discipline and unchecked flogging has been overblown. These historians argue that flogging was not considered cruel or unusual by the standards of the day, that most commanders used punishment judiciously and that despotic commanders who punished excessively were exceptional.[12]

We view the issue as one of social order. For the maritime nation of Britain, the Navy's reliability was of paramount importance. The Navy provided the country's bulwark against the threat of continental invasion. Its dominant role in providing the island's security made it the most important arm of the British state as well as the kingdom's largest employer. The Navy required large crews that had diverse skills, experience, conditions of recruitment, origins and ethnicity. In the dangerous world of warfare at sea, obedience to authority was a vital matter, and seamen needed to be motivated to perform their duties in sailing, operating and fighting the ship. Fear of the lash was far from the only inducement, of course; the Navy provided seamen with pay, victuals, alcoholic drink and opportunities for modest enrichment through the taking of prizes. Seamen had their own inducements flowing from an occupational culture that emphasized their skill and responsibility.[13]

The Navy had no coherent disciplinary policy in the modern bureaucratic sense. Rather, it adopted a set of loose conventions concerning obedience and punishment that were anchored by a partial and ambiguous legal code.[14] Nevertheless, both penal practice and naval law – the Articles of War – reflected eighteenth-century conceptions about the utility of punishment. The principle of general deterrence was taken as axiomatic by the ruling classes.[15]

The British elites regarded flogging as appropriate and practical; a punishment that was severe but short of lethal.[16] Prevailing views held that offenders should be dealt with harshly, even if few would be caught and even fewer punished because those few who were publicly flogged would serve as examples for the many. Naval officers hoped that a general deterrence strategy based on summary flogging would generate "the immediate, unhesitating, unquestioning reaction to orders – in one word: Obedience."[17]

The Articles of War and printed instructions to commanders provided the basis of criminal justice in the Georgian Navy, but they were unsystematic as a criminal code.[18] Although informed by the spirit of common law, the Articles served a military function and superseded civilian law, instructing that the law must defer "to the laws and customs in such cases used at sea."[19] They dealt with a variety of moral offenses, crimes against the Crown and the King's officers, and naval infractions. Reflecting legislative confidence in the principle of general deterrence, the Georgian-era Articles and related regulations were harsher than their predecessors because they were more comprehensive and specified flogging for many offenses. Commanders enjoyed nearly unlimited rights to inflict summary punishment by flogging seamen. The only substantive restriction was that commanders could only inflict flogging for offenses specified in the Articles; however, some of these were so broadly worded as to allow the punishment of nearly any kind of behavior.

The practice of flogging exemplified the logic of general deterrence. The public flogging ritual was designed to impress and overawe so that the seaman would see that the tremendous weight of authority would crush him if he should defy it.[20] In 1803 a Surgeon's Mate vividly described the practice of flogging:

> The carpenters are ordered to "rig the gratings," that is, to fasten two gratings to the gangways, in such a manner that the culprit stands upon one, to which his feet are fastened, and leans forward against the other, to which his hands are secured. The officers appear in their cocked-hats and side-arms, and the marines are "under arms," the ship's company is standing on the opposite side of the deck. Near the gratings the delinquent stands, and close to him the Master-at-Arms, with his sword drawn ... The arrangements being made, the First Lieutenant reports to the Captain, who usually comes upon the deck forthwith. The Captain sometimes addresses the crew, together with the culprit, and concludes by ordering him to "strip." When he has stripped the Captain says, "Seize him up," and he is instantly fastened to the gratings. An article of war, relative to the punishment, is then read by the Captain, who concludes by ordering the Boatswain's Mate to "give him a dozen." While the article of war is being read, the officers, including the midshipmen, stand uncovered [hats off]. The punisher, who is usually a powerful man, applies the cat strongly, and apparently with all his strength. It would appear that in some ships a Serjeant of Marines was employed to reckon the lashes, and regulate the time of infliction, by means of a sandglass of a quarter of a minute. At the conclusion of the dozen, another Boatswain's Mate is called, for the purpose of inflicting an equal number, and so on until the Captain suspends punishment.[21]

The impression made by such punishments could last a lifetime. Samuel Leech, who had been a serving-boy on the frigate *Macedonian* in 1811, recalled how, shortly after joining the ship, he witnessed a man receiving a severe flogging for drunkenness: "His flesh creeps ... the sufferer groans; lash follows lash ... Four dozen strokes have cut up his flesh and robbed him of all self-respect; there he hangs, a pitied, self-despised, bleeding wretch ... and the hands, 'piped down' by the boatswain, sullenly return to their duties."[22]

Sir Robert Steele, a distinguished Marine officer, witnessed many punishments in the Navy. He acknowledged the powerful example that floggings made, but was revolted by the potential abuse of power that flogging at will invited: "A Commander of a man-of-war can flog any man under his pennon [flag], without even the mockery of a trial. I never think of this without my blood running alternately hot and cold within me."[23]

Indeed, at least while the ship was at sea, naval commanders had nearly "absolute authority" over seamen. A standard manual called the Captain "like a King at Sea" and made clear that his authority depended on rules of discipline and subordination that had to be upheld by the threat of punishment.[24] In upholding shipboard order, the stakes for naval commanders were undeniably high. Naval officers saw themselves as in greater danger than their counterparts in the Army because they were frequently isolated at sea. Disorder had to be quashed before it grew to imperil a Captain or his command.[25] The well-known fate of commanders like Bligh who were turned out of their ships or, worse yet, Pigot, who lost his life, loomed large. The prospect of losing control was appalling, and it put not only a commander's life but the entire Navy's moral universe in peril.[26]

Despite the brutality of public flogging, the actual intent of the Articles was to moderate punishment. For rationalizing early modern governments, flogging was an attractive alternative to more traditional punishments such as gagging, branding, confinement in the stocks, keel-hauling and so forth. It could be standardized and calibrated to particular offenses by specifying the number of lashes; "a rough and ready and swift justice aimed at fitting the crime."[27] In fact, the penal reforms associated with the Articles and related instructions did succeed in reducing irregular forms of seagoing punishment, and they established conventions governing the size and weight of the cat-o'-nine tails used in flogging. Regulations that sought to limit punishments to no more than a dozen lashes per offense were routinely flouted, however. Even so, by insisting that flogging be carried out in routine ways and be reported in ships' logs, the Navy took important steps toward more a regular system of discipline.[28]

The reforms were intended to make punishment more uniform and reliable, but they also enhanced the capacity of Captains to punish at will. Although commanders had the power to refer offenders to naval courts-martial (which alone could impose the death penalty), public flogging on the decks of warships was the principal means to deter deviance and disobedience. "Starting" – delivering blows from knotted ropes or canes – could be spontaneously and casually applied.

In practice, moreover, many commanders who dealt with sea-men accused of an offense held informal hearings that would allow the accused to respond to the charges and call witnesses. Robert Wilson, a Petty Officer on the *Unite* from 1805 to 1809, recalled that the men accused of crimes were "called before the Captain one by one to make their defence; they are allowed a fair trial. If any officer speaks in their favour, they are acquitted or their punishment is mitigated; if they can clear themselves, well and good. In short, it is like a court of judicature."[29]

Whatever attractions it had to officers who believed in its deter-rent power, there were practical limits to flogging in addition to the rarely enforced formal regulations. First, commanders were ultimately accountable to the Admiralty and could face potentially ruinous inqui-ries into alleged brutality. Second, punishment was costly: severe flog-gings could leave seamen injured or debilitated, putting them on the sick-list and removing them from the ship's labor supply. Commanders and seamen alike understood that Captains who flogged excessively or too often risked their professional reputations and their shipboard legitimacy. As we have seen, those who punished excessively could provoke resistance, even mutiny.

Since Captains were entrusted with broad powers to inflict summary punishment, it was inevitable that they occasionally strayed into brutality. The great weakness of the Navy's disciplinary regime was that tyrannical officers like Pigot and Corbet had a virtual license to act on their prejudices and emotions. Lacking effective constraints on the exercise of their discretion, the insecurities of naval officers were largely unchecked while at sea.[30] Once the officer corps felt itself to be imper-iled by radical political change, the opportunity for commanders to inflict more frequent and severe punishment was already in place.

6.3 The Revolutionary Crisis and Naval Punishment

Despite the flaws in the Navy's disciplinary regime, for several decades after 1740 it seems to have worked tolerably well. Naval reformers' demands to rationalize punishment by normalizing flogging and deferring to the discretion of commanders resulted in a moderately severe disciplin-ary regime. Naval historians have noted that there was a shift in penal practices in the Napoleonic era, however. Discipline became tighter, tolerance for rowdiness and petty disorder declined and flogging became more common and more severe.[31] This transformation has been explained variously by intensifying class conflict between officers and seamen,[32] by the rapid expansion of the officer corps[33] and by the strains placed on the Navy by decades of wartime mobilization.[34]

These are all credible explanations. On the basis of new evidence, however, we can show that this shift resulted partly from a hitherto ignored factor: the coming of the revolutionary era. The fear of insurrection infected the political culture of Britain during the Age of Revolution. This fear also affected the sentiments of naval officers, altering shipboard social relations. There was a profound increase in tensions between officers and men and, as a result, more frequent and severe floggings.

The systematic data we collected shed new light on the issue. The incidence of flogging aboard ships increased sharply from the 1790s onward. Through the years 1740 through 1789, the average annual rate of punishment per member of a ship's company by number of lashes in our sample was only 1.34. From 1790 to 1820, flogging was much more common, rising to an annual rate of 4.35 lashes per seaman. Flogging was not only more frequent, it also was more severe. From 1740 to 1789, the average flogging consisted of 13.6 lashes – somewhat above the official norm of 12. From 1790 to 1820, however, the average flogging rose to 19.5 lashes – a 70 percent increase in severity.

Can the revolutionary crisis account for such a dramatic increase in corporal punishment aboard His Majesty's ships? The profound sense of crisis following the dawn of the Age of Revolution in Britain cannot be underestimated. The revolutionary events begun in France rocked all of Europe. The optimism and hopes for constitutional reform that initially led many Britons to sympathize with the revolution were soon replaced by fear and dismay as France radicalized. Public opinion was rent between the supporters of Tom Paine, who sympathized with France, and Edmund Burke's skepticism of the revolution. Meanwhile, in the midst of an agonizing constitutional crisis, France was convulsed by factionalism, royalist rebellions and Jacobin militancy.[35]

Even as Burke's pessimism gained ground, the matter soon became a life or death struggle for the British monarchy. Elite opinion swung decisively against the revolution from 1792 onward. The year of

1793 began with the execution of Louis XVI, an act that horrified the aristocracy as well as the British public. The French government devolved into dictatorship and the Reign of Terror, as thousands of noblemen, royalists and suspected enemies of the new state were arrested and gruesomely executed. French revolutionary armies turned back invaders and overran neighboring territories. The leaders of the revolution assailed the monarchies of Europe. In February, France declared war on Great Britain. This war was something new, an ideological struggle in which French goals were not limited to a conventional contest of arms but rather the "liberation" of "despotic" societies through invasion and support for domestic insurrections.[36]

In making the case to Parliament for financing a major war effort against the revolution, Prime Minister William Pitt decried France's "presumptuous attempts to interfere in the government of this country and to arm our subjects against ourselves; to vilify a monarch, the object of our gratitude, reverence, and affection," warning that, "We are at war with those who would destroy the whole fabric of our Constitution."[37] So grave was the sense of threat that, in the 1790s, Pitt was able to convince the British elite to impose the nation's first income tax on itself.

The government passed a series of repressive measures to throttle internal sedition and suppress insurrection. Even mild criticism of the monarchy or the government could lead to arrest. Facing what it perceived as an existential threat, Britain's leaders believed that the kingdom's democratic reformers, "Jacobin" radicals and Irish nationalists were all, to varying degrees, the inspired allies of France. Domestic pressures and civil unrest reinforced this impression. In addition to the severe economic strains of fighting a global war on land and sea against republican France and her satellites, the situation at home became highly unsettled. The late 1790s witnessed a variety of civil disturbances by radical reformers, growing labor unrest, desperate Irish rebellions backed by the French and the mass mutinies at Spithead and the Nore in 1797.[38]

Whereas reactionaries were quick to blame political discontent and social conflict on France and her agents, the evidence for large-scale collaboration is scant. Aside from Ireland's anti-colonial rebellions, the linkages between political dissent and domestic unrest and French Jacobinism were tenuous.[39] Despite this, the fear of social revolution and political radicalism among the British elites was real. Although the

Crown's spontaneous popular support should have been consoling, the government and leading public figures nevertheless had "grave concerns about the basic loyalty of the British population."[40] The ruling classes were obsessed with the idea that popular opposition of any kind was illegitimate, opening the door to Jacobinism and revolution.[41] These fears were certainly out of proportion to the actual threat of radical insurrection in Britain (at least outside of Ireland) but they nevertheless inspired demands for repression and order.

Once popular disorder was a tolerable feature of British life, but now the government treated it as a mortal threat. The alarmism surrounding the putative radical menace became manifest in a host of repressive laws, a muzzling of the press and, in practice, greater penal severity. Whereas the British elite once regarded rowdiness as a safety valve and saw the popular classes as posing little threat, this confidence had been shattered by the events of the French Revolution.[42] The fear that the Revolution had changed the world in adverse ways endured beyond the 1790s. In 1803–5 Britain experienced another invasion scare as Napoleon assembled forces on France's northern coast. Even as the egalitarianism of the Revolution ebbed away under Napoleon, his France remained a dire military and political threat.[43]

The same reactionary shift in elite attitudes occurred at sea. No change in laws governing the conduct of seamen aboard ships after 1789 accounts for greater resort to the lash. Nonetheless, the Navy was not spared the general spirit of reaction and repression that convulsed the rest of British society. Naval families shared the same anxieties as other well-off Britons. The French Revolution stirred fears of Jacobinism in the fleets and calls for tighter discipline by the officer caste.[44] Sea officers were strongly influenced by the Georgian establishment's ideals of hierarchy, deference and paternalism. The upper ranks of officers were drawn heavily from the aristocracy and landed gentry, but the naval career was also open to talented members of the middle classes. Priding themselves on loyalty to the Crown, they were no more sympathetic to democratic ideas than their upper-class peers.[45] Whatever the differences in their social backgrounds, officers as a whole feared the radicalization of seamen and were shocked by mutinies and insurrections.

Admiral Keith, who assumed control of the North Sea Fleet in the wake of the Nore mutiny, expressed the conventional wisdom when he attributed the great mutinies to "a dangerous spirit of republicanism, springing directly from the principles and examples of the French Revolution."[46] The brutal mutinies aboard the *Hermione* in 1797 and the *Danae* in 1800 were unusual cases in that political radicals were among the ringleaders, but even so they further shook confidence among officers.[47] Many were convinced that Jacobinism and "mob rule" could only be kept in check by tightening discipline and punishing any manifestations of disorder or disrespect.

Admiral Saint Vincent, commander of the Mediterranean Fleet in the late 1790s and of the Channel Fleet in 1800–1, was a prominent exponent of this view. In the name of "traditional values" and stern discipline, he expected strictness and frequent punishment by subordinate commanders.[48] In turning to flogging as a way to maintain control, such officers had broad support in English public opinion where many voices called for "unrestrained severity" to undo the supposed decay of naval discipline.[49] In this overheated context, the power to inflict summary punishment at a commander's discretion created conditions that made penal severity more likely. Brutal officers like Corbet could claim that the good order and combat readiness of the Navy depended on their unrestricted ability to inflict the lash.

6.3.1   Evidence for Changing Penal Severity

Qualitative evidence that shows the offenses that were punished prior to 1789 and after sheds further light on this greater penal severity. Figure 6.1 represents the data we coded from hundreds of logbooks suggesting that an increase in criminality or deviance cannot fully explain increased flogging; instead, it seems to indicate the officers' insecurity and growing distance from, and distrust of, seamen.

The data indicate that the share of floggings for serious violations – such as assault, theft, desertion and the sale of alcohol and other contraband – given by commanders during these two periods did not substantially differ. In the first period, punishment appears to have been focused more on offenses deleterious to the *performance* of the vessel, such as neglect of duty and mutiny (which rather broadly included individual defiance of command). In the second phase, however, commanders gave greater attention to seamen's *morality*, placing greater emphasis on drunkenness,

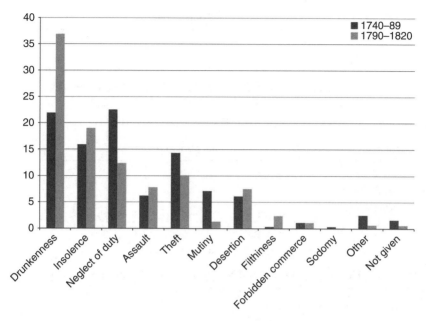

Figure 6.1 Reasons given by commanders for flogging by primary offense, 1740–89 and 1790–1820, by percentage
Source: Underwood et al. 2018.

insolence and filthiness (including "filthy" behavior and personal uncleanliness). A similar trend has been observed in court-martial prosecutions during this era.[50] Particularly noteworthy is the startling increase in the proportion of floggings given for drunkenness, which nearly doubled after 1789.

Moreover, the increase in penal severity that we have identified at the end of the eighteenth and early nineteenth centuries is not simply the result of a long-term secular increase in punishment. Prior to the revolutionary era, flogging seems to have increased modestly during wartime, but our data do not suggest a strong upward trend. Figure 6.2, which plots the observed punishment in the ships analyzed for this study over time, illustrates that there is no marked trend toward harsher punishment observed until after the mid-1790s, when it increases sharply.

Altogether, the data suggest that the increase in the frequency and severity of flogging after 1789 may have reflected less a change in the conduct of seamen than in the disposition of officers toward seamen. If

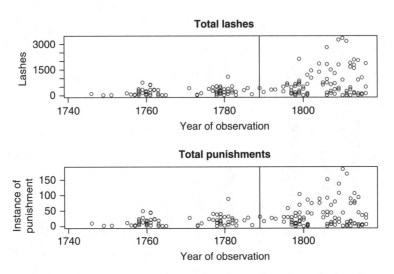

Figure 6.2 Floggings given on Royal Navy ships by total number of lashes given and total instances of punishment, 1740–1820
Source: Underwood et al. 2018.

the officers of the mid-century Georgian Navy had a live-and-let-live attitude toward the lower deck, the willingness to overlook minor forms of deviance is less evident in their counterparts at the end of the century.[51] As the amount of alcohol given to seamen did not change between the two periods, what does appear to have changed was commanders' tolerance of alcohol's potential to inspire rowdiness and disorder.[52]

Feeling themselves under threat, officers seem to have believed that morality – not just behavior per se – had to be upheld to preserve men's fighting spirit and discourage rebellion. A growing proportion of officers embraced Evangelicalism, becoming more serious about holding worship services aboard ships and enforcing the moral conduct of their men. Despite misgivings about the potential cruelty of flogging, Evangelical officers believed that it could only be relaxed once lower-deck morality improved. With the French Revolution in mind, many agreed with Captain (later Admiral) John Duckworth that seamen were worsening and that restoring good order called for more Bibles and more floggings.[53]

Robert Corbet was far from alone in believing that strict discipline and penal severity led to victories. As senior officers imposed a stricter regime, prosecutions mounted and harsher penalties for moral offenses were imposed at the end of the eighteenth century. Following his great victory over Napoleon's fleet at the Nile, Admiral Nelson opined that superior discipline gave the British Navy its military edge; this in contrast to the "riotous behavior of the lawless Frenchman."[54] Many agreed that British naval success owed to the stringent discipline of the Navy.[55]

Since seamen were entitled to a daily ration of strong rum or other alcoholic drink, drunkenness had always been commonplace aboard ships (including among the officers), as it was generally in British society.[56] Before 1789, it was usually punished only if it resulted in the neglect of duty. The tolerant attitude toward the lower deck that characterized the officers of the mid-century Georgian Navy appears to have been replaced with a new sternness at the end of the century, however. Increasing punishment for relatively trivial offenses further suggests that there was growing social distance between officers and men.[57]

Perhaps the seamen of the Royal Navy were becoming more insubordinate. The number of mutinies did increase after 1789. Bear in mind, however, that the wartime population of seamen in the Navy more than doubled between the 1740s and the 1810s, as did the number of battleships and cruisers in service, without a proportionate increase in the rate of mutiny.[58] Even so, the number of reported and prosecuted incidences of mutiny did increase in the 1790s, perhaps because officers became more scrupulous in referring insubordination to courts-martial, or because there was a change in the baseline rate of rebelliousness among seamen as a result of increasing grievances (see Chapter 4). In any event, it is probable that officers took note of large-scale insurrections such as the mutinies of 1797 and terrifying incidents like those aboard the *Hermione* or the *Marie Antoinette*, leading the impression that rebellion was on the rise regardless of its true rate. All this would have reinforced the idea that this was an age of crisis, social conflict and danger.

Sociologists have long argued that when a society is confronted by a challenge to its settled patterns of authority or moral boundaries, it will more aggressively prosecute perceived deviance.[59] In the Age of Revolution, the increasing tendency to punish seamen for drunkenness and similar affronts may be indicative of this kind of social crisis. Drunkenness may have always been a convenient pretext for inflicting the lash, as seaman Jacob Nagle recalled in his memoirs.[60] After 1789, however, the tolerance of the rowdiness that commanders associated with alcohol appears to have changed.

Beginning in 1806, Admiralty officials began to appreciate that punishment had become excessive and dangerous. They introduced a series of piecemeal regulations to rein in excessive flogging and better supervise officers. Enforcement was poor and historians argue that they did little to reduce flogging. The changes enacted indicate that the Admiralty was aware that summary punishment did not have its intended effects, and that excessive flogging was counterproductive.[61]

6.3.2 Testing the Threat Argument

The descriptive data on the frequency and severity of flogging over time and the shift in the offenses punished by commanders aboard ships after 1789 provide strong support for our proposition that perceived threats increased penal severity in the Royal Navy. Does the pattern hold given other possible causes of flogging?

Flogging could be associated with several factors other than threat that could have increased tensions or made it harder to manage the crews of naval ships. To assess these possibilities, we conducted a multivariate analysis of flogging. We analyzed the association between different factors and two measures of punishment, the total number of floggings (as a measure of frequency) in a given year on a given ship and the total number of lashes inflicted (as a measure of severity).[62] Appendix D provides details on our data and modeling strategy.

Several alternative explanations were considered. Prudent Captains should be attentive to local conditions and social relations aboard their own ships, rather than on global factors such as revolutionary conflict. If they believed that they had a "happy ship" made up of satisfied seamen, commanders could afford to be more magnanimous. Commanders might rely more heavily on flogging if they felt that the crew was restive, or when it faced unusual hardships – such as the burdens of long periods of wartime mobilization, too many foreigners and other grievances.

Discipline may have been more severe during wartime, when the demands for discipline and performance likely were greater. Perhaps long periods of warfare may have reinforced hierarchical power and created a greater propensity to punish.[63]

Commanders may have regarded native seamen as more coop-erative and loyal than foreigners. Co-ethnicity has been found to be an important source of obedience and military cohesion. Commanders may have felt more secure with crews that were predominantly British.[64] Greater social heterogeneity could increase the recourse to punishment because it undercuts a group's capacity for self-regulation. We have already seen how distrust for "foreigners" – which in the British mind included the Irish – was widespread among naval officers, who commonly regarded Irishmen and other foreigners as sources of opposition and disorder. Crews that were more ethnically diverse might have been less well integrated and more severely punished by commanders.

We have seen that grievances are the prime drivers of mutiny (Chapter 4). Such grievances include dissatisfaction with wages, as well as resentment against having been impressed, and foreign deployments. Foreign deployment was associated with longer voyages, greater inci-dence of illness and inferior rations. Collective hardships like these might have generated grievances among seamen that posed a challenge to command. Under these pressures, commanders may have been inclined to increase flogging.

In our analysis, we included measures relating to all of these explanations. Our findings suggest that the tendency to punish did not distinguish between strategies of infrequent but severe punishment, or frequent and less severe punishment. Consequently, most of the same factors associated with total lashes are also associated with the total number of floggings. The results indicate that the disposition to punish was affected by perceived threats to political authority and social control.

The analysis supports our argument about how global threats to social order posed by the French Revolution affected punishment. Even in the presence of other factors, the post-1789 period is positively and significantly associated with both measures of punishment. This rein-forces our confidence that Captains punished more frequently and severely in the revolutionary era than previously.[65]

Collective insubordination was also associated with the fre-quency and severity of flogging. Even if it fell short of full-fledged mutiny, collective insubordination is the greatest challenge to authority, and it was strictly forbidden under the Articles. Commanders made more profligate use of flogging when they experienced threats to their authority. Not only did they punish rebellious seamen individually, but they punished their crews more harshly when they experienced challenges to their authority.

The alternative explanations for penal severity have mixed results. As expected, the size of a ship's company indeed was associated with greater punishment – all other things equal, larger crews provide more opportunities for both deviance and punishment. We do not find that either wartime pressures or enhanced state power during war (as measured by years at war) affect the rate of flogging. Nor are ethnicity and seamen's social ties significant. Likewise, other factors that may have contributed to the difficulty of command (wage depreciation, impressments, etc.) were not responsible for increased flogging. Other contextual factors besides the Age of Revolution did matter, however. Captains may have perceived the need to punish seamen who were facing conditions that isolated them and made them less compliant. This may be why punishment increased when ships were in foreign waters.

To probe the strength of our findings, we also wanted to explore whether the effect of the French Revolution on punishment is limited temporally.[66] Perhaps the sense of threat subsided as the events of the most radical period of the French Revolution receded. In fact, we do find that the feeling of collective insecurity apparently attenuated over time. Figures 6.3 and 6.4 display estimates of the effect of time on expected number of punishments and expected lashes.[67]

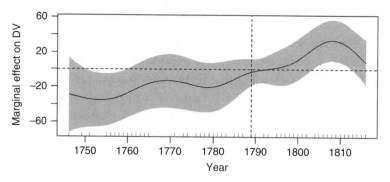

Figure 6.3 Estimated effect of time on expected number of punishments by flogging, 1740–1820

Source: Underwood et al. 2018. Note: DV = dependent variable.

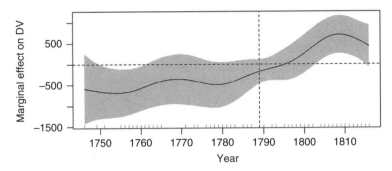

Figure 6.4 Estimated effect of time on expected number of lashes inflicted in punishments, 1740–1820
Source: Underwood et al. 2018. Note: DV = dependent variable.

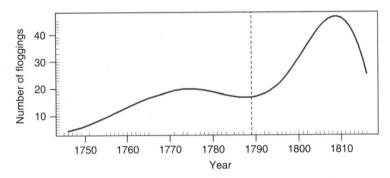

Figure 6.5 B-spline average of observed number of punishments by flogging, 1740–1820
Source: Underwood et al. 2018.

As can be seen in both figures, the pre-1789 period of our data contains a gradual downward trend in frequency and severity of punishment, holding all other determinants constant. Shortly following 1789, the marginal effect of time on the frequency and severity becomes positive, however – indicating a shift toward increasing frequency and severity of flogging over time. As seen in Figure 6.5, not until 1809 does the frequency and severity of flogging begin to fall.[68]

Further evidence in support of our explanation is provided by Figure 6.6, which shows the average number of floggings and average lashes per seaman in our sample over time.[69] The figure shows a clear increase in the frequency and severity of punishment following 1789.

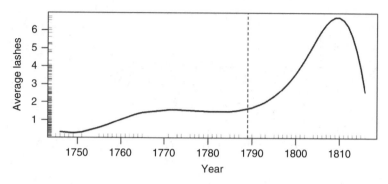

Figure 6.6 B-spline average of observed number of lashes in punishments by flogging, 1740–1820
Source: Underwood et al. 2018.

The figure also indicates that, following a peak near 1809, the frequency and severity of flogging began to decrease.

The analyses of the punishment presented here are consistent with the argument that commanders became increasingly punitive in response to the threat posed by the revolutionary age. The upward trend in punishment that is conspicuous from the 1790s onward reaches an inflexion point around 1809, both in terms of the frequency and severity of punishment. As the revolutionary crisis receded, the sense of threat among officers also seems to have ebbed. Napoleon's goals had become less revolutionary, and there was newfound confidence that France and her allies would be unable to repeat an invasion of Ireland (as it attempted in 1798), or invade England following the decisive defeat of the Napoleonic navies at Trafalgar in 1805. Although the observed level of punishment after 1810 is still greater than it was before 1789, a downward trend is conspicuous. The attenuation over time is consistent with our argument about the emotional dynamics driving punishment – as a threat recedes, the fear and anger that justify harshness also subside.

6.4   Punishment, Governance and Social Order

Herman Melville set *Billy Budd*, his parable of law and punishment in the Royal Navy, in the late 1790s. In the wake of the mass mutinies at Spithead and the Nore, relations have grown tense on the fictional warship HMS *Bellipotent*. Billy Budd, an impressed seaman of unsurpassed skill, is despised by Clegg, a Petty Officer, who plots the innocent man's downfall by accusing him of subversion. Called before Captain Vere to answer Clegg's charges, Budd, a severe stutterer, cannot defend himself. Goaded by his antagonist, Budd strikes out and Clegg falls backward, hitting his head and dying instantly.

With the shadow of the Nore mutiny looming over him, Vere is greatly alarmed by the incident. Readily acknowledging that Budd was innocent of stirring up mutiny, Vere nevertheless insists that Budd, has, in fact, become a mutineer by striking a killing blow against a superior officer. Against standard naval practice, Vere hastily organizes an improvised, "drumhead" court-martial aboard the ship because he is convinced that unless the popular sailor is swiftly punished, insurrection is imminent, as seamen will follow Budd's example and strike out against the officers of the ship.[70]

During the trial that follows, the officers of the jury resist convicting Budd in light of the irregularity of the proceedings, his innocence of the original charges and Clegg's obvious instigation. Nevertheless, Vere insists that they must destroy Budd as swiftly as possible or risk their own destruction. Thoughts of mercy must be put aside; the law that empowers them must prevail and be pitiless:

> How can we adjudge to summary and shameful death a fellow-creature innocent before God, and whom we feel to be so? ... When war is declared are we the commissioned fighters previously consulted? We fight at command. If our judgements approve the war, that is but coincidence. So in other particulars. So now. For suppose condemnation to follow these present proceedings. Would it be so much we ourselves that would condemn as it would be martial law operating through us? For that law and the rigour of it, we are not responsible. Our avowed responsibility is in this: That however pitilessly that law may operate, we nevertheless adhere to it and administer it.

Reluctantly, the jury condemns Budd. The next day, as Budd is about to be hanged before the assembled company of the *Bellipotent*, the outraged seamen are on the verge of mutiny. But as the noose is placed around his neck, innocent Billy shouts out "God bless Captain Vere" and leaps into the void. By Budd's sacrifice and words of benediction, authority is restored and the seamen return to duty.[71]

Melville set his tragedy at the close of the eighteenth century when British elites asserted that harsh forms of summary punishment were a necessary bulwark against revolution and disorder. Dramatic license allowed him to have Vere try and convict Budd in an irregular court-martial. We have shown, however, that the real evidence of increasing penal severity is not to be found in hangings but rather in the more routine and less formal domain of flogging aboard warships.

Early in the eighteenth century, naval authorities wanted to rationalize social control by normalizing flogging as a form of deterrent punishment placed in the hands of commanders who were permitted to flog at their own discretion. In most instances, summary flogging was the preferred alternative to the harsher punishments that could result from the judicial process. Although many offenses were punishable by hanging under the Articles, flogging was preferred at sea. Even capital offenses, such as desertion, insubordination, striking superiors and so on, were usually handled through summary punishment by flogging.[72] For example, after suppressing a potentially dangerous mutiny on the *Orion* in 1794, Captain Duckworth elected to deal with the matter himself and spared the ringleaders referral to a court-martial. Midshipman William Parker recorded in his diary,

> most of the ship's company got so drunk that they mutinisied, they said they would have liberty to go ashore; they released the prisoners out of irons; every officer of the ship was sent for; the Captain almost broke his heart about it; seven of the ringleaders were seized by the officers and twenty other men; they were put in irons, and the next morning when they were told of their night's proceedings they wept like children. The twenty were punished with 12 lashes each, and the seven were kept in irons and would have been tried by Court-Martial; but Captain Duckworth had them before him today and said that he was of a forgiving nature he gave them into the hands of the ship's company, that he restored to them with love for the services they had done him.[73]

The kind of forbearance shown by Duckworth was partly because commanders were loath to send men before courts-martial that might inflict fatal punishments and partly because believed they could tell the difference between misguided seamen and those who were true threats to their authority. However, part of the explanation is simply that convening courts-martial and serving on them were costly nuisances.[74] We would be on good ground to imagine that on Melville's *Bellipotent* had Budd's blow not unintentionally killed Clegg, it is very likely that Captain Vere would have had him soundly flogged and left the matter at that.

6.5 Social Control between Crisis and Rebellion

In the Royal Navy, commanding officers could inflict flogging at will. The Articles of War that bound them gave them much discretion in the area of discipline but not in others. As the case of the *Panther* discussed in Chapter 2 suggests, officers could get away with a lot, but not with cowardice or corruption. The way in which the officers were drummed out and the mutineers exonerated in the *Panther* case is indicative of that. One the reasons why the Articles were such a poor penal code in the domain of discipline is that their real focus was on the conduct of officers, not seamen. The rules concerning seamen were poorly drawn, requiring much discretion by officers on the scene and by courts-martial.[75]

The original data we collected from a randomly selected sample of vessels sheds new light on the role of discretion in debates surrounding discipline and punishment in the Georgian-era Navy. We have shown that commanders generally punished moderately, chiefly in order to enhance the performance of the ship's company and to ensure the security of their authority. These patterns are broadly consistent with a traditional deterrence framework predicated on the maintenance of social control.[76]

The incidence and severity of flogging increased sharply with contextual changes that threatened the British ruling classes. Increased penal severity departed from the preceding disciplinary regime that emphasized naval performance in favor of practices that stressed morality and subordination. Within customary limits, flogging was not regarded as cruel or unusual punishment in its time. In civilian merchant ships too, the law gave ships' masters the right to flog or beat seamen "in a reasonable manner" for "disobedience and disorderly conduct."[77]

Seamen evaluated the justice of punishment in terms of its predictability and proportion, accepting "due punishment" and "moderate correction" as an inevitable element of seagoing life.[78] It is telling that the seamen of the Nore did not include the abolition of flogging among their radical demands, but merely its reform (see Chapter 5). Seamen accepted that moderate, discriminating corporal punishment was part of the good governance of ships.

Yet our analysis suggests that the implicit compact between seamen and officers that undergirds discipline was altered by the Age of Revolution. Behaviors once largely tolerated in an informal compact between seamen and their officers became subject to harsher and more oppressive treatment after 1789, as the disposition toward punishment changed among members of the officer class. That the incidence and severity of punishment increased so sharply in the wake of revolution suggests that the prejudices and insecurities of naval officers were not kept in check by the Navy's policies.

The implications of our findings travel well beyond the confines of the Royal Navy. Threats to an established order can have profound consequences for social control. During periods of political crisis, the punitive measures taken to address perceived threats are frequently disproportionate to the scale of those threats. Societies facing generalized threats to social order impose more severe criminal and penal legislation and enforce greater penal severity in the courtroom.[79] Whereas the triggering events that give rise to a sense of threat may be ephemeral, the resulting attitudinal changes can influence discourses and practices for some time afterward. In the penal domain, beliefs justifying severity in maintaining security and inflicting punishment may become normative among enforcers, posing a substantial challenge to good government.

Not until the end of the Napoleonic era did flogging fall out of favor in the Royal Navy, but figures like Corbet had already brought it into public disrepute. Although it took decades for the campaign against flogging to result in its abolition, mutinies like those on the *Nereide* and the *Hermione* brought home the horror of the lash. In Chapter 7 we examine the consequences of mutiny beyond punishment and fear of disorder. Under what conditions did mutinies succeed in winning the redress of grievances? How did mutiny and insurrection influence reforms in the governance of the Navy and improve the welfare of seamen?

Notes

1. For a vivid description of the rituals surrounding the court-martial, see Byrn 1989, p. 56.
2. TNA: PRO ADM 1/5391 and ship's Captain's log, TNA: PRO, ADM 51/1941.
3. Claver 1954, p. 134; see also Malcomson 2016, pp. 198–204.
4. On Corbet's career and reputation, see Jones 1832; Laughton 2008; and Lavery 1998, pp. 401–8.
5. See Horne 2009 on the rewards of punishment.
6. See, e.g., studies by Goldberg, Lerner and Tetlock 1999; Lerner, Goldberg and Tetlock 1998; Rucker et al. 2004; and Tetlock 2002.
7. Rucker et al. 2004.
8. Haidt and Kesebir 2010.
9. On understandings of mutiny among naval officers, see Gilbert 1983 and Rodger 1982, 1986.
10. On the selection of the control sample for the case-control analysis, see Appendix A.
11. Claver 1954; Frykman 2009, 2010; Neale 1985; Rediker 1987.
12. Byrn 1989; Eder 2004; Rodger 1986.
13. On the incentives underlying social order, see Chapter 2.
14. Rodger 1986.
15. Corporal punishment's "undisputed function" in British society was deterrence; Eder 2004, p. 5; also see Byrn 1989, p. 55.
16. "From the elite point of view, whipping constituted a happy compromise between excessive leniency and the overreaction of the death penalty" (McLynn 1991, p. 282). See also King 2000 and Sharpe 1999.
17. Claver 1954, p. 1.
18. The Articles were a "haphazard assembly of regulations and admonitions, with a good deal of duplication and little order" (Rodger 1982, p. 8).
19. Rodger 1982, p. 12. Note that it was not only in the Navy that corporal punishment was used to gain obedience. Flogging and caning were widespread practices in British society and even upper-class children learned to fear the lash as part of their education.
20. See Foucault 1977 on "old regime" punishment.
21. Colburn 1844.
22. Leech 1847, p. 50.
23. Steele 1840, p. 205.
24. Rediker 1987, p. 208.
25. As Gilbert 1980, pp. 118–19, observes of naval commanders, "At sea, there was no place to turn for help. As a result, the naval justice system tried to nip disorder in the bud and punish its manifestations with rigor."
26. "First, there was the disorder of nature, exacerbated at sea by storms; second there was the disorder of men who were no longer working together to counteract and defeat the worst chaos of nature" (Gilbert 1980, p. 115).
27. Pope 1981, p. 215; see also Garland 1990, p. 241.
28. Eder 2004, pp. 66–7; see also Malcomson 2016 and Rodger 1986.

29. Lavery 2010, p. 277.
30. As discussed in Chapter 2, commanders' behavior could be monitored by subordinate officers (Masters, Lieutenants) who were also charged with maintaining logbooks. We found that Masters' logs were invaluable sources for confirming or correcting the punishments that Captains reported. In principle, such surveillance should have acted as an indirect check on commanders' discretionary powers, but it is impossible to say whether it did.
31. Byrn 1989; Gill 1913; Lavery 2010; Malcomson 2016.
32. Frykman 2009; Neale 1985.
33. Lavery 2010; Pope 1981.
34. Rodger 1986, 2004.
35. On British politics during the Age of Revolution, see Cookson 1997; Hobsbawm 1962; Jenks 2006; Philp 2006; and Thompson 1980.
36. Doyle 1990; Schama 1989.
37. Quoted in Churchill 1956, p. 287.
38. McLynn 1991; Philp 2006; Thompson 1980; Wells 1983.
39. On links between radicals and seamen, see Brown 2006; Goodwin 1979; Wells 1983.
40. Philp 2006, p. 4. Linda Colley 2003 argues that popular British nationalism overcame class conflict and political differences as the struggle with France progressed.
41. Cookson 1997, p. 182, observes that the ruling classes thought that "behind any popular opposition lurked a dangerously subversive secret radicalism."
42. Sharpe 1999, p. 198. Langford 1984, p. 383, observes that fear of revolution achieved "the destruction of the old tolerance" between the social classes and instilled "the popular riot among the bugbears of the propertied mind." See also studies by King 2000 and McLynn 1991.
43. As Colley 2003, p. 150, notes, "Even after Napoleon Bonaparte had muffled the egalitarianism of the early French Republic, the prospect of Britain's traditional rulers losing face (if not their heads) persisted … Napoleonic France could still be seen – and was seen by its British opponents – as a meritocracy."
44. Frykman 2009; Gill 2016, pp. 220–8.
45. On the social composition of the naval profession and its ethos, see studies by Lewis 1960, Rodger 1982 and Wilson 2017.
46. Allardyce 1883, p. 137.
47. Frykman 2010; Pope 1981.
48. La Fevre and Harding 2000, p. 337.
49. Jenks 2006, p. 108.
50. Gilbert 1976.
51. Rodger 1986.
52. Could the increase in punishment for drunkenness simply reflect greater alcohol consumption? During the eighteenth century, the range and average length of voyages increased. Ships in distant waters or at sea for long periods on blockade duty served out more spirits (principally rum), which might have led to greater alcoholic consumption. However, naval regulations governed the service of spirits in relation to other alcoholic beverages: "Half a pint of spirits replaced a gallon of beer, and was normally issued half in the morning and half in the evening, in the form of 'three-water-grog' (diluted with three parts of water)" (Rodger 2004, p. 496). Given this formula, greater service of rum instead of beer probably cannot account for an increase in drunkenness commensurate with the drastic increase in punishment. A gallon of "small" beer (ca. 3.5 percent ABV) would

contain 4.48 ounces of pure alcohol whereas a half pint of navy-proof rum (ca. 57 percent ABV) would contain 4.56 ounces.

53. Blake 2008, pp. 83, 290.
54. Gilbert 1976, p. 87.
55. See, e.g., Boucher 2012; Lloyd 1995; and Marshall 1823.
56. Byrn 1989, p. 127. Rodger 1986, p. 74, notes of the Navy during the era of the Seven Years' War, "Even excessive drinking was only a slight offence, and no man who was peaceably drunk would normally be punished for it."
57. Other historians observe similar changes in social relations, including nascent class conflict (Frykman 2009; Neale 1985), and an increasing moralism among officers (Blake 2008).
58. Rodger 2004, pp. 608, 637–9.
59. For example, Erikson 2005, p. 68, proposes that, "Whenever a community is confronted by a significant relocation of boundaries ... it is likely to experience a change in the kinds of behavior handled by its various agencies of control."
60. Nagle [1802] 1988, pp. 58–63.
61. Byrn 1989, p. 19; Malcomson 2016, pp. 198–204.
62. Note that our two measures of the dependent variable are closely correlated (at greater than 0.9), which suggests that officers were not pursuing rival strategies of selective deterrence (i.e., many moderate punishments) as opposed to general deterrence (i.e., a few very severe punishments).
63. Black 1976, pp. 101–2.
64. Costa and Kahn 2008.
65. On the basis of a Chow test, we found a structural break in the time series, which indicates that the relationship between variables changes after 1789. See Appendix D on the procedures and estimation strategies we used for these analyses.
66. To be more confident about period effects triggered by the French Revolution, we also estimated separate models that analyze observations up through 1789 with those after 1789 as we report in Appendix D. When we separated the data into two subpanels, the general impression as to the factors that increased punishment is much the same as when we combine the data, though there are some differing associations in the control variables.
67. The figures are visualizations of a semi-parametric regression model with all covariates from our model included as parametric terms and year of observation included as a nonparametric spline-based predictor. For more information on the use of this type of semi-parametric regression model, see Hastie 1992.
68. The solid line displays the marginal effect of time on flogging. The shaded region represents the 95 percent confidence interval of the spline-based estimate. The horizontal and dashed vertical lines are references to indicate a marginal effect of 0 and the year 1789, respectively. Tick marks on the inner x axis indicate the year of each observation.
69. The solid line shows a fit to the data, which here serves as a moving average. The dashed line in each figure is a visual reference showing the year 1789. Tick marks on the inner side of the axes indicate observed data values.
70. It is quite likely that Melville was aware of the mutiny on the *Hermione*. His novella *Billy Budd* was written near the end of his life; he died in 1891.
71. Melville 1924, especially chs. 22 and 26.
72. Byrn 1989; Eder 2004.
73. Phillimore 1876, p. 57.
74. Pope 1981, p. 221; also Rodger 1986.

75. On this point, see discussions in Rodger 1982, 1986.
76. The basic principle of deterrence is that the attractiveness of crime is influenced by the value of deviance offset by the probability of detection and punishment. See Gibbs 1977 and Matsueda 2013.
77. Earle 1998, p. 45.
78. Lavery 2010; Rodger 2004, 1986.
79. See, among many, studies on the politics of crime and social control by Baumer and Martin 2013; Beckett and Sasson 2004; Garland 1990, 2001; and Gottschalk 2006.

7 THE CONSEQUENCES OF MUTINY

During the night of May 13, 1741, "violent squalls" beset the storeship *Wager* off the Pacific coast of Patagonia. Tossed about on a "great sea," Lieutenant Robert Baynes, the acting commander, found that he could hardly sail the vessel. The great bulk of the ship's company having been disabled by sickness, he had just a dozen fit seamen available to battle the storm. "We were too weakly handed to have set the topsails," he later testified.

Sometime between four and five o'clock the next morning, the *Wager* struck a rock. The tiller was destroyed and Baynes just managed to bring the stricken ship onto a sandbank near an island. Amidst terrifying gales, the crew began using the ship's boats to evacuate and transport supplies to the island. In all, about one hundred officers and men were able to evacuate the ship, but some of the sickest and most incapacitated seamen and soldiers drowned.

Daylight revealed a stranded and battered ship. A few men remained onboard, drunk on looted wine and brandy. Ashore, the ship's company was exposed to wind, rain and bitter cold on a barren, marshy coast. With the Captain incapacitated by an injury suffered during the storm, Baynes and John Bulkeley, the Gunner, assumed control, organizing the transfer of the remaining stores to the island. In spite of efforts in the coming weeks to supplement these supplies by hunting and bartering with local Indians, food was to remain scarce.

Captain David Cheap had played a small role in coping with the shipwreck, but in the days that followed, a slow-motion mutiny began as Cheap attempted to reassert command. His officers thought him "inhuman and stupid," and the crew blamed him for the disaster. Nevertheless, Cheap announced a plan to construct boats from the wreckage of the ship to sail onward along the Chilean coast toward a planned rendezvous with a British squadron from which the ship had previously been separated. Baynes and Bulkeley refused to obey Cheap, arguing that the survivors should return to the Atlantic via the Straits of Magellan, and from there make their way back to England. Cheap's authority was weak – most of the officers and men backed Bulkeley and Baynes. Cheap did retain the support of a few officers (including Midshipman Byron, grandfather of the famous poet) and about two dozen seamen. As rival camps formed, the situation grew increasingly tense. After a drunken confrontation with a Midshipman, Cheap fatally shot the young man with a pistol.

The officers intervened to prevent further violence, but most of the crew now regarded Cheap as a murderer. Some demanded that he be arrested and returned to England for trial. Baynes and Bulkeley announced that they would construct boats from the wreckage of the ship and sail for England. Cheap denounced the plan as mutiny, but Baynes refuted the charge on the ground that Cheap's command had been nullified because the ship was wrecked. Bulkeley, moreover, drafted a petition charging that Cheap was incompetent, had abandoned the "publick good" and could no longer be obeyed.

Cheap stood on altogether shaky ground. In addition to being detested, naval regulations placed him in an ambiguous position when he tried to reassert command. Did his legal authority persist even though the ship he had been commissioned to was wrecked? The seamen knew that their entitlement to pay ended when the ship went out of commission. With Cheap clearly illegitimate in their eyes, on what basis were they obliged to obey him?

All told, the survivors spent five months on the island. First, they tried to repair the stricken *Wager* before demolishing her and building new vessels from surviving boats and the wreckage. A group of seamen deserted and tried to make their way overland to a Spanish colonial settlement. They failed to reach it, and most of the party died in the attempt. Finally, on October 12, 1741, Baynes's party, comprising the majority of the ship's survivors (about eighty men in total), set off for England in boats constructed from the wreckage. Cheap and his loyalist party set a northward course along the Chilean coast. After many months and much additional hardship, a handful of survivors led by Baynes and Bulkeley reached home. They thought that they would escape trial because everyone believed that Cheap and his companions were dead. Although Cheap and his men had failed to find the British ships they sought, they did manage to reach Valparaiso, where they were imprisoned until released by the Spanish four years later.

On Cheap's return to England, news of the *Wager* disaster spread. For the Navy, it was an embarrassing coda to an ill-conceived expedition. The ship had been one of a squadron of six warships under the command of Commodore George Anson. The squadron had departed from Portsmouth in September 1740 as part of a secret mission to attack Spain's Pacific possessions. The recently commenced War of Jenkin's Ear – which was later enveloped in the wider War of the Austrian Succession – pitted Britain against Spain in a conflict over colonial markets and imperial spoils. Anson was tasked with seizing, or at least disrupting, Spain's lucrative trade linking Europe, the New World and Asia.

Anson's squadron was meant to play havoc with Spain's complex colonial economy. Spain mined enormous quantities of silver in Peru. Some of it was carried over the Isthmus of Panama and then loaded onto ships at Portobello and sent to Spain. Spanish ships also brought New World silver to Manila and Macao where it was used to buy luxury goods. From Asia, ships carried the goods to Acapulco where they were unloaded and transported overland to Veracruz and from there shipped finally to Spain.

Anson was ordered to capture Callao, Lima's port, and from there to lead a revolt against Spanish rule in order to try to take the colony. He was further instructed to capture the Pacific Coast of Panama and seize treasure galleons and trade ships making their way between Asia and America. All this required Anson to carry hundreds of soldiers and an enormous quantity of supplies and military equipment over thousands of miles. Setting out, the ships were overburdened and overcrowded, a serious disability for ships obliged to round the Horn – the dreaded "Cape of Storms." Worse yet, a shortage of fit seamen and soldiers obliged Anson to man his expedition with hundreds of "invalids" – sick, injured or old men pressed into service. Under the best of circumstances, illness would have dogged Anson's squadron. But this expedition called for a sea journey of thousands of miles, condemning hundreds of men to death by typhus ("ship's fever") as well as the scourge of debilitating scurvy.

As the flotilla's main transport vessel, the overloaded *Wager* carried hundreds of seamen and soldiers. During the long voyage from England to Cape Horn, the ship became increasingly unsanitary and diseased. In November 1740 the ship's Captain died. His replacement died soon afterward. David Cheap, a senior Lieutenant from another ship in the squadron, assumed the command of the *Wager*.

In March of 1741, Anson's squadron finally reached the entrance to the path around Cape Horn but faced adverse currents and stormy weather. It became impossible for the ships to sail in company. Anson ordered the ships of the squadron to reunite off the west coast of Chile after rounding the Horn. The *Wager* faced mounting hardships, however, in trying to clear Cape Horn. Weeks passed as the ship tried to beat its way through the stormy passage.

By early May, the Horn had been rounded but social order on the *Wager* was collapsing. It was becoming nearly impossible to sail the storm-battered ship. The ship was in terrible repair, and the crew was so ravaged by fever and scurvy that sometimes only three men stood watch on deck. The crew pleaded with the officers to turn back and return to England, but Cheap insisted on making the planned rendezvous with Anson. Not long afterward, the ship was wrecked.

***

In June 1744, Anson arrived in England aboard his flagship, *Centurion*, having circumnavigated the globe. *Centurion* was the only ship of his squadron that returned. The suffering and loss of life endured by his men had been staggering, and his ship bore just a small fraction of those who had set out with him in 1740.[1] Nevertheless, having achieved an extraordinary feat of seamanship and loaded his ship with captured Spanish treasure, Anson was lionized as a hero.[2]

When Cheap finally returned from Spanish captivity in 1745, the Admiralty was obliged to convene a court-martial in the following year to inquire into the loss of the *Wager*. At trial Cheap accused Baynes and Bulkeley of negligent handling of the ship and fomenting mutiny. They defended themselves by painting Cheap as incompetent and inhumane. His poor leadership, lack of seamanship and stubbornness had made the loss of the ship inevitable. They said that this became obvious when, having finally rounded the Horn, the officers tried to convince Cheap to navigate a more westerly course before turning north along the coast of Chile. He chose to turn north toward land. In May of 1741, the ship's officers discovered that the *Wager* had not sailed far enough west and had strayed into a bay; this increased the chance that the ship would be wrecked along the coast. As they tried to beat their way back, Cheap was thrown from the storm-lashed deck and fell down a hatchway, breaking his shoulder. Retiring to his cabin with a bottle of laudanum, Cheap surrendered the quarterdeck to Baynes, whom he now blamed for losing the ship. Finally, Bulkeley and Baynes argued that Cheap's impulsive killing of the Midshipman destroyed whatever authority he still possessed.

The jury of officers found itself in a difficult position. Everyone would have rather forgotten the *Wager* affair and concentrated on celebrating Anson's circumnavigation and piratical success. In the end, the court's verdict excused Cheap of wrongdoing, but it also acquitted the mutiny charges. Because the crew was no longer in Admiralty pay following the shipwreck and not technically subject to naval discipline, defiance of Cheap did not constitute mutiny. The leaders of the mutiny did not go without censure, however, as the court reprimanded Baynes for negligence in the loss of the *Wager*, and he never again served as an officer at sea.[3]

George Anson went on to have a sterling naval career as an Admiral and member of the Admiralty Board that governed the Navy. He had learned powerful lessons from his Pacific expedition and from the fate of the ships under his command. An important voice for change, his "reforming zeal was given a keener edge by the memory of those galling experiences that had delayed and handicapped his expedition."[4] He was convinced that more had to be done to ensure the competence and effectiveness of naval officers. The health and welfare of seamen, particularly when at sea for long periods, were urgent priorities that demanded remediation. And the mutiny on the *Wager* taught him that institutional reforms were necessary to clarify issues of discipline and command.

Mutinies had consequences far beyond the immediate fate of the seamen and officers who were swept up into them. When the situation of seamen grew desperate, mutiny was one of the few avenues of recourse open to them. Although they were crude and uncertain instruments, mutinies often led to the redress of seamen's grievances when no other practical mechanism was available. Rebellion, however, was a threat to command and a challenge to governance.

In response to mutinies, senior officers and naval administrators were often divided between redressing "reasonable" grievances and crushing uprisings seen as dangerous to discipline and command. To deter collective action by seamen, commanders preferred to react harshly to mutiny. To our surprise, that harshness was sometimes tempered by the tendency of senior naval officials to make concessions, and by norms that prevented courts-martial from becoming instruments of judicial terror. Repression was the most common institutional response to mutiny, but in a few domains – particularly with respect to wages, discipline and health and welfare – mutiny inspired naval reforms.

7.1 Mutiny and the Redress of Grievances

Regardless of the forms that mutinies took – armed strikes, seizing and fleeing with the ship or rioting (see Chapter 3) – the seamen involved were motivated by specific grievances. They believed that rebellion might improve their lot. The evidence we have assembled on full-fledged mutinies shows that this belief was partially justified. In no less than half of the mutinies in our sample, seamen gained the redress of one or more of their grievances following their mutiny.

Nevertheless, mutiny was undeniably a dangerous and uncertain strategy. If grievances were redressed, at least to some extent for some large share of the ship's company, we can say that mutinies were a success. The successful redress of grievances depended on several factors, including the nature of the grievances at issue and the strategy adopted by seamen. In most cases, success was partial and substantial costs had to be paid by some of the seamen involved. Even in the most favorable cases, those resolved by negotiation with naval authorities, seamen might receive action on one of their stated grievances, but not on all of them. Moreover, in the aftermath of two-thirds of the mutinies in our sample, some of the seamen involved were indicted as ringleaders or as active mutineers and faced trial by court-martial.

Insurgents risked the harshest retribution for those mutinies where they seized control of their ships and tried to defect with them to foreign harbors. Even so, this kind of mutiny frequently succeeded in that most of the mutineers escaped from naval service. In two-thirds of the *organized exit mutinies* in our sample, seamen did manage to take the ship and reach a safe haven. In most instances, however, some of these mutineers were subsequently captured and tried for the double crime of piratical mutiny. In only three mutinies of the sixteen of this type – the *Lively* and the *Prince Edward* in 1782 and the *Shark* in 1795 – did the crew escape scot-free.

The most common type of mutiny in our sample was the *armed strike*. This kind of mutiny was predicated on gaining leverage in negotiations with senior naval officials aiming to redress specific grievances. As we saw in Chapter 3, these were in many ways the most thoroughly organized mutinies; they also adhered as closely as possible to the norms governing lower-deck voice. Armed strike mutinies were characterized by deliberation and moderation on the part of seamen and rarely involved deadly violence. Even so, their success depended heavily on the goodwill of senior officers and naval officials.

The case of the small battleship *Janus* provides a vivid example. In the winter of 1783, with the War of American Independence concluding, the morale of many ships' companies was low. *Janus* was moored at Spithead, being repaired and refitted for service. On February 25, the Captain read the "The Proclamations of Peace," announcing the end of the war. Two weeks passed and the crew became anxious because they had still not been paid off and released from service. Rumors began to circulate that the crew would be ordered back to the West Indies. The seamen selected a committee to plan a rebellion if the Navy was intent on denying them their pay or their liberty after many years at sea.

Without the prospect of satisfaction in sight, on March 11 the crew rebelled. The ship's officers were locked in their quarters and placed under armed guard. The mutineers loaded the ship's guns and prepared them for action. Their Captain was sent ashore to relay their demands to the Admiralty. Word of the mutiny began to spread at the nearby naval base at Portsmouth, where other returning ships were also crammed with restive seamen. In Whitehall, the Admiralty resolved to treat the matter delicately, so as to avert a general mutiny sweeping across the port.

In the following weeks, Admiral Richard Howe, the Commander-in-Chief of the Channel Fleet, acted cautiously. He isolated the *Janus* to prevent unrest from spreading to other ships in the fleet. He signaled his willingness to negotiate by coming aboard the *Janus* and personally appealing to the crew to return to its duty. Howe tried to mollify the ship's company by having its outstanding prize-money paid. Nevertheless, the crew was determined to have its central demands of being paid off and released satisfied.

The strikers held out until April 12, when an Admiralty commissioner boarded the ship and paid the seamen. Admiral Howe was then rowed out to the ship. On reaching it, the crew greeted him with all the appropriate honors and fell into formation while the fife and drums played the patriotic sailor's song "Heart of Oak." Howe addressed the men of the *Janus* declaring,

> I'm much grieved to hear of such mutinous conduct in British seamen. I have always found you orderly and obedient. I hope you know the deep interest I have always taken in your welfare. You are acting under the influence of a false report. The Janus will be paid off, although my predecessor decided she should be kept in commission.

The sailors cheered and the mutiny was over. No court-martial was convened, no sailors were punished and the crew dispersed.[5]

From the seamen's perspective, the *Janus* was an outstanding example of a successful mutiny. The favorable outcome owed much to the crew's organization and solidarity that permitted it to endure a lengthy standoff with the authorities. From the Navy's perspective, a peaceful resolution on the *Janus* was possible because the seamen acted to pursue legitimate objectives with moderation and restraint. The timing was right because, with the American war having come to a close, the imperative of maintaining unquestioning obedience had been relaxed. The resolution of the mutiny showed that judicious handling of seamen's legitimate grievances could keep a rebellion isolated and prevent a major insurrection in a home port – a notable lesson unlearned prior to the uprisings at Spithead and the Nore fourteen years later. Thanks to his handling of the *Janus* and his credibility as an honest broker, Howe became known as "The Sailor's Friend." As such, he was later called on to help negotiate a settlement of the mass mutiny at Spithead in the spring of 1797.

If mutinies conformed to certain norms – including that they did not take place on the high seas or in the face of the enemy, refrained from violence and sought only the redress of reasonable grievances – naval authorities might decide to accede to their demands and forgo punishment.[6] Although seamen's organization upped the chances of success, happy outcomes like that of the *Janus* were anything but assured. Whether the goal was exit or voice, well-organized mutinies usually achieved at least one of the stated goals of the mutineers (84 percent of organized mutinies). By contrast, mutinies that were *loosely organized or that devolved into rioting* were much less likely to succeed (40 percent of such mutinies).

If success partly depended on the conduct of the mutineers, the disposition of the authorities was as least as important. For example, when the men of the *Canada* staged a four-day armed strike in 1781 to demand that they be remitted wages in arrears before a new Captain assumed his commission, their demand was granted. Admiralty officials recorded that they had been "Ordered to be paid as they were within their rights." In other instances (such as the *Culloden* discussed in Chapter 3), negotiations could not even get off the ground because Captains were resolutely opposed to making any concessions at all. When commanders refused to negotiate, they usually tried to suppress unrest by a show of force, such as having the Marines load and aim their muskets at the mutineers, or by initiating deadly violence to retake the ship or cow the mutineers into submission.

The case of the mutiny aboard the ship-of-the-line *Terrible* in 1795 shows how important a commander's attitude was in determining the outcome of a mutiny. The crew staged an armed strike in response to having been routinely served spoiled food. From below decks, they passed up a letter to their commander, Captain Campbell, which read,

> May it Please Your Honour: We do not wish to incur your displeasure nor to create any disturbance in the ship, but as Men we would wish to be treated and to have wholesome bread as proper application has been made several times and no redress given we are under the disagreeable necessity to take those measures which are as obnoxious to us as they are to Your Honour. Our expectations are, an answer from under your hand that no one should be upbraided hereafter – No man to be punished, and serve us bread, and we will return to our Duty as usually.

In spite of their reasonable demands and deferential tone, Campbell was enraged, shouting down that "[by] my word and honour, everyone concerned in it should be punished, and that, very severely."

Campbell confided to his officers that his response was severe, but that he was unwilling to give into any demands. He had been especially irritated by the peaceful resolution of a mutiny in the same fleet aboard another warship in 1794. "It shall not be a *Windsor Castle*'s business," he assured the officers of his ship, adding that "if he gave into their plans, he would not think himself worthy to command a ship with near six-hundred [men]." Backed by a contingent of armed Marines, Campbell ordered that the barricades be stormed. Volleys of musket fire sufficed to end the rebellion.

Campbell severely flogged two presumed ringleaders on the spot and indicted a dozen men for mutiny, exempting several whose gunshot wounds had been severe enough to warrant amputations. By order of a court-martial, five of the *Terrible* mutineers were hanged. In addition, one of the flogged men was recommended for an additional trial despite the usual double-jeopardy protection. The handling of the matter was undoubtedly harsh, but Admiral Henry Hotham backed Campbell, writing to the Admiralty that repression "was a painful alternative [to negotiation] but the occasion required striking a blow and forcible example; and I hope the general impression it may have made upon the minds of many will conduce to allay that turbulent spirit and dissatisfaction which of late has been but too prevalent throughout the fleet."[7]

Uncertainty about the authorities' response complicated the strategy of mutiny. The Navy undermined the deterrent effect of making mutiny a capital crime by defining it so broadly as to include a wide range of behaviors traditionally understood as part of the (at least semi-legitimate) voice of the lower deck. The broadness of the definition made everyone unsure about the official response to disobedience or unrest.[8] Although seamen could take steps that enhanced the chances that they would escape the noose – either by staging orderly and moderate mutinies, or else by fleeing to safe havens – naval justice was not easily eluded. For most officers repression was the preferred response to mutiny. Only a third of armed strikes (nine of twenty-nine) achieved mutineers' twin goals of having their demands met and protecting every seaman from a trial. Two-thirds of the mutinies (67 percent) in our sample ended in a court-martial. As a result of most of those trials, someone would hang or otherwise be severely punished for the sin of mutinous behavior.

7.2   The Majesty of the Law: Judicial Repression of Mutiny

On January 24, 1802 Rear Admiral Cuthbert Collingwood wrote to his brother about his recent service as a jury member in the court-martial that prosecuted a score of accused mutineers from the battleship *Temeraire*. Collingwood confided that because the accused had fine service records and legitimate grievances he had sympathized with them. Despite this, he still had voted for harsh verdicts. "Twenty of them were tried, eighteen were condemned to die and eleven of them have suffered; a dreadful example but of absolute necessity to prevent individual convenience or opinion interrupting the course of public service," he explained.[9]

Collingwood's insistence on harshness is all the more striking when one considers his record as a commander. He was a talented and successful officer noted for his humanity toward his crews and his public stance against flogging.[10] Nevertheless, Collingwood's attitude toward judicial repression was hardly exceptional. In British military thinking the purpose of the law was to achieve obedience first and to secure justice second. Collingwood's harsh judgment points to a widely shared preference among naval commanders for repression in response to disorder and their reluctance to negotiate with disobedient seamen no matter how peaceful and moderate. The belief in the "absolute necessity" of courts-martial and hanging seems also to reflect the growing spirit of repression that originated in the crisis decade of the 1790s, as seen in the previous chapter on flogging.

At the same time, the severity displayed in a case like that of the *Temeraire* is also surprising. Although one might expect that courts-martial were dominated by "hanging juries," this is not generally what we found in scores of trial transcripts. Whereas there certainly were instances in which a spirit of vengeance animated the proceedings, the dominant logic at work was the finding of guilt and the relatively judicious assignment of punishment. If guilt could not be proved the accused were acquitted, and, where evidence of mitigation was evident, many demonstrably guilty men were spared the noose.

What we observed in naval trials is very much in keeping with the Georgian justice system more generally. The Georgian era is famous for its "Bloody Code"; a system of social control anchored by legislation mandating capital punishment for hundreds of offenses.[11] Despite the legislative willingness to inflict capital punishment, however, the threat of hanging vastly exceeded its actual use. In England, less than half of those convicted of capital crimes were executed. Many offenders avoided trial altogether or were acquitted.[12] One historian has deftly summarized the reality of crime and punishment in Georgian Britain: "Many offenders went uncaught: if caught, unprosecuted, if prosecuted, unconvicted; and if convicted, unhanged because of the granting of a pardon."[13]

As did the British elite more generally, naval officers believed in general deterrence. This implied that the punishment of a guilty few – especially by the dramatic act of gibbeting – would deter crime and deviance in the broader ranks of seamen.[14] As was typical of "old regime" systems of social control more generally, publicity and ceremony were vital parts of criminal justice.[15] The Navy made every effort to create ritualized punishment. Floggings and hangings were done in full view of the assembled fleet and seamen were required to watch from the decks of their ships.[16] Trials by court-martial were also conducted like theatrical events that would demonstrate the integrity of justice and the majesty of the law.

All of this public ceremony made procedure – the rule of law – very important, "insinuating the idea that every man was equal before the law, that the law was dispassionate, impartial, and blind to social stratification."[17] Although the rhetoric and practice of the rule of law was surely meant to legitimize authority, the norms surrounding the rule of law also constrained the authorities, helping to balance elite and popular interests and offering standards to judge poor governance.[18] This is evident in the prosecution of mutineers in naval courts-martial. Grievances could be framed in terms of a commander's accountability to the law – in the Navy "ill-usage," and violations of printed instructions – that sometimes helped to secure an accused mutineer's acquittal. Moreover, the occasional trial, conviction and disgrace of officers by courts-martial – as happened to Baynes of the *Wager*, the senior officers aboard the *Panther* (see Chapter 2) or Captain Corbet following the

Nereide mutiny (discussed in Chapter 6) – further bolstered the credibility of the rule of law, and actually ended the careers of some officers
who had earned the enmity of their crews.[19]

Although they displayed considerable prosecutorial bias, courts-
martial tended to adhere to general rules. The Articles of War, supplemented by printed regulations and instructions, provided the basis of
criminal justice in the Georgian Navy. They mandated a judicial process
that began with the arrest of a seaman accompanied by a letter of
complaint from a commanding officer to the Lords Commissioners of
the Admiralty specifying the charges. The decision to prosecute seamen
was not taken lightly, because courts-martial were inconvenient, time-
consuming and expensive. Admiralty officials and the Commanders-in-
Chief of foreign stations were permitted to dismiss charges they regarded
as "frivolous or improperly drawn" and sometimes did so.[20]

Courts-martial were advised by the office of the Judge
Advocate, which offered legal advice, kept a verbatim trial transcript,
administered oaths and advised the jury on legal or technical matters.
A jury consisted of at least five officers, all of whom had to hold
a minimum rank of Post-Captain, and conviction was by majority
vote, with ties decided in favor of the accused. Whereas the complaining
officer assisted by the Judge Advocate conducted the prosecution, the
accused conducted his own defense without aid of counsel.

Legal norms governed the proceedings. Evidence was given in
person. The jury deliberated secretly. The accused were presumed innocent, and a split jury resulted in acquittal. If guilty, a court could apply
the statutory penalty – in the case of mutiny, death by hanging for
seamen, or by firing squad for officers – or assign a lesser punishment,
usually flogging around the fleet. Naval justice gave one last great power
to its juries. In addition to finding guilt and assigning punishment, the
jury could recommend that convicted seamen be considered for "royal
mercy," that is, the commutation of the sentence by the Crown. Having
been convicted of a capital crime and assigned hanging, seamen awaited
either the granting of a royal pardon or their execution.[21]

The attention paid to certain elements of due process reveals the
influence of legal norms. Trials in absentia, self-incrimination and secret
witnesses were not allowed. To be accepted, eyewitness testimony had
to be corroborated. The members of jury did not provide testimony or
serve as character witnesses. Of course, there were clear limitations to

naval justice. The accused did not benefit from counsel or a jury of their peers (among the unmet demands of the uprising at the Nore in 1797).[22] No mechanism ensured that biased officers did not serve on a court. Unlike the norm that prevailed in common-law trials, in courts-martial conviction in capital cases only required a majority vote of the jury rather than unanimity.[23]

The eighteenth century has been called the golden age of discretionary justice in Britain.[24] Civilian magistrates and juries could be surprisingly forgiving of rioters, so long as unrest was framed in light of injustice and the poor's lack of political voice.[25] The wide berth for discretion is also clearly evident in naval courts-martial. Naval juries frequently engaged in nullification and mitigation in mutiny cases.[26] Courts-martial carefully questioned witnesses and sought exculpatory evidence. In some instances, as in the case of the *Panther*, juries effectively nullified the Articles by refusing to convict despite clear evidence of mutiny so long as it was clear that seamen had been effectively forced by circumstances to rebel. They were also surprisingly willing to consider a defendant's introduction of mitigating evidence. Seamen who were certainly guilty of taking part in mutinies were routinely acquitted if their roles in the rebellion were small. Juries were also prone to mitigation when testimony indicated that seamen were provoked or deceived, had not played leading roles in the mutiny, or demonstrated contrition.

Sometimes evidence of a seaman's past bravery and honorable service spared him. For example, two of the seamen convicted as "principal mutineers" on the *Winchelsea* in 1793 were given two hundred lashes instead of being hanged because the jury had not been convinced that they had been involved in plotting the rebellion or inducing others to join it.[27] In the *Albanaise* mutiny of 1800, seamen seized the ship by force, wounding several officers in the process, and took it to Malaga in enemy Spain. Eventually, several of the mutineers fell into British hands and were tried. Whatever may have been the desire to avenge this most heinous kind of mutiny, courts-martial displayed admirable restraint and discrimination in handling the accused. The two seamen who had played the most active role in the mutiny were convicted and hanged. Two seamen who had voluntarily returned to stand trial, however, were convicted but given lesser punishments (short terms of imprisonment, loss of back wages and flogging). Another seaman against whom charges were only "partly proven" was sentenced to three hundred lashes instead of the noose, and an "old salt" praised for his many years of loyal service was given only a short term of imprisonment.[28]

Another factor moderating the harshness of naval justice was the possibility of a pardon. As in civilian courts, courts-martial allowed jurors to recommend that the condemned receive a royal pardon. Although it was among the direst of naval crimes, courts-martial routinely recommended that some of those they found guilty in mutiny trials be pardoned, which, by legal convention, was always granted.[29] In the minds of juries, a convict's youth, mental illness or deficiency, or mitigating circumstances, such as the condemned having had endured punishment or a long period of confinement prior to trial, or having willingly cooperated with the court, favored clemency. Admiralty officials might also recommend pardon if trial deficiencies were obvious.[30]

Several examples help to illustrate the function of pardons. In the trial following the mutiny on the battleship *Adamant* in 1798, Cornelius Kelly was convicted as one of the "instigators" of the mutiny and sentenced to hang alongside two of his shipmates. Since Kelly was simple-minded and a hapless drunk, the jury thought that the other two were the real ringleaders. Having concluded that "Kelly was probably not aware at the time of the heinousness of the offence committed by him," the jury recommended his pardon.[31] In the trial of the mutineers on the *Saturn* in 1797, a Marine drummer-boy was convicted and sentenced to hang but recommended for mercy because he might have been manipulated by older seamen.[32] Courts even considered culture and language as mitigating factors against a capital sentence. In the trial of the mutineers on the *Dominica* in 1805, for example, a seaman named Suaré was convicted and sentenced to hang, but the jury thought a pardon was called for because of its inability to judge his motives and competence. The jury explained, "Sentenced by the Court to suffer death, is a black man, a native of Martinique, was cook of the vessel at the time of the mutiny and appears ignorant of the magnitude of the crime, and to have acted under the influence of fear, from the threats made against him by the Boatswain's Mate."[33]

Other seamen were pardoned due to evidence provided by character witnesses (nearly always given by officers of their ships) or because they had fine service records. Following the *Culloden* mutiny, three seamen were convicted as being principal mutineers but were "recommended to mercy" as acknowledgment of the "excellent character given to each of them by their officers."[34] In 1783 one of the seamen convicted for the mutiny on the *Jackal* won a pardon because the prosecution failed to establish that he was a ringleader, and because witnesses attested to his "general good character."[35] Similarly, after the mutiny on the *Dispatch* in 1815, the court "earnestly recommended" that three men convicted as instigators of the rebellion should nevertheless be pardoned because of their expressions of contrition and "in consideration of their excellent characters."[36]

The possibility of pardon was very important because there was no process to handle appeals in military justice. This explains why pardons sometimes resulted from interventions by Admirals or senior naval administrators who became concerned that indictments were too sweeping or that juries had displayed undue harshness. In the case of the *Jason* mutiny of 1807, the court-martial convicted eleven seamen and recommended five for a pardon. In view of the confused actions of the mutineers and the poor governance that had contributed to the uprising, however, the reform-minded Admiral George Berkeley, commander of the North American Station, intervened to grant royal mercy to an additional four seamen, leaving only the two apparent ringleaders to hang.[37] In the case of the *Santa Monica* mutiny in 1781, a vengeful Captain Linzee indicted more than sixty seamen for "mutinous assembly" and presented a muster list to prove that all of them had taken part in the armed strike. Under the Articles, these were capital charges. Judicial slaughter could have resulted if all or most of the mutineers had been convicted and sentenced. This horrifying outcome was averted by the commanding Admiral of the Leeward Islands Station, who set aside most of the charges. In the end, a single seaman convicted as the ringleader and spokesman of the mutiny was hanged.[38]

7.2.1 The Paradox of Severity: How Harsh Were Courts-Martial in Practice?

Given the mixed evidence of both harshness and mercy, is there a systematic way to assess how severely court-martials handled indicted mutineers? To answer that question, we have to begin by considering the outcome of trials sequentially. Once indicted, a seaman could be found guilty, or else acquitted. We think of acquittal broadly because conviction on lesser charges that did not carry a capital sentence was more or less equivalent to acquittal on the charge of mutiny. If found guilty, a seaman could be sentenced to death by hanging as specified under the Articles or be given a lesser punishment, generally flogging around the fleet.[39] If sentenced to death, the seaman could be hanged or else have his sentence commuted by pardon.

Our sample of single-ship mutinies (excluding those indicted for mutiny at the Nore) resulted in the indictment of 503 seamen, of whom 380 (75 percent) of those tried were found guilty. Given a guilty verdict, we found that 257 (68 percent) of the convicted were sentenced to death. The rest were given lesser punishments, generally floggings ranging from one hundred to six hundred lashes. Among those sentenced to die, not all were hanged. Courts sometimes made use of their power to recommend a royal pardon, with 61 of the 257 sailors sentenced to death for mutiny (24 percent) pardoned. Taken together, this means that, of the roughly five hundred seamen indicted for mutiny in our sample, fewer than two hundred (or about 40 percent) were actually executed as a result of trial by court-martial.[40]

Although many of the seamen who escaped the noose still had to face the lash, the outcomes of indictments for mutiny in our sample do not appear to support the Navy's reputation for unbridled judicial severity. Increasing judicial severity does become conspicuous, however, during the decades following 1789. Figure 7.1 displays the proportion of trials resulting in guilty verdicts, the proportion of seamen found guilty and sentenced to death, and the proportion of those sentenced to die but pardoned.[41] Of the three outcomes, the proportion of cases resulting in a guilty verdict varies least between 1740 and 1820. Over time there is a clear positive trend for the proportion of seamen found guilty sentenced to death, and the proportion sentenced to death who subsequently received a pardon (we observed no pardons in mutiny trials until 1779).

The sharply increasing proportion of death sentences resulting from court-martial trials during the crisis decade of the 1790s and beyond is consistent with the increasing penal severity observed in the previous chapter's analysis of flogging. Around the year 1780, less than half of those convicted in mutiny trials were condemned to die, whereas

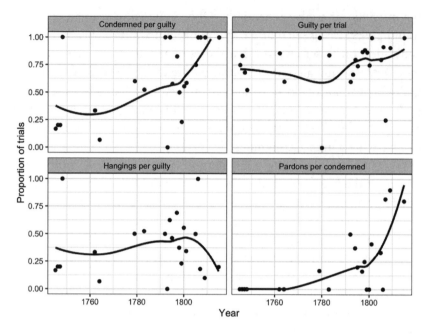

Figure 7.1 Outcomes of court-martial trials for major mutinies in the Royal Navy, 1740–1820
Source: Edwards and Pfaff 2016.

by 1800, more than three-quarters of those convicted were so condemned.

Why did courts become harsher in handing down capital sentences? The statements made by officers like Campbell, Hotham, Nelson and Collingwood suggest that the trend was caused, at least in part, by the same insecurities and fear of revolution that help to account for the increased severity of flogging in the previous chapter. With the prerogatives of command foremost in their minds, many commanders were worried that lenience by courts-martial and the willingness of senior naval officials to negotiate with mutineers were dangerous.

At the same time, however, the frequency of pardons markedly increased in the revolutionary era. Although sailors were more likely to receive capital sentences for mutiny after 1789, juries in courts-martial also more frequently recommended that condemned sailors be pardoned. Around the year 1780, about a tenth of men condemned to die for mutiny were pardoned, rising to more than a quarter of those condemned around the year 1800. The increasing willingness to grant pardons did not entirely offset the trend toward greater repression, but it did moderate it.

It may seem paradoxical that the same crisis that inspired a rise in judicial severity is also associated with the increasing willingness of naval juries to recommend pardons. Despite the narrow formalism of the Articles, the latitude afforded by the power to pardon gave officers serving on juries the symbolic opportunity to convict a wider range of accused mutineers without putting many more heads in the noose.

Our finding speaks to the "majesty of law" thesis of social control in Georgian society.[42] Some historians have argued that law was both an instrument of class conflict and, because of the room for discretion it provided, an effective means of ideological legitimation. The main function of the law was repression, but the ruling class also buttressed its moral authority by following legal norms and pardoning worthy offenders. Seen in this way, trials for mutiny were an ideal opportunity to express both logics. Inflicting the death penalty on those who threatened their status was an expression of the power of the officer caste. Seamen who raised a hand against their officers, whose disobedience stirred sedition in others or whose actions paved the way for insurrection could be indicted, tried and hanged as a salutary example to their shipmates.

At the same time, in granting pardons officers demonstrated their capacity for mercy and recognition of the worthiness of specific offenders. Remorseful seamen who had not breached the unwritten rules of lower-deck disorder and who could call upon officers to act as character witnesses could be spared. Rather than seeing such wayward seamen as threats to the established order, they were forced to confront the awful majesty of the law but ultimately be returned to the fold as wrongdoers who had received the strongest rebuke. Hangings and proclamations of royal mercy were thus manifestations of a system of repression that fell under the umbrella of general deterrence.

7.3 Mutiny as an Impetus to Reform

Mutinies repeatedly revealed problems of governance in the Navy. Beyond repression and the redress of specific grievances, sympathetic naval officers, public officials and moral reformers sometimes responded to mutiny by advocating for improvements in naval governance and seamen's welfare. The connection between mutiny and reform is not always straightforward, however, because the Navy was a fundamentally conservative institution in which resistance even to obviously beneficial reforms could be dogged. As one naval historian noted of many necessary reforms, "Every change was grudgingly accepted and sometimes dangerously delayed."[43] Nevertheless, mutinies inspired reforms in the domains of pay, discipline and punishment, and health and welfare.

7.3.1   Reforms to Recruitment and Pay

Following the Napoleonic Wars, some of the pressures that had posed such a challenge to governance in the Navy – the enormous size of the fleets, the great numbers of seamen borne, widespread impressment and long periods of continuous deployment at sea – were relaxed. Naval reforms had been proceeding in halting and piecemeal fashion since the Napoleonic Wars, but a wave of mutinies in 1859 and 1860 involving more than a dozen ships bolstered calls for improvements. The grievances that propelled these mutinies are familiar: objections to low wages, excessive discipline and deficiencies in health and welfare.[44]

In the wake of the final defeat of Napoleon in 1815, the Navy no longer required the enormous numbers of seamen that it had mustered for decades. The Navy substantially demobilized, falling from around a hundred and twenty-six thousand seamen in 1814 to thirty-five thousand in 1816 and nineteen thousand in 1817.[45] It was now able to abandon the widely despised practice of pressing merchant seamen into the Navy. The end of impressment was a relief to the officer corps that had always regarded it, at best, as a necessary evil.[46] In place of impressment, the Navy developed new ways of manning the fleets, including through volunteers with long periods of enlistment, internal specialization that created more predictable and attractive careers for seamen, and by creating a Royal Naval Reserve that instituted a reserve system for ratings similar to the one that kept officers on half-pay.[47] In 1860, the introduction of the first steam-powered ironclad warship in the Royal Navy, HMS *Warrior*, signaled the closing of the age of fighting sail. The great three-decker sailing ships bristling with guns that required such large crews gradually became a thing of the past.[48]

Whereas the evolution of the system for manning the fleets appears to have occurred without undue contention, the issue of wages reveals both ongoing exploitation and resistance to it. Wage policy presented a complicated administrative problem. For most of the eighteenth and nineteenth centuries, there was no substantial price inflation in Britain. Costs, and therefore wages, tended to be stable. Inflation tended to occur during wartime, with prices falling to prewar levels with the cessation of hostilities and demobilization.[49] Although this created short-term hardships for seamen and their families, a tendency toward price stability probably explains why the Admiralty did not seek a general wage increase for seamen during the period stretching from 1652 until 1797. For one thing, seamen's compensation included their victuals and entitlement to drink, which effectively boosted their incomes. For another, wage increases given to offset what was expected to be short-term inflation would have created budgetary hardships and would have been hard to rescind as prices fell.

Nevertheless, by the end of the eighteenth century, it was clear that the low average rate of inflation had steadily taken its toll on seamen's wages. Compared with the value of an Able Seaman's wage in 1740, in 1790 the buying power of his wage had fallen by about a third.[50] As we saw in Chapter 4, wage depreciation was not only a hardship for seamen, but it was also significantly associated with a greater risk of mutiny.

The level of military effort during the wars of the French Revolution and Napoleon was unprecedented. Military spending rose to roughly a third of gross domestic product. Prices increased sharply and remained stubbornly high.[51] Naval authorities did nothing to shield seamen or their families from the misery this wage erosion caused, but fear of domestic insurrection led the government to increase wages in the Army. Chapter 5 revealed that the great mutiny at Spithead in the spring of 1797 was a direct reaction to seamen's impoverishment. Parliament increased seamen's wages, raising the pay of an Able Seaman by about 12 percent as part of the negotiated settlement of the Spithead mutiny.

Figure 7.2 shows that although this was a substantial concession in the context of the fiscal crisis of the 1790s, it still left seamen with a wage substantially weaker in buying power than that enjoyed by the seamen of earlier decades. As the wars of the French Revolution gave way to the

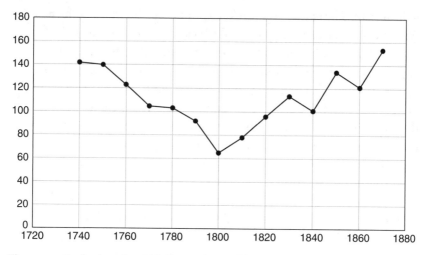

Figure 7.2 Real value of an Able Seaman's monthly wage in 2017 pounds, 1740–1870
Sources: Rates of pay reported in Rodger 2004, pp. 620–7, and Rasor 1976, p. 104.
Conversion to real terms via www.nationalarchives.gov.uk/currency-converter.

Napoleonic struggles, inflation again surged, eroding the buying power of
seamen's wages. Restiveness in the fleets remained a serious concern, and in
1807 the government once again raised seamen's wages by about 13 -
percent.[52] This probably forestalled more serious unrest.[53] Even so, the
buying power of seamen's wages remained at only about 60 percent of
what they had been in 1740.[54]

The end of the Napoleonic Wars brought a steep drop in prices that
restored much of the buying power of seamen's wages. The basic rate of pay
established in 1807 remained in place until 1852, when seamen benefited
from a wage increase of about 12 percent. In the context of a volunteer force
without recourse to impressment, the Navy had to improve wages if it
hoped to keep its fleets manned. Nevertheless, the pressure exerted by
mutinies may have continued to play a role. Following a wave of mutinies
in 1859–60, the government increased seamen's wages by nearly 20 percent
in 1862.[55] It was only with this boost in earnings that seamen modestly
exceeded the real buying power of their 1740 wage.[56]

Ironically, the improvement of working conditions in the Navy
was correlated with worsening conditions in much of Britain. The demobilization that followed the Napoleonic Wars seems to have displaced
militancy from the armed forces to society at large. Demobilized sailors

and soldiers flooded back to rural counties. This caused a severe decrease in wages and an increase in unemployment. Even as rural poverty rose steeply, new technologies like threshing machines and textile machines decreased the demand for rural labor. These proved fertile conditions for popular radicalism and outbreaks of rioting across Britain.[57]

7.3.2   Reforms to Discipline and Punishment

Many officers welcomed harsher discipline and the violent suppression of mutiny in the wake of the French Revolution. At the height of the Napoleonic Wars, however, some began to reconsider the role of discipline. The mutinies that came about as a result of the brutality of Pigot on the *Hermione* or Corbet on the *Nereide* provoked questions about the humanity and effectiveness of flogging. Gradually, attitudes toward seamen began to shift, and some began to propose that violent discipline had become counter-productive.

Cases such as the *Kingfisher* mutiny, which occurred at the peak of the crisis decade of the 1790s, revealed divisions among officers over the proper response to unrest. The men of the ship mutinied in August 1797 against ill-usage that included excessive discipline. With memories of Spithead and the Nore in mind, Captain John Maitland was afraid that the striking seamen would try to seize the quarterdeck. Impulsively, he flew past his officers and Marine guards into the midst of the crew, provoking a riot. Drawing his sword, he stabbed one seaman through the chest and, in a second blow, ran him through his side as he fell to the deck. Maitland then spun around, slashing at every seaman in sight. With one seaman dying at Maitland's feet and five other bloodied sailors staggering away from this ferocious show of force, the mutiny collapsed. Maitland triumphantly declared the crew a "parcel of villains" and warned that if they rose again, he would kill a half-dozen men.

As word of this confrontation spread, some lauded Maitland's ruthless effectiveness. His commanding officer, Admiral John Jervis, was delighted. Toasting Maitland's manly conduct, he recommended that other officers adopt "Doctor Maitland's radical cure" for the mutiny problem.[58] Not all of Maitland's brother officers agreed with the prescription, however. Maitland had insisted on courts-martial to try the alleged ringleaders of the mutiny and to judge his conduct, but the verdict did not produce the ringing exoneration that he (and Admiral Jervis) had expected. Although the jury acquitted Maitland of murder and assault, it faulted his conduct. It found that there had been no violence in the mutiny up to the point when Maitland charged the crowd. Moreover, Maitland failed to prove that the man he had killed was actively involved in the mutiny, much less a ringleader, as he claimed. The court admonished Maitland, finding that his actions were "spirited and successful but hasty and not tempered with that discretion which the nature of the case required."[59]

The case interested Edward Brenton, an officer who was a contemporary of Maitland's and later a keen historian of the Navy. Brenton's sympathies lay with reform, and he was appalled by the taste for repression among some senior naval officers. In his biography of Admiral Jervis, Brenton celebrated a successful and effective officer who had been elevated to the peerage after his famous victory at Cape St. Vincent and served as First Lord of the Admiralty. Nevertheless, Brenton criticized the intolerance of seamen's voice and the lust for discipline and violent retribution that he perceived in Jervis and fellow officers. Rather than flogging seamen into submission or crushing outbreaks of unrest, Brenton advised naval officers to eschew Jarvis's tyrannical streak: "Good management, kindness, firmness, attention to their [the seamen] needs, and a 'little indulgence,' these will seldom or never fail to keep down any spirit of mutiny."[60]

Admiral Philip Patton was another prominent voice raising concerns about discipline. After serving as an Admiralty commissioner and retiring from the Navy in 1795, he became an outspoken advocate of reform. Patton was an old, experienced commander who was concerned about what he saw as the increasingly rigid discipline and reliance on deterrent threats among officers unsettled by the revolutionary crisis. Before the outbreak of the great mutinies in 1797, Patton sent the Admiralty a memorandum on seamen's grievances pleading for immediate reform.

Patton's writings during this period are noteworthy because he argued that shipboard social order was contingent on good governance. Patton noted that a Captain's formal powers were all but useless without the consent of the seamen. In acknowledging rightful grievances and showing concern for their safety and welfare, the effective officer earns his subordinates' loyalty. With commanders like William Bligh of the *Bounty*, Hugh Pigot of the *Hermione*, Lord Proby of the *Danae*, John Linzee of the *Santa Monica* or Richard Corbet of the *Nereide* in mind, he decried the tendency of talented and promising officers to become tyrants who alienated the men under their command. It was bad leadership, not inadequate discipline, that was at the root of the Navy's chronic afflictions of mutiny and desertion. True discipline was based on the confidence that men had in the competence of the commander, his goodwill and his regard for their well-being. It was "that implicit confidence and perfect respect [on] which the discipline of ships must ultimately depend."[61]

Thinking like Patton's gradually gained ground in official circles. A reputation for brutality or complaints by ships' companies began to impede, if not halt, the progress of officers' careers. Admiral Collingwood was among the prominent voices who now backed reform, warning fellow officers that excessive flogging was "big with the most dangerous consequences and subversive of all real discipline."[62] Influenced by cases like that of Corbet's *Nereide*, Admiralty regulations prohibited starting in 1809. In 1811, the Admiralty revised its rules concerning a commander's power to inflict flogging at his discretion. Captains now would be required to specify the nature of the offense for which they had imposed punishment, as well as the number of lashes inflicted, in quarterly reports. Enforcement was poor, however.[63]

Naval reformers began to enjoy the backing of a loose public campaign against flogging in newspapers and periodicals. In 1812, opposition lawmakers introduced a motion in Parliament to abolish flogging.[64] Opposed by naval officers and administrators who saw corporal punishment as indispensable, the motion failed – as would similar efforts to abolish flogging in Parliament for decades to come.[65]

Fortunately for seamen, however, the decades after the defeat of Napoleon were a period of political opening. After the war, large-scale popular unrest had erupted against economic hardship, incipient industrialization and the closed British establishment.[66] Political agitation was backed by growing middle-class involvement in public affairs, yielding many milestone reforms, notably the Reform Acts of 1832 and 1867 that expanded the voting franchise, and the Abolition Act of

1833 that comprehensively banned slavery in the British Empire.[67] In 1835 the government empowered a Royal Commission "for the purpose of Inquiring into the several modes of Punishment now authorized and in use for the maintenance of discipline" in the armed forces. Although the commission's review did not lead to immediate reforms on land or at sea, as the "searching light of publicity" fell on the issue of naval discipline, corporal punishment was discredited.[68]

Perhaps just as important, the Navy's reputation for brutal discipline had become a liability in an era of voluntary enlistment. A wave of mutinies in 1860–1 brought renewed attention to the problem of flogging. Complaints about the treatment of ratings resulted in the Naval Discipline Acts of the 1860s, which more effectively regulated naval justice. New *Admiralty Instructions* in 1871 limited flogging as punishment to the offenses of mutiny and striking superior officers. A regulation mandating that no punishment could exceed twenty-five lashes followed in 1879.[69] Although the reform of naval discipline faced steady conservative resistance, from about 1820 onward it is clear that the practice of flogging was declining steadily under the weight of regulations and moral disapproval. By the end of the 1860s, flogging, one of the most important causes of mutiny, had become a rare and unusual punishment.[70]

7.3.3   Reforms to Health and Welfare

In Chapter 4 we showed that the proportion of a ship's crew that was recorded as sick is one of the most important predictors of mutiny. Widespread sickness and unchecked contagion increased grievances among seamen who interpreted the problem as a failure of governance. Horatio Nelson, for one, was convinced that sickness was the Royal Navy's greatest adversary. In the wars of the French Revolution and Napoleon, more than 80 percent of naval losses were to disease rather than the enemy. He insisted that the commanders under him put greater stock in the welfare of their crews, and pressured naval authorities to provide competent surgeons and fresh food. He remarked, "The great thing in all military service is health; and you will agree with me that it is easiest for an officer to keep men healthy, than for a physician to cure them."[71] He might as well have remarked also that it is easier for a commander to keep his men satisfied than it is to regain their goodwill following a mutiny.

In considering the malign effects of sickness on operations and social order, naval administrators realized that scurvy was a particular threat. Although many accounts of naval health have overstressed its lethality, scurvy chiefly bedeviled long-distance operations like Anson's expedition and other operations that kept ships at sea for long intervals, such as close (inshore) blockades of enemy ports and coasts.[72] The real killers of seamen were contagious diseases, especially typhus, yellow fever and malaria.

Officials and medical experts focused on diet and sanitation as solutions to the disease problem. One early remedy concentrated on improving ventilation in naval vessels. The Navy improved the training and status of Surgeons, who, by 1800, were better prepared for managing sickness and on the road to professionalization.[73] The Navy also established a Royal Naval Hospital at Haslar (in Hampshire) that opened its doors in 1761. It greatly improved the care of the sick, chiefly through diet and good sanitary conditions. Haslar could treat two thousand seamen, and it did much to limit the scourge of typhus, a disease of cold, damp and crowded conditions. Progress against typhus also was made by confining new recruits on receiving ships, where they could be cleaned and given fresh clothes prior to joining the fleets. Whereas periods of naval mobilization tended to foster devastating outbreaks of typhus, better care of the sick and the more orderly processing of recruits contained the problem beginning in the latter half of the eighteenth century.[74]

Diet was another concern. In some respect, the diet of seamen compared well to that of laborers ashore. The Navy provided abundant food; seamen were entitled to about 4,500 calories per day, which mostly came from sources of carbohydrate such as biscuit, peas, oatmeal and beer, supplemented by salt meat, butter and cheese. Compared with enemy navies, food was reliably supplied in the Royal Navy.[75] Even so, the seaman's diet was prone to spoilage during long voyages and was notably short of vitamin C.[76] Mutinous seamen, like those aboard the *Terrible*, repeatedly objected to spoiled provisions and the lack of fresh food, but comprehensive action only came after the mass mutinies of 1797. Alongside the demand for better pay, seamen at Spithead demanded better victuals, including "a sufficient quantity of vegetables." The Navy responded, resulting in a "dietetic revolution" based on healthier and more diverse victuals, including fresh foods and vegetables, better supplies of clean water, and improved barrel storage, which retarded spoilage.[77]

Scurvy did not always make mutinies but it did undercut the Navy's capacity to defend a global empire and impose blockades on enemy coasts. Defeating the disease was a priority for naval administrators, but the causes of scurvy were not well understood. Even the famous naval surgeon James Lind, who conducted the first clinical trial of treatments for scurvy by controlled experiment, suggested that it had many causes, and that citrus fruits were but one of many possible treatments. The Sick and Hurt Board that reported to the Admiralty suggested a variety of dietary measures to eradicate scurvy. Several were tried on James Cook's long-distance voyages of discovery in the 1760s and 1770s. Cook was a fastidious commander who attended carefully to the well-being of his crews. Scurvy and other sicknesses did not much afflict his men, although his insistence on cleanliness and fresh food rather than anti-scorbutic treatments of dubious value (wort, "portable soup," spruce beer, sauerkraut, etc.) seem to have been the chief reasons for his success.[78]

Citrus juice only gradually gained support. The crucial turning point occurred when Lind's disciples won the backing of Admiral Alan Gardner, a member of the Admiralty Board. In 1793, he began to strongly advocate for adding lemons to the diet of seamen, arguing that they were "deservedly acknowledged to be among the best anti-scorbutics and being usefully packaged will contain their good qualities for several months."[79] Beginning in 1795, the issuance of citrus became the standard practice in the Navy, with most of the fruit purchased in Spain or Italy. In spite of the expense and problems of supply, most senior naval officers were now convinced of the necessity of providing citrus as an anti-scorbutic measure on all the ships of Navy.[80]

The results were dramatic. Once one of great disablers of seamen, scurvy gradually disappeared in the fleets. Sailing to distant seas usually involved mortality rates of 10 percent or greater and had been dreaded – and sometimes resisted – by seamen.[81] Whereas the Navy had difficulty blockading North America during the War of American Independence, the defeat of scurvy enabled the close-in blockade of revolutionary and Napoleonic France and her allies, which choked their trade and prevented them from combining their fleets behind an invasion of Britain.[82]

In spite of solving the problem of scurvy and containing outbreaks of typhus in home waters, yellow fever and malaria still made tropical waters the graveyards of mariners. The West Indies Station, in particular, was vital in strategic terms, but the unhealthiest theater of naval operations. In the wars of the French Revolution and Napoleon, the Royal Navy lost tens of thousands of seamen to tropical disease, with an annual mortality rate of about one in every six seamen who served there.[83] Efforts to establish effective hospitals at tropical naval stations failed, partly because of inadequate investment, but partly because of the difficulties of understanding or preventing transmission of mosquito-borne diseases in wet climates.[84] As late as 1834, the mortality rate from disease in the Navy remained high, at about 2 percent per annum.[85]

7.4   The Tension between Rebellion and Reform

The *Wager* episode is unique, but the causes of the mutiny – sickness, the decay of social order, poor governance – are wholly consistent with the general explanation of rebellion presented in this book. In the wake of the *Wager* mutiny, the Admiralty changed the system of appointment for officers, and made steps toward battling scurvy through better diet and hygiene, as well. In 1749 it passed an act for "extending the discipline of the navy to the crews of his Majesty's ships, wrecked, lost, or taken, and continuing upon them their wages upon certain conditions."[86] Shipwrecked or captured seamen would remain in pay and commanders would never again face the ambiguous situation that confronted Cheap and Baynes of the *Wager*. In effect, the mutiny resulted in the clarification of the criteria defining mutiny.

The Royal Navy was stunningly successful in the Age of Sail. It allowed Britain to defeat all of her rivals, establish a global empire and defend it. Whatever their flaws, the Navy's institutions proved themselves more than adequate to the tasks of waging warfare, acquiring and outfitting ships, supplying and provisioning fleets and sustaining its enormous workforce. In view of this, resistance to reform was not necessarily unreasonable. Officers and naval officials recognized that tradition and conventional practices reinforced social order through stability and predictability.

Despite this understandable resistance, mutiny fostered social and institutional change in the Navy by calling attention to issues in need of urgent attention. The mass mutinies of 1797 led to the first general increase of seamen's pay in more than a century, and ongoing fears of insurrection inspired a second general wage increase in 1807. The fate of Anson's squadron and the mutiny on the *Wager* directly inspired efforts to clarify command authority and to improve the health of seamen. Mutinies on the *Hermione*, the *Nereide* and other ships brought naval discipline into disrepute. They inspired calls for reform, which eventually led to the abolition of starting and the progressive restriction of flogging.

Maintaining the health of a population under adverse circumstances is a major challenge for effective governance and the link between health and social order is starkly underlined by naval history. The remarkable operational effectiveness of the Royal Navy by the end of the eighteenth century came about, in part, because naval authorities strove more conscientiously to attend to seamen's welfare and improve their health in the wake of mutinies.

Reform did not occur solely because of the pressure exerted by mutineers, of course. Concern with operational success was enough of a reason to convince naval commanders and administrators that they had to improve governance to be assured of healthier and more satisfied seamen. The end of the Napoleonic Wars relieved many of the demands placed on the Navy. Nevertheless, mutinies and the *possibility* of mutiny seem to have been necessary conditions for the initiation and sustaining of many institutional reforms in the Navy. As the history of the slow erosion of wages in the Navy suggests, it is doubtful that the seamen in the sailing navy would have experienced substantial improvement of their situation absent the threat of lower-deck uprisings.

Notes

1. On its departure, Anson's squadron had borne about 1,600 men, of whom fewer than 200 returned to England. Of the roughly 1,400 men who died of

illnesses, 70 percent probably suffered from scurvy. See Bowden-Dan 2004, p. 262.

2. For accounts of the *Wager* mutiny and the Anson expedition, see Haine 1992; Pack 1964; and Williams 1999.

3. TNA: PRO ADM 1/5288.

4. Williams 1999, pp. 228–9; see also Baugh 1965 on Anson's career and role as a reformer.

5. See the Captain's and Master's logs from the *Janus* in TNA: PRO ADM 51/4226 and ADM 52/2359, as well as the account in Haine 1992, pp. 33–4.

6. On mutiny's "unwritten rules," see Rodger 1986, pp. 243–4.

7. TNA: PRO ADM 1/5333. Horatio Nelson was similarly outraged by the concessions given and the lack of punishment in the *Windsor Castle* case (discussed in Chapter 3). Nelson wrote to his wife decrying the "mistaken lenity" shown by senior naval officials (Naish 1958, p. 187).

8. As Gilbert 1983, p. 113, notes, "Since a wide variety of activities could possibly be defined as mutinous behavior, sailors never could be sure if twelve lashes or death would be the consequence." Earlier on, authorities may have been somewhat more tolerant of collective disobedience – so long as they saw it as justified – and more flexible concerning how rules were enforced than they were at the time of the wars of the French Revolution and Napoleon; see, e.g., Baugh 1977, p. 143.

9. Duffy 2003, pp. 175–6; also see Willis 2010.

10. Claver 1954, pp. 136–7; Rodger 2004, pp. 493–4.

11. On the code, see Hay et al. 1975; King 2000; McLynn 1991; Sharpe 1999.

12. McLynn 1991, p. 258.

13. Phillips 1980, p. 158. As Jeremy Bentham noted in his *Introduction to the Principles of Morals and Legislation* (1789), such practices undercut most of the deterrent function of punishment. For Bentham, the severity of punishment was much less important than its certainty.

14. "It was an axiom of the reigning penal theory of the day that criminals had to be dealt with severely to impress upon the rest of society the importance of obeying the law" (Byrn 1989, p. 10; see also Eder 2004).

15. On the logic of "old regime" punishment, see Foucault 1977 and Garland 1990.

16. Claver 1954, pp. 123–4.

17. McLynn 1991, p. xv.

18. On the role of the law in Georgian society see Brewer and Styles 1980; King 2000, 2006; and Sharpe 1999.

19. Rodger 2004, pp. 494–5.

20. Byrn 1989, p. 23; Rodger 1986, p. 218.

21. Byrn 1989, pp. 32–3.

22. Elitism was not peculiar to naval justice because the high property qualification for jury service meant that England's poor were also not tried by their peers under the common law. See Hay et al. 1975.

23. Eder 2004, pp. 58–62.

24. King 2000, p. 355.

25. McLynn 1991, p. 218; Sharpe 1999, p. 198.

26. Nullification refers to the action of a jury in a criminal case that disregards its own findings of fact by acquitting a defendant. Mitigation refers to the action of a jury moderating or relaxing the severity of a prescribed punishment.

27. TNA: PRO ADM 1/5330.

28. TNA: PRO ADM 1/5360–2.

29. When a jury recommended a pardon – "royal mercy" – it was "invariably granted" (Byrn 1989, p. 61).
30. Eder 2004, p. 145.
31. TNA: PRO ADM 1/5345.
32. TNA: PRO ADM 1/5340.
33. TNA: PRO ADM 1/5376.
34. TNA: PRO ADM 1/5331.
35. TNA: PRO ADM 1/5322.
36. TNA: PRO ADM 1/5452.
37. TNA: PRO ADM 1/5383.
38. TNA: PRO ADM 1/5318.
39. It could be argued that a seaman's sentence to hundreds of lashes was tantamount to a death sentence. In practice, however, floggings around the fleet rarely resulted in death. Seamen could not withstand floggings much above one hundred lashes. After which point, the ship's Surgeon would stop the punishment. The remaining punishment could be continued once the seaman had sufficiently recovered. Frequently, however, the remainder of the punishment would be remitted by petition (see Rodger 2004, p. 494; as well as Byrn 1989 and Claver 1954 on flogging).
40. Other studies of naval justice have reported similar findings. A study of court-martial trials at the Leeward Islands Station (in the Caribbean) in the 1784–1812 period finds that 54 percent of seamen receiving capital sentences were ultimately pardoned. A separate study of naval justice during the Seven Years' War finds that only a third of those given a death sentence were actually executed, with the remainder eventually benefiting from royal mercy (Eder 2004, p. 147). Gilbert's (1976, pp. 82–3) study of court-martial trials held between 1756 and 1806 found that in all cases of mutiny –including lesser forms like individual defiance and charges of striking a superior officer – less than a third of indicted seamen were ultimately executed.
41. The analysis of court-martial verdicts is based on Edwards and Pfaff 2016.
42. For expositions of the thesis, see, e.g., Hay et al. 1975 and McLynn 1991.
43. Lewis 1959, p. 198.
44. Rasor 1976, pp. 64–5.
45. Clowes 1901, p. 190; Lavery 2010, p. 291; Rodger 2004, p. 639.
46. Brunsman 2013; see also Rodger 2004, pp. 497–501.
47. Lewis 1959, pp. 204–5.
48. On the role of technological change, see Lewis 1959, pp. 198–206.
49. The economist Thomas Piketty (2014, pp. 103–9) has referred to the eighteenth and nineteenth centuries as the era of "the great monetary stability" when, despite rapid economic growth, prices and wages increased only very gradually.
50. An Able Seaman earned 288 pence per month (Rodger 2004, p. 624). In 1740, the buying power of the monthly wage was about £142 in 2017 terms. In 1790, it had fallen to £92 in 2017 terms. Values of the pound come from the British National Archive's currency converter at www.nationalarchives.gov.uk/currency-converter.
51. Oliver 1941; see also Twigger 1999.
52. The monthly wage of an Able Seaman improved from 288 to 354 pence in 1797 and to 402 pence in 1807. See rates of pay in Rodger 2004, pp. 624–7.

53. Lavery 2010, p. 281, suggests that improved pay was a factor in the prevalence of mutiny during the Napoleonic Wars, which accords with the analysis we presented in Chapter 4.
54. In 1810, the buying power of the Able Seaman's monthly wage was about £78 in 2017 terms.
55. The monthly wage of an Able Seaman rose to 492 pence in 1852 and to 588 pence in 1862; see Rasor 1976, p. 104.
56. Recall that the buying power of an Able Seaman's monthly wage in 1740 was about £142 in 2017 terms. His wage in 1862 was about £153 in 2017 terms. Expressed differently, a seaman's annual wage was about 63 percent of the national average in 1800 and about 65 percent in 1850 (Piketty 2014, pp. 105–6).
57. Hobsbawm and Rudé 1968. The wage stagnation we observe in the Navy was part of a more general social problem. As Piketty (2014, p. 7) observes of the late eighteenth and early nineteenth centuries, "In fact, all the historical data at our disposal today indicate that it was not until the second half – or even the final third – of the nineteenth century that a significant rise in the purchasing power of wages occurred."
58. Brenton 1837, p. 360.
59. TNA: PRO ADM1/5340.
60. Brenton 1837, p. 361.
61. See the discussion of Patton and selections of his writings in Lavery 1998, pp. 622–34.
62. Rodger 2004, p. 493.
63. Byrn 1989, p. 19; Claver 1954, pp. 132–4.
64. Rasor 1976, pp. 10–13, 51–5.
65. Claver 1954, pp. 196–8.
66. Calhoun 1982; Thompson 1980. However, as wages, living standards and employment gradually improved, popular unrest abated. See Eichengreen 2018, p. 37.
67. On the politics of this period and the reform movements that remade British society, see Briggs 2000 and Woodward 1958.
68. Claver 1954, p. 257.
69. Claver 1954, pp. 203, 257–67.
70. Rasor 1976, pp. 112–28. Even so, as Claver 1954 notes, corporal punishment in the Navy was not fully abolished for all categories of seamen and all manner of offenses until 1949.
71. Pope 1981, pp. 131–4.
72. Rodger 2004, p. 308.
73. Bowden-Dan 2004, p. 269.
74. Rodger 2004, p. 309.
75. Rodger 2004, pp. 304–6.
76. Ascorbic acid was not chemically identified until the early twentieth century by the Hungarian biochemist Albert Szent-Györgyi (1893–1986).
77. Bowden-Dan 2004, p. 264; on nutrition in the Royal Navy generally, see MacDonald 2006 and Watt, Freeman and Bynum 1981.
78. Bowden-Dan 2004, pp. 262–3; also see Hough 1994.
79. Vale 1998; for a more conventional view stressing the little man of science against the heedless bureaucrats, see Brown 2003.
80. Vale 1998, p. 172
81. Gill 1961, pp. 66–7.
82. Brown 2003. On health as a challenge for command, see Rodger 2004, pp. 399, 486.

83. Dull 2009, p. 141; Lewis 1960, p. 442.
84. Rodger 2004, pp. 308–9. In the late 1890s medical researchers led by US Army doctor Walter Reed proved the hypothesis of Carlos Finlay that mosquitoes were the transmission vector for yellow fever. The development of a vaccine would have to wait until the 1930s.
85. Rasor 1976, p. 103.
86. Williams 1999, p. 229.

8 CONCLUSION AND IMPLICATIONS

In reflecting on the events on the *Bounty*, William Bligh could not help but dwell on the social nature of mutiny. Not only was mutiny rebellion against a commander, but it was also a crime against the Crown. Mutineers overturned the hierarchy and deference that were foundations of eighteenth-century social order. Worse yet, from Bligh's perspective, mutiny was an indictment lodged against a commander's conduct and character. The sense of personal betrayal that he felt was practically inevitable because, at its heart, mutiny sprouted from sedition and conspiracy alien to the trust and cooperation that was so vital to the operation of a ship at sea.

Although Bligh suggested several reasons why the mutineers might have acted, he felt that the appalling social violation at the heart of mutiny would defy systematic explanation. "It is certainly true that no effect could take place without a Cause," Bligh argued, "but here it is equally certain that no cause could justify such an effect."[1] Many subsequent historians and military experts have agreed. Because it grows from peculiar conditions and interpersonal conflicts, it is claimed, mutiny cannot be systematically analyzed, but only described or unraveled on a case-by-case basis by reference to its particular players and unique events.

Taking a different course through social scientific investigation, this book contends that just two related factors, *grievances* and *governance*, can explain the outbreak of mutiny in the Royal Navy. We have shown that mutiny is the outcome of the conjunction of poor governance that creates grievances among seamen, their interpretation of these grievances as ill-usage that could be rectified by collective action, and their capacity to coordinate. This argument is backed by both careful narrative analysis and by systematic evaluation of evidence drawn from hundreds of naval vessels.

When seamen's situation grew desperate, mutiny was one of the few avenues of recourse available to them. Most of the mutinies we studied were not spontaneous. Strategic thinking shaped the actions of the leading mutineers. Two-thirds of the mutinies in our sample were predicated on taking control of a ship in order to communicate specific grievances to naval authorities, and to generate leverage sufficient to convince the authorities to redress them. Although driven by similar grievances, the remainder of the mutinies were propelled by the desire to escape naval service by seizing a ship and absconding en masse. Regardless of whether the goal was voice or exit, in most mutinies the rebels issued threats judiciously and tended to avoid deadly violence. Using violence to take vengeance against hated officers, as occurred on the *Hermione*, was exceptional.

Although they were crude and uncertain instruments by which to pursue their interests, mutinies often led to the redress of seamen's grievances. Nevertheless, even when their grievances were acknowledged and, to varying extents, redressed, the Navy usually responded to mutiny with repression. Commanding officers sought to maintain their authority by referring the principal mutineers to courts-martial to face capital charges. The force used to maintain discipline and deter insurrection became more intense in the wake of the French Revolution. The repressive impulses of naval officers were sometimes kept in check by the Navy's commitment to the rule of law, and by the discretionary powers granted to the juries of courts-martial. Courts-martial jurors had the option of granting pardons to convicted mutineers considered worthy of mercy, which they did with some regularity.

What were the consequences of shipboard rebellion? One of the most important was that mutinies inspired reforms in the Navy that improved the health, welfare and compensation of seamen. Although the mass mutinies of 1797 at Spithead and the Nore failed to attain the more radical reforms demanded by seamen, they nonetheless led directly to improvements in pay and victualing.

One of the benefits of focusing on grievances in explaining protest and rebellion is that it draws attention to the importance of the quality of shipboard governance. If grievances are omnipresent and organization and opportunity are really all that count, then there can be few policy implications. If grievances are ubiquitous, discontent can never be ameliorated enough to establish peace. There can be no case for institutional reforms that might improve organizational performance, make governance more responsive or alleviate deprivation. Rulers might well conclude that repression is their only means of averting rebellion. In reality, however, grievances sometimes inspire rebellions and good governance helps to forestall them.[2]

8.1 Governance and Grievances

Our book suggests that rebellion is ultimately a consequence of poor governance. But does this claim have any explanatory power? When social order faltered onboard a warship it was generally because failures of governance upset the customary equilibrium between officers and crew. Mutinies were driven by violations of the tacit consensus between officers and men, especially when seamen's welfare was compromised by factors such as sickness, excessive discipline and unpaid and deficient wages.

Social order in the Royal Navy relied on the interaction between commanders and crews. True enough, social order was imposed through vertical control. Hierarchy, formal rules, supervision of work and discipline all served to prop up the authority of the commander. At least as important to the running of a ship, however, was the horizontal social order fashioned by the seamen themselves. Life at sea was dangerous and difficult, and seamen knew that a ship could only succeed through teamwork. Professional sailors were a diverse group of craftsmen ranked by skill, experience and authority. The everyday social order of a ship was based on the natural incentives for cooperation between command and crew that were required on sailing warships.

Under ordinary conditions, seamen complied with command for a number of reasons, including training, habit, mutual dependence and the fear of punishment. Naval authorities realized that these were insufficient motives for compliance, however. Social order was much more robust if seamen also believed in the *legitimacy* of their commanders. Especially where cooperation is essential to group performance – as on a sailing ship at sea – people need to be motivated and coordinated. Governance relies on formal institutions of rule, but these are insufficient to provide optimal performance. If authorities are to govern well, they must have the autonomy and capacity to act in ways that advance the organization and its mission. The Royal Navy established a system that selected competent commanders and provided clear incentives for them to run their ships efficiently and with reasonable concern for the welfare of seamen. This was not enough, however, to ensure superior shipboard operation. Good governance draws as much on informal resources including customs and conventions as it does on bureaucratic resources like regulations and organizational competencies.[3]

Beyond the formal rules that governed the Navy in the Age of Sail, a set of expectations guided by the customs of the sea influenced how commanders ran their ships and whether seamen regarded them as fair and just. This is because those in command must seek at least some level of consent from the governed by adhering to normative expectations.[4] A government is legitimate insofar as rulers and ruled consider its actions to not only be effective but culturally appropriate. Rulers care about their legitimacy because it makes it easier to manage their agents and govern their subordinates.[5] The authorities are more likely to gain quasi-voluntary compliance from their subordinates – probably the best indicator that a regime has achieved some degree of legitimacy – when they treat them fairly and allocate resources efficiently.[6] Subordinates need to trust authorities to act in ways that do not endanger them or their basic interests. Particularly in situations in which subordinates are highly dependent on their rulers, rulers must be perceived to be attentive to subordinates' safety and well-being if rebellion is to be precluded.[7] Equality and representative government can enhance legitimacy but are not necessary to achieve it; the quality of governance probably matters more.[8]

Good governance can be assessed, in large part, by whether it meets the *expectations* of the governed; this means that measures of the objective conditions of those who are subject to rule are less important than their subjective evaluation of these conditions as fair and appropriate.[9] This means, of course, that "poor governance" does not have a fully objective definition that can be carried across time and place. Context and subjective evaluations matter when people perceive bad governance. Whatever its objective features – above all, providing security and welfare – good governance must also be culturally appropriate.[10]

Understanding grievances requires an interpretive evaluation of what the members of groups consider to be good governance.[11] In our study of the Royal Navy, we have shown how seamen understood poor governance through the subjective lens of their shared occupational culture. Does this mean that systematic analyses of the relationship between grievances and protest are impossible? Whereas it is difficult to make predictions based on subjective evaluations, analyses can make use of measurable indicators of grievances whose meaning is informed by qualitative assessment of evidence. In the case of the Royal Navy, seamen saw the failure to manage sickness, navigational accidents, serving spoiled food, inadequate wages, as indicative of poor governance. These are all measurable features of shipboard life that are observable in day-to-day administrative records preserved in the archives. Given the availability of appropriate data, culturally sensitive analyses of governance are possible in other settings, as well.

In explaining mutiny, we have shown that seamen understood grievances in the language of "usage" derived from their occupational culture. Seamen expected to work hard, and they expected that they would have to bear privation and discomfort. *Proper usage* meant that their work and the hardships they endured were valued, that their commanders acted to prevent extreme exploitation and that their basic safety and welfare were safeguarded. *Ill-usage* meant exploitation, abusive treatment, excessive discipline and neglect of their safety and welfare. These things not only induced hardship but were contrary to the norms of naval service and seamen's shared understandings. Obviously, ill-usage generated a sense of grievance, but it is also true that when seamen were angered about violations of occupational norms they became less tolerant of material hardships and failures of governance.

The sense of injury that seamen bore combined material and nonmaterial complaints. Whatever their source, grievances were framed in the language of ill-usage that expressed the seaman's conception of his proper duties and treatment. Put simply, contemporary social science has recognized that it is not a matter of "real" material grievances versus "subjective" cultural grievances – the two overlap and reinforce one another. Material grievances are interpreted through the feelings produced by our normative lenses.[12]

Full-fledged mutinies in the Royal Navy were rare, in part, because seamen ordinarily tolerated harsh lives and difficult conditions. Many of the hardships that are so shocking to modern readers – and that inspired Samuel Johnson's dyspeptic portrait of the sailors' lot – were tolerated by seamen, albeit with weary resignation and much grumbling. We have called these factors *structural* grievances because they were understood to be part of life at sea. The hardships that they imposed were part and parcel of the seaman's role. *Incidental* grievances generated by failures of command or official indifference to unusual conditions of suffering, however, were quite different. They were not understood as inevitable parts of the job. Commanders were expected to shield seamen from threatening incidents like outbreaks of deadly illnesses, navigational accidents, shortages and spoilage of food.

The genesis of rebellion hinges on the degree to which grievances are shared and considered to be ameliorable. If so, then authorities are at least partly responsible, and thus they should be held accountable for redressing the sources of these grievances. Discontent motivates rebellion when people believe that the authorities *should* be competent and effective and willing to assist or protect them, but that they have *fallen short*. The greater the dependence of people on rulers for their well-being, the more they will expect them to be at least minimally concerned with their security and welfare, to be responsive in times of crisis or emergency and to govern in ways that are culturally appropriate.[13]

8.2   Explaining High-Risk Collective Action

The factors that we have identified in the genesis of mutiny have parallels in causes of protest elsewhere. The conditions facing seamen in the Navy were not fundamentally different from those that face rebels today in circumstances as diverse as armed insurgencies, prison uprisings and militant strikes.

Mutinies are a specific type of high-risk collective action. To make them, seamen had to be able to act together. The obstacles they had to overcome and the dangers they faced were considerable. Armed officers ruled the ships and imposed surveillance and control on seamen. Naval law, backed by harsh discipline and the threat of the noose, deterred insubordination. Seamen, however, benefited from the strong bonds among shipmates that characterized the crews of sailing warships. Everyday relations among seamen, sailors' cultural practices and the social ecology of the ship undergird the capacity for cooperation that made mutinies possible. Seamen developed techniques that helped them to deter free riding and provide assurance of large-scale participation in mutinies. They signed petitions and round-robin letters stating grievances and demanding redress as ways of committing seamen to a prospective rebellion before it was launched. They also made each other swear secretive oaths to join the mutiny and stick by their shipmates until their grievances were addressed.

Although resource mobilization and rational action theorists broke with classical grievance models for good reasons, our book suggests that they threw the baby out with the bathwater. If a latent capacity for coordination exists in given population, as it did among eighteenth-century seamen in the Royal Navy, then grievances are necessary factors in explaining collective action – they designate the expected benefits that would flow from the mutiny's success. These expectations are shaped by beliefs about how and when rebellion is effective and by the value of the hoped-for payoffs.

The neglect of grievances in the literature on protest movements and revolution stems, in large part, from the classical theory of collective action and public goods. Mancur Olson's seminal model focuses on selective incentives to explain collective action and, among the many possible structural or situational factors that can affect participation, principally identifies group size as most relevant. In Olson's wake, resource mobilization theories tended to dismiss grievances as too ubiquitous to explain variation in protest. Moreover, they see the issue through the lens of public goods, whose nature invites free riding rather than widespread mobilization. If large-scale protest occurs, it is because of interest groups that provide organizational incentives and pay the upfront costs.[14]

Olson rightly identified free riding as a social dilemma that tends to obstruct collective action, but his analysis overpredicts it. Over time, the limitations of the Olsonian approach have become more evident. Small changes in how the model is specified and variations in the environment of action can invalidate its prediction of universal free riding. Empirically, the beliefs of people concerning the efficacy of protest, social influences on their choices, the magnitude of shared grievances, injustice frames and the tendency of social ties to contain free riding have all been demonstrated to have important effects on collective action.[15]

As an alternative, theorists have proposed a variety of models predicated on interdependent decision-making and social influence. Assurance-game models show that the choice to free ride is influenced by the choices of other actors, and that in collective action the best choice usually depends on what other people in the same situation do.[16] In the case of mutinies, we have shown that seamen's propensity to free ride was influenced by leading seamen and whether other seamen pledged to cooperate. In other models, social influence is paramount. People are thought to have protest thresholds – the number of other people that have to take part in collective action before they will join it – that explain why rebellions can take off. Once a small number of interested, resourceful and well-informed members of a group take action – as a critical mass – they can trigger a cascade of action in others as a social tipping point is crossed.[17] Social influence models like these are persuasive and, as we have shown, are effective in explaining the inception and spread of collective action when applied to specific instances of mutiny.

These explanations for collective action, however, also have notable limits. They usually do not generate specific predictions about when and where cooperation will emerge. Further, most empirical studies only apply these models to explain episodes of collective action after they occur. Whereas prevailing theories of collective action concentrate on factors internal to a group and tend to apply models in a post hoc fashion, our approach in this book has been different. In modeling the odds of historical episodes of rebellion in samples including both positive cases and controls, we find that the beliefs of actors and changes in the environment of action are robustly associated with collective action. Moreover, these factors explain more than do the structural properties of groups.

Why do factors external to the group explain so much? In studies of social movements it is virtually axiomatic to say that people respond to perceived opportunities when deciding whether to participate in rebellious collective action.[18] Instead, we have found that opportunities for rebellion are not closely associated with the *timing* of mutinies, but that they did influence the *type* of mutiny that occurred. Exit mutinies were most likely to break out on smaller ships at sea that could be seized and sailed into enemy harbors. By contrast, organized voice mutinies tended to occur at naval bases and anchorages where seamen could take the ship, or immobilize it in a strike, and then use it as leverage in negotiating with naval officials.

Taken together, our results suggest that seamen mutinied not so much opportunistically but because they wanted redress of grievances. Seamen targeted commanders and naval authorities because they attributed their grievances to the behavior of these local authorities. They were motivated to engage in collective action chiefly by the expected payoffs – improvements in their material conditions, or averting perceived threats to their welfare and safety – that they expected from undertaking the costs and hazarding the risks of mutiny. By establishing the payoffs to be won (or the ills to be avoided), the magnitude of grievances increased the odds of mutiny.

The grievances that matter for rebellion are shared and come in different types. The structural grievances that were a large focus of prior research far from exhaust the category. We have demonstrated that the combination of structural and incidental grievances better explains the genesis of rebellion than theories that rely exclusively on resources, opportunities, private incentives or structural deprivation. Grievances motivate radical protest to the extent that they inspire indignation among group members and focus their discontent. As seen in the case of the Royal Navy, incidents that convince seamen that the authorities are insensitive to their security and welfare put commanders at risk. Indignation was greatest where commanders were perceived as acting unfairly and in ways that violated the customs of the sea. Structural deprivation like wage erosion and excessive discipline creates a baseline level of discontent, but we have shown that incidental grievances like the outbreak of disease, accidents and scarce and spoiled food play the greater role in triggering rebellion. As we demonstrated in the analysis of the relationship between flogging and mutiny (Chapter 4), very severe grievances might be sufficient causes of rebellion. This is because at the highest levels, some grievances present such a dire threat to seamen's welfare that they raise the salience of group membership, convince people that there is little advantage to be had by inaction and make favorable opportunities all but irrelevant considerations.[19]

8.3   Mutiny in Comparative Perspective

In the Royal Navy mutiny was a relatively rare event but an important signal alerting the authorities to poor governance. The possibility of mutiny constrained commanders and naval authorities and limited, to some extent, the exploitation of seamen. On the rare occasions when full-fledged mutinies did occur, they made the Navy more aware of the danger of abusing seamen and neglecting their welfare. Occasional mutinies seem to have reinforced the implicit contract on which command and consent were based. Qualitative evidence from the mutinies in our sample suggests this – some mutinies were tacitly accepted by the Admiralty in that seamen's grievances were addressed without inflicting punishment in a third of our voice mutinies. Senior officials knew that mutinies served as a check on exploitative and abusive behavior. Compared with its contemporary rivals, the Royal Navy did better in ensuring the payment of seamen, reliably providing sound victuals and attending to the health and welfare of seamen. The result was not only better operational capacity, but, if the implications of our models are sound, it also meant far fewer mutinies than would have occurred otherwise.

The armed forces are never completely isolated from the broader currents of their societies. The seamen of the Royal Navy were influenced by the political developments around them. The crisis of the Age of Revolution placed strains on the British state that were also felt in the Navy. Fearful of the consequences of disorder and unsure of where their men's loyalties lay, officers in the revolutionary era became more concerned with moral enforcement, even at the cost of undercutting spontaneous compliance. They became less tolerant of petty deviance and used their statutory powers to punish seamen by summary flogging against those whom they regarded as troublesome.

This is not a pattern peculiar to the history of the Royal Navy. For instance, officers of the United States Army prosecuted drug offenses more zealously in the Vietnam War era, a period during which they felt threatened by a shifting political culture and perceived attacks on their status.[20] In the context of the "war on drugs" and the urban crises of the 1980s, police officers adopted policies of confrontation and aggressive enforcement targeting ethnic and racial minorities.[21] In both instances, the unintended consequence appears to have been a further erosion of the social compact between authorities and the governed.

In some instances, mutinies have been important events in revolutionary movements, including the Russian Revolution of 1905, the German Revolution of 1918 and colonial uprisings in India, Indonesia and elsewhere. In the case of the Royal Navy, we have shown, however, that it was not so much radicalization in the fleets as much as mounting grievances, especially those related to pay and discipline, that produced mutinies. Although there are conditions in which seamen and soldiers might become active in the civilian politics of their time, it is more common across time and place that grievances arising out of poor governance feature most prominently in motivating mutineers.[22]

Nevertheless, mutinies have played an important part in wars, revolutions and *coup d'états*. In the early modern era, mutinies plagued the military campaigns of great powers, like Spain, that struggled to pay and provision her troops in the Eighty Years' War against Dutch rebels.[23] In the wars of the French Revolution and Napoleon, mutinies undercut the naval operations of many of the participants, including Britain.[24] A rebellion of native troops nearly overthrew foreign rule in British India in the Sepoy Mutiny of 1857.[25] Mutinies rocked the exhausted armies and the navies of the belligerent powers in World War I and helped to hasten the capitulation of the Central Powers.[26] Since World War II, mutinies have become uncommon in the armed forces of most developed countries, however.[27] They played a far less substantial role in World War II compared with World War I, which is surprising in view of the hopeless strategic situations and appalling causalities facing the German and Japanese armed forces in the latter phases of that conflict.[28] The diminishing incidence of mutiny can be partly attributed to modern governance that addressed many of the failings that had led to previous mutinies – such as by professionalizing the officer corps, improving the surveillance and control of soldiers and sailors, improving health and welfare and avoiding triggering grievances like unpaid wages and inadequate provisions.

Whereas mutinies might seem like a thing of the past, across the developing world poor governance still causes mutinies by creating grievances and undercutting social order.[29] The mutiny of the Bangladesh Border forces (also known as the BDR) is a recent example that shows how potent grievances can be in undermining military organization. In a 2009 uprising that calls to mind the Nore mutiny of 1797, more than a thousand BDR enlisted men in Dhaka mutinied against their officers, protesting ill-treatment, embezzlement of their wages and an unjust promotion system. The rebellion began with a presentation of grievances that quickly escalated to a violent mutiny spreading to several installations around the city. More than seventy officers and hostages were killed before the rebellion collapsed when regular units of the Bangladesh Army surrounded BDR headquarters and the government offered an amnesty to peaceful mutineers. In the wake of the mutiny, thousands of guards were arrested and tried by courts-martial, resulting in hundreds of prison sentences, more than a hundred executions and promises to institute reforms that would address soldiers' grievances.[30]

8.3.1   Does the Study of Mutiny Generalize to Other Forms of Collective Action?

But are mutinies an exceptional type of insurgency? Can the study of the Royal Navy in the eighteenth and nineteenth centuries inform the analysis of collective action in other times and places? It is well known that premodern forms of collective action differed from modern forms in some regards. Whereas premodern collective action tended to be localized, reactive and small scale, modern social movements expand to national, regional or global scales. Does this limit this study's generalizability? Not necessarily. Although most collective action prior to the late eighteenth century was local in nature, this was not the case for war-connected struggles such as mutiny, which confronted state authority and had national implications, most notably in the mass mutinies of 1797. Moreover, many movements at the national scale begin with local rebellions triggered by incidental grievances.[31]

Nevertheless, mutinies are distinctive in at least three ways. Evidently, shipboard social structure provided some advantages for seamen's collective action by fostering a latent capacity for coordination. Seamen shared an occupational culture, social segregation and a community of fate – all circumstances shown to facilitate coordination in other studies of collective action.[32] If members of subordinate groups have common grievances and an elementary capacity to coordinate, they can mobilize in response to incidents that heighten collective identification and perceptions of injustice. In circumstances of oppression and deprivation, loosely structured groups rather than interest organizations are likely be vehicles of mobilization.[33]

But in other respects, seamen faced greater obstacles to collective action than many other kinds of insurgents. Mutineers, who served alongside officers in relatively small ships in which there is no anonymity, were much more *visible* than most other insurgents. Insurgency is aided when individuals are difficult for authorities to monitor and control; for example, civil wars are more likely to occur in mountainous terrain than in lowlands.[34] Mobility was extremely restricted onboard ship, however, and the authorities were cheek by jowl with the seamen.

Finally, unlike most other insurgents, mutineers could not profit from *selective recruitment*. Mutiny occurred among a set of individuals who were selected by commanders rather by the insurgents themselves. Save in limited instances – conspiracies to seize ships and turn them over to the enemy – mutineers were unable to exclude loyalist seamen opposed to insurgency, and hence they had to involve others with widely varying dispositions. As we showed in Chapter 5, this constraint undercut insurgent solidarity.

These last two features also hold for collective action in other coercive settings, evident in slave rebellions and prison riots, among other kinds of insurrections. Given the constraints of military discipline and the monitoring and control to which soldiers and seamen are subject, on balance, mutinies are probably more difficult to mount than most other kinds of collective action.

8.4   Rebellion and the Urgency of Reform

One of the major conclusions of this book is that incidental grievances are more prominent than structural ones as causes of collective action. The case of the Royal Navy during the Age of Sail is not the only one to suggest this.[35] For example, the factors that triggered the widespread urban unrest in hundreds of American cities in the late 1960s are also consistent with our argument concerning the role of incidental grievances in the genesis of rebellion. Analyses of the occurrence of race riots in American cities in the 1960s do not consistently support the interpretation that unrest was more likely in places worst affected by structural grievances like poverty, unemployment and segregation.[36]

Rather, the cause of rioting appears to lie in the relationship between long-standing grievances like these and poor governance in response to incidents that provoked conflicts between the authorities and minority communities. Although subsequent studies of the causes of urban uprisings in America focused almost entirely on structural grievances, the 1968 Kerner Commission report actually noted that, "When grievance-related incidents recurred and rising tensions were not satisfactorily resolved, a cumulative process took place in which prior incidents were readily recalled and grievances reinforced. At some point in the mounting tension, a further incident – in itself often routine or even trivial – became the breaking point, and the tension spilled over into violence."[37] Decades later, urban unrest in Ferguson, Missouri in 2014 and Baltimore, Maryland in 2015 was similarly motivated by a combination of long-standing structural grievances related to poverty, discrimination and urban decline, and specific incidents of police brutality.[38]

Provocative incidents cannot be predicted ex ante, but this does not mean that reforms that improve governance will not decrease the baseline propensity to rebel. In American cities, less confrontational policing strategies and better training, on the one hand, and an impression that authorities are respectful and mindful of residents' welfare on the other, might well reduce the odds that such incidents of excessive force by police officers will spark violent protest. It seems apparent that governments should rely less on repression and take grievances into account if they seek to mitigate unrest.

Beyond this nostrum, however, what implications does this lesson have for policymakers? The urban uprisings of the 1960s inspired calls for major reforms to alleviate grievances by improving the lives of inner-city African-Americans. Some improvements indeed were made – such as in better schooling, reducing discrimination in hiring and poverty alleviation – but conservative political resistance, resegregation and deindustrialization frustrated broader progress.[39] Assessing the general consequences of rebellion for institutional reforms suggests a mixed picture in a number of contexts. For instance, since the 1970s prison riots have led to reforms in the treatment of the incarcerated.[40] Nevertheless, the ongoing privatization of prison services in many states continues despite the poor performance, threats to the health and welfare of prisoners and violence against staff that prevail in many such facilities.[41]

These examples suggest that policy amelioration does not automatically follow from rebellion, but depends – as always – on political considerations. This was clearly the case in the Royal Navy. Whereas mutinies led the authorities to make some improvements in domains like pay and the health and welfare of seamen, fear of insurrection actually prompted an increase in penal severity beginning in the 1790s. Substantial reforms of naval discipline were not made until the revolutionary crisis and the Napoleonic Wars were victoriously concluded.

Even where the political will to make reforms exists, it is easier (but hardly ever easy) to create policies aimed at mitigating structural rather than incidental grievances. This is because the former tend to be more stable – and thus predictable – than the latter. This is even true of structural grievances that occur with some risk, and hence can be estimated with a known probability. Because incidental grievances are by definition unpredictable, authorities cannot readily design and enact plans to forestall their effects. Even so, planning may mitigate their consequences. An analogy can be drawn to earthquake preparedness. Although policymakers cannot know when a fault will slip, they do know where the fault lines are; they can enact policies to minimize loss of life (e.g., through building codes, investment in infrastructure and civil affairs training), and they can ensure an appropriate emergency response in areas most at risk.

Prior to triggering incidents, however, often there is too little political will to make sufficient investments in future security. In social life, policies to redress structural grievances tend to be considered only in the wake of unrest: authorities often find themselves shutting the stable door after the horse has bolted. This was also true in the Royal Navy, which did not act to improve seamen's structural grievances – such as inflationary pressure on their wages or arbitrary and excessive punishment – until after a spate of mutinies in the 1790s and mass insurrections at Spithead and the Nore that threatened to paralyze the country's defense.

Regimes that eschew reform in favor of repression to achieve social order may be strong in some regards, but they are notoriously brittle, as contemporary uprisings from Eastern Europe in 1989 to the Arab Spring in 2010 have demonstrated.[42] In many instances, addressing grievances arising from group-based discrimination and deprivation and improving governance might achieve more than repression.[43] The Syrian popular uprising of 2011 that evolved into a devastating civil war is indicative of the link between failures of governance and rebellion. The origins of the uprising, which turned violent in the wake of government repression, appear to have resulted as much from intolerance of dissent as from the combination of long-standing structural grievances in impoverished and neglected sections of the country. Incidental grievances related to the government's handling of a severe drought magnified this deprivation.[44] Government that was more honest, responsive and inclusive might not have prevented the demand for democratization that spread with the Arab Spring, but it may have averted its becoming a disaster on the scale and intensity of the Syrian civil war.

Rebellions are famously unusual events, but part of the explanation for their rarity lies in the tendency of people who suffer structural disadvantage and hardship to become accustomed to it and have little confidence in the prospect of attaining an alternative to the status quo. This fatalism can change, however, especially when widely shared incidental grievances impose unexpected injuries and inspire new beliefs. A latent capacity for coordination is a powerful undercurrent running through many kinds of social relations and institutions. The possibility of rebellious collective action implicitly constrains the actions of every polity. In many coercive institutions the fear of rebellion is a brake, and sometimes the only brake, on oppression and exploitation. The possibility of unrest, if not outright revolution, should be one of the most important factors that drive authorities to attend to the quality of governance.

The importance of good governance has become newly relevant.[45] Poor governance (or the perception of it) is one of the most important issues of our day, not only in developing countries and failing states, but in the advanced democracies as well. Around the world, the perception that the liberal elites and the institutions they constructed in the wake of World War II are not up to the task of governing has been a substantial factor driving political polarization and in inspiring populist rebellions around the world.[46] We have argued that discontent motivates rebellion when people believe that the authorities should be competent and effective and willing to assist or protect them, but that they have fallen short. The urgency of restoring or establishing good government and confidence in democratic leadership will be a defining challenge of this century.

Notes

1. Dening 1992, p. 8. On Bligh's campaign to exonerate himself, see Alexander 2003.
2. For example, on the causes of prison riots and the role of reform in averting them, see Carrabine 2005; Useem and Goldstone 2002; and Useem and Kimball 1991.
3. See Rothstein 2011.
4. This consent is advanced by the ruled in return for the authority's legitimacy; see Hechter 2009, fn. 30. On the role of historically derived expectations and the normative example set by leaders in establishing or undermining cooperative norms, see Acemoglu and Jackson 2015.
5. On the basic issue of legitimation and social order, see discussions in Finer 1997; North 1981 (especially ch. 5); Rousseau [1762] 1997; and, of course, Weber 1978.
6. Levi 1997.
7. On governance and its implications for social order and consent, see Hechter 2009, 2013; Levi 1997; and Levi and Braithwaite 1998. The limited state capacity typical of premodern regimes, as well as many contemporary developing societies, does not preclude consideration of legitimacy as a feature of good governance. On "good enough" governance as comprising security, basic welfare and culturally appropriate rules, see Brinkerhoff 2007 and Grindle 2007.
8. The quality of governance is independent of the ends it seeks. Delivering on its obligations to its subjects and limiting abuses of power may matter more to the governed than whether or not a government advances democracy; see Fukuyama 2013. On output as the key measure of governmental quality, see Rothstein 2009 and Rothstein and Teorell 2008.
9. On the importance of legitimating beliefs, see Levi, Sacks and Tyler 2009.
10. See Hechter 2013 for a related argument concerning the conditions under which the governed accept the legitimacy of alien rulers.
11. This interpretative understanding is what Max Weber 1978, pp. 7–10, notably designated as *verstehen*.
12. Such judgments are informed as much by social intuitions and emotional processes as they are by a rational assessment of objective conditions. See Haidt 2001; Haidt and Kesebir 2010; and Kahneman 2011.
13. See discussions in Carrabine 2005; Fry 2005; Hechter 2013; and Useem and Kimball 1991. Much of the literature on the failure of responsive governance concerns large national societies, in which policies are complex, and the relevant information, when not scarce, is subject to manipulation by media and the internet; see Achen and Bartels 2016 and Bartels 2008. These considerations did not hold in the Royal Navy in our period, hence under these conditions it was relatively feasible to gauge the quality of shipboard governance.

14. On resource mobilization theory's skepticism toward grievances as an explanation for mobilization, see, e.g., Jenkins and Perrow 1977, pp. 250–1, 266; McCarthy and Zald 1977, pp. 1214–15; Oberschall 1973, pp. 133–4, 194–5; and Tilly 1977, pp. 7–8, 200–7.

15. For studies directly challenging the limitations of the Olsonian paradigm see, among others, Marwell and Oliver 1993; Medina 2007; and Opp 1989, 2009.

16. See, e.g., Hardin 1982; Schelling 1978; Taylor 1987.

17. Examples of the social influence approach to understanding participation in collective action include Centola 2013; Granovetter 1978; Lohmann 1994; Macy 1991; Marwell and Oliver 1993; Schelling 1978; and Watts and Dodds 2009.

18. For a summary of political opportunity theory, see McAdam et al. 1996.

19. Kalyvas and Kocher 2007. On how extreme grievances can create adequate incentives for collective action in the absence of political opportunity, Einwohner 2003 and Einwohner and Maher 2011.

20. Not to mention their lives, if rumors of "fragging" can be taken as reliable. See Lennon 1991.

21. On "stop and frisk" and "broken windows" policing, see Geller and Fagan 2010; Gelman, Fagan and Kiss 2012.

22. For comparative and historical studies of mutiny, see, e.g., Dwyer 2017; Hathaway 2001; Lammers 1969, 2003; Smith 1994; Way 2003; and Woodman 2005.

23. Parker 1973; also see Way 2003.

24. Frykman 2009, 2010.

25. Rao and Dutta 2012.

26. On mutinies in World War I, see Hathaway 2001; Smith 1994; and Williams 1962.

27. See Guttridge 1992; Lammers 1969; Rose 1982; and Woodman 2005.

28. Despotic military discipline, the prior savagery inflicted upon the enemy that led to the belief that capitulation was more dangerous than fighting on and the hopeless feeling that the situation was irredeemable deterred widespread mutiny in German and Japanese forces in World War II; see, e.g., Dower 1987; Kershaw 2011; and Van Creveld 1983.

29. For example, Dwyer 2017, p. 181, finds in her survey of contemporary mutinies, "Mutineers often express the idea that their leaders have broken the implicit contract in which hierarchy will take care of soldiers' welfare and pay in return for discipline and obedience."

30. See news reports in www.bbc.com/news/world-south-asia-12123651; www.aljazeera .com/news/asia/2013/11/bangladesh-mutiny-verdict-due-201311561736760822.html; www.washingtonpost.com/world/bangladesh-sentences-152-to-death-for-2009-mutiny/2013/11/05/b02f6a1c-463c-11e3-a196-3544a03c2351_story.html? noredirect=on&utm_term=.95b70290a328.

31. See Calhoun 1982; Hale 2013; Rudé 1964; Tarrow 1998; and Tilly 1984, 1993.

32. See, e.g., the structural accounts in Gould 1995; Kerr and Siegal 1954; and Tilly 1977.

33. Pfaff 1996.

34. Fearon and Laitin 2003.

35. For example, the first Arab Spring uprisings were triggered by the self-immolation of the grocer Mohamed Bouazizi in Tunisia.

36. As Gooden and Myers 2018, p. 13, observe,

> The trajectories of the riot cities and the nonriot cities are remarkably similar. Thus, it is a bit more difficult to embrace the conclusion that

> this racial divide was the cause of the riots given that the racial divide was evident in both riot cities and nonriot cities and perhaps was even more pronounced in the nonriot cities than in the riot cities before the riots.

Also see the analysis in Olzak and Shanahan 1996.

37. See *Report of the National Advisory Commission on Civil Disorders*, p. 108.

38. On the origins of #BLM (Black Lives Matter), see Cobb 2016; LeBron 2017; and www .theguardian.com/world/2015/jul/19/blacklivesmatter-birth-civil-rights-movement.

39. On the consequences of deindustrialization in American cities, see Wilson 1997. Five decades after the 1960s uprisings in cities that were affected by rioting, "Some areas – educational attainment and poverty – show relative improvement but other areas – family income and unemployment disparities – show little change" (Gooden and Myers 2018, p. 2). Moreover, the reforms instituted by the Royal Navy in the early part of the nineteen century can only be partially attributed to the preceding wave of mutinies (see Chapter 7).

40. Useem and Goldstone 2002; Useem and Kimball 1991.

41. See, e.g., Bauer 2018.

42. On spontaneous rebellions against authoritarian regimes, see Goodwin 2001; Hale 2013; Kuran 1991; Pfaff 2006; Weyland 2016.

43. On material grievances as the main predictor of state instability, see Goldstone et al. 2010; on the role of state policies that aggravate ethnic inequality as the principal factor in the outbreak of violent insurrections, see Cederman et al. 2013. On the role of inclusive governance as a factor promoting peace and security, see Karell and Schutte 2018.

44. See De Chatel 2014 and DeJuan and Bank 2015.

45. See, e.g., Brinkerhoff 2005; Brinkerhoff and Brinkerhoff 2002; Starr 2008.

46. See, among other studies, Bartels 2008; Levitsky and Ziblatt 2018; Mounk 2018; and Rothstein 2011.

APPENDIX A
DRAWING THE SAMPLE AND ARCHIVAL SOURCES

Our study is unusual in research on mutinies and other forms of rebellion because we analyze both ships that experienced mutiny and a larger set of randomly selected control cases. In Chapter 4, we estimated models based on the case-control method for assembling a sample.

A.1   The Case-Control Method for Building a Sample

The case-control strategy allowed us to avoid the sample selection problem that so often compromises research on collective action. However, the low incidence of mutiny also poses a challenge for population-based statistical analysis. Since the standard statistical techniques for drawing samples and estimating probability do not efficiently handle the analysis of rare events, we employed the case-control method for obtaining a retrospective sample and estimated models predicting the odds of mutiny using logistic regression. In effect, we analyzed the factors that increased the risk that any given ship would belong to the case (mutiny) rather than the control (no-mutiny) group.

One of the great advantages of case-control methods is their efficiency with respect to sample size and the analytic leverage that would be absent otherwise. To employ case-control methods, controls ("negative" cases) must be at potential risk of positive occurrence and drawn from the study population. Case-based retrospective studies like ours select cases on the basis of known information and thus require smaller random samples of controls. Though larger control groups are preferable, because the return to power decreases sharply as the ratio of controls to cases grows, a modest ratio of cases to controls is a standard practice.[1]

The feasibility of case-control studies relies on obtaining a listing of units that experienced the rare event (cases) and the drawing of an appropriate control group from the larger at-risk population. For the case group, we were able to assemble a reliable set of completed mutinies from authoritative sources based on our stated definition of mutiny. Our sample includes all cases we could document in which seamen fully halt the normal operations of the vessel (either by seizing it or by refusing to perform their duties) that we could identify in historical accounts and in an official Admiralty register of mutinies.[2] Accordingly, our cases of mutinies and the information about them are diverse and drawn not only from court-martial transcripts, but also from official documents, surviving correspondence, diaries and memoirs of naval service.[3]

Although we may not have been able to capture every mutiny, our method does not require it. One of the obstacles confronting the systematic study of rebellions like mutiny is possible underreporting. Nevertheless, there are good reasons to suppose that many cases of full-fledged mutiny did not escape notice. Captains and masters kept separate logs of daily events and the Admiralty was keen to have information about unrest. Full-fledged mutinies were hard to cover up. Because of the possibility of selective prosecution, we did not confine ourselves to court-martial transcripts; our sources also include official documents, correspondence, diaries and memoirs. Our sample excludes the ships taking part in the fleetwide mutinies of 1797 at Spithead and the Nore, as those cases were not independent. We worked with a different sample, described in Appendix C, to inform the analysis reported in Chapter 5.

We identified sixty-two cases of mutiny meeting our definition that could be confirmed in naval records during the period of study. In our sample, mutinies occurred on ships of all kinds, from ships-of-the-line to small armed vessels (the average mutinous ship in our sample is 1,000 tons, carrying about 295 men). They were not simply crimes of opportunity that occurred when a crew was remote from possible sanctions (e.g., the *Bounty*). The majority of our mutinies took place in the home waters of the British Isles, and most (about 65 percent) occurred in harbors and anchorages. They tended to happen on ships close to centers of naval authority. Mutinies occurred around the globe, including the Mediterranean (twelve cases), the West Indies (seven), Africa (four), North America (three) and in the East Indies and the Pacific (four). Nearly all (fifty-eight) took place during wartime.

To select the control group, we drew a population-based sample from the risk-set of ship-years selected at random (without replacement) from the entire list of Royal Navy ships active during the period 1740–1820. Our sampling frame is Lyon's *Sailing Navy List* (1993). This list contains every ship (about 4,400 in total) and its years of service, permitting us to condition a ship's chance of being selected on the number of years it was in service. We sampled *ship-years*: each potential control appears as a particular ship in a particular year, e.g., *Crescent*-1805. A ship-year is defined as the period one year prior to the occurrence of mutiny in a positive case and a given calendar year in a control case. Limiting the observation to one year thus provides a conservative estimate of the effect of incidents. Theoretically, incidents that occurred far in the past are not expected to trigger contemporary incidental grievances.

Aiming to achieve a 4:1 ratio of controls to positive cases, we selected 284 ship-years from the resulting list of all valid ship-years. However, archival records proved too incomplete to allow reliable coding for 104 of these ship-years, resulting in a sample of 179 ship-years (akin to a 63 percent response rate) in our control group. Although this introduces the possibility of a biased sample because records of smaller ships might be less likely to be preserved than those of large, important warships, the resulting sample does not appear to be biased. · Our controls have an average rating of 5.43 (on a scale of 1–7 by class of ship) and weigh an average of 710 tons; the selected ships whose records were missing/incomplete have an average rating of 5.48 and a weight of 699 tons. The two groups are indistinguishable by class and size of ship, suggesting that absent records are missing at random.

In Chapter 5, we analyze a different study sample which consists of all of the ships that took part in the mass naval mutiny at the Nore in 1797 (the sample and analysis are described in Appendix C). For the analysis of punishment presented in Chapter 6, we used the randomly selected sample of ship-years that served as the controls for the analysis of the odds of mutiny as our population-based sample, excluding the positive cases of mutiny that might have biased our analysis (see Appendix D).

A.1.1   Data Sources

The source of the study sample and chief source of primary data for all of the analyses presented in this book were obtained from documents collected in the Admiralty files of the Public Records Office deposited at the British National Archives at Kew (TNA: PRO ADM). We coded variables through the systematic evaluation of:

1. *Captains' logs* and *Masters' logs* (TNA: PRO ADM 51 and ADM 52) record the proceedings of the voyage and daily events, including reported disciplinary violations, the name of the offender, and punishments given; and the navigation and management of the ship. Our dependent variables are coded from daily reports made in Captains' and Masters' logs over the course of a given ship-year.
2. *Muster books* (TNA: PRO ADM 36–39; ADM 41) containing information about all the individuals aboard a ship for each voyage, including surname, place of birth, age at entry, volunteer or impressed, previous ship served (if any), rank, sickness, nature of discharge and desertion. Musters were updated weekly. For ships experiencing mutiny, the last muster taken before the date of the mutiny was coded. For control cases, the muster taken in the middle of the month of June was coded.
3. *Courts-martial records* (TNA: PRO ADM 1) detailing prosecution of mutiny or inquiry into the loss of a ship. They are verbatim trial transcripts, including witness testimony, depositions and verdicts.
4. Physical characteristics as provided by Lyon 1993.

At minimum, coding of the variables we have identified required a ship's muster book, its entry in the Navy List and either Captains' or Masters' logs. Note that Admiralty records are not paginated.

In addition to the Admiralty records preserved in the British National Archives, we also consulted primary materials gathered at the Caird Library and Archive in the National Maritime Museum, Greenwich.

A.1.2   The Limitations of Archival Data

The logs, in their detail and completeness, provide an incomparable data source for study of social order and punishment in an early modern setting. All historical research on naval discipline has relied on them.[4] "For naval crime summarily punished on board ship, the best source is the logbooks of individual ships. The great value of this source material lies in the fact that it provides a more representative description of day-to-day offences, whereas courts-martial mainly focus on serious infractions." Moreover the reasons recorded for the floggings run the full gamut from petty to dire offenses.[5]

Despite their richness, naval data sources do have limitations.[6] For example, the reported number of men pressed in a ship's muster is probably undercounted because some officers gave pressed men the opportunity to enter the books as "volunteers" so as to be eligible for a wage bonus. Another limitation is that Captains were not always scrupulous in reporting embarrassing episodes or every flogging or its severity. Fortunately, we code events and punishment from both Captains' logs and Masters' logs. Where available, redundant sources provide greater reliability; Masters were not responsible for inflicting punishment and had little incentive to neglect reporting punishments (in fact, we found Masters to be more likely to list the number of lashes inflicted than Captains).

Notes

1. See Gail et al. 1976; Haroutune and Lilienfeld 1994; Lasky and Stalley 1994; Lilienfeld and Stolley 1994; Newman 2001; Schlesselman 1982.
2. See Gossett 1986; Haine 1992; Hepper 1994; Lyon 1993; Rodger 2004.
3. Lammers 2003 explicitly endorses this approach.
4. See, e.g., Byrn 1989; Eder 2004; Rodger 1986.
5. Eder 2004, p. 16; also see discussion on p. 64.
6. See the discussion in Cock and Rodger 2006 and May 1976.

APPENDIX B
PREDICTING THE ODDS OF MUTINY

B.1 Predicting Mutinies on Ships

Chapter 4 presents the results of logistic regression models based on the sample of cases and controls described in Appendix A. The *dependent variable* is measured as 0 or 1 depending on whether we could document a mutiny meeting our definition aboard that ship during a given year. Our analysis includes a number of independent variables.

B.1.1 Indicators of Incidental Grievances

Percent sick is measured as the proportion of the ship's company reported as "sick" in the muster book. The sick were judged incapacitated for service by the ship's Surgeon; hence this probably provides a conservative estimate that does not indicate malingering or trivial complaints. Mortality would be of obvious interest, but it cannot be reliably measured, because the seriously ill were usually transferred to naval hospitals or other sites prior to their death.

Reduced rations measures whether a ship's crew had been placed on reduced or restricted rations of food or drink by a ship's commander for a period greater than one day over the course of a relevant ship-year, as reported in ships' logs. Seamen generally received less than their statutory rations because of shortages or spoilage of provisions.

Sailing accident measures whether ships' logs reported an accident that endangered the operation of the ship or the crew (e.g., grounding, a collision, a lost mast or a drowning) over the course of a relevant ship-year. By custom as well as naval law, a ship's commander was considered responsible for all failures of navigation and ship-handling.

Last year of a war measures whether a relevant ship-year was during the disruptive period of demobilization of fleets at the conclusion of Britain's wars. Seamen tended to blame officers for delays in mustering out and receiving their back pay. The wars in our period of study are the Austrian Succession (1740–8), the Seven Years' War (1756–63), the War of American Independence (1775–83) and the wars of the French Revolution (1793–1802) ending with the Treaty of Amiens, followed shortly by the Napoleonic Wars (1803–15).

B.1.2   Indicators of Structural Grievances

We measure *punishment* as a per capita rate of floggings for each of our cases and controls by taking the total number of lashes inflicted on a crew over the course of a given ship-year and dividing it by the number of seamen in the ship's company. If "running the gauntlet" was recorded, we treated this as two dozen lashes. Punishment reports were missing for twenty-two ships; to ensure missing data have not biased our estimates, we attributed missing values by multiple imputations in our final model.

We measure *crowding* by dividing a ship's company as reported in the muster book by the ship's total tonnage as reported in Lyon 1993.

Inflation-adjusted wages is a dynamic measure of the value of seamen's wages; we adjusted the nominal monthly wage of an Able Seaman by the previous year's change in the buying power of the pound (consumer price index). Inflation could substantially erode the value of a seaman's wages, which were not regularly adjusted and remained basically fixed at seventeenth-century levels until a general wage increase was granted by Parliament in 1797 and again in 1807. The monthly wage of an Able Seaman was 320 pence until 1797, when wages increased to 354 pence. Wages rose to 402 pence in 1807.[1]

Impressments are the share of a ship's company reported as being pressed into service as recorded in ships' muster books. If an entry read "see former books," we matched the members of our mustered company to the last preceding book that noted recruitment.

Foreign station is a variable measuring whether a ship served in foreign waters for all or part of a relevant ship-year, as reported in ships' logs. Foreign deployments were typically lengthier, more dangerous and more arduous than local deployments. For coding purposes, foreign stations include operations anywhere outside the English Channel, the eastern North Atlantic (excluding the Americas) and the North and Baltic Seas.

In addition to our grievance measures, we include variables that measure the social-structural characteristics of ships, and variables that might have influenced the opportunity for and context of mutiny.

B.1.3   Social Structural Indicators

Irish is the proportion of seamen born in Ireland. In cases in which place of birth was not reported in the muster book, it is inferred from the seaman's last name. In the event that a surname's origin is indeterminate ethnically (e.g., the surname Green), we coded the name as English.[2]

Prior service is the share of the ship's company reported as having served with at least one other seaman on another ship prior to transfer to the current vessel. If the entry read "see former books," we matched the members of our mustered company to the last preceding book that noted recruitment. Our measure is a proxy for social network structures, as these social ties may have facilitated participation in mutiny.

Rank heterogeneity measures the stratification of the ship by rank and qualities as reported in muster books and calculated according to a Shannon entropy measure. We calculated the score for each ship's company using the following groups by rank/quality: Officers, Warrant Officers, Petty Officers, Able Seamen, Ordinary Seamen, Landsmen, Marines and other (e.g., servants). Lower scores indicate less rank diversity.

B.1.4   Opportunity Variables

Marines is the share of a ship's company composed of Marine soldiers, if any, as reported in ships' muster books. Marines were supposed to engage the enemy in battle and serve as an onboard security force.

Fleet or detached service is a variable measuring whether a ship was assigned to a fleet or squadron or engaged in detached service over the course of a relevant ship-year as reported in ships' logs.

B.1.5   Contextual Variables

Wartime is a variable measuring whether Britain was at war during a given ship-year. *Number of years at war* is a continuous variable measuring the number of years Britain had been at war in a given ship-year. Long periods of uninterrupted warfare could have increased burdens on seamen, increased tensions and fatigue and made the command of warships harder. For each ship-year, we calculated the corresponding number of years of hostilities in which the Navy was engaged.

Table B.1 summarizes the variables we use in the analysis.

B.2   Findings

Given a dichotomous dependent measure, we estimated logistic regression models. Table B.2 reports model coefficients and measures of fit. In Model 1, we regress several social structural variables as proxies for the social heterogeneity among seamen expected to increase their capacity to coordinate collective action. Only the share of a ship's company that is Irish is positively and significantly associated with the risk of mutiny. In Model 2, we add variables as proxies for opportunities that could have increased the odds of mutiny by increasing its perceived efficacy or lowering expected costs. Although the presence of Marines did not deter mutiny, ships that were part of a fleet or squadron had significantly greater odds of mutiny than did solitary ships. This finding concurs with the qualitative evidence that seamen often seized ships to negotiate with senior naval authorities to redress their grievances.

In Model 3, we include proxies for structural grievances. Many of the factors usually considered to be onerous to seamen – impressments, crowding and foreign deployments – are not significantly associated with mutiny. However, the value of inflation-adjusted wages

Table B.1 *Covariates used in the analysis predicting mutiny*

Variable	Mean	Median	SD	Interpretation	Expectation on odds of mutiny
Percent Irish	0.13	0.11	0.07	Social structural	+
Rank heterogeneity	1.65	1.76	0.96	Social structural	+
Percent prior service	0.31	0.22	0.03	Social structural	+
Marines	0.15	0.16	0.02	Opportunity	−
Fleet or squadron	0.51		0.03	Opportunity	−
Inflation-adjusted wages	353.67	335.36	47.49	Structural grievance	−
Crowding	28.56	26.00	24.64	Structural grievance	+
Percent impressed	0.07	0.033	0.02	Structural grievance	+
Foreign deployment	0.67		0.03	Structural grievance	+
Per capita flogging rate	2.99	1.72	3.90	Structural grievance	+
Percent sick	0.03	0.0068	0.01	Incidental grievance	+
Reduction in rations	0.09		0.02	Incidental grievance	+
Accidents at sea	0.12		0.02	Incidental grievance	+
Last year of war	0.12		0.02	Incidental grievance	+
Years at war	4.69	4.00	2.93	Contextual variable	+
Wartime	0.90		0.02	Contextual variable	+

Table B.2 *Logistic regression models predicting mutiny*

	Social structural	Opportunity	Structural grievance	Incidental grievance	Contextual variable	Interaction terms
Percent Irish	5.730**	5.578**	6.438**	7.756**	7.680**	15.938***
	(2.040)	(2.126)	(2.310)	(2.695)	(2.716)	(4.655)
Percent prior service	0.093	−0.047	−0.577	−1.119	−1.137	2.226
	(0.563)	(0.578)	(0.700)	(0.816)	(0.818)	(1.682)
Rank heterogeneity	−0.465	−0.398	−0.300	−0.137	−0.120	−0.101
	(0.359)	(0.417)	(0.332)	(0.274)	(0.274)	(0.294)
Share Marines		−1.628	−0.553	0.411	0.416	−0.157
		(1.756)	(1.982)	(2.153)	(2.164)	(2.296)
Fleet or squadron		1.159***	1.575***	1.804***	1.789***	1.785***
		(0.330)	(0.396)	(0.469)	(0.483)	(0.492)
Inflation-adjusted wage			−0.012*	−0.014	−0.014	−0.013*
			(0.005)	(0.006)	(0.006)	(0.006)
Population density			0.017	0.012	0.011	0.012
			(0.013)	(0.013)	(0.012)	(0.012)
Percent impressed			0.234	0.683	0.745	1.907
			(1.653)	(1.833)	(1.839)	(2.222)
Foreign deployment			−0.319	−0.802	−0.814	−0.717
			(0.373)	(0.447)	(0.449)	(0.462)
Per capita floggings			0.117	0.172**	0.173**	−0.216
			(0.053)	(0.060)	(0.061)	(0.196)
Percent sick				20.917***	20.858***	19.484***
				(5.400)	(5.382)	(5.405)

Reduction in rations				2.004**	2.034**	2.017**
				(0.676)	(0.682)	(0.687)
Accidents at sea				1.654**	1.640**	1.800**
				(0.614)	(0.620)	(0.641)
Last year at war				1.751**	1.916*	1.776*
				(0.661)	(0.817)	(0.873)
Years at war					-0.040	0.021
					(0.105)	(0.113)
Wartime					0.344	-0.159
					(0.819)	(0.850)
Per capita flogging^2						0.022
						(0.012)
Percent Irish × percent prior service						-21.802*
						(9.848)
Intercept	-1.070	-1.556*	1.244	0.567	0.348	-0.213
	(0.621)	(0.661)	(1.706)	(1.917)	(1.999)	(2.070)
AIC	270.651	260.911	229.964	194.448	198.228	192.547
Log likelihood	-131.325	-124.455	-103.982	-82.224	-82.114	-77.273
LR test(X^2)	10.977*	13.740**	12.495*	43.378***	0.220	9.681**
N	239	239	220	219	219	219

Note: Likelihood ratio tests for significance of interaction effects were $X^2 = 3.521$, $p = 0.061$ for percent Irish × percent prior service and $X^2 = 4.897$, $p = 0.027$ for per capita flogging^2 (both tests single tailed). AIC = Akaike Information Criterion.
* $p < 0.05$; ** $p < 0.01$; *** $p < 0.001$ (two-tailed tests).

significantly decreased the odds of mutiny, and high per capita flogging rates also significantly increased the odds. These associations are consistent with the qualitative evidence, which shows that rebellious seamen frequently cited low wages and excessive discipline as motivating grievances.

Model 4 includes proxies for incidental grievances. All the indicators of incidental grievances are positively and significantly associated with the odds of mutiny. Whereas reduced rations, seafaring accidents and the last year of a war are all highly significant predictors of mutiny, the association between mutiny and sickness is especially strong. Contextual variables related to the pressures of warfare and the duration of conflicts included in Model 5 are not significantly associated with the risk of mutiny.[3]

In Model 6, we add terms to explore possible interaction and nonlinear effects. Although we see no significant interaction effects between classes of grievances, we do find an interaction between the share of Irishmen in a ship's crew and the share of the crew that had previously served together. Adding this interaction effect significantly improves the predictive ability of the model (likelihood ratio $X^2 = 3.52$, $p = 0.06$).

More specifically, when holding all other variables in the model at their means, on a ship with a mean level of sailors who previously served together, increasing the proportion of Irish seamen one standard deviation above the mean is associated with an 8.1 percent increase in the probability of mutiny. Because we have specified a logistic model, the effects of the predictor variables on the outcome are inherently nonlinear, which is why we specify the marginal effects at specific levels of the interacting variables.

On ships one standard deviation below the mean level of sailors previously serving together, the same change in the proportion of Irish seamen is associated with a 15 percent increase in the probability of mutiny. Finally, on ships one standard deviation above the mean level of sailors previously serving together, the same change in proportion of Irish seamen is associated with only a 3 percent increase in the probability of mutiny.

Consistent with our argument that structural grievances motivate rebellion when experienced at higher magnitudes that violate expectations about proper treatment, there is a nonmonotonic effect of flogging on the probability of mutiny. Analysis of a semi-parametric regression model replacing the traditional parametric estimate with a smoothing spline for per capita flogging supports our expectation of an increasingly positive effect on the probability of mutiny at successively higher levels. Model 6 includes a squared term for per capita flogging that significantly improves the fit of the model (X^2 = 4.90, p = 0.027). Because flogging was an expected part of maintaining order at sea, at very low levels increasing flogging decreases the probability of mutiny. Holding all other variables in the final model at their means, increasing the instances of flogging per capita from 0 to 3 reduces the probability of mutiny by 5.9 percent. Near the mean levels of per capita flogging (2.99), the effect of a one-unit increase in flogging is essentially zero. Seamen expected discipline and tolerated moderate levels of flogging. However, at one standard deviation above average flogging levels (approximately seven floggings per capita), the effect is positive: for instance, going from seven to eight per capita floggings raises the probability of mutiny by 1.5 percent. The effect continuously increases: at two standard deviations above average (approximately eleven floggings), increasing per capita flogging by one point raises the expected probability of mutiny by 5.9 percent. At three standard deviations above average, raising per capita flogging by one point (from fifteen to sixteen) increases the probability of mutiny by 10.9 percent.

Because there are missing data for some ships on some variables, we also estimate a final grievance model using multiple imputations. After checking that data were missing at random, we used the Multivariate Imputation with Chained Equations approach, because it allows for separate probability models to be used in the imputation of different missing variables and utilizes the full likelihood for estimation.[4] The results of the analysis are reported in Table B.3 and are nearly identical to those reported in Model 5, indicating that our findings are not biased by missing data.

B.3   Predicting Individual Seamen's Participation in Mutiny

In Chapter 4 we also present the results of an analysis of a subsample of mutinies for which we have complete lists of which seamen in a ship's

Table B.3 *Final model with imputation*

	β	Number missing	FMI
Percent Irish	15.740***	0	0.025
	(4.165)		
Percent prior service	2.875*	2	0.022
	(1.370)		
Rank heterogeneity	−0.129	0	0.013
	(0.297)		
Share Marines	−0.625	0	0.017
	(2.063)		
Fleet or squadron	1.274**	0	0.014
	(0.425)		
Inflation-adjusted wage	−0.009	0	0.043
	(0.005)		
Population density	0.012	0	0.010
	(0.009)		
Percent impressed	2.533	1	0.031
	(1.833)		
Foreign deployment	−0.742	0	0.024
	(0.418)		
Per capita floggings	−0.125	21	0.208
	(0.177)		
Percent sick	12.862**	2	0.020
	(4.042)		
Reduction in rations	1.608**	0	0.011
	(0.588)		
Accidents at sea	1.723**	0	0.012
	(0.531)		
Last year at war	1.330	0	0.039
	(0.725)		
Years at war	0.030	0	0.027
	(0.102)		
Wartime	−0.092	0	0.020
	(0.797)		
Percent Irish × percent prior service	−21.879**	0.024	
	(8.159)		

Table B.3 *(Cont.)*

	β	Number missing	FMI
Per capita flogging²	0.015	0.150	
	(0.010)		
Intercept	-1.527	0.040	
	(1.881)		

Note: Number missing refers to number of missing values for each covariate. FMI is fraction of missing information and indicates what proportion of information used to estimate each coefficient was imputed.
$^*p < 0.05$; $^{**}p < 0.01$; $^{***}p < 0.001$ (two-tailed tests).

company participated and whether they also served as a ringleader in the mutiny.

Given a dichotomous dependent measure, we estimated logistic regression models predicting whether seamen were identified as active participants in the mutiny and whether they were identified or indicted as ringleaders. For this analysis we include a variety of individual covariates that may have influenced the odds that a seaman took part in mutiny or served as a leader. These variables were drawn from the relevant ship's muster books and from its logs.

From the ship's muster book, we coded the rank of the seamen. Seamen's ranks are coded as Petty Officers, Able Seamen, Ordinary Seamen, Landsmen, Marines and Supernumeraries (passengers, servants and others present on the ship but not regular members of the ship's crew). The omitted category in the analysis is officers, including both commissioned and warrant officers. We also include the age of the seamen as reported in the muster, whether he was non-British (born somewhere other than England, Wales or Scotland), whether he had been pressed into service, whether he had been promoted in the last year and whether, prior to his enrollment in the muster, he had served on the same ship as had the greatest proportion of his fellow shipmates. Finally, from the ship's logbooks, we coded whether the seaman had been flogged in the year preceding the mutiny.

The results of the analysis predicting participation are reported in Table B.4. They show that although Petty Officers were important

Table B.4 *Logistic regression model predicting active mutineers*

	β	df	Sig.	Exp(β)
Petty Officer	0.21	1	0.413	1.234
Able Seaman	0.911	1	0	2.486
Ordinary Seaman	0.479	1	0.03	1.615
Landsman	0.832	1	0	2.299
Marine	−1.227	1	0.001	0.293
Supernumerary	−0.469	1	0.159	0.625
Age	−0.032	1	0.001	0.968
Foreign	0.564	1	0	1.758
Pressed	0.445	1	0.016	1.56
Promoted	−0.395	1	0.073	0.674
Flogged	0.293	1	0.125	1.34
Prior ship	0.221	1	0.113	1.247
Constant	−0.819	1	0.006	0.441

Cox and Snell R square 0.085
Nagelkerke R square 0.123
N = 1,787

sources of leadership in mutinies, they were not more likely to have joined them as ordinary participants. Able Seamen, Ordinary Seamen and Landsmen were at greater odds of joining a mutiny. Marines and outsiders were, not surprisingly, less likely to have played active roles in mutiny. Younger seamen were more prone to be mutineers than older seamen. Having been pressed increased the odds of becoming a mutineer. Other factors are not statistically significant.

Table B.5 shows the results when we estimated the odds of being a mutiny ringleader. They show that, as expected, Petty Officers were about four times more likely to have been among the ringleaders of mutinies and Able Seamen were nearly three times likelier than the omitted baseline category. Among ringleaders, personal grievances loom large. Both having been pressed and having been flogged increased the odds of being a ringleader. Given the added risks borne by ringleaders, it is not surprising that they appear to have had personal reasons for rebellion. Having served with other seamen on a previous ship

Table B.5 *Logistic regression model predicting mutiny ringleaders*

	β	S.E.	Sig.	Exp(β)
Petty Officer	1.389	0.441	0.002	4.011
Able Seaman	0.97	0.35	0.006	2.638
Ordinary Seaman	0.558	0.449	0.214	1.748
Landsman	0.073	0.534	0.892	1.075
Marine	−1.305	1.068	0.222	0.271
Supernumerary	−17.173	3515.706	0.996	0
Age	−0.017	0.019	0.374	0.983
Foreign	0.159	0.267	0.553	1.172
Pressed	1.029	0.299	0.001	2.798
Promoted	−0.116	0.393	0.767	0.89
Flogged	0.714	0.256	0.005	2.041
Prior ship	0.42	0.261	0.108	1.521
Constant	−3.544	0.619	0	0.029

Cox and Snell R square 0.032
Nagelkerke R square 0.102
N = 1,787

increased the odds of being a ringleader but the variable narrowly misses statistical significance.

Notes

1. The historical CPI data for Britain from 1750 is reported in Twigger 1999. For the years before 1750, we use the London grain price as a proxy. Rodger 2004 reports wage levels.
2. We use Neafsey's (2002) surname dictionary. Inferring ethnicity from surnames has been used in other studies of military organization (see, e.g., Costa and Kahn 2008). There were seamen from many countries in the Royal Navy; however, as a share of the total number of seamen aboard ships, outside of the Irish, their numbers were trivial.
3. As a robustness check, we also estimated models predicting mutiny using nonparametric random-forest modeling (see Siroky 2009). These models also prominently indicated an association between our grievance measures and our outcome measure.
4. On the estimation of these models, see Van Buuren and Oudshoorn 1999.

APPENDIX C
ESTIMATING TIME TO DEFECTION
AT THE NORE MUTINY

In Chapter 5, we report the results of Cox proportional hazards models to estimate the time to defection.[1] Tests of the proportional hazards assumption both globally and for each variable indicate that the proportional hazards assumption underlying the Cox model is tenable for our data.

C.1   The Sample

Our study sample is of thirty-three ships that were identified in primary and secondary accounts as having taken part in the mutiny at the Nore and that could be verified in naval records. The data are coded from documents collected in the Admiralty files of the Public Records Office deposited at the British National Archives at Kew (TNA: PRO ADM). Because muster books (TNA: PRO ADM 36–39; ADM 41) and ships' logbooks (TNA: PRO ADM 51 and ADM 52) are complete, we were able to code both cross-sectional and time-varying variables for every ship. For each of the thirty-three ships we assessed a variety of variables on social structural and situational factors that may have influenced the duration of mutiny aboard that ship. Logbooks allow us to make daily observations of every ship that was part of the mutiny, whereas muster books allow us to code features of the social structure of the crew at the time of that ship's joining the mutiny. These data provide measures of ethnic composition, the distribution of ranks and qualifications onboard ships, mode of recruitment and prior service of seamen.

C.2   Dependent Variable

Duration is measured in days from when a ship entered the mutiny until its defection. The average duration is 22.33 days. There are thirty-three ships all of which have mutiny entrance and defection dates. Thus, there is no left or right censoring. This results in a case-day file with a total of 671 observations.

We do not hypothesize time dependence (i.e., that the hazard rate varies across the duration of a ship's mutiny) and therefore we avoid specifying the baseline hazard rate by using the Cox semi-parametric proportional hazards model.

C.3   Independent Variables

Because muster books and ships' logbooks are complete, we were able to code both cross-sectional and time-varying variables for every ship. For each of the thirty-three ships at the Nore we assessed a variety of variables on social structural and situational factors that may have influenced the duration of mutiny aboard that ship. The coding was accomplished using ships' logs and muster books (a weekly census of everyone onboard and his characteristics). Logbooks allow us to make daily observations of every ship that was part of the mutiny, whereas muster books allow us to code features of the social structure of the crew at the time of that ship's joining the mutiny. These data provide measures of ethnic composition, the distribution of ranks and qualifications onboard ships, mode of recruitment and prior service of seamen.

To test community ties explanations, we use three proxy measures: the share of the ship's company rated as Landsmen, the share of a ship's company that was Irish and the share of the ship's crew that had previous service with at least one other seaman on the same ship prior to assignment to their vessel. Men rated as Landsmen in muster books were inexperienced, unskilled and, usually, recent recruits to the fleet who may have undercut the cohesion of crews.

Archival sources allowed us to measure a host of other variables, as well. In addition to sociodemographic variables, we also coded variables from ships' logs for the year preceding the mutiny in order to explore factors that might have influenced mutiny duration, including how the ship joined the mutiny, the rate of punishment experienced by ships' companies, desertion rate, rate of impressments, conditions of their service (time spent at sea, service outside of home waters, reported shortages of rations, etc.) and so on. None of the unreported sociodemographic or other variables from either source is significantly correlated with mutiny duration.

By dint of their occupational histories and term of service, Landsmen were the least likely to have been instilled with the community norms. About a fifth of the men at the Nore were Landsmen. To calculate the share of Landsmen on a ship, we divided the reported number by the size of the ship's company. Coethnicity may be one of the most robust bases for community solidarity. Republican forms of organization, like that which governed the Nore mutiny, may be especially facilitated by a high degree of likeness among members that reinforces consensus. In fact, research on the coherence of military units has found that ethnic differences can undermine group solidarity and increase defection. At the Nore, the sense of community aboard ships may have been especially affected by the tension between Britons and the Irish as a result of incipient nationalism. Those born in Ireland were by far the largest and most important group of "foreigners" in naval service, composing about 12 percent of the ships' companies at the Nore and about 11.5 percent of all seamen in the Navy in the late 1790s.[2] To calculate the variable, we took the number of men identified as Irish in muster books and divided it by the size of the ship's company.

The degree of community aboard ships was probably affected by the long-standing social ties among seamen. Ships varied substantially in terms of the sailors' previous experiences with one another. Whereas some ships' companies had been assembled from diverse recruitment sources so that few of the men had served with one another before, on other ships many of the sailors had served with their shipmates before, often giving them many years' prior acquaintance. The community ties argument suggests that the greater the share of the ship's company that had previous joint service, the greater the duration of the mutiny will be.

For indicators of dependence and control, we coded the share of active mutineers that faced indictment for their avid participation as a share of a ship's company and the date aboard a ship that details of the royal pardon were communicated to seamen. To assess the relative size of the mutinous faction on Nore ships, we took the number of men indicted for active or leading roles onboard a ship divided by the size of the ship's company.[3]

The date on which the pardon was read is a time-varying variable. To measure it, we identified ships in which the details concerning the settlement at Spithead and the terms of the royal pardon were read to the crew by officers or Admiralty officials. On some ships, the details were read in the midst of the initial unrest on the ship, and on others they were read at later points during the confrontation with the authorities. The date of these events (if they occurred) is reported in each ship's Captain and Master logs. Ships have a value of 0 up until the day in which the pardon was read (if it was read). From that day onward, a ship receives a value of 1 for the rest of the duration of its mutiny. Ships that never had the pardon read receive a value of 0 for their entire mutiny duration. There is no pattern in the evidence that suggests that this variable is endogenous to our dependent variable.

Finally, as control variables we included two cross-sectional measures. First, to assess possible differences in achieving and maintaining solidarity in groups of different sizes, we measure the size of the ship's company that is reported in each ship's muster book at the last date of a muster prior to the ship joining the mutiny. Much of the historical literature emphasizes the importance of pressed and Quota-men in the mutiny. To assess the share of a ship's company that had been pressed or compelled to serve through a Quota Act, we examined each ship's muster book that indicates the conditions of a man's recruitment. If the entry read "see former books," we matched the members of our mustered company to the last preceding book that noted recruitment. The resulting number of coerced recruits is divided by the size of the ship's company.

As we do not expect decisions by ships' companies to be taken independently, we also include the spread of defection in the mutiny as a diffusion variable that measures the influence of previous defections by other ships. A dichotomous variable $D_{j\tau}$ is coded 1 if a defection occurred in ship j in time τ, and 0 if it did not occur. The first diffusion variable is merely a cumulative count of the number of ships that defected prior to time t. Since the defection of other ships might have the largest influence in the days immediately following their defection, the second diffusion variable counts the number of ships that defected in the three days prior to time t.

The third diffusion variable counts the number of ships that defected the day prior to time t. Table C.1 provides descriptive statistics for these variables.

Table C.1 *Descriptive statistics of the variables used in the event-history models*

Cross-sectional variables (for thirty-three ships)	Definition	Mean	SD	Min	Max
Ship's company	Size of ship's company	245.42	156.75	38.00	491.00
Active mutineers	Proportion of ship's company who are active mutineers	0.06	0.06	0.00	0.21
Share Irish	Proportion of ship's company who were born in Ireland	0.12	0.06	0.03	0.38
Share unskilled Landsmen	Proportion of ship's company who were unskilled Landsmen	0.23	0.12	0.00	0.61
Share previous service	Proportion of ship's company who served with at least one other seaman on the same ship prior to their current assignment	0.32	0.21	0.01	0.91
Share pressed men	Proportion of ship's company who are pressed men	0.07	0.08	0.00	0.38
Time-varying variables (for 671 spells)					
Pardon read	1 = day the pardon is read and thereafter; 0 = otherwise	0.37	0.48	0.00	1.00
S1: Cumulative prior defection	Count of the number of ships that defected prior to time t	3.70	4.19	0.00	32.00
S2: Defection within the past three days	Count of the number of ships that defected within the three days prior to time t	1.40	2.28	0.00	22.00
S3: Defection within the past day	Count of the number of ships that defected the day prior to time t	0.61	1.53	0.00	13.00

C.4   Findings

Table C.2 presents the hazard models of the rate of defection from the mutiny with active mutineers, share Irish, pardon read, and the diffusion variables as the predictors. Alternative bivariate and multivariate hazard models were also estimated for size of the ship's company, share unskilled landsmen, share previous service and share pressed men (results not shown). Since the coefficients of these models never reached statistical significance, these variables were excluded from the final models.

Across all the models, the coefficient for the variable share Irish is positive and significant, indicating that the larger the proportion of Irish on a ship, the higher a ship's hazard rate of defection from the mutiny. The share of active mutineers on a ship has a significant and

Table C.2 *Hazard models predicting the rate of defecting from the Nore mutiny*

	Model		
	(1)	(2)	(3)
Active mutineers	-6.302†	-6.797†	-7.855^{*}
	(3.724)	(3.646)	(3.642)
Share Irish	6.554†	6.913^{*}	7.830^{*}
	(3.553)	(3.478)	(3.306)
Pardon read	1.028^{*}	1.033^{*}	0.967^{*}
	(0.444)	(0.062)	(0.434)
S1: Cumulative prior defection	0.157^{***}		
	(0.043)		
S2: Defection within the past three days		0.200^{**}	
		(0.062)	
S3: Defection within the past day			0.353^{***}
			(0.095)
X^2	31.67	27.48	31.64
df	4	4	4
No. of spells	671	671	671
No. of ships	33	33	33

Note: Two-tailed significance tests: † $p < 0.10$; * $p < 0.05$; ** $p < 0.01$; *** $p < 0.001$.

negative effect on the hazard rate in each model. As the proportion of active mutineers on a ship increases, the hazard of defecting decreases. The coefficient for pardon read is positive and significant in all three models. For example, in Model 1 the risk of defecting is roughly 180 percent higher for ships in which the pardon was read compared to ships in which it was not read (e1.028 = 2.80).

All three diffusion variables have a positive and significant effect on the hazard rate. The hazard of defecting increases as the number of ships that defected increases, whether measured as all defections prior to time t (Model 1), defections three days prior (Model 2) or defections one day prior (Model 3).

Our findings indicate some support for the community ties explanation. A large share of a ship's company being composed of Irishmen – by far the largest group of non-English seamen on ships at the Nore – did indeed undercut mutiny solidarity, as the theory of coethnicity would lead us to expect.

Our findings do not provide support for the other community-based accounts of solidarity, however. In our models predicting duration of the mutiny, neither the proportion of Landsmen aboard a ship (which should have undercut solidarity according to a community explanation) nor the proportion that had served with other seamen previously (which should have enhanced solidarity) is significant (results not shown).

Finally, the analysis provides strong support to our propositions that dependence and control were the main factors that ensured solidarity in the Nore mutiny. Both ignorance of the terms of the settlement at the Nore and a large cadre of committed mutineers prolonged the mutiny aboard ships at the Nore. Particularly striking is the finding that learning the details of the royal proclamation reduced the duration of mutinies net of other factors.

Notes

1. On event-history modeling, see Allison 1984 and Box-Steffensmeier and Jones 2004.
2. Gill 1913, p. 330.
3. The numbers of men indicted are reported in Manwaring and Dobrée 1987.

APPENDIX D
ESTIMATING THE FREQUENCY
AND SEVERITY OF PUNISHMENT
IN THE ROYAL NAVY

In our analysis of punishment by flogging in the Royal Navy, we include measures indicative of our hypotheses alongside a number of variables intended to explore alternative factors that may have influenced commanders' decisions to inflict punishment.

We restrict our analysis to the control group sample described in Appendix A that comprises 179 ship-years. The diversity of ship types in our sample is also comparable to the characteristics of the population of Royal Navy ships. Although our sample is not large, it is random and diverse. Nevertheless, given its size statistical power is limited and generalizations must be made with caution.

D.1   Dependent Variables

Total lashes given: This measures the number of lashes inflicted in all episodes of flogging during a ship-year as noted in Captains' and Masters' logs. In a few instances, floggings are noted in logs but the number of lashes is unreported. In those instances, we use an estimate of twelve lashes, as it was the standard punishment in naval regulations. In the very rare instances in which flogging is inflicted by running the gauntlet, we treat it as twenty-four lashes.

Total punishments given: This variable measures the total number of floggings inflicted on all crew members (of whatever number of lashes) by summary punishment on board a ship during a ship-year as reported in Captains' and Masters' logs.[1]

D.2   Independent Variables

Post-1789: To test our argument about the effect of the Age of Revolution on sentiments concerning social control, an indicator of whether a case is observed after 1789, the year that the French Revolution commenced, is included.[2]

Collective insubordination: One of the most direct challenges to authority was collective insubordination, which under naval conventions could capaciously be defined as mutiny. This indicator variable measures if defiant collective action occurred on a ship during the relevant ship-year. It is defined as incidents in which two or more seamen were involved in defying command and which was described in ships' logs as mutinous or insubordinate conduct.

% British: We measure the share of the ship's company that was English, Welsh and Scottish – the peoples included in Britain's emerging sense of nationality. The ethnicity of ship's company is coded by the place of birth for each seaman as reported in the muster book. In cases in which it does not record the place of birth, then ethnicity is inferred from the crew member's surname. In the event that a surname's origin is indeterminate ethnically (e.g., the surname "Green") then the name is coded as English. All surnames originating from continental European ethnicities are coded as European. Estimating ethnicity from surnames, although imperfect, has been used in other studies of military organization.[3]

Years at war: To explore the possibility that wartime pressures account for penal severity, we calculated for each ship-year the corresponding number of years of hostilities in which the Royal Navy was engaged. The wars in our period of study are the Austrian Succession (1740–8), the Seven Years' War (1756–63), War of American Independence (1775–83), and the wars of the French Revolution (1793–1802) that ended with the Treaty of Amiens, followed fourteen months later by the Napoleonic Wars (1803–15).[4]

% pressed: As a control for impressment, we calculated the share of a ship's company reported as having been pressed into service in a ship's muster book.

Foreign station: We employ an indicator variable measuring whether a ship was in foreign waters for all or part of a relevant ship-year, as reported in logbooks. For coding purposes, foreign stations include operations in the Mediterranean, the West and East Indies, Africa, the Americas and the Pacific. Excluded are the English Channel, the North Atlantic and the North and Baltic Seas.

CPI: As a control for wage grievances that might have created tension aboard ships, we measure the change in the consumer price index in the year previous to the observation of the case.

We also include measures as proxies for group cohesion and shipboard security and a control for the size of a ship's crew.

% joint service on a prior ship: This variable measures the proportion of the ship's crew that had served with other crew members on the same vessel prior to their assignment to the ship that is the unit of analysis. A high degree of cohesion among seamen on a given vessel may have enabled it to maintain order horizontally. Alternatively, high social solidarity among seamen may have been seen as a challenge to the commander's authority, particularly after 1789. It is coded from the muster book.

Marines: One of the roles of Marines was to be an armed guard in support of the officers. This indicator variable reports whether a detachment of Marines was part of the ship's company as reported in muster books.

 # in the ship's company: As a control for the size of a ship's crew, we included it as recorded in its muster book. All things being equal, the larger a ship's crew the greater the opportunity to inflict punishments.

D.3 Estimation and Findings

In our analysis we regress selected independent variables on two measures of punishment: the total number of floggings (as a measure of frequency) in a given ship-year and the total number of lashes inflicted (as a measure of severity). We utilize a two-part regression model to explore and properly account for the discontinuity after 1789. Although this results in a modest increase in Type I error, it is necessary in order to model the potential changes in the underlying social processes driving the phenomena under study prior to and after the onset of the Age of Revolution that would be lost if we modeled a single stationary time.

We faced three challenges in conducting the analysis. First, the size of our random sample of ship-years is modest (179 cases). Second, there are missing data on the dependent variable for 15 cases. Given our sample size, we did not want to eliminate these cases and so elected to utilize a multiple imputation strategy. After checking that data were missing at random, we employed the Multivariate Imputation with Chained Equations (MICE) approach since it allows for separate probability models to be used in the imputation of different missing variables and utilizes the full likelihood for estimation. We employed the *R* package MICE for the imputation procedure.[5]

Table D.1 displays means and standard deviations for all variables for both raw and imputed data. The differences in means are very

Table D.1 *Variables used in the analysis of flogging*

	No imputation		With imputation	
	Mean	SD	Mean	SD
Total lashes given	483.38	649.27	477.26	640.87
Total floggings	26.60	32.62	26.42	32.25
Inflation (previous year change in CPI)	3.02	9.93	3.02	9.93
% recently pressed	8.96	11.59	8.91	11.58
% previously served together	58.84	78.01	58.27	77.62
Foreign station	0.67	0.04	0.67	0.04
% British	0.77	0.11	0.77	0.11
# in the ship's company	188.35	160.64	188.35	160.64
Post-1789	0.50	0.04	0.50	0.04
# years at war	4.70	3.02	4.70	3.02
Marines	0.75	0.03	0.75	0.03
Collective insubordination	0.20	0.03	0.20	0.03

small, which suggests that there are no outsized effects on estimates owing to imputed values.

The third issue is that our sample includes several ship-years in which no punishments were inflicted. For both dependent variables we must answer two questions: (1) are punishments/lashes administered and (2) given that punishments/lashes are administered, how many are administered? Statistically, these questions take the form of (1) the probability that punishments/lashes are administered and (2) given that punishments/lashes are administered, what is the expected amount given?

Statistical structures like this are commonly represented using a class of models grouped under the label of "hurdle models." A common use of such models is to estimate whether an outcome is greater than zero (the "hurdle") and, if so, the expected value of the outcome.[6] In our case, we model the probability of the number of punishments/lashes being greater than zero with a probit distribution and we model the expected number of punishments/lashes as a negative binomial distribution (also commonly referred to as a zero-inflated negative binomial model). For the sake of brevity, the probit coefficients and measures related to the imputation process are not reported in the tables.

Tables D.2 and D.3 show the effect of each independent variable on the expected value of total number of punishments/lashes, given that the number is greater than zero. We estimated regression models for our two dependent variables, the total number of lashes inflicted on a ships' company in a given ship-year and the total number of all episodes of floggings in a given ship-year. Whereas the total number of lashes is meant to capture the severity of punishment and the total number of floggings its frequency, the measures are very highly correlated (0.96). This suggests that the tendency to punish did not divide between strategies of infrequent but severe punishment (perhaps indicative of a general deterrence strategy) or frequent and less severe punishment (perhaps indicative of specific deterrence). Consequently, most of the same factors associated with total lashes are also associated with the total number of floggings, though there are a few differences.

For both the models estimating the total number of lashes given and for the total number of punishment events (floggings), the results are in line with our hypotheses that the disposition to punish is

Table D.2 *Regression coefficients for total lashes given*

Predictor	All years	Up to 1789	Post-1789
Inflation (change in CPI)	−0.008	−0.018	−0.004
	(0.008)	(0.012)	(0.008)
% recently pressed	0.009	−0.002	−0.004
	(0.009)	(0.009)	(0.008)
% previously served together	0.001	0.066	1.087**
	(0.001)	(0.363)	(0.342)
Foreign station	0.423*	0.336	0.279
	(0.168)	(0.204)	(0.193)
% British	−0.970	−2.326†	0.287
	(0.830)	(1.285)	(0.910)
# ship's company	0.002**	0.002*	0.004***
	(0.001)	(0.001)	(0.001)
Post-1789	0.879***	–	–
	(0.191)	–	–
# years at war	0.020	0.045	−0.019
	(0.027)	(0.044)	(0.026)
Marines	0.261	0.325	0.933**
	(0.267)	(0.245)	(0.263)
Collective insubordination	0.302†	0.402†	0.299
	(0.172)	(0.217)	(0.210)
Constant	5.053***	6.182***	4.158***
	(0.702)	(1.079)	(0.757)

Note: $N = 179$ for each full imputed dataset.

* $p < 0.05$, ** $p < 0.01$, *** $p < 0.001$, † $p < 0.10$.

affected by perceived threats to political authority and social control. They provide support for our principal argument that global threats to social order affect dispositions toward punishment. Even in the presence of covariates associated with rival explanations, the indicator variable for the post-1789 period is positively and significantly associated with both measures of punishment. This finding is in accordance with the descriptive evidence we found that commanders punished more frequently and severely in the revolutionary era than they had before. Our finding is robust to a Chow test of our models of flogging frequency and severity. When we partition the data on the year 1789, both frequency ($X^2 = 74.25$, $p < 0.001$) and severity ($X^2 = 2.16$, $p = 0.004$)

Table D.3 *Regression coefficients for total episodes of punishment by flogging*

Predictor	All years	Pre-1789	Post-1789
Inflation (change in CPI)	−0.004	−0.020	0.002
	(0.008)	(0.013)	(0.008)
% recently pressed	0.003	−0.002	−0.006
	(0.008)	(0.010)	(0.007)
% previously served together	0.002	0.052	1.055**
	(0.001)	(0.376)	(0.310)
Foreign station	0.355*	0.380†	0.155
	(0.158)	(0.211)	(0.184)
% British	−0.772	−1.918	0.705
	(0.796)	(1.371)	(0.861)
# ship's company	0.002***	0.002†	0.004***
	(0.001)	(0.001)	(0.001)
Post-1789	0.605**	–	–
	(0.181)		
# years at war[a]	0.017	–	−0.018
	(0.026)		(0.025)
Marines	0.258	0.210	0.883**
	(0.240)	(0.263)	(0.264)
Collective insubordination	0.376*	0.479*	0.369†
	(0.163)	(0.222)	(0.192)
Constant	2.210***	3.375	0.919
	(0.671)	(1.149)	(0.716)

Note: $N = 179$ for each full imputed data set.
[a] Relationships among this covariate, the DV and other covariates necessitated its removal to maintain computational tractability in the pre-1789 subsample.
* $p < 0.05$, ** $p < 0.01$, *** $p < 0.001$, † $p < 0.10$.

yield significant associations, indicating a structural break in the relationship between the dependent variables and the covariates in the year 1789.

We also see that collective insubordination is positively and significantly associated with both measures of punishment. Commanders punished more severely on ships in which this occurred. This association is consistent with our contention that commanders used flogging to stave off threats to their authority – that is, they not only punished rebellious seamen specifically but punished their crews more harshly *generally* when they felt challenges to their authority.

The variables we included in our models as proxies for alternative explanations for penal severity have mixed associations with the dependent variables. As expected, the size of a ship's company is associated with greater punishment – all other things being equal, larger crews provide more opportunities for both deviance and punishment. We do not find that the pressures unleashed by warfare or the enhancement of state power during wartime as measured by years at war are significantly associated with flogging.

The share of the crew that was British is negatively associated with both measures of punishment, although the relationship is not statistically significant. The share of a ship's company that had served with others on a previous ship is positively associated with both measures of punishment but likewise is insignificant.

Our models also provide some support for the alternative explanation that Captains perceived the need to flog seamen when they were facing conditions that made command more difficult and seamen less compliant. This conclusion is indicated by the positive and significant association between serving in a foreign station and both measures of punishment. However, other measures of stresses that may have made command more difficult (wage depreciation, impressments, the pressures associated with long periods of warfare), as well as alternate models with indicator variables for wartime and 1797 not shown here, have no significant association with flogging.

So as to be more confident about period effects, we also estimated separate models that analyze observations up through 1789 with those after 1789. When we separate the data into two subpanels, the general impression as to the factors that increased punishment is much the same as when we combine the data, though there are some differing associations.

Both the expected effect of time and the observed average levels of flogging presented here are consistent with our argument that Captains became increasingly punitive in response to the threat posed by the revolutionary age. The upward trend in punishment that is conspicuous from the 1790s onward reaches an inflexion point around 1809. Whereas the observed level of punishment after 1810 is still greater than it was before 1789, a downward trend is observable. The attenuation over time is consistent with our understanding of the underlying social-psychological dynamics that inform our explanation of threat and penal severity.

Notes

1. Note that our two measures of the dependent variable are closely correlated (at above 0.9); this suggests that officers generally were not pursuing rival strategies of selective deterrence (i.e., many moderate punishments) as opposed to general deterrence (i.e., a few very severe punishments).

2. Britain did not enter armed hostilities with the French Republic until 1793, when, following the execution of Louis XVI, France declared war on Great Britain. One could argue that this event, rather than the Revolution itself, would have created collective insecurity in Britain. To explore this possibility, we estimated models using an indicator variable for 1793 in place of 1789 and the variable has the same positive and significant association with our measures of the dependent variable. It might also be argued that the War of American Independence was the start of the revolutionary era. The fact that the leaders of the rebellion never sought to challenge the domestic power of the British monarchy and eschewed social radicalism argues against this interpretation. To be certain, we estimated our models with 1776 and 1783 as indicator variables and found no positive or significant association with our measures of the dependent variable.

3. See, e.g., Costa and Kahn 2008.

4. Although one could treat the Peace of Amiens (March 1802–May 1803) that divides the wars of the French Revolution from the Napoleonic Wars as a brief interlude and not a real cessation of hostilities, this argument strikes us as retrospectively biased. The motives for the peace were genuinely driven by the desire to end the war that, on the British side, was shaped by "financial, political and strategic exhaustion" (Rodger 2004, p. 472). Moreover, the peace was marked by substantial naval demobilization; total manpower fell by about 50 percent between 1801 and 1803 (from 131,959 to 67,148) and financial expenditure fell by about a third. Indeed, so thorough was demobilization that manning levels in the Royal Navy would not exceed those reached on the eve of the peace until 1808 (Rodger 2004, pp. 638–9, 645).

5. See Van Buuren and Oudshoorn 1999.

6. See Wooldridge 2009.

BIBLIOGRAPHY

Abrams, D. E. and Hogg, M. A. (1990). *Social Identity Theory*. New York: Springer.

Abrams, D. E. and Hogg, M. A. (2006). *Social Identifications: A Social-Psychology of Intergroup Relations and Group Processes*. London: Routledge.

Acemoglu, D. and Jackson, M. O. (2015). History, Expectations and Leadership in the Evolution of Social Norms. *Review of Economic Studies*, 82/2, 423–56.

Acemoglu, D. and Robinson, J. A. (2006). *Economic Origins of Dictatorship and Democracy*. New York: Cambridge University Press.

Achen, C. and Bartels, L. M. (2016). *Democracy for Realists*. Princeton, NJ: Princeton University Press.

Ahlquist, J. and Levi, M. (2013). *In the Interest of Others: Organizations and Social Activism*. Princeton, NJ: Princeton University Press.

Alam, S. (2007). *Rethinking the Mau Mau in Colonial Kenya*. New York: Palgrave Macmillan.

Alexander, C. (2003). *The Bounty: The True Story of the Mutiny on the Bounty*. New York: Penguin.

Allardyce, A. (1883). *Memoirs of the Honourable George Keith Elphinstone, Viscount Keith, Admiral of the Red*. Edinburgh: Blackwood.

Allen, D. (2002). The British Navy Rules. *Explorations in Economic History*, 39, 204–31.

Allison, P. D. (1984). *Event History Analysis*. Newbury Park, CA: Sage.

Allison, R. S. (1943). *Sea Diseases*. London: Bale.

Almeida, P. D. (2005). Multi-Sectoral Coalitions and Popular Movement Participation. *Research in Social Movements, Conflicts and Change*, 26, 67–102.

Ashton, T. (1955). *An Economic History of England: The Eighteenth Century.* London: Routledge.

Asongu, S. A. and Nwachukwu, J. C. (2016). Revolution Empirics: Predicting the Arab Spring. *Empirical Economics,* 51, 439–82.

Ausubel, L., Cramton, P. and Deneckere, R. (2002). Bargaining with Incomplete Information. In R. Aumann and S. Hart, eds., *Handbook of Game Theory with Economic Applications.* Vol. 3. Amsterdam: Elsevier, pp. 1897–1945.

Bartels, L. (2008). *Unequal Democracy.* Princeton, NJ: Princeton University Press.

Bates, R. H. (2008). *When Things Fell Apart: State Failure in Late-Century Africa.* New York: Cambridge University Press.

Bauer, S. (2018). *American Prison: A Reporter's Undercover Journey into the Business of Punishment.* New York: Penguin.

Baugh, D. A. (1965). *British Naval Administration in the Age of Walpole.* Princeton, NJ: Princeton University Press.

Baugh, D. A. (1977). *Naval Administration, 1715–1750.* London: Naval Records Society.

Baumer, E. and Martin, K. (2013). Social Organization, Collective Sentiment, and Legal Sanctions in Murder Cases. *American Journal of Sociology,* 119, 131–82.

Beckett, K. (1999). *Making Crime Pay.* New York: Oxford University Press.

Beckett, K. and Sasson, T. (2004). *The Politics of Injustice.* 2nd edn. New York: Sage.

Beissinger, M. (2011). Mechanisms of *Maidan*: The Structure of Contingency in the Making of the Orange Revolution. *Mobilization,* 16, 25–43.

Bell, C. and Ellemann, B. (2003). *Naval Mutinies of the Twentieth Century.* London: Cass.

Bellin, E. (2012). Reconsidering the Robustness of Authoritarianism in the Middle East: Lessons from the Arab Spring. *Comparative Politics,* 44/2, 127–49.

Benford, R. and Snow, D. (2000). Framing Processes and Social Movements. *Annual Review of Sociology,* 26, 611–39.

Bennett, A. (2010). Process Tracing and Causal Inference. In H. Brady and D. Collier, eds., *Rethinking Social Inquiry.* 2nd edn. Lanham, MD: Rowman & Littlefield, pp. 207–19.

Bergstrand, K. (2014). The Mobilizing Power of Grievances: Applying Loss-Aversion and Omission Biases to Social Movements. *Mobilization,* 19, 123–42.

Berman, B. (1991). *Control and Crisis in Colonial Kenya.* Columbus: Ohio State University Press.

Berman, E. (2009). *Radical, Religious and Violent*. Cambridge, MA: MIT Press.

Bethlehem, J. (2009). The Rise of Survey Sampling. CBS Discussion Paper 1572-0314. The Hague: Statistics Netherlands.

Black, D. (1976). *The Behavior of Law*. New York: Academic Press.

Blake, R. (2008). *Evangelicals in the Royal Navy, 1775–1815*. London: Boydell.

Bligh, W. ([1792] 1962). *An Account of the Mutiny on Board H.M.S. "Bounty."* New York: New American Library.

Boix, C. (2003). *Democracy and Redistribution*. New York: Cambridge University Press.

Boswell, J. ([1791] 1934–50). *Boswell's Life of Johnson*. Oxford: Clarendon Press.

Boucher, J. (2012). *Memoir of the Life of Admiral Sir Edward Codrington*. Vol. I. New York: Cambridge University Press.

Bowden-Dan, J. (2004). Diet, Dirt and Discipline: Medical Developments in Nelson's Navy. *The Mariner's Mirror*, 90, 160–72.

Box-Steffensmeier, J. M. and Jones, B. S. (2004). *Event-History Modeling*. New York: Cambridge University Press.

Brady, H. E. and Collier, D. (2010). *Rethinking Social Inquiry*. 2nd edn. Lanham, MD: Rowman & Littlefield.

Brenton, E. P. (1837). *Naval History of Great Britain: Vol. I, 1783–1836*. London: Colburn.

Brewer, J. (1976). *Party, Ideology and Popular Politics at the Ascension of George III*. New York: Cambridge University Press.

Brewer, J. (1989). *The Sinews of Power: War, Money and the English State, 1688–1783*. New York: Knopf.

Brewer, J. and Styles, J. (1980). *An Ungovernable People: The English and Their Law in the Seventeenth and Eighteenth Centuries*. New Brunswick, NJ: Rutgers University Press.

Briggs, A. (2000). *The Age of Improvement, 1783–1867*. 2nd edn. London: Longman.

Brinkerhoff, D. W. (2005). Rebuilding Governance in Failed States and Post-conflict Societies: Core Concepts and Cross-Cutting Themes. *Public Administration and Development*, 25, 3–14.

Brinkerhoff, D. W. (2007). *Governance in Post-Conflict Societies*. New York: Routledge.

Brinkerhoff, D. W. and Brinkerhoff, J. M. (2002). Governance Reforms and Failed States: Challenges and Implications. *International Review of Administrative Sciences*, 68, 511–31.

Brown, A. G. (2006). The Nore Mutiny: Sedition or Ships' Biscuits? *The Mariners' Mirror*, 92, 60–74.

Brown, S. (2003). *Scurvy*. Markham, ON: Thomas Allen.

Brunsman, D. (2013). *The Evil Necessity: British Naval Impressment in the Eighteenth-Century Atlantic World*. Charlottesville: University of Virginia Press.

Brush, S. G. (1996). Dynamics of Theory Change in the Social Sciences: Relative Deprivation and Collective Violence. *Journal of Conflict Resolution*, 40/4, 523–45.

Byrn, J. D. (1989). *Crime and Punishment in the Royal Navy: Discipline on the Leeward Island Station, 1784–1812*. Aldershot, UK: Scolar Press.

Byrn, J. D. (2009). *Naval Courts Martial, 1793–1815*. Farnham, UK: Navy Records Society.

Calhoun, C. (1982). *The Question of Class Struggle*. Chicago: University of Chicago Press.

Calhoun, C. (1991). The Problem of Identity in Collective Action. In J. Huber, ed., *Macro-Micro Linkages in Sociology*. Los Angeles: Sage Publications, pp. 51–75.

Calhoun, C. (1997). *Neither Gods Nor Emperors: Students and the Struggle for Democracy in China*. Berkeley: University of California Press.

Calhoun, C. (2012). *The Roots of Radicalism*. Chicago: University of Chicago Press.

Caputo, S. (2018). Scotland, Scottishness, British Integration, and the Royal Navy, 1793–1815. *Scottish Historical Review*, 97/1, 85–118.

Card, D. and Olson, C. (1995). Bargaining Power, Strike Durations, and Wage Outcomes: An Analysis of Strikes in the 1880s. *Journal of Labor Economics*, 13/1, 32–61.

Carrabine, E. (2005). Prison Riots, Social Order and the Problem of Legitimacy. *British Journal of Criminology*, 45, 896–913.

Cederman, L.-E., Gleditsch, K. S. and Buhaug, H. (2013). *Inequality, Grievances and Civil War*. New York: Cambridge University Press.

Centola, D. (2013). Homophily, Networks, and Critical Mass: Solving the Start-Up Problem in Large Group Collective Action. *Rationality and Society*, 25/1, 3–40.

Chai, S-K. and Hechter, M. (1998). A Theory of the State and of Social Order. *Homo Oeconomicus*, 15, 1–26.

Chong, D. (1991). *Collective Action and the Civil Rights Movement*. Chicago: University of Chicago Press.

Churchill, W. (1956). *A History of the English-Speaking Peoples: Vol. III, The Age of Revolution*. New York: Dodd, Mead and Co.

Claver, S. (1954). *Under the Lash: A History of Corporal Punishment in the British Armed Forces*. London: Torchstream.

Clowes, W. L. (1901). *The Royal Navy, a History from the Earliest Times to the Present: Vol. VI, 1812–1856*. London: Oaks.

Coats, A. V. (2004). Joyce, Valentine (1768/9–1800). In T. Wareham, ed., *Oxford Dictionary of National Biography*. Oxford: Oxford University Press.

Coats, A. V. (2008). Parker, Richard (1767–1797). *Oxford Dictionary of National Biography*, https://doi.org/10.1093/ref:odnb/21333.

Coats, A. V. (2011). The Delegates: A Radical Tradition. In A. V. Coats and P. MacDougall, eds., *The Naval Mutinies of 1797*. Woodbridge, UK: Boydell, pp. 39–60.

Coats, A. V. and MacDougall, P. (2011). *The Naval Mutinies of 1797: Unity and Perseverance*. Woodbridge, UK: Boydell.

Cobb, J. (2016). The Matter of Black Lives. *The New Yorker*; March 14.

Cock, R. and Rodger, N. A. M. (2006). *A Guide to the Naval Records in the National Archives of the UK*. London: Institute of Historical Research.

Colburn, H. (ed.). (1844). *United Service Magazine and Naval and Military Journal*. London: Henry Colburn.

Colley, L. (2003). *Britons: Forging a Nation, 1707–1837*. 2nd edn. London: Pimlico.

Collier, P. (2000). Rebellion as a Quasi-Criminal Activity. *Journal of Conflict Resolution*, 44, 839–53.

Collier, P. and Hoeffler, A. (2004). Greed and Grievance in Civil War. *Oxford Economic Papers*, 56/4, 563–95.

Collins, R. (1995). Prediction in Macrosociology: The Case of the Soviet Collapse. *American Journal of Sociology*, 100, 1552–93.

Convertito, C. (2011). The Health of British Seamen in the West Indies, 1770–1806. Unpublished dissertation, Department of History, University of Exeter.

Cook, K., Hardin, R. and Levi, M. (2005). *Cooperation without Trust*. New York: Russell Sage.

Cookson, J. E. (1997). *The British Armed Nation, 1793–1815*. Oxford: Clarendon.

Corbett, J. (2004). *Private Papers of George, Second Earl Spencer, First Lord of the Admiralty: 1794–1801*. Vol. II. London: Adamant.

Cordingly, D. (2003). *The Billy Ruffian: The Bellerophon and the Fall of Napoleon*. New York: Bloomsbury Press.

Costa, D. and Kahn, M. (2008). *Heroes and Cowards: The Social Face of War*. Princeton, NJ: Princeton University Press.

Cox, D. R. (1972). Regression Models and Life Tables. *Journal of the Royal Statistical Society*, ser. B., 34, 187–202.

Cramton, P. and Tracy, J. (2003). Unions, Bargaining and Strikes. In J. Addison and C. Schnabel, eds., *International Handbook of Trade Unions*. Cheltenham, UK: Edward Elgar, chapter 4.

Crimmin, P. P. (2004). Troubridge, Sir Thomas, First Baronet (c.1758–1807). In T. Wareham, ed., *Oxford Dictionary of National Biography*. Oxford: Oxford University Press.

Dana, R. H. (1911). *Two Years before the Mast*. Rev. ed. New York: Houghton Mifflin.

Davey, J. (2012). *The Transformation of British Naval Strategy: Seapower and Supply in Northern Europe, 1808–1812*. Woodbridge, UK: Boydell.

Davies, J. C. (1962). Toward a Theory of Revolutions. *American Sociological Review*, 27, 5–19.

Davies, J. C. (1969). The J-Curve of Rising and Declining Satisfactions as a Cause of Some Great Revolutions and a Contained Rebellion. In H. D. Graham and T. R. Gurr, eds., *The History of Violence in America*. New York: Bantam Books, pp. 690–730.

De Chatel, F. (2014). The Role of Drought and Climate Change in the Syrian Uprising: Untangling the Triggers of Revolution. *Middle Eastern Studies*, 50, 521–35.

DeJuan, A. and Bank, A. (2015). Baathist Blackout: Selective Goods Provision and Political Violence in the Syrian Civil War. *Journal of Peace Research*, 52, 91–104.

DeJuan, A. and Wegner, E. (2017). Social Inequality, State-Centered Grievances and Protest: Evidence from South Africa. *Journal of Conflict Resolution*, 62, 31–58.

Dening, G. (1992). *Mr. Bligh's Bad Language*. New York: Cambridge University Press.

Diani, M. and McAdam, D. (2003). *Social Movements and Networks*. New York: Oxford University Press.

Dowding, K. (2016). *The Philosophy and Methods of Political Science*. London: Palgrave.

Dowding, K., John, P., Mergoupis, T. and Van Vugt, M. (2000). Exit, Voice and Loyalty: Analytic and Empirical Developments. *European Journal of Political Research*, 37, 469–95.

Dower, J. (1987). *War without Mercy*. New York: Norton.

Doyle, W. (1990). *The Oxford History of the French Revolution*. Oxford: Oxford University Press.

Duffy, M. (1987). *Soldiers, Sugar and Seapower: The British Expeditions to the West Indies and the War against Revolutionary France*. Oxford: Clarendon.

Duffy, M. (ed.) (2003). *The Naval Miscellany*. Vol. VI. Aldershot, UK: The Navy Record Society.

Dugan, J. (1965). *The Great Mutiny*. New York: Putnam.

Dull, J. (2009). *The Age of the Ship of the Line*. Lincoln: University of Nebraska Press.

Durkheim, E. ([1897] 1966). *Suicide*. New York: The Free Press.

Dwyer, M. (2017). *Soldiers in Revolt: Army Mutinies in Africa*. New York: Oxford University Press.

Earle, P. (1998). *Sailors*. London: Meuthen.

Easton, C. (2017). The Unusual Afterlife of Richard Parker. *History Today*, www.historytoday.com/history-matters/unusual-afterlife-richard-parker.

Eder, M. (2004). *Crime and Punishment in the Royal Navy of the Seven Years War, 1755–1763*. Aldershot, UK: Ashgate.

Edwards, F. and Pfaff, S. (2016). Political Crisis and Penal Severity: Mutiny and Capital Punishment in the Royal Navy, 1740–1815. Paper presented at the Annual Conference of the Law and Society Association, New Orleans.

Edwards, R. (1979). *Contested Terrain: The Transformation of the Workplace in the Twentieth Century*. New York: Basic.

Eichengreen, B. (2018). *The Populist Temptation: Economic Grievance and Political Reaction in the Modern Era*. New York: Oxford University Press.

Einwohner, R. L. (2003). Opportunity, Honor, and Action in the Warsaw Ghetto Uprising of 1943. *American Journal of Sociology*, 109, 650–75.

Einwohner, R. and Maher, T. (2011). Threat Assessment and Collective-Action Emergence: Death-Camp and Ghetto Resistance during the Holocaust. *Mobilization*, 16, 127–46.

Ekirch, A. R. (2017). *American Sanctuary: Mutiny, Martyrdom, and National Identity in the Age of Revolution*. New York: Pantheon.

Elias, N. (2007). *The Genesis of the Naval Profession*. Dublin: University College Dublin Press.

Elster, J. (1984). *Ulysses and the Sirens*. New York: Cambridge University Press.

Erikson, K. (2005). *Wayward Puritans: A Study in the Sociology of Deviance*. Rev. ed. Boston: Pearson.

Fantasia, R. (1988). *Cultures of Solidarity*. Berkeley: University of California Press.

Fearon, J. D. and Laitin, D. D. (2003). Ethnicity, Insurgency, and Civil War. *American Political Science Review*, 97, 75–90.

Field, C. (1924). *Britain's Sea-Soldiers*. Liverpool: Lyceum.

Finer, S. E. (1997). *The History of Government: Vol. I, Ancient Monarchies and Empires*. New York: Oxford University Press.

Fiorentini, G. and Peltzman, S. (1995). *The Economics of Organised Crime*. Cambridge: Cambridge University Press.

Fortescu, J. W. (1902). *History of the British Army*. London: Macmillan.

Foucault, M. (1977). *Discipline and Punish*. New York: Vintage.

Fry, S. E. (2005). When States Kill Their Own: The Legitimating Rhetoric and Institutional Remedies of Authority Crises. Unpublished dissertation, Department of Political Science, New York University.

Frykman, N. (2007). Slave Ship Sailors and Their Captive Cargoes. *Labor*, 4, 24–6.

Frykman, N. (2009). Seamen on Late Eighteenth-Century European Warships. *International Review of Social History*, 54, 67–93.

Frykman, N. (2010). The Mutiny on the *Hermione*: Warfare, Revolution and Treason in the Royal Navy. *Journal of Social History*, 44, 159–87.

Fukuyama, F. (2013). What Is Governance? *Governance*, 26, 347–68.

Fukuyama, F. (2016). Governance: What Do We Know, and How Do We Know It? *Annual Review of Political Science*, 19, 89–105.

Gail, M., Williams, R., Byar, D. and Brown, C. (1976). How Many Controls? *Journal of Chronic Disease*, 29, 723–31.

Gambetta, D. (2011). *Codes of the Underworld: How Criminals Communicate*. Princeton, NJ: Princeton University Press.

Gamson, W., Fireman, B. and Rytina, S. (1982). *Encounters with Unjust Authority*. Belmont, CA: Dorsey.

Gandhi, J. and Przeworski, A. (2006). Cooperation, Cooptation and Rebellion under Dictatorships. *Economics & Politics*, 18, 1–26.

Garland, D. (1990). *Punishment and Society: A Study in Social Theory*. Chicago: University of Chicago Press.

Garland, D. (2001). *The Culture of Control: Crime and Social Order in Contemporary Society*. New York: Cambridge University Press.

Gates, S. (2002). Recruitment and Allegiance: The Microfoundations of Rebellion. *Journal of Conflict Resolution*, 46, 111–30.

Gause, F. G. (2011). Why Middle East Studies Missed the Arab Spring: The Myth of Authoritarian Stability. *Foreign Affairs*, 90, 81–90.

Gehlbach, S. (2006). A Formal Model of Exit and Voice. *Rationality and Society*, 18, 395–418.

Geller, A. and Fagan, J. (2010). Pot as Pretext: Marijuana, Race, and the New Disorder in New York City Street Policing. *Journal of Empirical Legal Studies*, 7, 591–633.

Gelman, A., Fagan, J. and Kiss, A. (2012). An Analysis of New York City Police Department's "Stop-and-Frisk" Policing in the Context of Claims of Racial Bias. *Journal of the American Statistical Association*, 102, 813–23.

Gerring, J. (2007). *Case Study Research*. New York: Cambridge University Press.

Gerring, J. (2012). *Social Science Methodology: A Unified Framework*. New York: Cambridge University Press.

Gerstenberger, H. (2007). Shipboard Life. In *The Oxford Encyclopaedia of Maritime History*. Vol. III. New York: Oxford University Press.

Gibbs, J. P. (1977). Social Control, Deterrence, and Perspectives on Social Order. *Social Forces*, 56, 408–23.

Gilbert, A. N. (1976). Buggery and the British Navy, 1700–1861. *Journal of Social History*, 10, 72–98.

Gilbert, A. N. (1980). Crime as Disorder: Criminality and the Symbolic Universe of the 18th Century British Naval Officer. In R. W. Love, ed., *Changing Interpretations and New Sources in Naval History*. New York: Garland, pp. 110–22.

Gilbert, A. N. (1983). The Nature of Mutiny in the British Navy in the Eighteenth Century. In D. M. Masterson, ed., *Naval History: The Sixth Symposium of the U.S. Naval Academy*. Wilmington, DE: Scholarly Resources, pp. 111–20.

Gill, C. (1913). *The Naval Mutinies of 1797*. Manchester: Manchester University Press.

Gill, C. (1961). *Merchants and Mariners of the 18th Century*. London: Arnold.

Gill, E. (2016). *Naval Families, War, and Duty in Britain, 1740–1820*. Martelsham, UK: Boydell Press.

Gilroy, P. (1993). *The Black Atlantic*. London: Verso.

Givan, R., Roberts, K. M. and Soule, S. A. (2010). *The Diffusion of Social Movements*. New York: Cambridge University Press.

Glasco, J. (2004). The Seaman Feels Himself a Man. *International Labor and Working-Class History*, 66, 40–56.

Glynn, W. (1999). *The Prize of All the Oceans: The Triumph and Tragedy of Anson's Voyage Round the World*. London: HarperCollins.

Godard, J. (1992). Strikes as Collective Voice. *Industrial and Labor Relations Review*, 46, 161–75.

Goldberg, J. H., Lerner, J. S. and Tetlock, P. E. (1999). Rage and Reason: The Psychology of an Intuitive Prosecutor. *European Journal of Social Psychology*, 29, 781–95.

Goldstone, J. A. (1991). *Revolution and Rebellion in the Early Modern World*. Berkeley: University of California Press.

Goldstone, J. A. (2000). Predicting Revolutions: Why We Could (and Should) Have Foreseen the Revolutions of 1989–1991 in the USSR and Eastern Europe. In R. O'Kane, ed., *Revolution*. London: Routledge, 383–416.

Goldstone, J. A. (2003). Comparative Historical Analysis and Knowledge Accumulation in the Study of Revolutions. In J. Mahoney and D. Rueschemeyer, eds., *Comparative Historical Analysis in the Social Sciences*. New York: Cambridge University Press, pp. 41–90.

Goldstone, J. A. (2014). *Revolutions: A Very Short Introduction*. New York: Oxford University Press.

Goldstone, J., Bates, R., Epstein, D., Gurr, T. R., Lustick, M., Marshall, M., Ulfelder, J. and Woodward, M. (2010). A Global Model for Forecasting Political Instability. *American Journal of Political Science*, 54, 190–208.

Goldstone, J. and Useem, B. (1999). Prison Riots as Micro-Revolutions. *American Journal of Sociology*, 104, 985–1029.

Gooden, S. T. and Myers, S. L. (2018). The Kerner Commission Report Fifty Years Later. *Russell Sage Journal of the Social Sciences*, 4, 1–17.

Goodman, R. (2005). *A Brief History of Mutiny*. London: Robinson.

Goodwin, A. (1979). *The Friends of Liberty: The English Democratic Movement in the Age of the French Revolution*. Cambridge, MA: Harvard University Press.

Goodwin, J. (2001). *No Other Way Out: States and Revolutionary Movements, 1945–1991*. New York: Cambridge University Press.

Gossett, W. (1986). *The Lost Ships of the Royal Navy, 1793–1900*. London: Mansell.

Gottschalk, M. (2006). *The Prison and the Gallows: The Politics of Mass Incarceration in America*. New York: Cambridge University Press.

Götz, N. (2015). Moral Economy: Its Conceptual History and Analytical Prospects. *Journal of Global Ethics*, 11, 147–62.

Gould, R. (1995). *Insurgent Identities*. Chicago: University of Chicago Press.

Granovetter, M. (1978). Threshold Models of Collective Behavior. *American Journal of Sociology*, 83, 1420–43.

Greif, A. (2006). *Institutions and the Path to the Modern Economy*. New York: Cambridge University Press.

Grindle, M. S. (2007). Good Enough Governance Revisited. *Development Policy Review*, 25, 533–74.

Gurr, T. R. (1970). *Why Men Rebel*. Princeton, NJ: Princeton University Press.

Guttridge, L. (1992). *Mutiny*. Annapolis, MD: Naval Institute Press.

Habyarimana, J., Humphreys, M., Posner, D. and Weinstein, J. (2007). Why Does Ethnicity Undermine Public Goods Provision? *American Political Science Review*, 101, 709–25.

Habyarimana, J., Humphreys, M., Posner, D. and Weinstein, J. (2009). *Coethnicity: Diversity and the Dilemmas of Collective Action.* New York: Russell Sage.

Haidt, J. (2001). The Emotional Dog and Its Rational Tail: A Social Intuitionist Approach to Moral Judgment. *Psychological Review*, 108, 814–34.

Haidt, J. and Kesebir, S. (2010). Morality. In S. T. Fiske, D. T. Gilbert, G. Lindzey and A. E. Jongsma, Jr., eds.,*Handbook of Social Psychology.* Hoboken, NJ: Wiley, pp. 797–832.

Haine, E. (1992). *Mutiny on the High Seas.* New York and London: Cornwall.

Hale, H. E. (2013). Regime Change Cascades: What We Have Learned from the 1848 Revolutions to the 2011 Arab Uprisings. *Annual Review of Political Science*, 16, 331–53.

Hardin, R. (1982). *Collective Action.* Baltimore: Johns Hopkins University Press.

Hardin, R. (2007). *David Hume: Moral and Political Theorist.* New York: Oxford University Press.

Haroutune, K. A. and Lilienfeld, D. E. (1994). Applications of the Case-Control Method. *Epidemiologic Reviews*, 16, 1–5.

Hart, O. (1989). Bargaining and Strikes. *The Quarterly Journal of Economics*, 104, 25–43.

Hathaway, J. (2001). *Rebellion, Repression and Reinvention: Mutiny in Comparative Perspective.* Westport, CT: Praeger.

Hattendorf, J. B., Knight, R. J. B., Pearsall, A., Rodger, N. A. M. and Till, G. (1993). *British Naval Documents, 1204–1960.* Aldershot, UK: Scholar Press.

Hastie, T. J. (1992). *Generalized Linear Models in S.* Pacific Grove, CA: Wadsworth.

Hay, D., Linebaugh, P., Rule, J. G., Thompson, E. P. and Winslow, C. (1975). *Albion's Fatal Tree: Crime and Society in Eighteenth Century England.* New York: Pantheon.

Hechter, M. (1978). Group Formation and the Cultural Division of Labor. *American Journal of Sociology*, 84, 293–318.

Hechter, M. (1987). *Principles of Group Solidarity.* Berkeley: University of California Press.

Hechter, M. (1992). The Insufficiency of Game Theory for the Resolution of Real-World Collective Action Problems. *Rationality and Society*, 4, 33–40.

Hechter, M. (1995). Reflections on Historical Prophecy in the Social Sciences. *American Journal of Sociology*, 100, 1520–7.

Hechter, M. (1998). *Internal Colonialism: The Celtic Fringe in British National Development.* Rev. ed. New Brunswick, NJ: Transaction.

Hechter, M. (2009). Legitimacy in the Modern World. *American Behavioral Scientist*, 53, 279–88.

Hechter, M. (2013). *Alien Rule*. New York: Cambridge University Press.

Hechter, M. (2018). Norms in the Evolution of Social Order. *Social Research*, 85, 23–51.

Hechter, M. and Horne, C. (2009). *Theories of Social Order*. Stanford, CA: Stanford University Press.

Hechter, M. and Kanazawa, S. (1997). Sociological Rational Choice Theory. *Annual Review of Sociology*, 23, 191–214.

Hechter, M. and Opp, K.-D. (2001). *Social Norms*. New York: Russell Sage.

Hechter, M., Pfaff, S. and Underwood, P. (2016). Grievances and the Genesis of Rebellion: Mutiny in the Royal Navy, 1740–1820. *American Sociological Review*, 81, 165–89.

Heckathorn, D. (1996). Dynamics and Dilemmas of Collective Action. *American Sociological Review*, 61, 250–77.

Hendrix, C. and Haggard, S. (2015). Global Food Prices, Regime Type and Urban Unrest in the Developing World. *Journal of Peace Research*, 52, 143–57.

Hepper, D. (1994). *British Warship Losses in the Age of Sail*. Rotherfield, UK: Boudriot.

Hill, C. (1969). *Reformation to Industrial Revolution: The Pelican Economic History of Britain: Vol. II, 1530–1780*. New York: Penguin.

Hirschi, T. and Gottfredson, M. (1983). Age and the Explanation of Crime. *American Journal of Sociology*, 89, 552–84.

Hirschman, A. O. (1970). *Exit, Voice and Loyalty: Responses to Decline in Firms, Organizations and States*. Cambridge, MA: Harvard University Press.

Hobbes, T. ([1651] 1996). *Leviathan*. Edited by J. C. A. Gaskin. New York: Oxford University Press.

Hobsbawm, E. (1962). *The Age of Revolution, 1789–1848*. London: Weidenfeld and Nicholson.

Hobsbawm, E. and Rudé, G. (1968). *Captain Swing*. New York: Pantheon.

Hogg, M. A., Abrams, D. E., Otten, S. and Hinkle, S. (2004). The Social Identity Perspective: Intergroup Relations, Self-Conception, and Small Groups. *Small Group Research*, 35, 246–76.

Horne, C. (2009). *The Rewards of Punishment: A Relational Theory of Norm Enforcement*. Stanford, CA: Stanford University Press.

Hough, R. (1994). *Captain James Cook*. London: Hodder & Stoughton.

Hovi, J. (1998). *Games, Threats, and Treaties*. London: Pinter.

Howard, P. N. and Hussein, M. M. (2011). The Upheaval in Egypt and Tunisia: The Role of Social Media. *Journal of Democracy*, 3, 35–48.

Hughes, E. (1957). *The Private Correspondence of Admiral Lord Collingwood.* London: Naval Records Society.

Jaffer, A. (2015). *Lascars and Indian Ocean Seafaring, 1780–1860.* Woodbridge, UK: Boydell.

James, W. (1837). *Naval History of Great Britain, 1793–1827.* Vol. I. London: Harding, Lepard and Co.

Jenkins, J. C. (1983). Resource Mobilization Theory and the Study of Social Movements. *Annual Review of Sociology,* 9, 527–53.

Jenkins, J. C. and Perrow, C. (1977). Insurgency of the Powerless: Farm Worker Movements. *American Sociological Review,* 42, 249–68.

Jenks, T. (2006). *Naval Engagements: Patriotism, Cultural Politics and the Royal Navy, 1793–1815.* New York: Oxford University Press.

Johnson, N. and Koyama, M. (2017). States and Economic Growth: Capacity and Constraints. *Explorations in Economic History,* 64, 1–20.

Jones, J. (1832). Character and Conduct of the Late Captain Corbet Vindicated, in a Letter to the Editor. *United Service Journal,* 3, 162–71.

Kahn, H. (1960). The Arms Race and Some of Its Hazards. *Daedalus,* 89, 744–80.

Kahneman, D. (2011). *Thinking, Fast and Slow.* New York: Farrar, Strauss & Giroux.

Kalyvas, S. (2006). *The Logic of Violence in Civil War.* New York: Cambridge University Press.

Kalyvas, S. and Kocher, M. (2007). How "Free" Is Free Riding in Civil Wars? Violence, Insurgency and the Collective Action Problem. *World Politics,* 59, 177–216.

Kanazawa, S. and Still, M. C. (2000). Why Men Commit Crimes (and Why They Desist). *Sociological Theory,* 18, 434–47.

Karell, D. and Schutte, S. (2018). Aid, Exclusion and the Local Dynamics of Insurgency. *Journal of Peace Research,* 55/6, 711–25.

Kawalerowicz, J. and Biggs, M. (2015). Anarchy in the UK: Economic Deprivation, Social Disorganization, and Political Grievances in the London Riot of 2011. *Social Forces,* 94, 673–98.

Keevil, J. J. (1958). *Medicine and the Navy, 1200–1900.* Vol. II. Edinburgh: Livingstone.

Kemper, T. (2001). A Structural Approach to Social Movement Emotions. In J. Goodwin, J. Jasper and F. Polletta, eds., *Passionate Politics: Emotions and Social Movements.* Chicago: University of Chicago Press, pp. 58–73.

Kennedy, W. B. (1990). The United Irishmen and the Great Naval Mutiny of 1797. *Eire,* 25, 7–18.

Kerner, O. (1968). *Report of the National Advisory Commission on Civil Disorders*, Washington, DC: United States Government Printing Office.

Kerr, C. and Siegal, A. (1954). The Interindustry Propensity to Strike. In A. Kornhauser, R. Dugan and A. M. Ross, eds., *Industrial Conflict*. New York: McGraw-Hill, pp. 89–111.

Kershaw, I. (2011). *The End: Hitler's Germany, 1944–1945*. New York: Penguin.

King, G. and Zeng, L. (2001). Logistic Regression in Rare Events Data. *Political Analysis*, 9, 137–63.

King, P. (2000). *Crime, Justice and Discretion in England, 1740–1820*. New York: Oxford University Press.

King, P. (2006). *Crime and Law in England, 1750–1840*. New York: Cambridge University Press.

Kiser, E. (1995). What Can Social Theories Predict? *American Journal of Sociology*, 100, 1611–5.

Kiser, E. (1999). Comparing Varieties of Agency Theory in Economics, Political Science, and Sociology. *Sociological Theory*, 17, 146–70.

Kitts, J. (2000). Mobilizing in Black Boxes: Social Networks and Participation in Social Movement Organizations. *Mobilization*, 5, 241–57.

Klandermans, B. (1997). *The Social Psychology of Protest*. Oxford: Blackwell.

Knight, R. and Wilcox, M. H. (2010). *Sustaining the Fleet, 1793–1815: War, the British Navy and the Contractor State*. Woodbridge, UK: Boydell.

Kollock, P. (1998). Social Dilemmas: The Anatomy of Cooperation. *Annual Review of Sociology*, 24, 183–214.

Kopstein, J. (1996). Chipping Away at the State: Workers' Resistance and the Demise of East Germany. *World Politics*, 48, 391–423.

Kuran, T. (1991). Now out of Never: The Element of Surprise in the East European Revolutions of 1989. *World Politics*, 44, 7–48.

Kuran, T. (1995). The Inevitability of Future Revolutionary Surprises. *American Journal of Sociology*, 100, 1528–51.

Kuran, T. (1997). *Private Truths, Public Lies: The Social Consequences of Preference Falsification*. Cambridge, MA: Harvard University Press.

La Fevre, P. and Harding, R. (2000). *Precursors of Nelson: British Admirals of the Eighteenth Century*. London: Stockpole.

Lamb, J. (2002). *Preserving the Self in the South Seas, 1680–1840*. Chicago: University of Chicago Press.

Lamb, J. (2016). *Scurvy: The Disease of Discovery*. Princeton, NJ: Princeton University Press.

Lammers, C. (1969). Strikes and Mutinies. *Administrative Science Quarterly*, 14, 558–72.

Lammers, C. (2003). Mutiny in Comparative Perspective. *International Review of Labor History*, 48, 473–82.

Land, I. (2009). *War, Nationalism and the British Sailor, 1750–1850*. New York: Palgrave Macmillan.

Landa, J. (1994). *Trust, Ethnicity, and Identity*. Ann Arbor: University of Michigan Press.

Langford, P. (1984). The Eighteenth Century. In K. O. Morgan, ed., *The Oxford Illustrated History of Britain*. Oxford: Oxford University Press.

Lasky, T. and Stalley, P. D. (1994). Selection of Cases and Controls. *Epidemiologic Review*, 16, 6–17.

Laughton, J. K. (1899). Troubridge, Thomas (1758?–1807). In S. Lee, ed., *Dictionary of National Biography*. London: Smith, Elder & Co.

Laughton, J. K. (2008). Corbet, Robert (d. 1810). In T. Wareham, ed., *Oxford Dictionary of National Biography*. Oxford: Oxford University Press.

Lavery, B. (1998). *Shipboard Life and Organisation, 1731–1815*. London: Navy Record Society.

Lavery, B. (2010). *Royal Tars: The Lower Deck of the Royal Navy, 875–1850*. Annapolis, MD: Naval Institute Press.

Lawrence, J. (1987). *Mutiny in the British and Commonwealth Forces, 1797–1956*. London: Buchan and Enright.

Le Bron, C. J. (2017). *The Making of Black Lives Matter*. New York: Oxford University Press.

Leech, S. (1847). *Thirty Years from Home, or, A Voice from the Lower Deck*. Boston: Whittemore.

Leeson, P. (2009). *The Invisible Hook: The Hidden Economics of Pirates*. Princeton, NJ: Princeton University Press.

Leeson, P. (2010). Rational Choice, Round Robin, and Rebellion. *Journal of Economic Behavior and Organization*, 73, 297–307.

Leeson, P. (2017). *WTF? An Economic Tour of the Weird*. Stanford, CA: Stanford University Press.

Lennon, D. (1991). A Communitarian Army? Status and Role Considerations in the Use of Courts-Martial in the United States Army. *Deviant Behavior*, 12, 31–79.

Lerner, J. S., Goldberg, J. H. and Tetlock, P. E. (1998). Sober Second Thoughts: The Effects of Accountability, Anger and Authoritarianism on Attributions of Responsibility. *Personality and Social Psychology Bulletin*, 24, 563–74.

Levi, M. (1997). *Consent, Dissent, and Patriotism*. New York: Cambridge University Press.

Levi, M. and Braithwaite, V. (1998). *Trust and Governance*. New York: Russell Sage.

Levi, M., Sacks, A. and Tyler, T. (2009). Conceptualizing Legitimacy, Measuring Legitimating Beliefs. *American Behavioral Scientist*, 53, 354–75.

Levitsky, S. and Ziblatt, D. (2018). *How Democracies Die*. New York: Crown.

Lewis, M. A. (1959). *The History of the British Navy*. New York: Essential.

Lewis, M. A. (1960). *A Social History of the Navy, 1793–1815*. London: Allen and Unwin.

Lichbach, M. (1998). *The Rebel's Dilemma*. Ann Arbor: University of Michigan Press.

Lilienfeld, D. E. and Stolley, P. (1994). *Foundations of Epidemiology*. 3rd edn. New York: Oxford University Press.

Linebaugh, P. and Rediker, M. (2001). *The Many-Headed Hydra*. Boston: Beacon.

Lipset, S. M., Trow, M. and Coleman, J. (1956). *Union Democracy*. New York: Doubleday.

Lloyd, C. (1995). *The Keith Papers: Selected Papers of Admiral Viscount Keith*. London: Naval Records Society.

Lohmann, S. (1994). The Dynamics of Informational Cascades. *World Politics*, 47, 42–101.

London, D. (2001). Mutiny in the Public Eye: The Role of Newspapers in the Spithead Mutiny. Unpublished PhD thesis, History Department, King's College, London.

Long, J. S. (1997). *Regression Models for Categorical and Limited Dependent Variables*. Thousand Oaks, CA: Sage.

Loveman, M. (1998). High Risk Collective Action: Defending Human Rights in Chile, Uruguay, and Argentina. *American Journal of Sociology*, 104, 477–525.

Luongo, K. (2011). *Witchcraft and Colonial Rule in Kenya, 1900–1950*. New York: Cambridge University Press.

Lyon, D. (1993). *The Sailing Navy List: All the Ships of the Royal Navy – Built, Purchased and Captured – 1688–1860*. London: Conway Maritime Press.

Mabee, F. (2007). The Spithead Mutiny and Urban Radicalism in the 1790s. *Romanticism*, 13, 133–44.

MacDonald, J. (2006). *Feeding Nelson's Navy*. London: Chatham.

MacDougall, P. (2011). Reporting the Mutinies in the Provincial Press. In A. V. Coats and P. MacDougall, eds., *The Naval Mutinies of 1797*. Woodbridge, UK: Boydell, pp. 161–8.

MacKenzie, N. (1967). *Secret Societies*. New York: Holt, Rinehart and Winston.

Macy, M. W. (1991). Chains of Cooperation: Threshold Models in Collective Action. *American Sociological Review*, 83, 1420–43.

Maddison, A. (2001). *The World Economy: A Millennial Perspective*. Paris: OECD.

Mahoney, J. (2007). Qualitative Methodology and Comparative Politics. *Comparative Political Studies*, 40, 122–44.

Mahoney, J. (2008). Toward a Unified Theory of Causality. *Comparative Political Studies*, 51, 412–36.

Malcomson, T. (2016). *Order and Disorder in the British Navy, 1793–1815*. Woodbridge, UK: Boydell.

Manwaring, G. E. and Dobrée, B. (1987). *The Floating Republic: An Account of the Mutinies at Spithead and the Nore in 1797*. London: Cresset Reprints.

Marshall, J. (1823). *Royal Navy Biography, or Memoirs of the Services*. London: Longman.

Martin, D. (1980). *An Ownership Theory of the Trade Union*. Berkeley: University of California Press.

Marwell, G. and Oliver, P. (1993). *The Critical Mass in Collective Action*. New York: Cambridge University Press.

Marx, K. (1977). On Strikes. In D. McClellan, ed., *Karl Marx: Selected Writings*. New York: Oxford University Press, pp. 213–15.

Matsueda, R. (2013). Rational Choice Research in Criminology. In R. Wittek, T. Snijders and V. Nee, eds., *Handbook of Rational Choice Social Research*. Stanford, CA: Stanford University Press, pp. 283–321.

May, W. E. (1976). Notes for Historical Research on the Royal Navy. *Military Affairs*, 46, 186–7.

McAdam, D. (1982). *Political Process and the Rise of Black Insurgency, 1930–1970*. Chicago: University of Chicago Press.

McAdam, D. (1988). *Freedom Summer*. Oxford: Oxford University Press.

McAdam, D. and Boudet, H. (2012). *Putting Social Movements in Their Place*. New York: Cambridge University Press.

McAdam, D., McCarthy, J. D. and Zald, M. N. (1996). *Comparative Perspectives on Social Movements*. New York: Cambridge University Press.

McAdam, D., Tarrow, S. and Tilly, C. (2001). *Dynamics of Contention*. New York: Cambridge University Press.

McAdam, D. and Paulsen, R. (1993). Specifying the Relationship between Social Ties and Activism. *American Journal of Sociology*, 99, 640–67.

McCarthy, J. D. and Zald, M. N. (1977). Resource Mobilization and Social Movements. *American Journal of Sociology*, 82, 1212–41.

McKee, C. (1978). Fantasies of Mutiny and Murder: A Suggested Psycho-History of the Seaman in the United States Navy, 1798–1815. *Armed Forces and Society*, 4, 293–304.

McLauchlin, T. (2015). Desertion and Collective Action in Civil Wars. *International Studies Quarterly*, 59, 669–79.

McLynn, F. (1991). *Crime and Punishment in Eighteenth-Century England.* Oxford: Oxford University Press.

McVeigh, R. (2009). *The Rise of the Klu Klux Klan: Right-Wing Movements and National Politics.* Minneapolis: University of Minnesota Press.

Mead, G. H. (1934). *Mind, Self and Society.* Chicago: University of Chicago Press.

Medina, L. F. (2007). *A Unified Theory of Collective Action and Social Change.* Ann Arbor: University of Michigan Press.

Melville, H. (1924). *Billy Budd and Other Prose Pieces by Herman Melville.* London: Constable.

Melville, H. ([1847] 2007). *Omoo: A Narrative of Adventures in the South Seas.* New York: Penguin.

Moore, B. (1978). *Injustice: The Social Bases of Obedience and Revolt.* Armonk, NY: M.E. Sharpe.

Mounk, Y. (2018). *The People vs. Democracy.* Cambridge, MA: Harvard University Press.

Nagle, J. ([1802] 1988). *The Nagle Journal: A Diary of the Life of Jacob Nagle, Sailor, from the Year 1775 to 1841.* Edited by J. C. Dann. New York: Weidenfeld & Nicolson.

Naish, G. P. B. (1958). *Nelson's Letters to His Wife and Other Documents, 1785–1831.* London: Routledge & Keegan Paul.

Neafsey, E. (2002). *Surnames of Ireland.* Kansas City: Irish Genealogical Society.

Neale, J. (1985). *The Cutlass and the Lash: Mutiny and Discipline in Nelson's Navy.* London: Pluto.

Newman, S. C. (2001). *Biostatistical Methods in Epidemiology.* New York: Wiley.

Nicol, J. ([1822] 1997). *The Life and Adventures of John Nicol, Mariner.* Edited and introduced by T. Flannery. New York: Grove.

North, D. (1981). *Structure and Change in Economic History.* New York: Norton.

Oberschall, A. (1973). *Social Conflict and Social Movements.* Englewood Cliffs, NJ: Prentice-Hall.

Oberschall, A. (1980). Loosely-Structured Collective Action. *Research in Social Movements, Conflict and Change*, 3, 45–68.

Oberschall, A. (1994). Rational Choice in Collective Protest. *Rationality and Society*, 6, 79–100.

O'Donnell, M. (1838). *A Brief Treatise on the Law of Combinations, on Unlawful Societies, and on the Administration of Unlawful Oaths*. Dublin: Hodges and Smith.

Oliver, H. (1941). War and Inflation since 1790 in England, France, Germany, and the United States. *American Economic Review*, 30, 544–51.

Oliver, P. and Marwell, G. (2001). What Ever Happened to Critical Mass Theory? *Sociological Theory*, 19, 292–311.

Olson, M. (1965). *The Logic of Collective Action*. Cambridge, MA: Harvard University Press.

Olzak, S. and Shanahan, S. (1996). Deprivation and Race Riots. *Social Forces*, 74, 931–61.

Opp, K.-D. (1989). *The Rationality of Political Protest*. New York: Westview.

Opp, K.-D. (2009). *Theories of Political Protest and Social Movements*. New York: Routledge.

Opp, K.-D., and Gern, C. (1993). Dissident Groups, Personal Networks and Spontaneous Mobilization: The East German Revolution of 1989. *American Sociological Review*, 58, 59–80.

Østby, G. (2008). Polarization, Horizontal Inequalities and Violent Civil Conflict. *Journal of Peace Research*, 45, 143–62.

Ostrom, E. (1990). *Governing the Commons: The Evolution of Institutions for Collective Action*. New York: Cambridge University Press.

Ownby, D. and Heidhues, M. S. (1993). *Secret Societies Reconsidered*. Armonk, NY: M.E. Sharpe.

Pack, S. W. C. (1964). *The Wager Mutiny*. London: Redman.

Parker, G. (1973). Mutiny and Discontent in the Spanish Army of Flanders, 1572–1607. *Past and Present*, 58, 38–52.

Pearson, M. (2017). Places in the Indian Ocean World. *Journal of Indian Ocean World Studies*, 1, 4–23.

Pfaff, S. (1996). Collective Identity and Informal Groups in Revolutionary Mobilization. *Social Forces*, 75, 91–118.

Pfaff, S. (2006). *Exit-Voice Dynamics and the Collapse of East Germany*. Durham, NC: Duke University Press.

Pfaff, S., Hechter, M. and Corcoran, K. E. (2016). The Problem of Solidarity in Insurgent Collective Action: The Nore Mutiny of 1797. *Social Science History*, 40, 247–70.

Pfaff, S. and Kim, H. (2003). Exit-Voice Dynamics in Collective Action: An Analysis of Emigration and Protest in the East German Revolution. *American Journal of Sociology*, 109, 401–44.

Philips, D. (1980). A New Engine of Power and Authority: The Institutionalisation of Law Enforcement in England, 1780–1830. In V. A. C. Gattrell, B. Lenman and G. Parker, eds., *Crime and the Law: The Social History of Crime in Western Europe since 1500*. London: Europa, pp. 155–89.

Phillimore, A. (1876). *The Life of Admiral of the Fleet Sir William Parker*. London: Harrison.

Philp, M. (2006). *Resisting Napoleon: The British Response to the Threat of Invasion, 1797–1815*. Aldershot, UK: Ashgate.

Pierson, P. (2004). *Politics in Time*. Princeton, NJ: Princeton University Press.

Piketty, T. (2014). *Capital in the Twenty-First Century*. Boston: Harvard University Press.

Pinard, M. (2011). *Motivational Dimensions in Social Movements and Contentious Collective Action*. Montreal: McGill-Queen's University Press.

Pope, D. (1963). *The Black Ship*. London: Weidenfeld and Nicholson.

Pope, D. (1981). *Life in Nelson's Navy*. London: Unwin Hyman.

Pope, D. (1987). *The Devil Himself: The Mutiny of 1800*. London: Alison Press.

Popkin, S. L. (1979). *The Rational Peasant: The Political Economy of Rural Society in Vietnam*. Berkeley: University of California Press.

Porter, R. (1991). *English Society in the Eighteenth Century*. 2nd edn. London: Penguin.

Rao, H. and Dutta, S. (2012). Free Spaces as Organizational Weapons of the Weak. *Administrative Science Quarterly*, 57, 625–68.

Rasmussen, E. (2007). *Games and Information*. Oxford: Blackwell.

Rasor, E. L. (1976). *Reform in the Royal Navy: A Social History of the Lower Deck, 1850–1880*. New York: Anchor.

Rediker, M. (1987). *Between the Devil and the Deep Blue Sea*. New York: Cambridge University Press.

Rediker, M. (2004). *Villains of All Nations: Atlantic Pirates in the Golden Age*. New York: Verso.

Richardson, W. (1908). *A Mariner of England: An Account of the Career of William Richardson*. London: Murray.

Richerson, P. and Henrich, J. (2009). Tribal Social Instincts and the Cultural Evolution of Institutions to Solve Collective Action Problems. Context and the Evolution of Mechanisms for Solving Collective Action Problems Paper. Available at SSRN: https://ssrn.com/abstract=1368756 or http://dx.doi.org/10.2139/ssrn.1368756.

Rodger, N. A. M. (1982). *The Articles of War: The Statutes Which Governed Our Fighting Navies, 1661, 1749, and 1886*. Havant, UK: Mason.

Rodger, N. A. M. (1986). *The Wooden World*. New York: Norton.

Rodger, N. A. M. (2001). Commissioned Officers' Careers in the Royal Navy, 1690–1815. *Journal for Maritime Research*, 3, 85–129.

Rodger, N. A. M. (2002). Honour and Duty at Sea, 1660–1815. *Historical Research*, 75, 425–47.

Rodger, N. A. M. (2003). Mutiny or Subversion: Spithead and the Nore. In T. Bartlett, D. Dickson, D. Keogh and K. Whelan, eds., *1798: A Bicentenary Perspective*. Dublin: Four Courts, pp. 549–64.

Rodger, N. A. M. (2004). *The Command of the Ocean: A Naval History of Britain, 1649–1815*. London: Penguin.

Rose, E. (1982). The Anatomy of Mutiny. *Armed Forces and Society*, 8, 561–74.

Ross, A. M. (1948). *Trade Union Wage Policy*. Berkeley: University of California Press.

Rothstein, B. (2009). Creating Political Legitimacy: Electoral Democracy versus Quality of Government. *American Behavioral Scientist*, 53, 311–30.

Rothstein, B. (2011). *The Quality of Government*. Chicago: University of Chicago.

Rothstein, B. and Teorell, J. (2008). What Is Quality of Government? A Theory of Impartial Government Institutions. *Governance*, 21/2, 165–90.

Rousseau, J.-J. ([1762] 1997). *The Social Contract and Other Later Political Writings*. Cambridge: Cambridge University Press.

Rubin, D. B. (1987) *Multiple Imputation for Nonresponse in Surveys*. New York: Wiley.

Rucker, D. D., Polifroni, M., Tetlock, P. E. and Scott, A. (2004). On the Assignment of Punishment: The Impact of General-Societal Threat on the Moderating Role of Severity. *Personality and Social Psychology Bulletin*, 30, 673–84.

Rudé, G. (1964). *The Crowd in History*. New York: Wiley.

Rule, J. B. (1988). *Theories of Civil Violence*. Berkeley: University of California Press.

Schama, S. (1989). *Citizens: A Chronicle of the French Revolution*. New York: Knopf.

Scheidel, W. (2017). *The Great Leveler: Violence and the History of Inequality*. Princeton, NJ: Princeton University Press.

Schelling, T. (1960). *The Strategy of Conflict*. Cambridge, MA: Harvard University Press.

Schelling, T. (1978). *Micromotives and Macrobehavior*. New York: Norton.

Schlesselman, J. (1982). *Case-Control Studies*. New York: Oxford.

Scott, J. (1976). *The Moral Economy of the Peasant*. New Haven, CT: Yale University Press.

Scott, J. (1985). *Weapons of the Weak*. New Haven, CT: Yale University Press.

Scott, J. (1990). *Domination and the Arts of Resistance*. New Haven, CT: Yale University Press.

Seawright, J. (2016). *Multi-Method Social Science*. New York: Cambridge University Press.

Selbin, E. (2010). *Revolution, Rebellion and Resistance: The Power of a Story*. London: Zed.

Sewell, W. (1980). *Work and Revolution in France: The Language of Labor from the Old Regime to 1848*. New York: Cambridge.

Sewell, W. (2005). *Logics of History*. Chicago: University of Chicago Press.

Sharpe, J. A. (1999). *Crime in Early Modern England, 1550–1750*. New York: Addison.

Shils, E. and Janowitz, M. (1948). Cohesion and Disintegration in the Wehrmacht. *Public Opinion Quarterly*, 12, 280–315.

Siegel, D. A. (2009). Social Networks and Collective Action. *American Journal of Political Science*, 53, 122–38.

Simmons, E. (2014). Grievances Do Matter in Mobilization. *Theory and Society*, 43, 513–46.

Siroky, D. (2009). Navigating Random Forests and Advances in Algorithmic Modeling. *Statistics Surveys*, 3, 147–63.

Skocpol, T. (1979). *States and Social Revolutions*. New York: Cambridge University Press.

Smith, L. V. (1994). *Between Mutiny and Obedience*. Princeton, NJ: Princeton University Press.

Smith, V. L. (2003). Constructivist and Ecological Rationality in Economics. *American Economic Review*, 93, 465–508.

Sobel, M. E. (1996). An Introduction to Causal Inference. *Sociological Methods and Research*, 24, 353–79.

Sondhaus, L. (2001). Austro-Hungarian Naval Mutinies of World War I. In J. Hathaway, ed., *Rebellion, Repression and Reinvention: Mutiny in Comparative Perspective*. Westport, CT: Praeger, pp. 195–214.

Starr, H. (2008). *Dealing with Failed States*. London: Routledge.

Steele, R. (1840). *The Marine Officer, or, Sketches of Service*. Vol. I. London: Colburn.

Stewart, F. (2008). *Horizontal Inequalities and Conflict*. Basingstoke, UK: Palgrave Macmillan.

Stinchcombe, A. L. (1995). *Sugar Island Slavery in the Age of Enlightenment*. Princeton, NJ: Princeton University Press.

Tarrow, S. (1998). *Power in Movements*. New York: Cambridge University Press.

Tausch, N., Becker, J., Spears, R., Christ, O., Saab, R., Singh, P. and Siddiqui, R. (2011). Explaining Radical Group Behavior: Developing Emotion and Efficacy Routes to Normative and Nonnormative Collective Action. *Journal of Personality and Social Psychology*, 101, 129–48.

Taylor, M. (1987). *The Possibility of Cooperation*. New York: Cambridge University Press.

Tetlock, P. E. (2002). Social Functionalist Frameworks for Judgment and Choice. *Psychological Review*, 109, 451–71.

Theal, G. M. (1898). *The Records of the Cape Colony from December 1796 to December 1799*. Vol. II. London: Clowes.

Thompson, E. P. (1971). The Moral Economy of the English Crowd in the Eighteenth Century. *Past & Present*, 50, 76–136.

Thompson, E. P. (1980). *The Making of the English Working Class*. Rev. edn. London: Vintage.

Thomson, H. (2017). Food and Power: Agricultural Policy under Democracy and Dictatorship. *Comparative Politics*, 49, 273–93.

Thrale, M. (1983). *Selections from the Papers of the London Corresponding Society 1792–1799*. New York: Cambridge University Press.

Thursfield, H. G. (1951). *Five Naval Journals*. London: Naval Records Society.

Tilly, C. (1977). *From Mobilization to Revolution*. New York: McGraw-Hill.

Tilly, C. (1984). Social Movements and National Politics. In C. Bright and S. Harding, eds., *Statemaking and Social Movements*. Ann Arbor: University of Michigan Press, pp. 297–319.

Tilly, C. (1993). Contentious Repertoires in Great Britain, 1758–1834. *Social Science History*, 17, 253–80.

Tilly, C. (1995). To Explain Political Processes. *American Journal of Sociology*, 100, 1594–1610.

Tilly, C. (1996). *European Revolutions: 1492–1992*. New York: Wiley.

Tocqueville, A. de ([1856] 1955). *The Old Regime and the French Revolution*. New York: Doubleday.

Tracy, N. (2012). The British Expedition to Manila. In M. H. Hanley and P. J. Speelman, eds., *The Seven Years War: Global Views*. Leiden: Brill, pp. 461–86.

Trotsky, L. ([1932] 1959). *The History of the Russian Revolution*. Garden City, NY: Doubleday.

Turner, R. and Killian, L. (1972). *Collective Behavior*. 2nd edn. Englewood Cliffs, NJ: Prentice-Hall.

Twigger, R. (1999). Inflation: The Value of the Pound 1750–1998. Research Paper 99/20, Economic Policy and Statistics Section, House of Commons Library.

Underwood, P., Pfaff, S. and Hechter, M. (2018). Threat, Deterrence, and Penal Severity: An Analysis of Flogging in the Royal Navy, 1740–1820. *Social Science History*, 42, 411–39.

Useem, B. (1998). Breakdown Theories of Collective Action. *Annual Review of Sociology*, 24, 215–38.

Useem, B. and Goldstone, J. (2002). Forging Social Order and Its Breakdown: Riot and Reform in U.S. Prisons. *American Sociological Review*, 67, 499–525.

Useem, B. and Kimball, P. (1991). *States of Siege: U.S. Prison Riots, 1971–1986*. New York: Oxford University Press.

Vale, B. (1998). The Conquest of Scurvy in the Royal Navy, 1793–1800: A Challenge to the Current Orthodoxy. *Mariner's Mirror*, 94, 160–75.

Valle, J. (1980). *Rocks and Shoals: Naval Discipline in the Age of Fighting Sail*. Annapolis, MD: Naval Institute Press.

Van Buuren, S. (2012). *Flexible Imputation of Missing Data*. Boca Raton, FL: Chapman & Hall.

Van Buuren, S. and Oudshoorn, C. G. (1999). *Flexible Multivariate Imputation by MICE*. Leiden: TNO.

Van Crefeld, M. (1983). *Fighting Power: German and U.S. Army Performance, 1939–1945*. London: Arms and Armour Press.

Van Dyke, N. and Soule, S. A. (2002). Structural Social Change and the Mobilizing Effect of Threat. *Social Problems*, 49, 497–520.

Van Stekelenburg, J. and Klandermans, B. (2013). The Social Psychology of Protest. *Current Sociology*, 6, 886–905.

Van Zomeren, M., Postmes, T. and Spears, R. (2008). Toward an Integrative Social Identity Model of Collective Action. *Psychological Bulletin*, 134, 504–35.

Viterna, J. (2013). *Women in War: The Micro-Processes of Mobilization in El Salvador*. New York: Oxford University Press.

Walder, A. (2009). Political Sociology and Social Movements. *Annual Review of Sociology*, 35, 393–412.

Wallace, J. (2013). Cities, Redistribution and Authoritarian Regime Survival. *Journal of Politics*, 75, 632–45.

Walsh, E. (1981). Resource Mobilization and Citizen Protest around Three Mile Island. *Social Problems*, 29, 1–21.

Watt, H. and Hawkins, A. (2016). *Letters of Seamen in the Wars with France, 1793–1815*. Woodbridge, UK: Boydell.

Watt, J., Freeman, J. and Bynum, W. F. (1981). *Starving Sailors: The Influence of Nutrition upon Naval and Maritime History*. London: National Maritime Museum.

Watts, D. J. and Dodds, P. (2009). Threshold Models of Social Influence. In P. Hedstrom and P. Bearman, eds., *The Oxford Handbook of Analytical Sociology*. New York: Oxford University Press, pp. 475–97.

Way, P. (2003). Class and the Common Soldier in the Seven Years' War. *Labor History*, 44, 455–81.

Weber, M. ([1918–21] 1978). *Economy and Society*. Berkeley: University of California Press.

Weinstein, J. M. (2007). *Inside Rebellion: The Politics of Insurgent Violence*. New York: Cambridge University Press.

Wells, R. (1983). *Insurrection: The British Experience, 1795–1803*. London: Allen and Unwin.

Weyland, K. (2016). Patterns of Diffusion: Comparing Democratic and Autocratic Waves. *Global Policy*, 7, 557–62.

Williams, G. (1999). *The Prize of All the Oceans: The Triumph and Tragedy of Anson's Voyage Round the World*. London: Harper Collins.

Williams, J. (1962). *Mutiny 1917*. London: Heinemann.

Willis, S. (2010). *The Fighting Temeraire*. London: Pegasus Books.

Wilson, E. (2017). *A Social History of British Naval Officers, 1775–1815*. Woodbridge, UK: Boydell.

Wilson, W. J. (1997). *When Work Disappears: The World of the New Urban Poor*. New York: Vintage.

Wolcott, S. (2008). Strikes in Colonial India, 1921–1938. *Industrial and Labor Relations Review*, 61, 460–84.

Wood, E. J. (2003). *Insurgent Collective Action and Civil War in El Salvador*. New York: Cambridge University Press.

Woodman, R. (2005). *A Brief History of Mutiny*. London: Robinson.

Woodward, E. L. (1958). *The Age of Reform, 1815–1870*. Oxford: Oxford University Press.

Wooldridge, J. M. (2009). *Introductory Econometrics*. 4th edn. Mason, OH: Cengage-Learning.

INDEX